This book is written for two women:

To Junko, my partner in life,

and to Sachiko, our gift to the future.

And, of course, for you.

# Acknowledgments

Though a book might *start* when a writer puts pen to paper (or a modern equivalent thereof), it takes the cooperation of people dedicated to excellence to bring its pages to the reader. The team at Cengage Learning, with whom I've had the pleasure of working on many books, are just such people. Thanks go to the entire Cengage Learning group, especially Mark Garvey, Cathleen Small (for her superb editing), and Brent Heber (for keeping me honest on the technical bits).

As this book goes to press, Digidesign is in the process of a transformative integration with its parent company, Avid. Fortunately for us all, the spirit that created Pro Tools at Digidesign (and has kept it growing through the years) is alive and well in its new unified home. The skill and dedication of Avid's people are behind the company's success, and thanks to their passion, the creative world is a better place. My gratitude goes out to Avid colleagues such as Andy and Claudia Cook, Greg Robles, and Bobby Lombardi—you guys prove that it's possible to be brilliant and cool at the same time.

Last but certainly not least, I have to thank the people in my life who inspire me and nourish my soul. Brian Smithers and Dave Oxenreider stand out among them— their faith in me has at times exceeded my own and gave me the confidence to begin writing in the first place. Finally, my heart belongs to Junko Hagerman and our daughter Sachiko, who reminds me that some jokes are funny at *any* age.

# About the Author

**Andy Hagerman** has been a professional musician, composer, arranger, and teacher for the majority of his 40+ years. While studying at the prestigious Northwestern University in Chicago, he also discovered a passion for MIDI and computer music, still in their infancy. As a performer, he has performed in numerous ensembles of all types, including many years of playing at Disneyland, Walt Disney World, and Tokyo Disneyland. As a composer, he is active in the creation of planetarium and science center soundtracks, and his work can be heard worldwide, including at the renowned American Museum of Natural History in New York City.

# Contents

# Introduction

First of all, congratulations on becoming a Pro Tools user, and welcome (or welcome back, if you're an existing Pro Tools user)! I suppose that similar salutations are on page one of many product user guides and manuals, but when Avid says that their powerful Digital Audio Workstation (DAW) is the industry standard—and for good reason—you can believe it. Indeed, you'll find Pro Tools, from the humble Mbox all the way up to high-end HD systems, hard at work in every facet of audio and musical production. It's a serious, professional product, and your decision to buy it (and learn it) is a step in the right direction.

The Chinese philosopher Lao-Tsu once said, "A journey of a thousand miles begins with a single step." That's where this book comes in—it's that first step. Gaining a solid fundamental understanding of the basics of Pro Tools will ensure that your journey starts off well prepared and heads in the right direction. In this book, you'll learn the basic techniques of creating, recording, editing, and mixing digital audio and MIDI (Musical Instrument Digital Interface). You'll learn how to harness the power of Pro Tools' impressive array of features, from software effects, to virtual instruments, to mixes that are automated and edited with some of the best tools in the business.

This is my fifth book about Pro Tools, the first being about version 6 of the software, followed by books on Pro Tools 7 and 7.4. The book you're holding stands on the shoulders of those previous books (including some of the same material as the earlier titles) but will also cover the exciting new features of Pro Tools 8. Even though Pro Tools has been a world leader for many years, I think you'll find that the radical improvements in Pro Tools 8 are especially exciting for LE users, and particularly those who are musically creative (or would like to be!). These new features, combined with the solid design of Pro Tools in general, open the door to inspiring possibilities indeed.

If your aim is to create and produce audio, Pro Tools is an excellent choice, and *Pro Tools LE 8 Ignite!* will be your companion during those critical first steps on the road to discovery!

# Who Should Read This Book?

Essentially, this book is geared toward beginners with little or no experience in working with a DAW. You'll find that this book's highly visual and plainly worded style makes it easy to follow. Nearly every step in the processes discussed is accompanied by clear illustrations, so you won't have to spend your time hunting around the screen for tools and menus. (What fun is *that*?) Furthermore, once you're finished with the chapters and exercises, this book will be a valuable reference later on as well.

Don't worry if you're not a formally trained musician or if you haven't really dealt with digital audio before. The beauty of Pro Tools—and computer music in general—is that even untrained (but creative) musicians can enjoy great success in this kind of environment. In fact, many of the new features in Pro Tools version 8 make it even easier and more fun to be creative than in previous versions! Of course, any general music or audio knowledge you bring to the table is an added advantage, but it is certainly not a requirement for this book.

Now with that being said, Pro Tools is a *deep* program, and even those of us who have been using it for years are still finding new tidbits now and then. For that reason, I can't dedicate the limited space I have in this book to covering basic computer operations. That means it's up to you to understand the most basic ins and outs of your particular platform (Mac or PC). Don't worry too much, though—the general computer knowledge required to use Pro Tools is pretty basic, and if you can locate, launch, and close programs already, you're probably in fine shape.

# How to Use This Book

Music is fundamentally a progressive process—from creation to performance, it's the result of many small steps taken in order. A solid mastery of Pro Tools works much the same way. This book is laid out to mirror the creative process, from setup, through the recording process, to editing, mixing, and putting on the final touches. Additionally, the first sections of the book will also include a bit of information about the nature of DAWs in general, so that you understand the logic of these devices and can work most efficiently. If you're just beginning with DAWs, you'll find this information valuable in the long run.

Because this book is arranged sequentially according to the production process, you'll be able to follow along from the very start of a project through its completion. However, if you're interested in some areas more than others (which is pretty common with more experienced users), feel free to take the book out of order and just concentrate on those sections first—this book will work that way as well.

You'll find that most of this book is laid out in a tutorial-style format; there are even tutorial files you can use side by side with the book's examples (on the included disc). Of course, you can also use this book as a point of reference source as well, using the clear, illustrated style of this format to your advantage as you locate information on specific functions.

Last but not least, you'll note that peppered throughout this book are a number of Notes and Tips. Take a look at these to find additional ways to increase your efficiency, additional information on key functions, and even warnings that point out common pitfalls and how to avoid them.

> **NOTE**
>
> Speaking of Notes, there's no time like the present to start!
>
> If you already have some experience with previous versions of Pro Tools, you might be particularly interested in checking out what's new in Pro Tools 8. This book has been updated to show the latest features, including updated screenshots, shortcuts, and other general information throughout the text.
>
> Additionally, you'll find sections dedicated to features introduced in Pro Tools 8. Section titles will call attention to these features.

# Finally, a Little Background...

Pro Tools systems can be broken down into two families: HD and LE. HD systems are based upon a hardware-based architecture, which means that there are dedicated PCI or PCIe cards designed for the sole purpose of providing a powerful engine for running Pro Tools. This means two things: First, Pro Tools|HD is a reliable, scalable, and powerful system—an obvious choice for professional facilities. Second, it costs more (and it can be a *lot* more).

LE systems aren't hardware-based; they're host-based, which simply means that the host computer (meaning the computer that you're using to run the software) is charged with all the tasks of running Pro Tools, from recording and playback to effects and automation. This allows an LE system to be a good deal more economical than its HD counterpart. Of course, since your computer's CPU is doing *everything*, you won't get the same kind of power from an LE system, and there are a few features that are reserved for HD systems only.

The good news—and it's great news, really—is that the software environments in HD and LE are nearly identical. This means that you can take advantage of one of the most powerful and well-developed user interfaces on the market without breaking the bank. What's more, when it comes time for you to upgrade to HD, you'll already know the software.

For more than 20 years, Digidesign has been a leader in Digital Audio Workstation technology, and the professional community has chosen Pro Tools as the clear industry standard. Now, Avid has released Pro Tools 8 (for PC and Mac), which incorporates some real advances, especially for LE users. Among these are:

* A radically redesigned user interface and a well-designed reorganization of menus and tools
* Brand-new MIDI editing environments (MIDI Editor and Score Editor)
* New editing features and workflows, including a great new way to work with multiple "takes" of a section, and a feature called Elastic Audio
* An improved Mix window, with 10 insert slots per channel, track lanes for improved mixing workflow, and new plug-ins and virtual instruments

If a lot of this sounds like Greek right now, don't worry—we'll cover it in the chapters to come. Ready? Let's go!

# 1 } Welcome to Pro Tools LE 8

Congratulations, and welcome to the world of Pro Tools! Throughout Digidesign's 20+ year history, Pro Tools (now part of Avid Technology) has established itself at the forefront of the DAW (*Digital Audio Workstation*) community, and version 8 elevates this platform greatly—particularly for Pro Tools LE users. As a result, Pro Tools 8 will be found in virtually every level of the audio industry, from music production for CDs to surround sound for movie soundtracks. Now, armed with Pro Tools LE's powerful array of functions and features, *you'll* be able to tap into this world of digital audio for yourself to realize your own creative vision. Welcome to the party!

The first step in the process is to set up your system and master the essential functions of Pro Tools. In this chapter, we'll discuss the structure and most basic operations of Pro Tools LE 8, and you'll learn how to:

* Identify and assemble the hardware and software components of a Pro Tools LE system and understand their functions
* Organize sessions and data in Pro Tools
* Use Pro Tools' most basic functions
* Create, open, play, and close a session

# What Makes Up a Pro Tools System?

Avid's Pro Tools systems fall into one of three families—M-Powered, LE, or HD. Pro Tools LE, which we'll discuss in this book, is a *host-based* type of DAW, which means that the power of your Pro Tools system is based entirely on the processing power of your computer. Your computer's CPU (the *host*) handles important operations, such as mixing and effects processing. HD systems, on the other hand, have dedicated PCI hardware cards added to the computer, which take care of those kinds of functions.

HD systems, because of their added processing horsepower, higher mix precision, and greater flexibility, tend to be more commonly found in professional recording studios, whereas LE systems have found their niche in the growing number of home and project studios worldwide. It bears mentioning, though, that both types of systems are certainly pro-level in their own right, and the broad compatibility of Pro Tools allows projects to be started in LE-based home studios and then completed in more powerful HD-powered studios with ease!

Let's talk about your new Pro Tools LE system. LE systems, regardless of their specific configurations, all rely on a few key components.

## The Heart of Your DAW: The Computer

The host computer is the cornerstone of your Pro Tools LE system. Your computer—particularly your computer's CPU (*Central Processing Unit*)—will be called upon to do everything from mixing and automation to effects processing, so the more speed your CPU has, the more powerful your Pro Tools software will be as a result. The host computer can be either a PC (running Windows XP or any 32-bit Vista OS) or a Mac (with OS X Leopard for Pro Tools 8).

In addition to CPU speed, your computer's RAM (*Random Access Memory*) plays an important role in how your digital audio work-station will perform. It probably comes as no surprise to learn that the more RAM your computer has, the better. More RAM will allow your Pro Tools session to run more real-time effects and will make for an overall more powerful DAW. Avid stipulates a minimum of 1 GB of RAM, with 2 GB or more recommended.

Ideally, your DAW computer should be dedicated solely to music-related tasks. Other applications running on your system can steal from your computer's overall efficiency when running Pro Tools. The task of recording and playing back digital audio can be demanding on your computer's CPU, and other programs interrupting the steady stream of data to and from your hard drive can cause major problems. Of course, having such a dedicated computer can be impractical for many users; in that case, you should avoid resource-sapping applications (particularly games) and limit the number of active programs during your Pro Tools sessions.

## Pro Tools Audio Interface

Your Pro Tools audio interface (which you purchased with your system) is the doorway for audio going to and coming from your computer. Generally speaking, your computer will connect directly to the audio interface, and your various audio devices (mixing boards, keyboards, or microphones) will connect to the interface's available audio inputs. To listen to your session, you should connect the main audio outputs of your interface to an amplifier, and from there to monitor speakers (or to powered speakers, which have built-in amplification). Following is a brief rundown of the audio interfaces available for Pro Tools LE systems and their key features.

### Mbox 2 Micro

The Mbox 2 Micro is Avid's newest addition to the LE family, and it's made quite a splash. The real attractiveness of this particular inter-face is its size—it's roughly the size of a USB flash drive, which allows Pro Tools users to work virtually anywhere (in combination with a laptop).

There's one limitation that you should be aware of with the Micro, however, and that lies in its I/O complement: There are *no* inputs on the Mbox 2 Micro (not surprising, given its compact size), so you won't be able to use it for typical recording purposes.

However, if you're looking to take a previously recorded session on the road, or you are only concerned with composing with virtual instruments and pre-made bits of audio, this is an interface worth looking at. Here's what you'll get:

* USB connection to the host computer, which also powers the unit. An extension USB cable is included. (You'll want to use this if your USB ports are very close together.)
* Two channels of analog output, combined in a 1/8-inch stereo jack. This jack can be connected to either headphones or monitor speakers and has a volume control on the interface.
* Support for up to 24-bit/48-kHz digital audio.

### Mbox 2 Mini

What makes the Mbox 2 Mini so great is its balance of power and portability. It has just enough I/O to take care of the basics, and with its size and USB power, it is a perfect travel companion to a laptop. Here are some of the notable features of the Mbox 2 Mini:

* USB connection to the host computer, which also powers the unit.
* Two analog inputs/outputs, including one XLR connection (usually used for a microphone, and including switchable phantom power), and two 1/4" connections that can be used for line-level signals or instruments.
* A sturdy metal chassis. This might not sound like a particularly special feature, but if you're going to use the Mbox 2 Mini when traveling, you'll really appreciate the robust housing. The housing also includes a Kensington security lock so you can cable the interface to your desk and so on.
* Headphone outputs.
* Support for up to 24-bit/48-kHz digital audio.

## Mbox 2

The Mbox 2 is a nifty little interface that delivers much for its modest price. Though it doesn't have the number of inputs and outputs of some of the larger Pro Tools interfaces, its portability and MIDI support are very attractive features for many users:

❋ USB connection to the host computer, which powers the unit in addition to transferring audio information.

❋ Two analog inputs/outputs (Mic, Line, or DI instrument level), plus one stereo S/PDIF input/output, all of which can be used simultaneously.

❋ Two microphone preamps with switchable phantom power for condenser mics.

❋ Headphone outputs.

❋ Support for up to 24-bit/48-kHz digital audio.

❋ MIDI In and Out ports.

> **❋ WHAT ABOUT MY ORIGINAL MBOX?**
>
> The Mbox 2, as you might guess from the name, is the next generation of the original Mbox (which was an immensely popular LE interface in its day). Do you have one of those original Mboxes? Not to worry—it will work just fine with Pro Tools LE 8!

## Mbox 2 Pro

The Mbox 2 Pro is the most advanced member of the Mbox 2 family. Though this interface is a bit bigger than the Mbox 2, it will give you higher audio quality and more inputs and outputs. Take a look at the features:

❋ IEEE 1394 (FireWire) connection to the host computer. If you use a 6-pin connection to the host computer, the Mbox 2 Pro can receive power from the computer. (Be careful, though—the Mbox 2 Pro requires a good bit of power and can deplete a laptop battery quickly in some cases!)

❋ Six analog inputs/eight analog outputs, including two XLR connections (for microphones) and two instrument connections conveniently located on the front of the interface.

* A phono preamp for turntable connections.

* Switchable phantom power for condenser microphones.

* MIDI In and Out ports. (These support MIDI Time Stamping (MTS) for greater accuracy.)

* Two headphone outputs with independent volume control.

* BNC word clock connections.

* Support for up to 24-bit/96-kHz digital audio.

### Digi 003 Factory

Just as the Mbox 2 family is the next generation of the original Mbox, the new Digi 003 is the evolution of a previous device called the Digi 002. The 003 Factory interface is the flagship of the LE hardware line, and it features not only expanded I/O, but a very cool mixer-style control surface. The core features of the Digi 003 interface include the following:

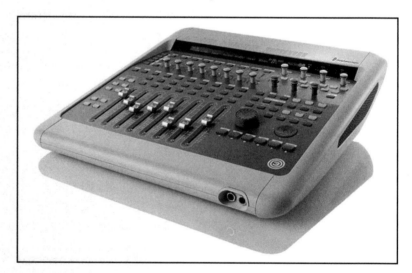

* IEEE 1394 (FireWire) connection to the host computer.

* Eight analog inputs/outputs, one stereo S/PDIF digital input/output, and eight channels of ADAT optical input/output.

* Built-in control surface, including eight touch-sensitive motorized faders, and rotary encoders (a fancy term for knobs) for controlling pans, plug-ins, and so on.

❄ MIDI I/O.

❄ Four microphone preamps with switchable phantom power.

❄ Headphone outputs.

❄ BNC word clock connections.

❄ Support for up to 24-bit/96-kHz digital audio.

As I mentioned, the 003 Factory is the newer version of the 002. Among numerous small improvements, there are a few particularly notable differences between the two:

❄ The 002 features a standalone digital mixer mode, whereas the 003 can function as a standalone MIDI controller.

❄ The 002 has a single headphone jack located in the upper-right corner of the control surface. Though this was convenient enough, it resulted in the headphone cable laying over the control surface. The 003 has improved this by giving you two headphone jacks and moving them to the very front of the control surface.

❄ The 003 adds a dedicated jog/shuttle wheel. This is very useful for navigation and playback.

## Digi 003 Rack

The Digi 003 is available in two versions. In addition to the full-blown 003 Factory discussed previously, there's the rackmount version, called the *Digi 003 Rack*, which is a two-rack space module sporting the same I/O complement as the 003, but without the control surface component.

## New: Digi 003 Rack Factory

To answer the call for more microphone preamps, Avid has created the 003 Rack Factory, which doubled the complement of microphone preamps to eight. The unit is similar to the two-rack space module (no control surface) in other respects, but the additional mic preamps can accommodate more involved recording environments.

### New: Eleven Rack

The new Eleven Rack interface is a departure from the other Pro Tools LE interfaces, able to act as not only an audio interface, but also a stand-alone guitar amp head. Within this versatile device are not only the basic audio and MIDI I/O complement of an Mbox 2, but also DSP (*digital signal processor*) chips that provide a wide range of guitar amp models that are equally at home in the studio or onstage.

Here are just a few of the features of the Eleven Rack:

* USB 2.0 connection to the host computer
* Two channels of line-level input, one XLR microphone input, plus an impedance-matching guitar input
* Two channels of AES/EBU and S/PDIF digital I/O
* One headphone output
* MIDI I/O

### WHERE CAN I LEARN MORE?

If you want to learn more about the specifications of any Pro Tools hardware, the Avid website (www.avid.com) is a great place to start. There is currently a link back to the Digidesign.com page on the lower half of the main Avid.com page, and that will take you to a page where you can browse for the current Pro Tools LE line and explore the entire range of products available, from the highest-end ICON system to the most basic plug-in.

## Hard Drive(s)

Just as traditional tape-based recording studios rely on magnetic tape as a storage medium, Pro Tools relies on hard drives for the recording and playback of its digital audio. The drives can be SCSI, IDE/ATA, Serial ATA, or even FireWire based.

It is important to remember two factors when choosing a hard drive for Pro Tools—size and speed. First, a larger-capacity drive will allow you to store more audio data. This will translate into more minutes of audio that you can store, higher-quality digital audio, or both. A fast drive will allow for more efficient transfer of data (also called *throughput*) when you are recording and/or playing back audio. This can translate into higher track counts and more reliability when working with complex sessions.

### Using a Second Hard Drive

Adding a second drive dedicated to the storage of your Pro Tools sessions will greatly increase your Pro Tools system's performance. You'll still want to install the Pro Tools application on your computer's system drive, but when you create your sessions (something we'll get into later in this chapter), put them on your "audio" drive. That way, you'll have one hard drive occupied with the nominal tasks of your computer and another separate drive (with its own read/write head and throughput) dealing only with your Pro Tools session and audio.

❋ WILL PARTITIONING MY DRIVE DO THE TRICK?

Partitioning a single hard drive may give the outward appearance of creating a second drive, but in reality there is still only one physical hardware device. Although partitioning can be a convenient way of organizing your data, it *doesn't* add another physical drive with its own read/write head, so it won't give Pro Tools the same benefit with real-time tasks as a second physical drive would.

❄ HFS+ DRIVE SUPPORT

If you're like me, you spend a lot of time working on both PCs and Mac computers. In the past, that's meant that my Mac-formatted (HFS+) drives were useless on a PC, but those days are over. Pro Tools LE 7.3 introduced an HFS+ Disc Support option in Pro Tools' installation process. Just click the appropriate check box when you install Pro Tools, and your PC will be able to read and write to Mac-formatted drives (regardless of whether Pro Tools is running).

Though it's quite a handy feature, there's one caveat: If you're using a Mac-formatted drive for audio recording, you'll want to have all of your session's related files (a concept we'll talk about later in this chapter) also on Mac-formatted drives. Recording and playback of a single session using a combination of both PC- and Mac-formatted discs is not recommended.

## A Great Resource: Avid's Compatibility Documents

You might have noticed that though I've talked about desirable qualities of a powerful DAW system, I haven't mentioned many specific details about what kind of hardware you should be using (things such as minimum CPU speed and chipset types). I apologize if I seem evasive on the subject, but the truth of the matter is that the ever-changing landscape of computer-based products transforms and grows so rapidly that any specs I quote here might well change over time. Don't despair, though—Avid has provided the help you need to build the Pro Tools system you want!

Avid keeps an up-to-date list of compatible hardware on its website. To get to the compatibility section, just click the Support link located at the top-center area of the Avid website (www.avid.com), and you'll find loads of useful technical information at your fingertips. Simply click on the Digidesign tab near the top of the screen for Pro Tools support options, and you'll see a Compatibility & Upgrades link about halfway down the page. You will find a comprehensive list of minimum system requirements and information.

To view more compatibility information and alerts, you can also take a look at the Quick Links section on the right side of the Support home page. Click the Compatibility & Upgrades link, and you'll be able to see more information. It's a quick and easy way to find compatibility between operating systems and Pro Tools software versions.

# A Word about Installation

When it comes to installing your Pro Tools software, I've got good news and bad news. First the bad news: Because installation can vary from interface to interface and system to system, the installation procedure is another topic that's tough to describe in a book like this. Not only are there many different configurations possible (with different audio interfaces, computers, and so on), but Avid is constantly upgrading and tweaking their products. Bottom line: The specifics of installation are subject to change, and though your installation will probably go smoothly, sometimes there are issues to be dealt with.

The documentation you received with your Pro Tools LE software and hardware is the first place to look for late-breaking information on installation. In the ever-changing world of computers, though, even that documentation could be slightly out of date! Once again, the Avid website is also an invaluable resource for the latest software version updates and information on installation and troubleshooting. In particular, I'd recommend checking out the FAQ and Tech Docs sections—they're great resources for hunting down all the latest information.

The documentation that came with your Pro Tools hardware, combined with a little Net surfing (if needed), should allow you to successfully install and configure your Pro Tools LE system. Once that's finished, you're ready to move on.

# New in Pro Tools 8: Check for Software Updates

Wouldn't it be great if there were a way for Pro Tools to help you out with software updates? Good news—Pro Tools 8 adds exactly that functionality and can search for any updates, bug fixes, and so on that are relevant to your system. Better yet, Pro Tools can also check to see whether there are any updates needed or available for your installed plug-ins—how cool is that? Pro Tools will even differentiate between paid and non-paid updates, so you can choose to make the larger version leaps at your discretion.

Using this new feature is very easy—so easy, in fact, that there's virtually nothing you need to do. Pro Tools 8 by default will quickly check for updates when you launch the program. All you need to do is make sure that your computer is connected to the Internet, and this will happen automatically. (Don't worry—this check is very quick and doesn't add too much time to the Pro Tools launch.)

If you want to do an update check manually, you can do that as well, and it's also a simple process:

**1** Once Pro Tools is launched (something we'll go into later in this chapter), **click** on **Help**. The Help drop-down menu will appear.

**2** **Choose Check for Updates.** The Software Update progress window will appear.

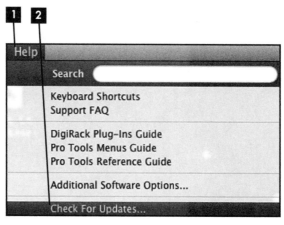

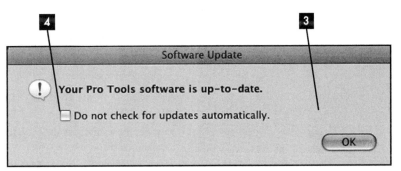

**3** If there are updates to be installed, you will be directed to a website with links for the appropriate download(s). If you are up to date, you'll see the window shown here. **Click** on **OK** to finish the process.

**4** If you don't wish for Pro Tools to perform automatic update searches upon startup in the future, just **click** the **Do Not Check for Updates Automatically check box.**

# A Word about Pro Tools M-Powered

A few years ago, Avid Technology acquired a company called M-Audio, which has been a leader in the home studio market. This has resulted in a version of Pro Tools called Pro Tools M-Powered—which can run on M-Audio interfaces!

The list of supported M-Audio interfaces is impressive and growing all the time. To get a completely up-to-date list, take a look at www.m-audio.com to see all the different kinds of devices available. For many users, the different options (for example, a combined keyboard/MIDI interface/audio interface like the Ozonic) are quite attractive. But what about the software?

The good news is that the Pro Tools M-Powered software (which is *not* included with the interface—it must be purchased separately) is largely identical to Avid's Pro Tools LE. There are a few differences, however, that do bear mentioning:

※ Avid's high-end Ethernet control surfaces won't work with Pro Tools M-Powered.

※ Avid video hardware doesn't work with Pro Tools M-Powered.

※ Pro Tools M-Powered does not support DV Toolkit (an Avid bundle product for producing audio in sync with video material) or the Complete Production Toolkit.

※ Pro Tools M-Powered doesn't support DigiTranslator (which provides file interchange between Pro Tools and other media production applications, such as Avid systems, Logic Audio, and others).

Generally speaking, the differences between Pro Tools LE and Pro Tools M-Powered are really not great hardships for many beginning Pro Tools users. In fact, if you've got Pro Tools M-Powered, you'll be able to use the vast majority of this book as a production resource, with little concern about these small differences.

# Understanding Sessions and Files

Now you've got your system set up, and Pro Tools is installed. Before you get any deeper into the world of Pro Tools, you should take a moment to understand the general principles behind this powerful digital audio workstation. An understanding of Pro Tools' overall architecture and how different elements work together will serve you well as you continue to grow in this environment.

## Pro Tools Is a Pointer-Based Application

It's common to refer to a cursor as a *pointer*, but when you're discussing a *pointer-based* application, such as Pro Tools, you're referring to the way the program deals with digital audio data. In Pro Tools' case, this pointer-based structure can be broken down to three interdependent elements—session files, folders, and audio files. In this situation, the term "pointer" refers to the way your Pro Tools session file will access (or "point") to other files on your hard drive as your session plays.

A session folder is created when you create a new session; it contains the following items (as needed):

✳ **Session file.** The session file is at the top of the Pro Tools hierarchy. This is the file created by Pro Tools when you create a new session, and it's the file you open to return to a session you already created. Although this file is relatively small, it is the master of all your session elements. Session files have the .ptf extension and contain the following elements of your session:

  ✫ The names, types, and arrangement of all tracks in your session

  ✫ All MIDI data

  ✫ Essential settings, such as inputs and outputs

  ✫ All edits and automation data

## ✳ SESSIONS AND AUDIO

It might sound as if the only thing you need is a session file, but that's not quite true. Although session files contain all the important aspects of a project listed above (and more), they don't actually contain any audio. Instead, a session file refers (or *points*) to audio files located elsewhere on your audio hard drive.

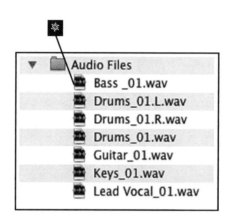

✳ Audio Files subfolder. As soon as audio is recorded, it's stored in an Audio Files subfolder within the session folder. Different takes are stored in this folder as individual audio files. When you play a session, Pro Tools accesses, or points to, the audio files in this folder.

## ✳ HOW DO AUDIO FILES GET THEIR NAMES?

When you record audio in Pro Tools, the name of the file you created follows the name of the track on which it was recorded. For example, if you record onto a mono (one-channel) Audio track named Bass, the files created by Pro Tools in the Audio Files folder will be named Bass.01, Bass.02, and so on as you record takes on this track. In the case of stereo Audio tracks, two mono files (one for the left side and one for the right) are created. If you record onto a stereo Audio track named Drums, two files named Drums_01.l and Drums_01.r will be created.

There are additional folders that can be created by Pro Tools as needed:

✳ **Fade Files subfolder.** When you start creating fades (including fade-ins, fade-outs, and crossfades), Pro Tools renders the created fades to files on your hard drive. Audio files are again created, but they're not stored in the Audio Files folder this time. Instead, they're stored in a folder named Fade Files. It's important to keep in mind that even though fades are audio files, they are significantly different in function from the audio files you record or import into your session (in ways that you'll learn about later); thus, they are stored separately.

❋ **Region groups.** Beginning with version 7, Pro Tools allows you to select multiple regions and link them together in a single *region group*. Digital audio, MIDI, and video regions can be grouped together, making editing much faster and easier. You'll learn more about region groups later, but for now just know that groups you create are stored in this folder. (If you don't create any region groups in a given session, a folder won't be created.)

❋ **Rendered files.** Pro Tools 7.4 introduced a great feature called *Elastic Audio*. This is a very cool new addition indeed, and one you'll learn about in Chapter 10, "Moving to the Next Level: Tips and Tricks." For now, though, all you need to know is that when you're working with Elastic Audio, you have the option of "rendering" your elasticized audio to an audio file—and when you do, it will be stored in this folder.

❋ **Session file backups.** Depending upon your preference settings, Pro Tools can automatically create backups of your sessions and store them in this folder. By default, a new session backup is created every five minutes, and the folder keeps the last 10 backup files. This is highly recommended, particularly for new users to Pro Tools, and can help you recover quickly if you encounter technical trouble.

If you start using video files and/or creating custom plug-in settings, Pro Tools may create additional subfolders as needed:

❋ **Plug-In Settings subfolder.** In Pro Tools, you have the option of using plug-ins, which are programs designed to work within the Pro Tools environment and function as virtual effects. (You'll learn more about plug-ins in Chapter 8, "Basic Mixing.") When you create specific plug-in presets, you have the option of saving them in this session subfolder.

❋ **Video Files subfolder.** When your session calls for a video track, you can save it in this session subfolder.

❋ WHAT ABOUT THE WAVECACHE?

There's one more file you'll often find in your session folder that we haven't talked about yet. It's a small file named WaveCache, and it stores all the waveform overviews for any audio in your session. *Waveform overview* is a fancy way of describing the visual representation of audio waves that you might see on an Audio track. This small file is automatically created and updated, so there's nothing you need to worry about with it!

### Regions versus Files

Given the fact that Pro Tools records audio to individual files on your hard drive, how do you later access these files? Simply put, when audio is recorded to an Audio track (or even MIDI data to a MIDI track), Pro Tools creates an object or region in the Edit window. In the case of Audio tracks, these regions refer (or *point*) to files on your hard drive, triggering them to sound as your session plays.

Here's a close-up of Pro Tools' Edit window. There's one Audio track in this session, and only one region on that track. That region is referring to a file named Vocal Comp.

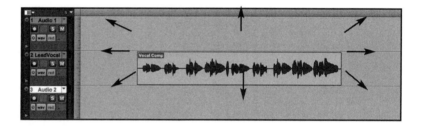

Working with regions has many advantages. One of the first you'll discover is that you have the ability to move them earlier or later on the session's timeline, allowing you to precisely position the regions in time. An environment like this, in which you have the ability to manipulate elements independently on the timeline, is commonly known as *nonlinear*. In addition to moving regions earlier or later in time, you have the option of moving them to other similar tracks. (In other words, you can move a region on a mono Audio track to another mono Audio track, and so on.)

## Nondestructive Editing

Another great advantage of using regions in this way is that you can *nondestructively* trim the audio that's being used in your session (meaning that no audio data is being lost, so you can always undo what you've done). This can be a tricky concept, especially for those who have grown up using analog tape, so let's take a look:

In this example, let's assume that the region named Vocal Comp is playing an audio file of the same name in the Audio Files subfolder. What if you don't want to use the whole region in your session? No problem—you can just adjust the start or end boundary of that region, effectively taking the unwanted bits of audio out of your session.

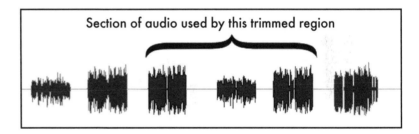

Section of audio used by this trimmed region

Does this mean that you've changed the file on your hard drive? No! You've only changed the *region* that is pointing to that file, so only a portion of that file will be heard in the session. Don't worry; because you haven't changed the audio file (only the region that is pointing to it), you can always drag the region boundaries back out if you change your mind later!

In addition to being able to trim data, there are other situations in which nondestructive editing can aid you in your production work, and you'll discover them as this book proceeds. The bottom line is that a nonlinear pointer-based environment coupled with non-destructive recording and editing gives an educated Pro Tools user a huge amount of flexibility and power, and the ability to undo changes and operations when needed.

# Basic Pro Tools Operation

The end of the beginning: You've set up your system efficiently, taken some time to understand the way Pro Tools works, and now, based on that understanding, you're ready to start working. The last step before you dive deeper into Pro Tools is to open a preexisting session.

❋ THE CHAPTER 1 TUTORIAL SESSION

At this stage, you might not have a preexisting Pro Tools session to work with, but that's not a problem. Just insert the CD included in this book and copy the folder named Chapter 1 Session to your hard drive.

When you open your session, you may see a few message boxes, including one that mentions that the "original disc allocation" can't be used. It's not a problem— it simply means that the drive you're using isn't the drive upon which it was created (*my* hard drive). You can safely pass through this window with no problem. If you do happen to run into difficulty, though, please take a look at the "Setting Up Your Session" PDF document, also included on this book's CD.

## New in Pro Tools 8: Quick Start Dialog Box

A feature has been added (and granted, it's not unique to Pro Tools) that makes opening and creating sessions easy. The Quick Start dialog box will come up when Pro Tools launches and gives you a number of useful options. Let's run through them one by one:

**1** Click the **Create Session from Template radio button**. A list of template categories and template files will be displayed to the right of the radio button cluster. What's a template? We'll get into that later in this chapter and book, but for now, just know that opening a template session will create a new session complete with basic tracks, plug-ins, and so on, so that you can get straight to work.

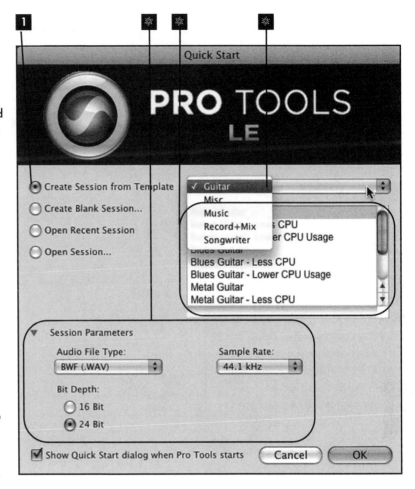

❁ Your template list can be organized into different categories. (You can change these, which we'll go into later in this chapter.) Just click on the template category menu to reveal a list of categories, as shown here.

❁ After choosing a category, the list below the drop-down menu will be populated by the templates in that category. Click on the template you want to load.

❁ Once you click a template, the session parameters will be updated in the lower section. If you want to change any aspects of the session, such as sample rate or bit depth (aspects we'll talk about later in this chapter), you can do it here.

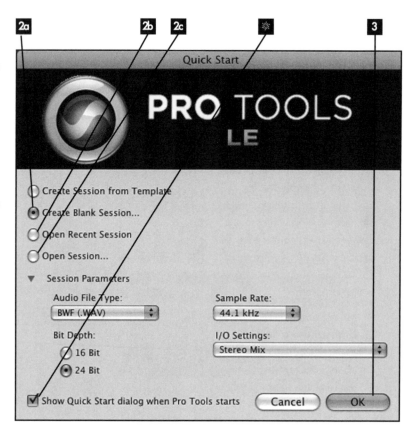

**2a** Click the **Create Blank Session radio button** to create a session from scratch. We'll go through the details of creating a new session later in this chapter.

OR

**2b** Click the **Open Recent Session radio button** to choose from a list of your most recently opened sessions.

OR

**2c** Click the **Open Session radio button** to launch a standard File Open window. This is the same window you can access from the File drop-down menu in Pro Tools, which we'll go through in the next section.

**3** Once you've made your choice, **click** on **OK** to open or create the session. (Clicking the Cancel button will bypass the Quick Start window.)

✳ If you don't want to see the Quick Start dialog box when you start Pro Tools (in which case you'll go directly to Pro Tools with no session loaded), just click the Show Quick Start Dialog When Pro Tools Starts box to remove the check mark. (This box is checked by default.)

### BUT WHAT IF I DON'T WANT TO SEE THE QUICK START DIALOG BOX⁉⁇

You can also prevent the Quick Start dialog box from being displayed when Pro Tools starts through a window in Pro Tools called the Preferences window (which you'll learn quite a bit about as this book progresses). Once Pro Tools has launched, go to the Setup drop-down menu and choose the Preferences menu item. The Preferences window will open, and you will find the Show Quick Start Dialog When Pro Tools Starts check box in the lower-right corner of the Operation tab.

## Opening a Session When Pro Tools Is Running

Suppose that Pro Tools is already running, and you've already gone past the Quick Start window. Here's how to open a session:

**1** Click on **File**. The File menu will appear.

**2** Click on **Open Session**. A standard File Open dialog box will appear, depending on the operating system you're using.

### ✻ YOUR FIRST SHORTCUT

Pro Tools includes shortcut keys that enable you to work more efficiently. The shortcut for Open Session (Command+O on a Mac and Ctrl+O in Windows) is very useful—and easy to remember as well!

**3** If necessary, **select** the **drive** that contains the audio session. The drive will be selected, and the folders on that drive will appear.

**4** Click on the **folder** that contains the session folder. The folder will be selected, and the scroll bar will automatically move to display the contents of that folder.

**5** If necessary, **click** on the **subfolder** that contains the session file. The contents of the subfolder will be displayed.

**6** Click on the desired **session file. The file will be selected.**

**7** Click on **Open**. The session will be loaded into Pro Tools.

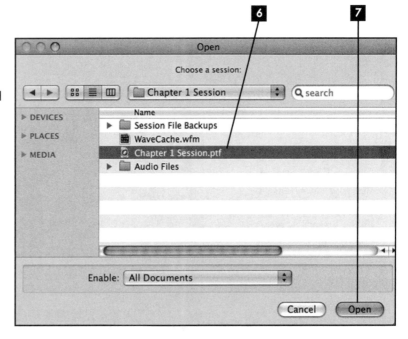

✳ OPEN RECENT SESSIONS

The ability to select a recently opened file from a list is fairly common in the software world, and most users will be familiar with this idea from other applications. You've already seen the Open Recent Session option in the Quick Start window, but you also have this available in Pro Tools itself. The Open Recent item can be found immediately below the Open Session menu item. Simply click Open Recent, and you will see a list of up to 10 of your most recently opened sessions.

## Opening a Session When Pro Tools Is Not Yet Launched

In this case, suppose Pro Tools is *not* yet launched. To open a session, follow these steps:

**1** Select the **hard drive** that contains your session. On a PC, this will involve using My Computer or Windows Explorer. On a Mac, you can use the Finder or simply click on the hard drive icon on your desktop.

**2** Open any **folder** that contains your session folder. The contents of the folder will be displayed.

**3** Open the **folder** that contains the session file. The contents of the folder will be displayed.

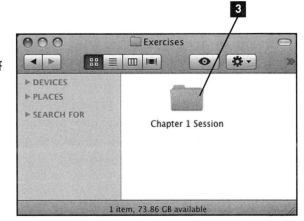

**4** Double-click on the desired **session file**. Pro Tools will launch automatically, and the session will be loaded.

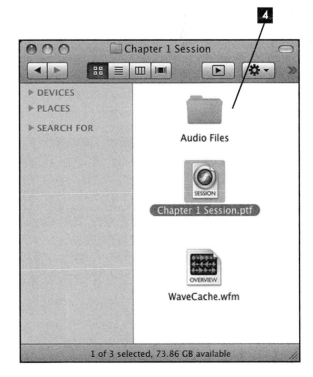

Now, let's take a closer look at the important process of creating a blank new session. (Many of these topics also apply to opening template sessions.)

# Creating a New Session

Now that you've got your system put together and everything's installed, you can create a new session (as opposed to opening a preexisting session, as you did in the previous section of this chapter). Our earlier discussion of how Pro Tools works will come in handy here. In addition to these previous concepts, you'll want to start thinking about how you can best set up your new session and maximize your computer's resources.

## Starting the Process

In the previous section, you learned that you can create a blank new session from the Quick Start window, but you can also create a new session from within Pro Tools itself. After you've launched Pro Tools, you'll see the program's basic array of drop-down menus. Here's where the important process of creating a session can begin.

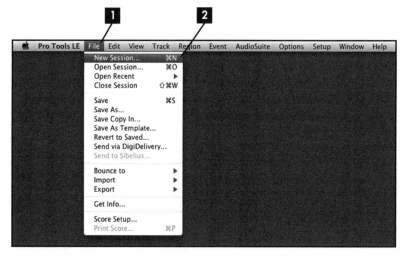

**1** Click on **File**. The File menu will appear, containing a list of Pro Tools' basic functions.

**2** Click on **New Session**. The New Session dialog box will open. In a sense, it is a smaller version of the Quick Start window.

❀ MORE SHORTCUTS!

As you explore Pro Tools further, you'll notice that there are many functions that have shortcut keys associated with them. These shortcut key combinations are displayed to the right of the functions (such as the shortcut for creating a new session—+N (Mac) or Ctrl+N (PC)—shown in the previous image). Although there are far too many shortcuts to learn all at once, learning the combinations for popular functions, such as opening or creating a session, can help you work more efficiently.

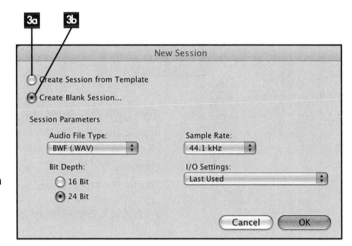

**3a** Click the **Create Session from Template radio button** to gain access to your session templates, just as you did in the Quick Start window.

OR

**3b** Click the **Create Blank Session radio button** to create a new session, just as you can do in the Quick Start window. Because that's what we'll be doing in this section, this is the button you'll want to select.

## Choosing Session Parameters

Whether you're creating a new session from the Quick Start window or from the File drop-down menu, your next task is to choose your session parameters, which will determine other important aspects of your session.

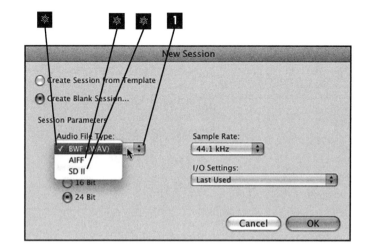

**1** Click on the **Audio File Type menu arrows**. A drop-down menu will appear. Choose a file type from the following options:

✷ **BWF (.WAV).** A WAV file is a Windows standard file, and the Broadcast Wave Format (BWF) is a version of this file type that is particularly suited to television and film production. (The file extension is still .wav.) This is a good format choice for session files that will be used in both Mac and Windows systems.

✷ **AIFF.** This is the standard audio file format for Macs.

✷ **SD II.** This format (which used to be the default format for Pro Tools in older versions) is available only on Mac-based Pro Tools systems.

❊ CHOOSING A FILE FORMAT

Pro Tools' default file format is BWF (.WAV), and this generally works well in most situations. If you are planning to share files between Mac and Windows systems, this is the preferred file format.

On the other end of the compatibility spectrum is SD II, or Sound Designer 2, and it's worth noting that not only is it a Mac-only file type, but it also only supports sample rates up to 48 kHz.

**2** Click on the **Sample Rate menu arrows**. A menu will appear, showing the sample rates supported by your audio interface.

**3** Select a **sample rate** for your session.

**4** Select either **16 Bit or 24 Bit audio** as the bit depth for your session.

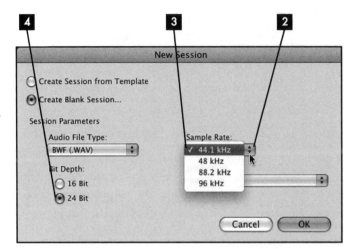

### WHAT ABOUT IMPORTING AUDIO?

Once selected, the sample rate and bit depth will become the overall sample rate and bit depth for all audio in this session. This means that any audio you import into the session (a process we'll go through in Chapter 3, "Getting Started with Audio") will have to either match these specs or be converted to match the session (something that Pro Tools does automatically when conversion is needed).

**5** Click on the **I/O Settings menu arrows**. The I/O Settings drop-down menu will appear.

**6** Select your **I/O (Input/Output) settings** for this session. For now, choose Stereo Mix. The option will be selected.

**7** You've made some very important choices, and the next step is to choose a name and location for your session. Click OK to proceed.

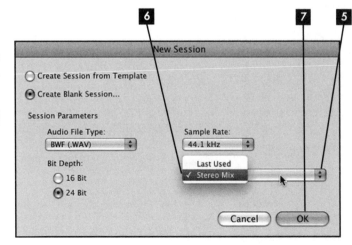

❋ WHERE CAN I LEARN MORE ABOUT I/O SETTINGS?

Your I/O settings determine the assignments and names of inputs, outputs, inserts, and busses. Don't worry if this doesn't make a lot of sense now—you'll learn more about how to make the most of your I/O settings in Chapter 3.

## Choosing the Name and Place

Two of the most important skills you can learn as a DAW user are file management and documentation. Though these are fairly simple and straightforward tasks, you shouldn't underestimate their importance. The last thing you want is to misplace a session and waste valuable time trying to find it—or worse, inadvertently delete a session because it was in the wrong place!

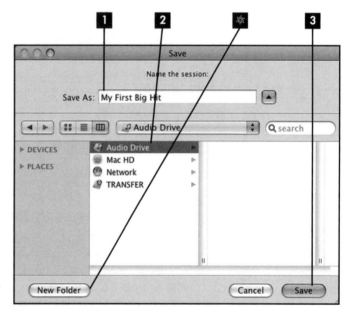

**1** The first thing you have to do is to choose the name of your session. **Type** the **name** in the Save As text box.

**2** According to your operating system, **navigate** to the desired **drive**. (If you have a hard drive devoted to digital audio, choose that drive.)

❋ In some cases, you might want to create a new folder to put your session folder in. If you do, create a new folder according to the normal conventions of your operating system.

**3** Once you've set your name and location, **click** the **Save button**. Your session will be created and loaded into Pro Tools. Good job!

❋ WHERE TO CREATE YOUR SESSION

According to this screen, this new session will be created on my audio hard drive.

# Playing a Session

Let's assume that you've got Pro Tools running and you've opened up a preexisting session (for example, the Chapter 1 session that you opened earlier). Wondering how to play it? No problem—it's easy!

A transport section is in the top area of a window that Pro Tools calls the *Edit window* (which you'll learn more about in the next chapters). It will help you with basic play and record operations. It looks very much like the controls you would find on almost any media player. Let's take a look at the basic functions:

❄ HOW TO GET TO THE EDIT WINDOW

If you're not seeing any transport-style controls at the top of your Pro Tools window, you've probably opened your session into the other main window (called the Mix window, which looks very much like a mixing console). Getting to the Edit window is very easy—just go to the Window drop-down menu at the top of the Pro Tools window and choose the Edit menu item.

If you are in the Edit window and you are still not seeing any transport controls, click the small triangular button in the upper-right corner of the Edit window and select Transport from the list. (This is a section of the Edit window that we'll go into in greater detail in Chapter 2, "Getting Around in Pro Tools.")

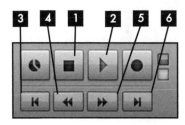

**1** The Stop button—you guessed it—stops playback.

**2** The Play button will play back your session from the current position.

**3** The Return to Zero button takes you directly to the beginning of your session.

**4** Rewind quickly moves your playback point earlier in your session.

**5** Fast Forward quickly moves your playback point later in your session.

**6** The Go to End button takes you directly to the end of your session.

# Saving Your Work

Now that you've got the very basics down, it's time to think about how to wind things up. This is a crucial stage, and it's important to do the job correctly. There are a number of ways to save your work, each with its own specific advantages.

## Save

This is a pretty standard feature and as straightforward as they come:

**1** Click on **File**. The File menu will appear.

**2** Click on **Save**. Your work will be saved, and you can continue to work on the saved session.

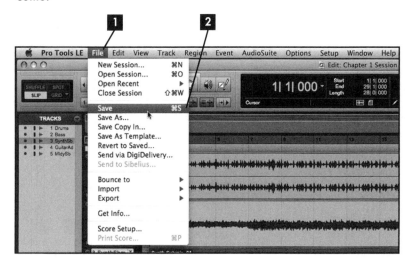

## Save As

If you use the Save command, the previous version of the session will be overwritten with the new one. What if you don't want to overwrite the old session? That's where Save As comes into play.

**1** Click on **File**. The File menu will appear.

**2** Click **Save As**. The Save Session As dialog box will open.

**3** Type a **different name** for your session in the Save As text box to avoid overwriting the original session.

**4** Click on **Save**. The new version of the session will be saved with the name you specified in Step 3. You are all set at this point to continue work on the newly saved session.

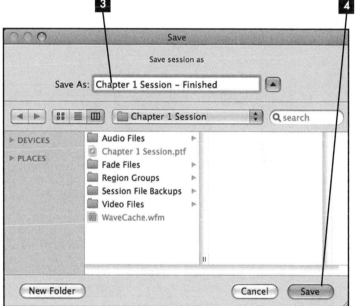

❋ **WHERE DO I SAVE THE NEW "SAVE AS" SESSION FILE?**

It's important to note that both the original session file and the new version of the file can reside in the same session folder and can access the same source audio files.

## Save Copy In

If you want to save your session with a different name *and* create a new folder, complete with all the dependent audio files, the Save Copy In feature is for you! This is commonly a part of the final archiving process when a project is complete (which you'll learn more about later).

> ### THE IMPORTANCE OF BACKING UP YOUR WORK!
>
> Backing up (or *archiving*) your work is a tremendously important part of production. It might not be terribly exciting, but you'll be glad you established good file-saving habits when something unexpected happens.
>
> The Save Copy In feature is particularly suited to archiving because it makes copies of your original session in a separate (and hopefully safe) place. Additionally, this process can intelligently gather all the elements your session needs (assuming you selected them in the Items to Copy section) and save them in one central location. Bottom line: When you're backing up your session, Save Copy In is a very smart way to go!

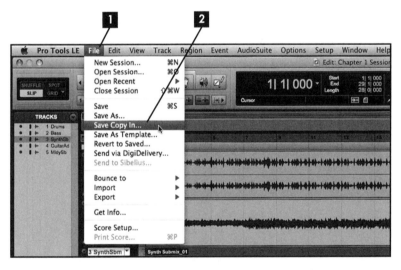

**1** Click on **File**. The File menu will appear.

**2** Click on **Save Copy In**. The Save Session Copy dialog box will open.

Save Copy In gives you the option to save elements of your session (audio files, fade files, and so on), which gives you a whole new dimension of flexibility. Here are some things you can specify:

❄ **Session Format menu.** This drop-down menu contains options for previous versions of Pro Tools. Select one of these formats if you intend to open this session in an older version of Pro Tools.

❄ **Session Parameters section.** These are the same options you saw when you initially created your session. You can select different file types, sample rates, and/or bit depths for your session. Pro Tools will automatically convert audio files as needed in your new session's Audio Files folder.

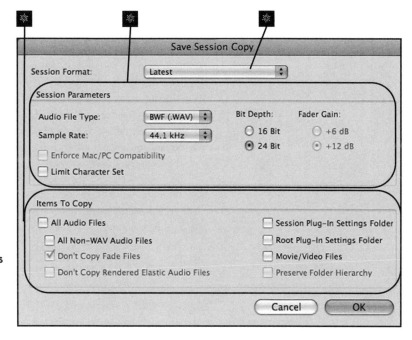

❄ **Items to Copy section.** You can choose the elements of your original session that you want to copy over to your new session folder. Click the appropriate boxes to copy aspects of your old session to your new session folder.

**3** In the Save As text box, **type** a descriptive **session name** that is different from the original session name.

**4** **Select** a **location** for your session from the Save In menu. This section is identical to the related sections in the dialog boxes when you choose Save or Save As. This time, a new folder will be created for your new session, though.

**5** **Click** the **Save button.**

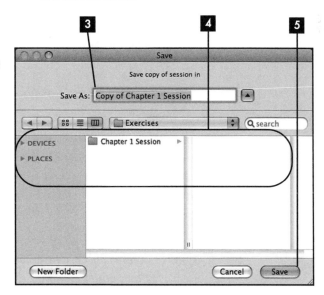

❄ ❄ ❄

**PRESERVE FOLDER HIERARCHY**

Sometimes (particularly in sessions with higher track counts) you'll want to record audio to multiple hard drives at once (something we'll discuss in Chapter 4, "Recording Audio"). By default, the Save Copy In process will gather all your session's audio files into a single new Audio Files folder. Most times this is desirable, but you might want to keep these audio files separate, so that you can move them back to their original drives at a later time. In that case, click the Preserve Folder Hierarchy check box (at the bottom-right corner of the Save Session Copy dialog box). Checking this box will create separate Audio Files folders within your new session folder, each placed within folders named for your audio drives. For example, instead of a single subfolder named Audio Files in your session, as you've seen earlier in this chapter, you might have folders named Audio Drive 1/Audio Files, Audio Drive 2/Audio Files, and so on.

**CAUTION: VERSIONS AND FEATURES**

When you use Save Copy In to save a Pro Tools session as an older version, it probably comes as no surprise that any of the new features that aren't sup-ported in the older version will be lost. Here's another scenario to consider—it *is* possible to open a Pro Tools 8 session file in Pro Tools 7 without any special Save Copy In process. Of course, you'll lose any of the new features specific to Pro Tools 8. Here's the rub: If you save the session in Pro Tools 7, you'll save the session as a *Pro Tools 7 session*, and though you can open it in Pro Tools 8 again, you'll have to redo any work you had originally done that used features exclusive to Pro Tools 8.

## New in Pro Tools 8: Session Templates

The idea of using templates to save time is by no means a new concept—savvy Pro Tools users in all sorts of situations have used template sessions to bypass the time-consuming tasks of track creation, plug-in setup, and mixer configuration. In Pro Tools 8, however, the functionality and ease of use of templates has been raised to a new level.

As you saw in the Quick Start window, you already have a list of useful templates that are installed with Pro Tools, but you also have the ability to create templates of your own. It's easy!

**1** Click on **File**. The File menu will appear.

**2** Click on **Save As Template**. The Save Session Template dialog box will open.

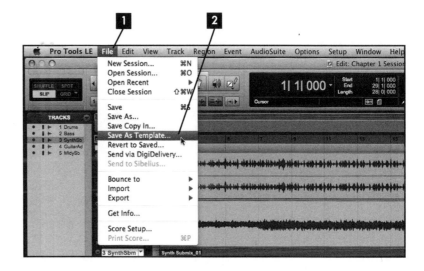

You have two options as far as location is concerned:

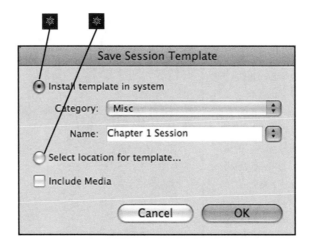

❊ Choosing the Install Template in System radio button will automatically create your template in the default system location. This will allow you to easily access the template from the Quick Start window in the future.

❊ Choosing the Select Location for Template radio button will allow you choose any name and location for your template file once you click the OK button. This is particularly handy for Pro Tools users who work in multiple studios. (An inexpensive USB drive can hold many session templates, and you can carry it with you easily.)

Let's assume that you want to want create this template on your system, and that you've chosen the Install Template in System radio button. Let's take a look at the different options you'll get:

1. **Click** the **Category menu arrows.** A list of category options will appear.

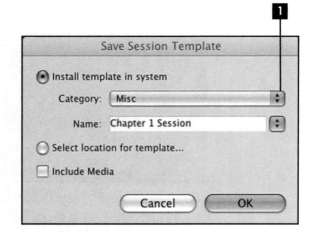

* The top section of the list will show you preexisting categories, into which you can place your template. Just click the desired category to select it.

* The Add Category menu item will allow you to create a new category and add it to the list shown in the top section. Just click this option, and you will be prompted to name your new category.

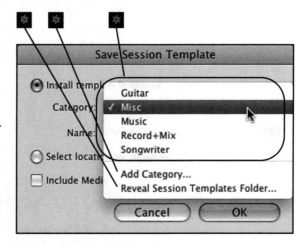

* The Reveal Session Templates Folder menu item will open the template folder using your computer's file browser (Mac's Finder or Windows' Explorer, depending on your platform). This is useful for managing your template files (renaming, deleting, and so on). It's worth mentioning at this point that Pro Tools template files are not session files themselves, and they will have a .ptt file extension.

**2** Once you've chosen the appropriate category, just **type** a **name** for your template in the Name text box. (Clicking the arrows button will display a list of all the templates currently in that category.)

**3** When you're finished, just **click** on **OK** to create your template.

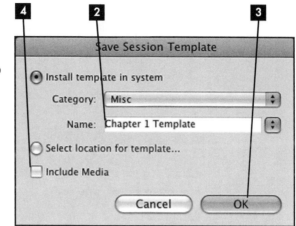

**4** In many cases, you won't want your template to include any audio or video files, but if you *do*, just **select** the **Include Media check box**.

# Closing Your Session

The last basic procedure you have to complete is to close down your session.

**1** **Click** on **File**. The File menu will appear.

**2** **Click** on **Close Session**. Pro Tools will shut down the current session and make itself ready for the next step.

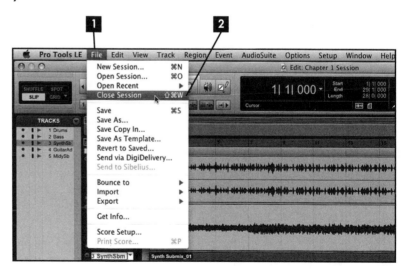

❋ DO YOU WANT TO SAVE YOUR CHANGES?

Before your session closes completely, a message box might prompt you to save your changes. This message box appears when you make *any* changes to your session and then try to quit Pro Tools before saving those changes. You can choose Save or Don't Save and move on.

# Quitting Pro Tools

Actually quitting Pro Tools varies slightly depending upon the operating system you use:

**1a** For Mac users, quitting Pro Tools is just like quitting any other application. **Click** on the **Pro Tools LE menu** and **select Quit Pro Tools LE.**

OR

**1b** If you're using Pro Tools on a PC, closing the software is exactly the same as the process in virtually every other program you've used in Windows. Simply **click** on the **File menu** and **select Exit.**

That's it—good job!

# 2 } Getting Around in Pro Tools

In Chapter 1, you took the time to install and set up your Pro Tools system. You've gone the extra mile and learned how Pro Tools "thinks" regarding sessions and files. You've even gotten to the point of creating, opening, and playing session files. Now, let's go to the next level of using Pro Tools and get better acquainted with the layout of the Pro Tools environment.

Think of this chapter as a brief primer in the "Pro Tools way" of getting the job done. Based upon the general architecture discussed in this chapter, you'll be able to efficiently navigate through the operations and features we'll go through later.

Some more experienced computer-based producers will immediately see similarities between Pro Tools LE and other well-designed DAWs, but it will still be a good use of your time to learn the proper names and layouts of these new workspaces. There are a number of windows in Pro Tools, many with specific functions, and you'll find that getting acquainted with the most common ones will really pay off later. In this chapter, you'll learn how to:

※ Recognize the main sections of the Edit window and how to customize them

※ Recognize the basic layout and functions of the Mix window

※ Access other useful windows, such as the Big Counter, System Usage windows, Playback Engine window, and Workspace Browser

※ Make the most of your regions

# The Edit, Mix, and Transport Windows

When you open a session, it will display any number of window configurations. This layout will reflect the windows that were displayed the last time you saved that session. In most cases, one of Pro Tools' two main windows, the Edit window or the Mix window, will be shown. It's important to know what these two windows do and how to navigate within them. There's one more window that's crucial for all kinds of Pro Tools operations, called the Transport window. (You used a smaller version of that window when you played a session in Chapter 1.) Let's take a quick look at the general layout of these important windows.

### ✵ A NEW LOOK

Any reader who's used previous versions of Pro Tools will notice that there's not just a small change in Pro Tools' GUI (*Graphical User Interface*)—it's a *big* change. Pro Tools has a much slicker look overall, but the new GUI is more than just a pretty face. The new colors reduce eye fatigue, particularly in the low-light conditions that are popular in recording studios. The new graphic design also has some built-in flexibility (which we'll go into throughout this chapter), so it not only looks cooler, but it works better as well!

### ✵ A QUICK WAY TO CHANGE WINDOWS

You'll be making the switch between the Edit and Mix windows often, so doing so as quickly as possible can be very useful. The shortcut to toggle between the Mix and Edit windows is Command+= for the Mac or Ctrl+= for Windows.

# Working with the Edit Window

If there's a primary window in Pro Tools, it's the Edit window. This environment is packed with useful tools and information about your Pro Tools session—so much so that it can be a little daunting at first! If you break it down into the basics, though, you'll find it easy to understand and use.

## The Playlist Area

❋ USING THE TUTORIAL SESSION

To follow along, just open the session named Chapter 2 Session, which is included on your book's CD. (Remember, you'll have to copy the session files to your computer's hard drive first.)

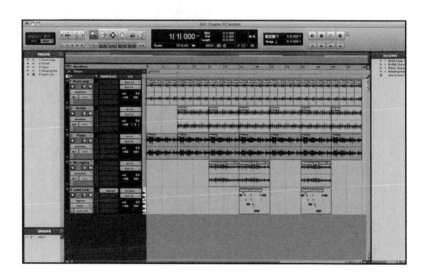

When you begin a new session from scratch, the Playlist area will be an empty area in the middle of your Edit window. Any kind of track you create will appear in this area as a horizontal row. Here, for example, there are four stereo Audio tracks and one stereo Instrument track (the Lead Line track). As discussed in Chapter 1, the colored blocks are called *regions*.

## The Tracks and Edit Groups Column

Immediately to the left of the Playlist area, you'll notice a column including the Tracks list and the Groups list. Let's take a look at the Tracks list first:

❊ For each track there is a specific track name (located in the upper-left corner of each track strip). When you want to select a track, you can do so by clicking on the track name button. Tracks that are selected will be indicated with a highlighted name. (In this case, the Piano track is selected.) Each track strip shows a lot of information besides regions and track names, which we'll get into in Chapter 3, "Getting Started with Audio."

❋ You'll find the Tracks List button in the upper-right corner of the Tracks list. Think of this as a sort of "control center" for showing and hiding tracks. You have options to show or hide all tracks, only selected tracks, or track types. (For example, with the Show Only submenu, you can show only Audio tracks.) There is another submenu for sorting tracks (shown here), which allows you to arrange your tracks in a variety of orders.

All the tracks in your session, whether visible or hidden, are listed in the Tracks list area. In Pro Tools 8, this list is divided into sections, each giving you important information about your session:

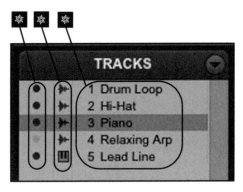

※ The left-hand column will indicate which tracks are shown and which are hidden. The shown tracks are marked with a dark dot, and tracks that are hidden will be indicated with a light-gray dot. (In this example, all the tracks are being shown except the Relaxing Arp track.) This column will give you not only information, but control as well—just click any track's dot (technically called the Track Show/Hide icon) to change its state.

※ Moving to the right, you'll see a column of icons indicating track type. (Track types are something we'll go into in the next chapter.) In this case, the first four tracks are *Audio* tracks, and the bottom track is called an *Instrument* track.

※ Of course, you want to be able to see the track names, and you'll find them in the right-hand column.

**WILL HIDDEN TRACKS BE HEARD?**

All active and unmuted tracks, whether they are shown or hidden, will sound during playback. The ability to hide or show tracks is simply a feature to help you manage your editing and mixing desktop. (But it's a feature for which you'll be grateful when your tracks start adding up!)

**TRACK COLOR COLUMN**

In some cases, you may see a fourth column, indicating track color, between the Show/Hide column and the Track Type column. This is a common column to see, and we'll talk specifically about track colors (and how to use them) later in this chapter.

Just below the Tracks list, you'll find the Groups list. An edit group is a selection of tracks that can be edited as one. The layout of this list is similar to the Tracks list:

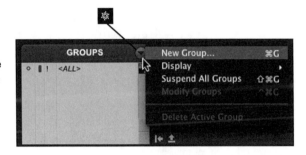

❊ You'll find the Groups button in the upper-right corner of the Groups list. Like the Tracks List button, you'll see a list of group-related functions when you click on the button at the top of the Groups list.

As you create edit groups, they'll show up here in the Groups list. (Active groups will be highlighted.) Here again, this list is divided into columns. (We'll go into how to use edit groups in Chapter 6, "And More Editing.")

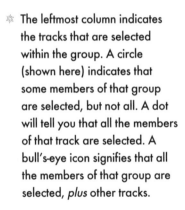

❊ The leftmost column indicates the tracks that are selected within the group. A circle (shown here) indicates that some members of that group are selected, but not all. A dot will tell you that all the members of that track are selected. A bull's-eye icon signifies that all the members of that group are selected, *plus* other tracks.

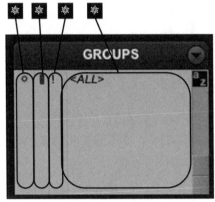

❊ The next column will show the group's color assignment. When a group is active, it will be indicated in your Mix window, using this color.

❊ Immediately to the left of the group name is a column that will show the group's letter. Every group you create will have a letter assigned to it. (The All group shown here is special and is indicated by an exclamation mark.)

❊ Group name.

> ❋ THE EVER-PRESENT ALL GROUP
>
> When you create a new session, you'll notice that there's already a group
> shown in this list (named All), even though you didn't create it. The All group
> is created automatically when a session is created. Highlighting the word "All"
> will allow you to quickly edit all the tracks in your session simultaneously.
> (We'll cover the creation and use of additional edit groups in Chapter 6.)

## The Regions List

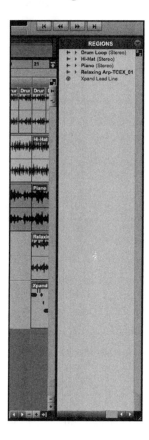

To the right of the Playlist area, you'll find another vertical column.
This is the Regions list—a storage area for regions that are (or will
be) used in your session.

❄ **Regions List button.** At the upper-right corner of the Regions list, you'll find the Regions List button. Clicking this button will display a drop-down menu of region-related functions.

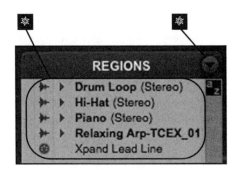

❄ **Regions list.** This is a complete collection of all the regions (audio and MIDI) available in your session, regardless of whether they're being used actively in a track. From here, you can drag and drop regions onto the appropriate tracks. This list is broken down into columns as well, which can vary depending on the options you choose in the Regions List menu.

❄ **WHAT'S MIDI?**

You might notice that I've been mentioning a thing called MIDI (*Musical Instrument Digital Interface*) from time to time. We'll go into MIDI and how to use it in Pro Tools in Chapter 7, "Using MIDI."

## Rulers

The Ruler area allows you to view the passage of time in your session in a number of different ways. Different scales, such as minutes and seconds or bars and beats, can be useful to you depending on the kind of work you are doing in Pro Tools. Any combination of the following rulers can be shown:

❄ Timeline ruler types (Bars|Beats, Min:Secs, or Samples)

❄ Conductor ruler types (Tempo, Meter, Key, Chords, or Markers)

The timeline can be displayed simultaneously in many time scales, with each visible ruler's format displayed to the left of the timeline.

## Edit Tools

There are a number of tools that can be displayed in the top row of the Edit window. What tools you choose to see and their placement in this area is up to you to decide (and you'll do just that later in this chapter), but here are some basic tool clusters:

❋ Edit modes.

❋ Zoom tools.

❋ Basic Edit tools.

> ❋ Grid and Nudge settings: These will allow you to choose the resolution of your region movements.

The location and selection displays can give you location information.

❋ The time scale will tell you exactly where you are in your session.

> ❋ The selection area will tell you the beginning, end, and duration of your selection. (The format for this section is based upon the format you've chosen for the time scale.)

## New in Pro Tools 8: Universe View

Experienced Pro Tools | HD users will recognize the term "Universe." For some time, Pro Tools | HD has included a Universe window that allows users to navigate complex sessions with ease. With the advent of Pro Tools 8, everyone has this power, and it's been made even more convenient!

**1** Click the **Edit Window button**. A list of display options will appear.

**2** Click on **Universe**. The Universe view will appear.

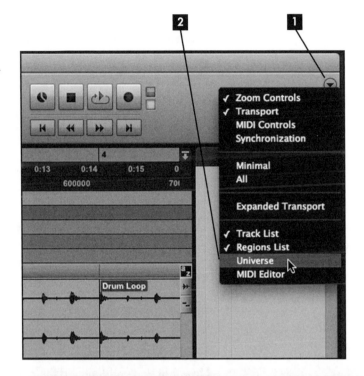

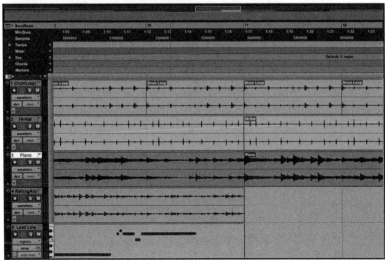

The Universe view will appear just above the ruler(s) and will show your session in its entirety. Let's take a closer look:

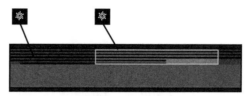

* Regions in your sessions (audio or MIDI) will be represented as colored horizontal lines. (The color will reflect the color of the corresponding regions in your session.)

* The Universe view will be divided into a dark area and a light area, with the light area representing what you're actually seeing in your Edit window's Playlist area. Here's where it really gets interesting: Just click within this light area and drag it to the desired position in your session. You'll immediately see your Playlist area updated to reflect the movement of the light-colored area.

## Customizing the Edit Window

Now that you've identified the overall layout of the Edit window, the following sections describe a few ways to set up the window to make working easier.

### Adjusting List Size

If your session calls for more groups than tracks, you might want to give a little more space to the Groups list on your desktop.

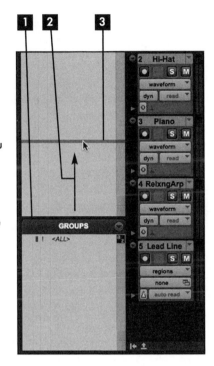

**1** **Move** your **cursor** to the boundary between the Tracks list and the Groups list.

**2** **Click and drag** the **boundary** up or down as needed. As you drag, you'll see a light-gray line marking the movement of the boundary.

**3** **Release** the **mouse button**. The boundary will be "dropped," and the lists will be reorganized.

❄ **RESIZING THE LISTS**

You can similarly adjust any of the horizontal or vertical boundaries for the Tracks list, Groups list, and Regions list. Be careful, though—adjusting the vertical edges of these areas can affect how much space you have on your screen for tracks.

## Hiding Lists

In addition to adjusting the sizes of these lists, you can hide them entirely when you're not using them.

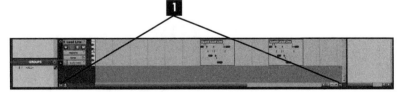

**1** **Click** on the **arrow** at the inner-bottom corner of either vertical section. The appropriate column will be hidden immediately, and more of your Edit window will be usable by your Playlist area.

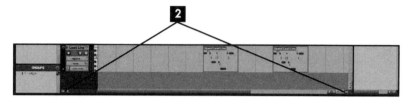

**2** Not seeing your lists? That means that they're currently hidden. **Click** on the **arrow** in either lower corner of the Edit window. The corresponding column will reappear immediately.

> ❄ **WHAT WILL I SEE WHEN I OPEN A SESSION?**
>
> Remember, the window arrangements that appear when you open a session are the same as they were in the session when you last saved it. It might be a bit surprising to open a session and see no Tracks or Regions list in your Edit window. Don't worry, though—you can always follow the previously mentioned steps to display the lists.

## Displaying Track Columns

There are a number of columns in the Edit window's Track area that provide track-specific information on things such as inputs, outputs, inserts, sends, comments, and more. We'll go into each of these in due course, but for now, here's how to show or hide the columns you want:

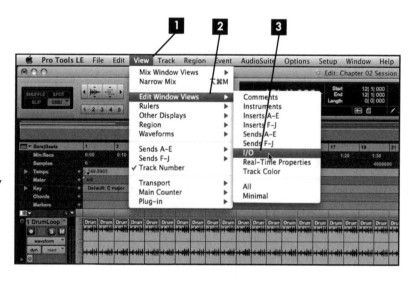

**1** **Click** on **View**. The View menu will appear.

**2** **Click** on **Edit Window Views.** A submenu of the available columns that can be shown in the Track area will appear. Checked columns are currently displayed.

**3** **Click** on any **menu item** to check or uncheck it, and the appropriate column will be displayed.

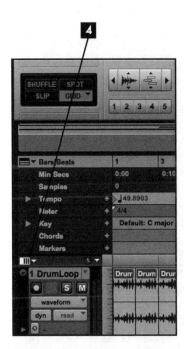

**4** Here's another way to get to the same list. **Click** the **Edit Window View Selector icon**, which you'll see just above the top track in your session and below the rulers section.

> ❄ **TOTALLY EXTREME VIEWING, DUDE!**
>
> In addition to selecting columns individually, you can select All or Minimal to show or hide all columns.

## Displaying Rulers

You can also choose which rulers are to be shown.

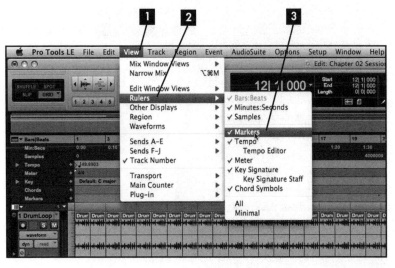

**1** **Click** on **View**. The View menu will appear.

**2** **Click** on **Rulers**. A list of available rulers will appear. (A check mark by a ruler indicates that it's being shown.)

**3** **Click** any **ruler** to change its state (shown versus hidden).

**4** There's another way to get to the same list. **Click** the **Ruler View selector** to show the Ruler View menu. You'll find this button to the left of the highlighted ruler.

## Adjusting Track Heights

In Pro Tools, you have the ability to change the height of individual tracks. This can come in handy, particularly when you have many tracks in your session and you want to see them all, or when you really want to do some microsurgery on one track in particular. Here's how:

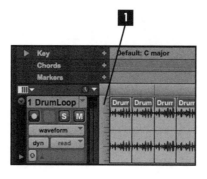

**1** Between each track's columns (I/O, Inserts, Sends, Comments) and the Region area is a small vertical area (in this case showing the amplitude scale). **Right-click** in this **area**. The Track Height drop-down menu will appear.

**2** **Select** the desired **track height**. The track will immediately change to match your height choice.

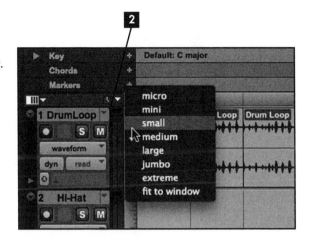

## ✳ CHANGING THE TRACK HEIGHT FOR DIFFERENT TRACK TYPES

You can change the height of any Pro Tools track (including MIDI and aux tracks, which you'll explore in later chapters). However, the thin vertical area for other types of tracks looks a little different than the amplitude scale of an Audio track. MIDI tracks, for example, show a keyboard-like display. In any case, right-clicking in this area will bring up the same Track Height menu.

✳ There's an even easier way to change track heights. Simply move your cursor to the bottom of the desired track, in the columns area. You'll see your cursor turn into a double-arrow icon (shown here). Once you see this cursor icon, just click and drag up or down to decrease or increase that track's size.

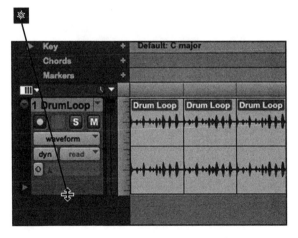

✳ ✳ ✳

> ❄ MAKING GLOBAL CHANGES
>
> Here's another useful shortcut: Hold the Option key (Mac) or the Alt key (PC)
> while you change the height of any one track, and the heights of all shown
> tracks will change at once.

## Custom Colors

The ability to apply the color of your choice to a track, region, or group isn't a new feature in Pro Tools 8 (it was introduced back in version 6), but like so many other features, it has been greatly improved upon. Like other Edit window customizations, this won't change the *sound* of your session, but it can really help you work more efficiently. Users of all levels will find this sort of control a powerful ally in organizing tracks, regions, and more!

Let's take a look at how this feature can be used to mark your tracks. The first step is to make sure that you're able to view track colors:

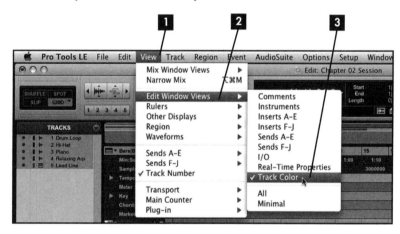

**1** Click on **View**. The View menu will appear.

**2** Click the **Edit Window Views menu item**. The Edit Window Views submenu will appear.

**3** Select the **Track Color menu item** if it is not already selected. Track colors will only be visible if this menu item is checked. If there is no check mark by this item, click it to enable this view.

You will now see a colored tab to the left of each track, but that's only the beginning of the power you have over the appearance of your tracks. Let's start off by changing the color of a specific track.

**1a** From the Window menu, **choose Color Palette**. The Color Palette window will appear.

OR

**1b** **Double-click** the **Track Color column** (at the leftmost edge of the track). The Color Palette window will appear.

**2** Click the desired **color box**. The selected track's color column will immediately change its color-coding to match.

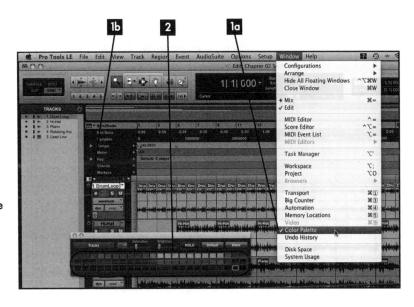

But wait, there's more!

**1** Click the **Apply to Selected menu** (which currently reads "Tracks"). This menu will allow you to color different elements of your session.

❋ **Tracks.** As you just saw, this menu item will enable the Color Palette window to change a track's color tab.

❋ **Regions in Tracks.** This will change the color of regions that have been selected in the Playlist area of the Edit window.

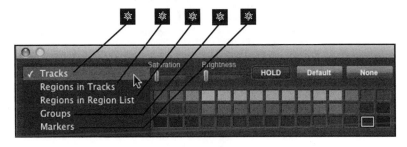

❋ **Regions in Region List.** Selecting this menu item will allow you to color-code selected regions in the Regions list area.

❋ **Groups.** This will allow you to change the color-coding of selected groups.

❋ **Markers.** Markers may also be color-coded, which you'll learn more about in Chapter 6.

## New in Pro Tools 8: Movable Tools

Not only do you have the ability to show or hide different tool clusters in the top row of the Edit window (by clicking the Edit Window button in the upper-right corner), but you also have the ability to move them to suit your particular work style.

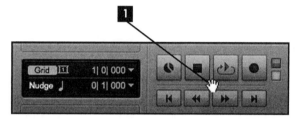

**1** **Hold** down the **Command key (Mac) or Ctrl key (Windows)** and move your cursor over the tool cluster that you wish to move. (In this case, I want to move the Transport cluster.) The cursor will turn into a hand icon to indicate that the cluster is ready to be moved.

**2** **Click and drag** the **cluster** horizontally to the desired location. You will see a semi-transparent representation of the tool cluster as you drag it.

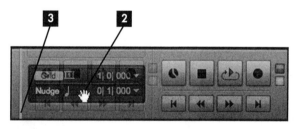

**3** A vertical yellow line will indicate where the cluster will be inserted. When you get to the desired location, just **release** your **mouse button**, and the clusters will be rearranged to reflect your changes.

## New in Pro Tools 8: Waveform Views

The graphic representation of audio within an audio region is technically referred to as the *Waveform overview*, and it's worthwhile to note that this overview is stored in the *WaveCache* file (which we discussed briefly in Chapter 1). Prior to Pro Tools 8, this overview had an 8-bit resolution, and it's been upgraded to 16-bit in Pro Tools 8. Additionally, you now have the ability to look at your waveforms in a number of different ways.

**1** **Click** on **View**. The View menu will appear.

**2** **Click** on **Waveforms**. The Waveforms submenu will appear. The top section of this submenu will allow you to view the waveform in two different ways:

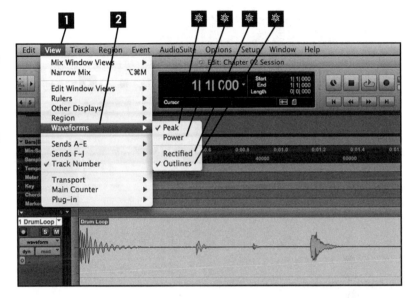

❋ Peak is perhaps the most common way of looking at your waveform. It is a faithful representation of the amplitude of each sample of your audio. This is important, because it will give you a sense of how you're using your dynamic range and when you're in danger of clipping (something that is particularly nasty when dealing with digital audio).

❋ Though viewing your waveforms in Peak view is certainly useful, it often doesn't match with the perceived loudness of a sound. For a waveform view that looks a bit more like it sounds, choose Power from the Waveforms submenu.

In addition to these two ways of looking at your audio waveforms, you have a couple more view options:

❋ Pro Tools has long had the ability to show you waveforms in a rectified manner, but with Pro Tools 8, this has been made even more accessible in this submenu. (If the term *rectified* doesn't sound familiar, don't worry—we'll cover that in just a bit.)

❋ Particularly when you are working with a light-colored region, the difference between the color of the waveform and the background
- color of the region can be pretty subtle, and this can make the waveform a bit difficult to distinguish. Select the Outlines menu item to view your waveforms with a very thin dark line—I think you'll appreciate how this makes your waveforms easy to read!

### ✳ RECTIFIED WAVEFORMS

The term "rectified waveform" might be unfamiliar to many readers, but once you see it, it's easy enough to understand. To understand what a rectified waveform shows, though, it's useful to take a second look at the traditional un-rectified view:

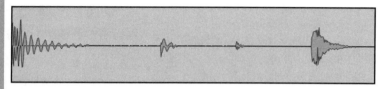

You'll notice that the waveform is centered around a virtual axis going through the middle of the wave. This axis represents zero volts, or silence. If you zoom into the waveform you'll find that the wave oscillates above and below this zero-volt line, indicating positive and negative voltage.

Now let's take a look at a rectified waveform:

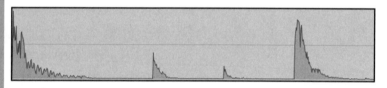

When you look at rectified waveforms, the zero-volt line is at the bottom of the waveform display. Whether the voltage is positive or negative, the visual representation ascends with increasing voltage. In many cases, this makes peaks and transients much easier to distinguish, particularly when you are working with drums or spoken words.

# Working with the Mix Window

After the Edit window, another one you'll use extensively in Pro Tools is called the *Mix window*. Although there's a good bit of common ground between the Mix and Edit windows, the layout and function of the Mix window is geared toward the mixing and automation phases of your production.

## Understanding the Mix Window Layout

Much of the general layout of the Mix window is similar to the Edit window's layout.

❄ **Tracks list.** This area functions identically in both the Edit and Mix windows and will allow you to select and show/hide specific tracks.

❄ **Mix Groups list.** As you create mix groups, they will show up in this area, just as edit groups showed up in the Edit window's Groups list.

❄ **Channel Strips area.** When you create any kind of track (Audio, Aux, Master Fader, MIDI, or Instrument), it will appear here as a vertical strip. (You'll learn more about the elements that make up these channel strips in Chapter 8.)

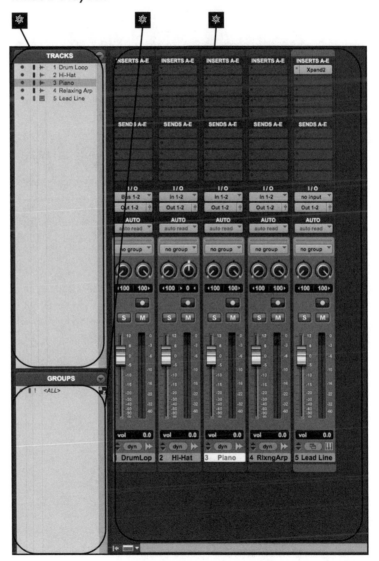

### TRACK ORDERS IN THE EDIT AND MIX WINDOWS

Tracks that appear at the top of the Edit window will appear on the left side of the Mix window. As tracks descend in the Edit window, they move from left to right in the Mix window's Channel Strips area.

### TRACK SHOW/HIDE IN THE EDIT AND MIX WINDOWS

There is a one-to-one correspondence between tracks that are shown (or hidden) in the Mix window and those in the Edit window. Also, remember that whether a track is shown or hidden doesn't affect that track's audibility.

## Customizing the Mix Window

Tailoring your Mix window for maximum ease of use will make mixing much more efficient and fun. This section explores some of the most common customizations for the Mix window.

### HIDING THE LISTS COLUMN IN THE MIX WINDOW

As in the Edit window, clicking on the double arrows in the corner of the Mix Groups list will hide Tracks list/Mix Groups column. This can give you more space on your desktop for channel strips.

**1a** Click the **View menu** and then choose **Mix Window Views**. The Mix Window Views submenu will appear.

OR

**1b** Click the **Mix Window View Selector icon**. The Mix Window Views menu will appear.

**2** Click on any **element** (Comments, Inserts, Sends, Track Color, or Instruments) to check or uncheck it. As with the Edit window, checked items will be shown.

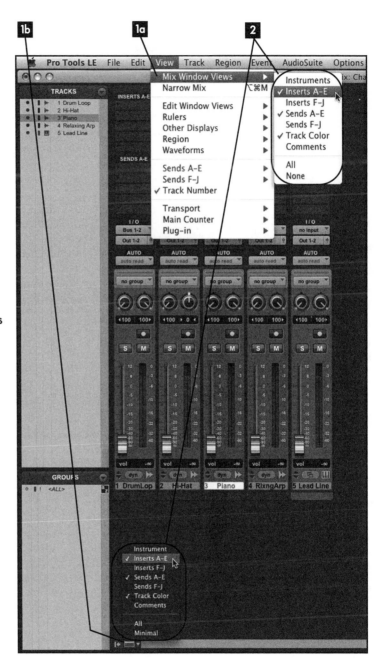

❄ SENDS AND INSERTS

Sends and inserts are essential to the mixing process, and the ability to show and hide them will be helpful as you tweak your mix. You'll learn more about mixing techniques in Chapter 8, "Basic Mixing."

Suppose you have a lot of tracks in your session, and you'd like to see as many of them as possible in the Mix window. Here's how to squeeze more tracks onto a limited desktop.

**1** Click on **View**. The View menu will appear.

**2** Select **Narrow Mix**. Technically, the Mix window itself won't narrow, but the individual channel strips will, allowing you to fit more tracks within a given space.

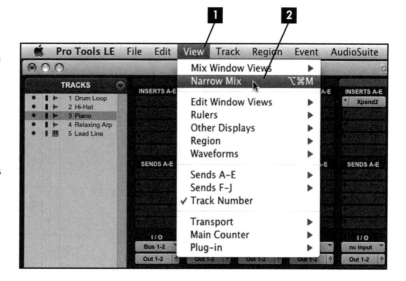

You might be wondering whether you can use track color-coding in the Mix window as you did previously in the Edit window. The answer is a resounding yes, and you'll find that coloring your channel strips will be particularly useful in organizing more complex mixes.

❋ Double-click on either of the color-code areas of a given track to open the Color Palette window. From there, you can change the color-coding of selected tracks just as you did in the Edit window.

❋ You can also click the Window drop-down menu to access the Color Palette window (again, just as we discussed earlier with the Edit window).

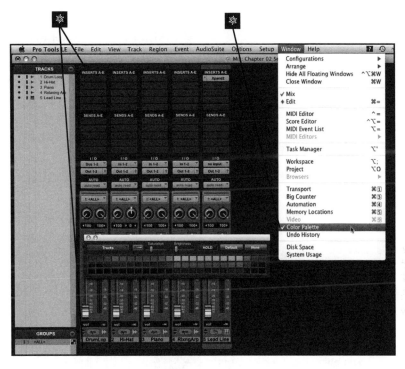

In addition to coloring the tabs on channels, you also have the ability to color the entire channel strip. This applies to the Edit window as well, but it is particularly useful in the Mix window. You'll find the controls for doing this in the Color Palette window itself.

❋ The Apply to Channel Strip button, when activated, will apply the track's color to the entire track column (or the track row in the case of the Edit window). The button will be blue when channel strip coloring is active.

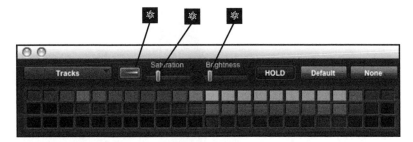

❋ Once the Apply to Channel Strip button is activated, you'll have the ability to choose the color's strength with the Saturation slider. As the slider is moved from left to right, the channel strip's color becomes less subtle. (Note that this slider is only accessible when the Apply to Channel Strip button is activated.)

❋ You can change the overall brightness of your channel strips by adjusting the Brightness slider.

> **COLOR-CODING AND THE MIX WINDOW**
>
> Because the Mix window doesn't deal with regions, you will probably want to limit your color-coding to tracks and groups in this window. Color changes made in this window will be applied to the Edit window as well.

# The Transport Window

Yet another window, called the *Transport window*, will be useful in playing your session.

**1** Click on **Window**. The Window menu will appear.

**2** Click on **Transport**. The Transport window will appear. Like the Edit and Mix windows, the Transport window has a number of functions, but for now we'll just focus on basic transport controls.

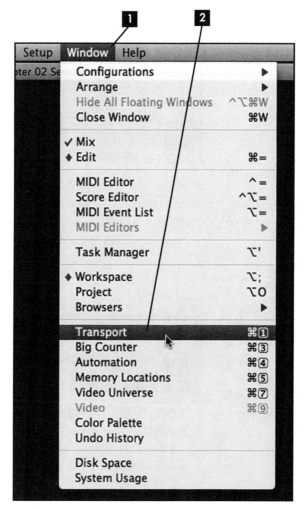

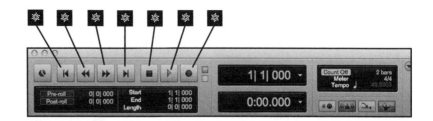

❄ Go to Beginning.

❄ Rewind.

❄ Fast Forward.

❄ Go to End.

❄ Stop.

❄ Play.

❄ Record.

❄ Main Time Scale.

❄ Sub Time Scale. (Think of this as a way to view the passage of time in a different format from the main time scale—you'll learn how to work with both scales in Chapter 5, "Editing.")

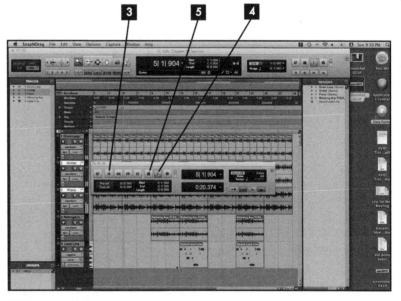

**3** Click on the **Go to Beginning button** to make sure you're at the beginning of your session.

**4** Click on the **Play button**. Your audio will begin playing, as shown in this illustration. You'll notice that a long vertical line travels from left to right in the Playlist area of the Edit window. This is called the *timeline insertion*, and you'll notice that as it intersects with different regions, sound will be produced.

**5** Click on the **Stop button** when you're finished. The playback will stop.

## Customizing the Transport Window

The Transport window is especially useful when you're working in the Mix window, because the Mix window has no built-in transport controls. Though it is fairly intuitive, this window bears discussion, as does how to customize it.

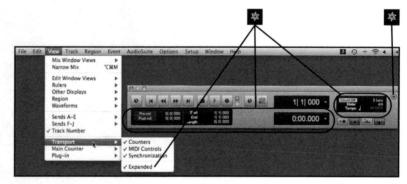

**1** Click on **View**. The View menu will appear.

**2** Click on **Transport**. The Transport submenu will appear with the following options:

* **Counters.** This option will add the main counter to the Transport window.

* **MIDI Controls.** This option will add basic MIDI controls to the Transport window (which will be discussed in detail in Chapter 7, "Using MIDI").

* **Synchronization.** Pro Tools has the option of being controlled remotely or of controlling other devices. You'll learn how to use these features in Chapters 4 and 7.

* **Expanded.** This option will show secondary transport controls, including pre-roll and post-roll, the sub-counter, and secondary MIDI controls.

* Clicking on the triangle icon in the upper-right corner will also show the Transport window view options list.

# Other Useful Windows

Even though you'll spend the majority of your Pro Tools life working in the Edit and Mix windows, there are a number of other windows that serve more specific purposes. These windows usually operate in conjunction with either the Edit or the Mix window (whichever one you're using). You can access these secondary windows through the Windows menu, like so:

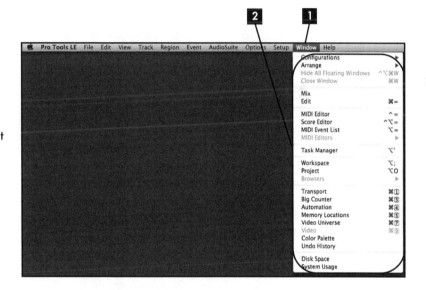

**1** Click on **Window**. The Window menu will appear, displaying an assortment of choices.

**2** Click on the **window** you want to display. The following list details some of the available windows.

❋ GETTING TRANSPORT CONTROL IN THE MIX WINDOW

You've already worked with the Transport window. (Remember, the shortcut is Command+1 [on your computer's numeric keypad] on the Mac or Ctrl+1 [on your computer's numeric keypad] on the PC.) Like the Transport window, the windows discussed here will open on top of either the Edit or the Mix window.

Let's take a first look at some of the more popular windows.

## Big Counter

※ **Big Counter.** The Big Counter window is simply a larger display of your main counter, but it really comes in handy when you want to watch your session's progress from across a room! The shortcut for the Big Counter window is Command+3 (on your computer's numeric keypad) on a Mac or Ctrl+3 (on your computer's numeric keypad) on a PC.

※ **RESIZABLE!**

Longtime users of Pro Tools will be very happy to hear that the Big Counter window is now resizable, and by dragging the lower-right corner of the window, you can adjust it to fill as much of your screen as you like!

## Automation Enable

※ **Automation.** Automating Pro Tools is a topic you'll work with later in this book. Simply put, it's a way for you to make your mixes more dynamic by changing settings as your session plays. The Automation window shown here allows you to enable or disable these changes for various aspects of your session. The shortcut for the Automation window is Command+4 (on your computer's numeric keypad) on a Mac or Ctrl+4 (on your computer's numeric keypad) on a PC.

## Memory Locations

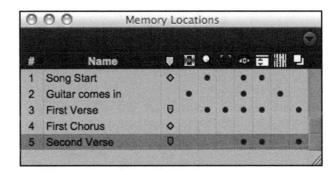

❋ **Memory locations.** As you become more experienced, your sessions will tend to become more complex. You'll find that navigating around intricate sessions will start taking more and more time and effort. Wouldn't it be great if there was a way to immediately jump to a specific location, or even a specific region of your session? That's exactly what memory locations can do. As you'll learn in Chapter 6, memory locations are a powerful and flexible way to get from place to place instantly! For those readers who will use this feature frequently, you can open it by pressing Command+5 (on your computer's numeric keypad) on a Mac or Ctrl+5 (on your computer's numeric keypad) on a PC.

## Video

❋ **Video.** Pro Tools is an audio application, but that doesn't mean you can't work with video. Although your video editing options are limited to be sure, importing video files into your session is easy, and viewing your movie as your session plays is as simple as opening the Video window from the Window drop-down menu. You can also get to this window quickly by pressing Command+9 on a Mac or Ctrl+9 on a PC.

## Session Setup

Those of you who are experienced with Pro Tools version 6 or earlier might notice that the Session Setup window, which was under the Window menu, is no longer there! Not to worry; it just moved to another menu. Here's how to open the window:

1. **Click** on **Setup**. The Setup menu will appear.

2. **Click** on **Session**. The Session Setup window will appear.

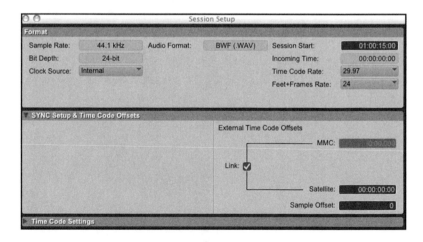

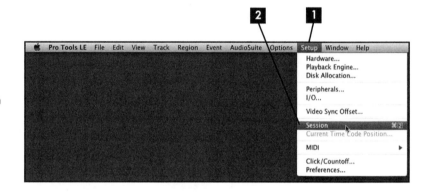

The Session Setup window displays useful information about your session's configuration. The shortcut for the Session Setup window is Command+2 on a Mac or Ctrl+2 on a PC.

## System Usage and Disk Usage

Last but not least among the historically popular windows, the System Usage and Disk Usage windows will give you important information about how your system is doing. There are no shortcut keys for these windows (you'll have to open them from the Window menu), but they're critical windows nonetheless!

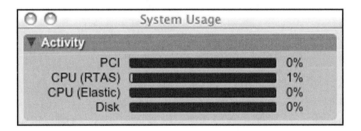

❊ **System Usage.** As you learn more about how to efficiently use Pro Tools, you'll want to refer to the System Usage window from time to time to check on how your computer is dealing with the tasks associated with Pro Tools. This window gives a simple and efficient view of the workload your session is dealing with, broken down into categories.

❊ **ELASTIC AUDIO CPU METER**

Those of you familiar with versions of Pro Tools prior to 7.4 will notice that the System Usage window has changed just a bit. In previous versions, there was a single CPU meter, which showed RTAS plug-in activity in your session. Now, with the introduction of Elastic Audio (which we'll get into in Chapter 10, "Moving to the Next Level: Tips and Tricks"), there is a second meter that will tell you how hard your computer's CPU is working on Elastic Audio–related tasks.

| Disk Usage | | | | |
|---|---|---|---|---|
| Disk Name | Size | Avail | % | 44.1 kHz 24 Bit Track Min. |
| TRANSFER | 4.9G | 4.3G | 87.9% | 588.3 Min |
| Audio Drive | 926.6G | 824.3G | 89.0% | 111505.5 Min |
| Mac HD | 186.0G | 72.5G | 39.0% | 9810.9 Min |

❄ **Disk Usage.** The size of a hard drive in a DAW is kind of like the amount of tape in an analog recording studio—the more you have, the more you can record. The Disk Usage window will let you know how much free space you have on each drive for recording audio and how much time that space represents (at your session's sample rate and bit depth).

❄ DISK SPACE VERSUS DISK ACTIVITY

You'll notice that there's a disk meter in the System Usage window as well as a stand-alone Disk Usage window. What's the difference? The System Usage window's disk meter will tell you the activity of the hard drives in your system (in terms of data throughput), whereas the Disk Usage window will give you information about storage capacity.

## New in Pro Tools 8: MIDI Editor and Score Editor

Perhaps the most important advances in Pro Tools 8 have been in the world of music creation, and working with MIDI data has changed significantly in this version. At the heart of these changes are two new windows (which we'll talk more about in Chapter 7)— the MIDI Editor and the Score Editor.

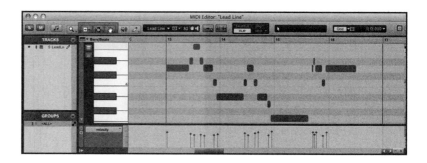

The MIDI Editor window is more than your typical floating window—for many users, it will become their primary creative environment. To the left, you'll see the familiar-looking Tracks and Groups lists, and you'll be able to view MIDI data in a number of different days in the main section of the window. The top row of the MIDI Editor window will also show you some familiar-looking editing tools, so you can work with MIDI data in the MIDI Editor in the same way you work with data in the Edit window.

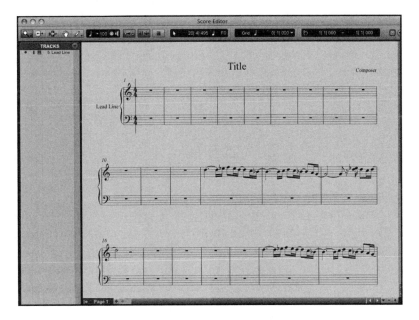

If you want to print music for your musicians (or even if you just feel more comfortable creating music in a more traditional environment), the Score Editor window will serve you well. Here, as with the MIDI Editor, you'll see the familiar Tracks and Groups lists on the left side and editing tools on the top row. What makes the Score window really unique, though, is its ability to add notational aspects, such as song title, composer, chord symbols, and so on, that musicians will need to see in order to play your music.

# Window Management

We've covered a lot of important introductory ground in this chapter, but if you'll indulge me just a bit longer, I'd like to walk you through some features you can use to get the most out of your desktop!

## Window Configurations

One of Pro Tools' most useful features is the ability to recall specific arrangements of windows. With window configurations, you can quickly change the windows being displayed, as well as their sizes and positions. The process is as simple as it is useful.

**1** **Arrange** your **windows** in any way that suits your workflow. In this case, I've chosen a simple arrangement of both Edit and Mix windows.

**2** The next step is to capture this arrangement of windows. From the Window menu, **choose Configurations** and then **New Configuration**. The New Window Configuration window will appear.

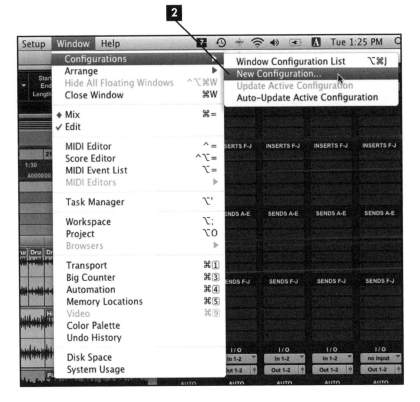

**3** In the New Window Configuration window, you have the option of capturing either the entire layout by clicking the top radio button or specific aspects of your desktop as shown in the bottom radio button's drop-down menu. In this case, **choose** the **top radio button** and **type** a descriptive name in the Name field.

**4** Click **OK**. The window will close, and your screen arrangement will be ready to be recalled at a moment's notice!

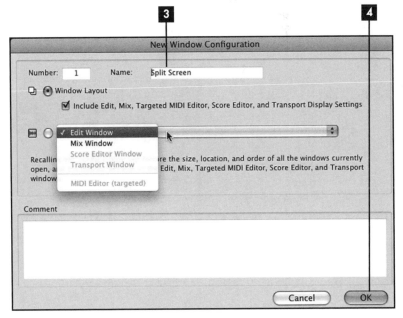

Recalling a window configuration is easy, and as with most things in Pro Tools, there are a number of ways to do it.

**1** From the Window menu, **choose Configurations**. The Window Configurations submenu will appear.

**2** Any existing window configurations will appear at the bottom of the submenu. Just **click** the **layout** you want to recall.

**3** There is also a convenient floating window that shows a list of your window configurations (similar to the Memory Locations window that you saw earlier in this chapter). **Choose Window Configuration List** to show this window.

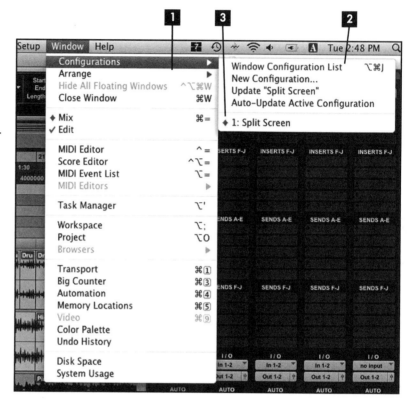

**4** This window will not only show you a list, but it will also show you the aspects that are recalled with each configuration through the icons that are to the immediate right of the configuration name (window layout, Edit window, Mix window, Score Editor, Transport window, and MIDI Editor). Just **click** on the **configuration** you want to recall.

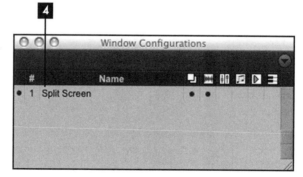

❄ WINDOW CONFIGURATIONS SHORTCUT

Here's a shortcut for recalling a window configuration, but be careful—the key order is important. First, press the period key on your numeric keypad, then press the number of the window configuration that you want to call up (again on your numeric keypad), and then finally press the asterisk key (yet again on your numeric keypad).

❄ UPDATING A WINDOW CONFIGURATION

In the Window Configurations submenu, you'll note that there is an Update "[configuration name]" option, which will allow you to change a given configuration to reflect the current window arrangement. Auto-Update Active Configuration will do this automatically.

## Hiding Floating Windows

From time to time, your desktop may get a bit cluttered with floating windows of all kinds, getting in the way of seeing the Edit or Mix window clearly. There are two ways to quickly hide (and bring back) all floating windows in one fell swoop.

❄ From the Window menu, choose **Hide All Floating Windows**. All floating windows will immediately disappear, and the menu item will be checked. Re-clicking Hide All Floating Windows (when it is checked) will reveal all hidden floating windows.

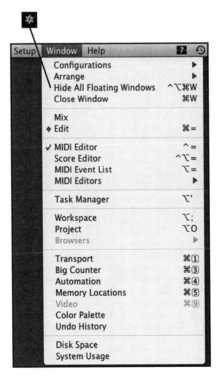

HOW TO HIDE ALL YOUR FLOATING WINDOWS—FAST!

Press Command+Option+Control+W (Mac) or Ctrl+Alt+Start+W (PC) to hide or show all floating windows.

You'll find that this feature, though simple, is particularly useful when you're using plug-in effects and virtual instruments, and it will allow you to quickly shift your focus.

## New in Pro Tools 8: Window Arrangements

Like many multi-window applications, Pro Tools 8 gives you the ability to quickly arrange your windows in some standard configurations. This last bit is very straightforward, but let's take a look before we move on to the next chapter.

**1** Click on **Window**. The Window menu will appear.

**2** Click on **Arrange**. The Arrange submenu will appear.

❋ Tile will arrange all active windows on the desktop in a standard tile pattern.

❋ Tile Horizontal will arrange windows from top to bottom. Note that this option is not available when too many windows are currently active.

❋ Tile Vertical will arrange windows side by side. Here, too, this option will be grayed out if there are too many active windows in your session.

❋ Cascade will lay all active windows on top of each other, arranging them in a standard cascade pattern (showing the title bar of each window, so that you can easily see what windows are currently open).

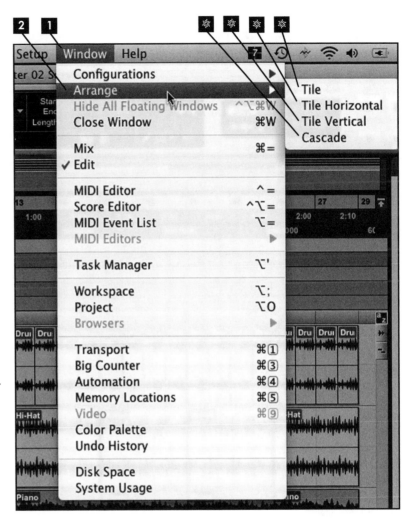

Congratulations! You now have a fundamental understanding of what Pro Tools is and how it functions, which will help you be a more intelligent user as you delve deeper into this powerful environment. Now you're ready to begin actively using Pro Tools LE and start working with audio!

# 3 } Getting Started with Audio

Now that you have a solid basic understanding of what Pro Tools is and what it can do, it's time to start making things happen. The first step on the path to Pro Tools proficiency is to set up a session and start using audio. In this chapter, you'll learn how to:

* Configure Pro Tools to make the most of your computer system
* Set up and customize your inputs, outputs, inserts, and busses
* Create Audio, Aux Input, and Master Fader tracks
* Import audio into your session
* Play your session in a variety of ways to suit different circumstances

# Setup

Before you can get the show on the road, you'll need to call upon knowledge that you gained in the first chapter to create a session on which you can work.

**1** Launch Pro Tools.

**2** Click on File.

**3** Click on New Session.

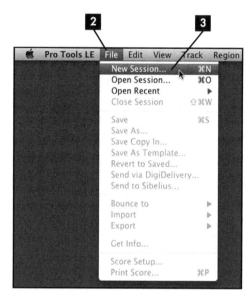

**4** Choose the Create Blank Session radio button.

**5** Select BWF (.WAV) from the Audio File Type menu.

**6** Select 44.1 kHz from the Sample Rate menu.

**7** Select the 24 Bit radio button in the Bit Depth area.

**8** Select Stereo Mix from the I/O Settings menu.

**9** Click on Save. The Save dialog box will appear.

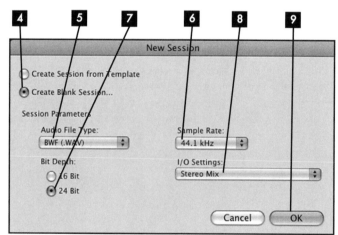

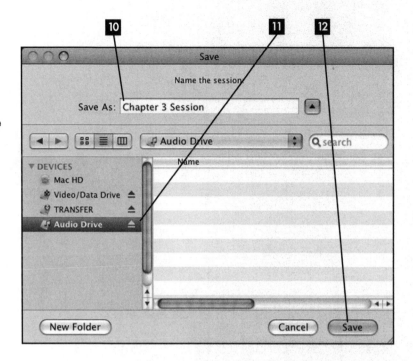

**10** Type a descriptive **name** for your session in the Save As field.

**11** **Choose** an appropriate **place** for your session. (In this case, I'm saving the session to my Audio hard drive.)

**12** **Click** the **Save button**. Your session will be created.

# The Playback Engine Window

Every DAW application has a certain amount of code devoted to the tasks of digital audio recording and playback. This bit of programming is so important that it has its own name—it's called the *audio engine*. Pro Tools' audio engine is appropriately called the *DAE*, or *Digidesign Audio Engine*. The DAE is at the very heart of Pro Tools' operations, and the quality of its construction is a big reason for Pro Tools' popularity.

Let's start this chapter by taking a look at the Playback Engine window, where you can choose settings for the DAE and make the most of your overall system. We'll start by locating the Playback Engine window.

1. **Click** on **Setup**. The Setup menu will appear.

2. **Click** on **Playback Engine**. The Playback Engine window will appear.

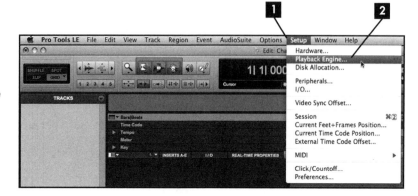

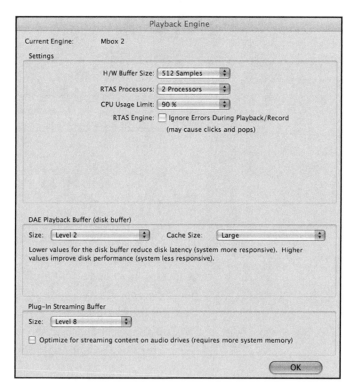

Let's take these sections one by one:

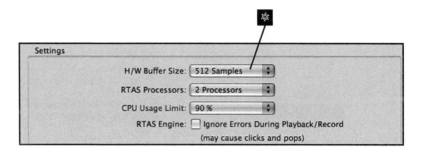

❄ The **H/W Buffer Size** (hardware buffer size) essentially affects all host-based real-time processes in your Pro Tools system. This is particularly important when talking about Pro Tools LE systems. With Pro Tools LE, your computer's CPU (the *host*) is responsible for all of the processes, including recording, playback, and plug-in effects. The hardware buffer will allow you to set aside some of your CPU's power to create a data buffer for these important tasks. Just click the arrow button at the right of the setting to reveal a drop-down list of options.

### ❄ WHAT'S A BUFFER?

You've probably heard the term "buffer" tossed about in discussions about computers, but you might be a bit foggy on what exactly a buffer is and what it does. A buffer is a certain amount of computer memory (generally RAM memory is used due to its high speed) that a processor uses for short-term data storage during operations.

Though buffers are used in different ways for different kinds of applications, as a general rule buffers will allow a processor to work with large amounts of data more efficiently.

## THE PROS AND CONS OF HARDWARE BUFFER SETTINGS

Having a higher hardware buffer setting can certainly enable you to have more simultaneous audio processes (such as plug-in effects, for example), but there's a catch: High buffer settings can also increase recording *latency*, or the delay between a signal going into Pro Tools and the audio heard out of the monitor speakers (in Pro Tools LE systems). High recording latency can be a real bother during Pro Tools LE recording sessions. (The delay can be very distracting to musicians when they are trying to hear their live performance through the headphones.)

Here's a good rule of thumb for you: Set your hardware buffer as low as possible when recording. (This may or may not be the first setting on the list, depending on your computer's power.) After the recording phase of your project is finished, you can set the buffer higher, so you can take advantage of more plug-ins during the editing and mixing stages.

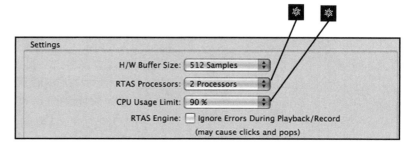

※ The RTAS Processors list (which you'll see if you click the arrow button to the right of the setting) will allow you to utilize any number of CPUs in a multi-processor system. If you have multiple CPUs, choosing to use them (as I've done in this image) will give you the option of launching more RTAS plug-ins. However, if other applications on your system (such as video editing applications) have higher priority, or if your session has a great deal of mix automation, then consider using fewer CPUs to free up processing power.

※ The CPU Usage Limit allows you to set a cap on the amount of CPU power to be used by Pro Tools. When you click the arrow button indicated, you'll see a drop-down menu showing a series of percentages. A higher percentage (for example, the 90% shown here) will give Pro Tools more power, though it may rob power from other applications (again, such as a video editing application) that may also be running. A lower limit will restrict Pro Tools somewhat, but it can also ensure adequate power for other applications. This setting works in combination with the RTAS Processors setting we just discussed.

❄ One of the things I personally like about the DAE is that it's a stickler for quality. If there are any errors in the recording or playing back of your audio, the DAE will stop everything and tell you about the problem. I do find, however, that these messages (which will stop playback or recording) can get a bit bothersome when I'm working in a noncritical situation (for example, when I'm launching plug-ins during playback, just to see which effect suits my needs). In these situations, where a few clicks or pops are tolerable, check the RTAS Engine—Ignore Errors During Playback/Record box.

### ❄ WHEN NOT TO IGNORE THE ERRORS!

As a general rule, you should only check the Ignore Errors During Playback/Record box when you run into problems in noncritical situations (such as editing). When you're in the important recording or final mixdown stages of your project, remember to uncheck the Ignore Errors During Playback/Record box—you certainly don't want to hear clicks and pops then!

Now let's take a look at the DAE Playback Buffer settings:

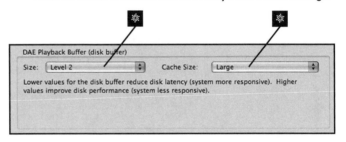

❄ The DAE Playback Buffer Size allows you to change (by clicking the arrow button to the right of the Size value) the storage capacity of the buffer Pro Tools uses for playing back audio. The default value (Level 2, or 1500 milliseconds) is fine for the vast majority of situations, but if you run into disk playback errors (errors telling you that your disk is too slow to continue playback of your session), you can choose a higher buffer setting to treat the symptom.

### ❄ WILL THE DAE PLAYBACK BUFFER AFFECT RECORDING?

As the Playback Engine window states, higher buffer settings can make Pro Tools less responsive. (In other words, you might perceive a bit of a lag between the time that you click the Play button and the time that Pro Tools actually starts playback.) This should not be confused with recording latency—in fact, the changes you make to the DAE Playback Buffer won't affect recording latency one way or the other.

❄ The Cache Size is a relatively new addition to Pro Tools (it was introduced in version 7.4), allowing the user to allocate memory specifically for Elastic Audio–related tasks. (We'll talk more about Elastic Audio in Chapter 10.) If you click the arrow to the right of the Cache Size setting, you'll be able to choose from three settings: Minimum (reduces memory use), Normal, and Large (improves performance).

❄ ❄ ❄

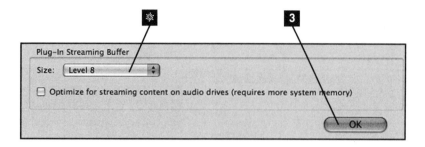

❋ If your system happens to be running the Structure software sampler, you will also see a Plug-In Streaming Buffer Size section, which will allow you to choose the amount of memory the DAE reserves for sample playback. If you don't see this section in your Playback Engine window, don't worry—that simply means you haven't installed Structure.

**3** When you're finished, just **click** the **OK button** (at the bottom-right corner of the window), and your settings will take effect.

# Customizing Your Session: I/O Setup

An understanding of Pro Tools' signal flow is critical to using this powerful DAW, and at the heart of signal flow is the I/O (Input/Output) Setup window.

## Setting Up Inputs

When you created this session, you chose Stereo Mix as your I/O (Input/Output) setting. This I/O setting is Pro Tools' generic setup for stereo work, and although it works fine as is, you can customize it to match your own studio's setup and boost your productivity right from the start! Let's start by taking a closer look at the input setup for your studio—in other words, the connections going *into* your audio interface, and from there to the Pro Tools software environment.

**1** Click on **Setup**.

**2** Click on **I/O**. The I/O Setup dialog box will open.

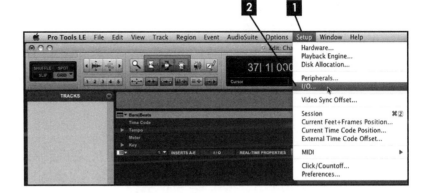

**3** Click on the **Input tab**. The tab will move to the front.

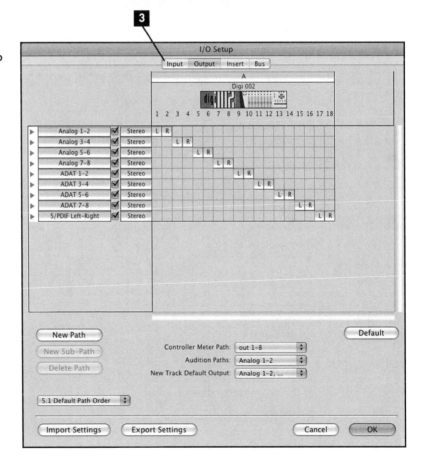

※ **A WORD ABOUT THE SCREENSHOTS**

The examples in this section show the windows you'll see if you have a Digi 002 system. If you have any other kind of interface, the window will look a little different (although the functions will be the same). At the top of the window, you'll see a picture of your audio interface. Directly below the interface, you'll see a listing of all the available inputs for that interface.

## Customizing Your Inputs

The grid area and the labels to the left represent input paths, which will allow you to match the virtual inputs in the Pro Tools software to the physical inputs of your Pro Tools hardware. The dialog box currently displays a default input setup. In this section, we'll go through the process of creating a custom I/O setup from the ground up. To make sure we're creating everything from scratch, let's delete the existing paths.

**1** Click on the top **path name**.

**2** Press the **Shift key** and **click** on the remaining **path names** until all the paths are highlighted.

**3** Click on the **Delete Path button.** All the input paths will disappear.

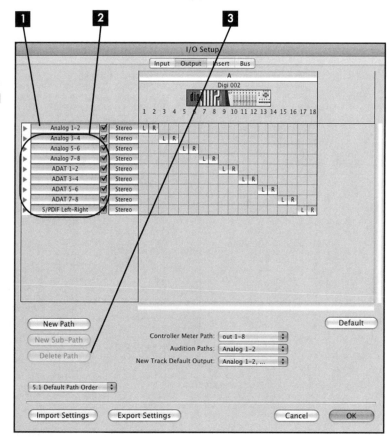

**4** Click on the **New Path button**. A single new path will appear with the default name of Path 1.

**5** Click on the **New Path button** 11 more times. Additional paths will be created, again with default names.

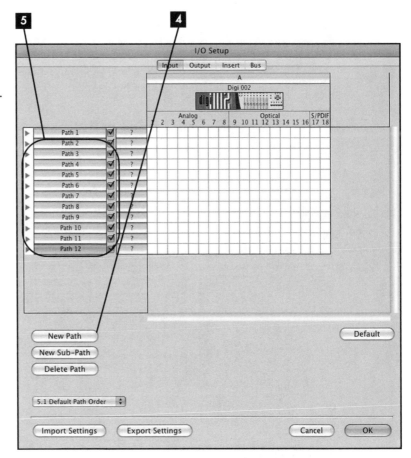

**6** Although you've created input paths, they're not much use until they've been configured and assigned to physical inputs on your interface. That's your next job. **Double-click** on the top path name. **The path name** will be highlighted.

**7** **Type** a descriptive **name** for this path.

**8** **Repeat Steps 6 and 7** for the other paths as appropriate (remember, you might not have that many available inputs on your interface), naming each input descriptively.

❄ **HOW SHOULD I NAME MY INPUTS?**

A good rule of thumb is to name your inputs for the devices that are connected to your system. As you list these devices, keep track of which inputs are coming from stereo sources and which are coming from mono sources—It'll come in handy later!

## Configuring a Path as Stereo or Mono

Now you need to configure each path as being either stereo or mono.

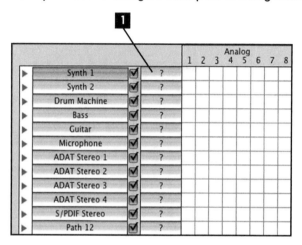

**1** Click on the **question mark (?)** to the right of the path name you want to set up. The path type pop-up menu will appear.

**2** **Choose** a **type** for each path (stereo or mono).

## Assigning Your Path

Now it's time to assign each path (in this case, Synth 1) to specific inputs of your audio interface (in this case, Analog 1 and 2 of my 002).

**1** **Move** your **cursor** to the grid area in the top row. Your cursor will change from an arrow to a pencil.

**2** **Click** in the **square** that matches the input you desire. Because this happens to be a stereo path, two blocks will appear, marked L and R (for left and right). Don't worry if you click in the wrong box—you can click and drag each block to the appropriate cell.

**3** Repeat Step 2 for all your paths.

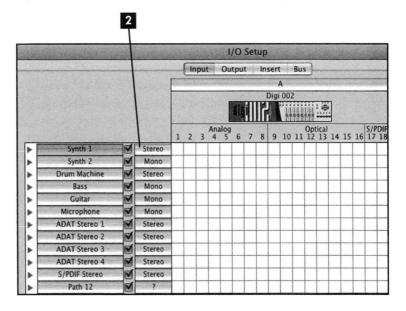

| | | | Analog | | | | | | | | Optical | | | | | | | S/PDIF |
|---|---|---|---|---|---|---|---|---|---|---|---|---|---|---|---|---|---|---|
| | | | 1 | 2 | 3 | 4 | 5 | 6 | 7 | 8 | 9 | 10 | 11 | 12 | 13 | 14 | 15 | 16 | 17 | 18 |
| Synth 1 | ☑ | Stereo | L | R | | | | | | | | | | | | | | | |
| Synth 2 | ☑ | Mono | | | M | | | | | | | | | | | | | | |
| Drum Machine | ☑ | Stereo | | | | L | R | | | | | | | | | | | | |
| Bass | ☑ | Mono | | | | | | M | | | | | | | | | | | |
| Guitar | ☑ | Mono | | | | | | | M | | | | | | | | | | |
| Microphone | ☑ | Mono | | | | | | | | M | | | | | | | | | |
| ADAT Stereo 1 | ☑ | Stereo | | | | | | | | | | | L | R | | | | | |
| ADAT Stereo 2 | ☑ | Stereo | | | | | | | | | | | | | L | R | | | |
| ADAT Stereo 3 | ☑ | Stereo | | | | | | | | | | | | | | | L | R | |
| ADAT Stereo 4 | ☑ | Stereo | | | | | | | | | | | | | | | | | L | R |
| S/PDIF Stereo | ☑ | Stereo | | | | | | | | | | | | | | | | | | L | R |
| Path 12 | ☑ | ? | | | | | | | | | | | | | | | | | |

When you've set up your I/O window, you might see something like the image shown here. (This is the input page I created using the steps we just covered.)

## Setting Up Sub-Paths

You've set up your paths, and now it's time to think about sub-paths. *Sub-paths* are individual assignments within a path. For example, take a look at the first ADAT path—ADAT Stereo 1. If you will only ever have a stereo signal going into those two inputs, you're all set. However, if you want to also be able to use each input separately, you might consider setting up a couple of sub-paths within that stereo path.

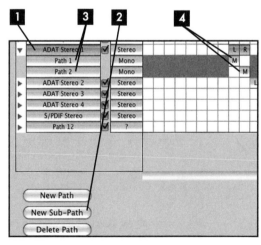

**1** Click on the desired **stereo path name**. The name will be highlighted.

**2** Click twice on the **New Sub-Path button**. Two sub-paths will be created below the path, with default names (Path 1 and Path 2).

**3** Double-click on each **sub-path** and **name it**, just like you did with the paths.

**4** As you did with paths, you need to assign a physical output to each sub-path. **Click** on the desired **grid square**. A block with an M (for mono) will appear.

PATHS, SUB-PATHS, AND OVERLAPPING

There is an extra flexibility that comes with sub-paths—sub-paths can overlap, while paths cannot. In other words, two active paths cannot both use the same physical output. (If you try to do this, Pro Tools will give you a gentle reminder message.) This might not mean much if you're only working with stereo paths, but when you move on to surround sound projects, you'll find that by creating multiple sub-paths that overlap, you'll be able to really control your mix!

 AND SPEAKING ABOUT SURROUND SOUND...

With a basic Pro Tools LE system, you're limited to creating mono or stereo paths, which effectively limits you to mono or stereo production. Actually, this isn't a serious limitation for many users, but there is a segment of LE users that craves the ability to create surround mixes. Don't despair—you can add surround functionality (up to 7.1 mixes!) by picking up the Complete Production Toolkit, an optional add-on for Pro Tools LE. You can learn more about the Complete Production Toolkit at www.avid.com.

## Changing a Path's Assignment

When you've created a path (or sub-path) and assigned a physical interface input to that path, you're all set. But what if you want to change that assignment? For example, let's assume that the bass in my studio is actually plugged into Input 7, and the guitar is actually plugged into Input 6. Changing the inputs is extremely easy, and it is one of the real beauties of the I/O Setup window:

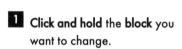 Click and hold the block you want to change.

2 Drag the block until it is directly over the desired input. A hollow box will show where your input path will be deposited.

3 Release the mouse button. The path's input block will be moved to the selected interface channel.

## Setting Up Outputs

You've set up your system to deal with incoming audio—good job! The next step is to customize how audio exits your audio interface. For the examples shown in this section, we'll once again create a basic setup that works in my studio and that you can adapt to reflect your personal needs and I/O capabilities. The good news is that the Output tab of the I/O Setup dialog box is laid out very similarly to the Input tab, so this should go a lot more quickly!

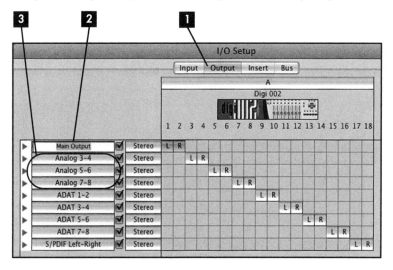

**1** Click on the **Output tab** in the I/O Setup window. The tab will move to the front.

**2** Double-click on the first **output path name** and **type Main Output.** (This is the same method you used to name input paths.) The path will be renamed.

**3** Repeat Step 2 for the next three output paths (if your interface has them) and **rename** the **paths** as follows:

❊ Drum Cue Mix

❊ Bass Cue Mix

❊ Guitar Cue Mix

❊ GENERAL RULES FOR OUTPUTS

This kind of setup is pretty common for stereo projects. In this case, you would typically use Main Output for your studio monitors. Use the Cue Mix outputs for individual headphone mixes for your recording musicians. Remember, though, that these are all line-level signals, and they will need amplification before they go to speakers or headphones. Also keep in mind that different interfaces have different numbers (and types) of outputs, so it's a good idea to check your interface's documentation to see what it supports.

**4** Click on the **triangle** to the left of each path (on a Windows machine, it will show as a plus [+] sign) to show any existing sub-paths they might contain. In this case, because you simply renamed the paths that existed in the first place, each stereo path should have a couple of sub-paths, which will be automatically renamed as well.

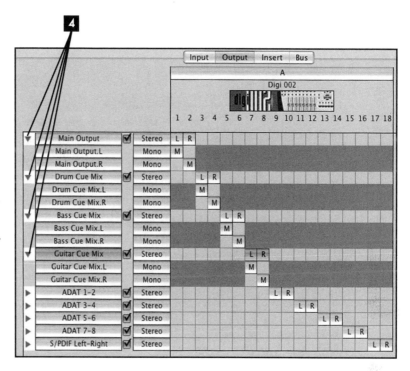

❋ **AUDITION PATHS**

You'll want to be able to "audition" audio files before you import them into your session (something we'll talk about later in this chapter). If you look at the bottom of the I/O Setup window's Output tab, you'll see a drop-down menu for Audition Paths. From this menu, you can choose the output path you want to use when auditioning files. For many Pro Tools LE users, the main output path (the same one that you use to monitor your mix) is a good choice. You'll hear any auditioned files through your main monitor speakers.

❋ **NEW TRACK DEFAULT OUTPUT**

Have you got a favorite output path—one you usually use when creating new tracks? If you do, you can choose it from the New Track Default Output menu, which you'll find in the bottom-center section of the Output tab.

## Setting Up Inserts

In the world of DAWs, you're able to use a wide variety of software effects (reverbs, delays, and so on) called plug-ins. Does that mean you won't be able to use any of the rackmount effects you've got in your studio? Not at all—you can bring them into the Pro Tools environment through a configuration of your inputs and outputs called *hardware inserts* or *I/O inserts*. You'll learn more about inserts and how to use them in Chapter 8, "Basic Mixing," but right now, our job is to set things up correctly.

One thing you need to know about hardware inserts is how to connect your gear. The rule is simple: Use the same number of inputs that you used for the outputs. For example, if you have a rackmount stereo reverb unit that you want to use with Pro Tools, you have to use a pair of outputs (for example, #17 and #18) to send signal to the reverb unit, and you have to use the same numbers (#17 and #18) on the input side to get audio from the reverb back into Pro Tools.

As we did when we configured our inputs, let's start by deleting everything and then build things up from scratch. Technically this isn't necessary, but it will make it easier to work with in the long run.

**1** Click on the **Insert tab** in the I/O Setup dialog box. The tab will move to the front.

**2** Click on every **path name** to select it and then click on the Delete Path button, just like you did with the inputs earlier in this chapter. The paths will be deleted.

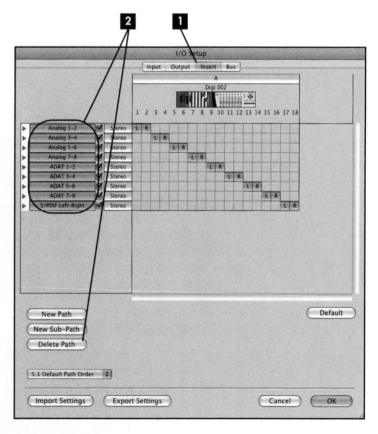

**3** Click on the **New Path** button to create a new path for each of your effects units (to the extent that your audio interface has the available physical inputs and outputs, of course) and **name** each **path** the same way you did on the Input and Output tabs (and configure each as either stereo or mono).

**4** Again, using the same method you used for setting up your inputs and outputs, **assign** each **path** to the inputs/outputs to which your effect is connected. In this case, my EQ is connected to I/O #17 and #18. As mentioned before, you are setting an input and output pair, with signal leaving your computer through interface outputs and returning to the Pro Tools environment through the same numbered inputs.

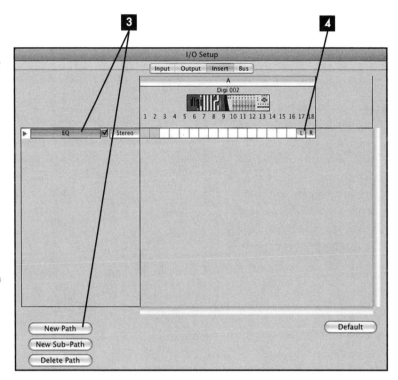

## Setting Up Busses

Last but not least is the Bus tab. Busses are like virtual audio cables that you can use within the Pro Tools mixing environment. You'll use them for all sorts of internal routing, such as sending dry audio from an Audio track to a reverb on an Aux track. Don't worry if that sounds like Greek—you'll be doing this sort of thing in Chapter 8, using Pro Tools' trusty busses. You have 32 of these virtual audio cables at your disposal, and unlike physical audio cables, they won't add noise to your mix!

Often the default naming of the busses will suffice, and their generic names will suit their multipurpose functions. Sometimes, though, you might decide to name your busses more descriptively. Here's how.

**1** Click on the **Bus tab**. The tab will move to the front.

**2** Because busses are so multi-functional, you really don't *need* to name them all. In this case, let's just name the last pair so you'll know to reserve it to use later for your vocals. **Double-click** on the last **path name** and **type Vocal Verb**. The path will be renamed.

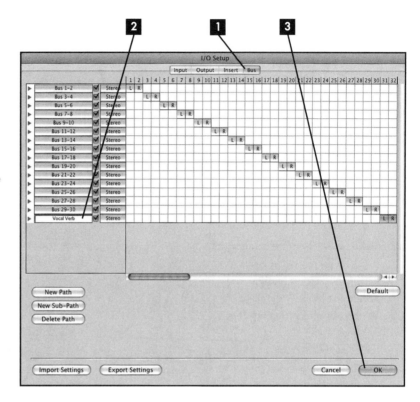

<table>
<tr><td>BUSSES AND PHYSICAL INPUTS</td></tr>
</table>

**※ BUSSES AND PHYSICAL INPUTS**

Notice how this tab is different from the others. There aren't any references to your interface's physical inputs or outputs at the top of the window. That's because your busses are entirely virtual—a part of your Pro Tools software—and not physical in any way!

**3** Click on **OK**. The dialog box will close. You're finished!

## Managing Your I/O Settings

Now that you've created a tailor-made I/O setup, you might want to save your settings so you can use them in other sessions. Here's how.

### Saving Your I/O Settings

To save your I/O settings to an I/O settings file, follow these steps.

**1** Click on **Export Settings**. The Save I/O Settings As dialog box will open.

**2** Type a **name** for these settings in the Save As text box.

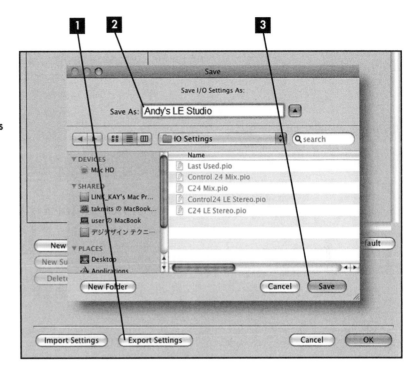

Choose a descriptive name for your settings so you can recall them easily when you want to use them in another session.

❄ I/O SETTINGS AND NEW SESSIONS

There's another benefit to exporting your tweaked I/O settings. If you save the I/O settings to the default location (which you just did if you were following the steps outlined here), when you create a new session, your new setup will be an option in the I/O Settings drop-down menu.

**3** Click on **Save**. Your settings will be saved to Pro Tools' default I/O location.

## Recalling Your Settings

After you've customized and exported your I/O settings, you can easily recall them. That means that the time you spend tweaking your I/O settings to work in a variety of situations is easily integrated into any session. In this workflow example, you'll delete all of the existing paths in the session and then reload your previously saved settings. (Strictly speaking, you don't have to delete existing paths before importing, but for the purpose of this example, it makes the process easier.)

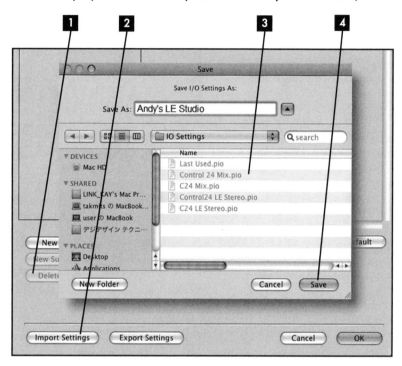

**1** Select all the **paths** and then click on the **Delete Path button**. In the interest of being thorough, repeat this step for all of the tabs (Input, Output, Insert, and Bus). Again, this step isn't absolutely required, but is a convenience in this case.

**2** To load previously saved I/O settings, click on the **Import Settings button**. The Select I/O Settings to Import dialog box will open.

**3** Select the desired **I/O settings file**.

**4** Click the **Save button**. The I/O settings you selected will be loaded.

# Tracks

Whether you're looking at the Edit window or the Mix window, you'll notice that your new session opened up without any tracks in it. It's up to you to create the tracks you'll need in your session.

## Making Tracks

No matter what kind of track you want to create, you'll start with the following steps.

**1** **Click** on **Track**. The Track menu will appear.

**2** **Click** on **New**. The New Tracks dialog box will open.

❋ NEW TRACK SHORTCUT

Because you'll be making many tracks as you work more and more in Pro Tools, you might want to learn the "new track" shortcut. Command+Shift+N (Mac) or Ctrl+Shift+N (PC) will launch the New Tracks dialog box.

**3** As soon as it's launched, the New Tracks dialog box is set up to create one mono Audio track. For this example, let's create four tracks instead. **Double-click** in the **Create field** to highlight it (if it isn't already highlighted) and then **type** the **number of tracks** you want to create (in this case, you'll type 4).

❋ MORE ABOUT THE NEW TRACKS DIALOG BOX

You'll notice that there are a few drop-down menus in the New Tracks dialog box. The first drop-down menu (the Track Format menu) allows you to specify whether your track will be stereo or mono. The second drop-down menu (the Track Type menu) allows you to select the *kind* of track you'll create. We'll be covering these menus (and what they mean) in just a bit, so read on!

**4** **Click** the **Create button**. The New Tracks dialog box will close, and the tracks will be created in your session.

❋ ❋ ❋

Now let's create a couple of stereo Audio tracks.

**1** **Open** the **New Tracks dialog box** as you did in the previous section.

**2** **Type 2** in the Create field to create two tracks.

**3** **Click** on the **Track Format drop-down menu**.

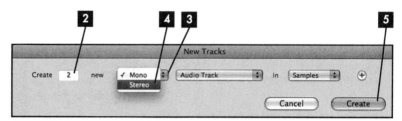

**4** **Click** on **Stereo**. The option will be selected.

**5** **Click** on **Create**. Two stereo Audio tracks will be created, just as you specified.

> ❄ **TRACKS AND TOOLKITS**
>
> You've just created six Audio tracks (four mono and two stereo). How many more can you make? Well, that depends—with a basic Pro Tools LE system, you can make up to 48 Audio tracks (stereo or mono, or any mix of the two). If that's not enough for the work that you do, you can add a toolkit (a software upgrade to Pro Tools LE). The Music Production Toolkit 2 adds music functionality (which we'll talk more about later), and the DV Toolkit 2 adds video production-related features. When it comes to Audio tracks, either toolkit will increase the number you can create from 48 to 64.
>
> And if *that's* not even enough, there's the Complete Production Toolkit. This software upgrade will give you up to 128 voices. A voice is used by each channel of a track—for example, a mono track will use one voice, a stereo track will use two, and so on. So, with the Complete Production Toolkit, you could create 128 mono Audio tracks, or 96 stereo tracks, or any combination in which the number of channels totals 128.
>
> You can learn more about the features of all the toolkits on Avid's website (www.avid.com).

## Creating an Auxiliary Input Track

An Auxiliary Input track (also commonly called an *Aux Input* or simply an *Aux* track) is similar to an Audio track in many respects, except that it doesn't contain any audio regions. Its main function is to serve as a means of routing audio from a source to a destination or as a means to process one or more audio signals with plug-in effects.

You'll learn how to use Aux tracks in Chapters 7 and 8, and you'll find them very handy indeed, particularly when you get down to the business of mixing. In this chapter, though, let's start with the process of creating a couple of stereo Aux tracks, a process almost identical to creating Audio tracks.

**1** Open the **New Tracks dialog box** as you did in the previous sections.

**2** **Type 2** in the Create field to create two tracks.

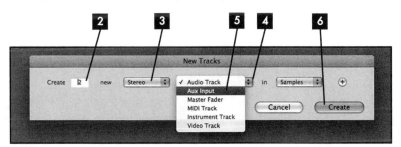

**3** Click on **Stereo** in the Track Format drop-down menu to make these Aux tracks *stereo* Aux tracks. The option will be selected.

**4** Click on the **second drop-down menu**. A list of all the different track types available in Pro Tools will appear.

**5** Click on **Aux Input**. The option will be selected.

**6** Click on **Create**. Two stereo Aux tracks will be created, just as you specified.

## Master Faders, MIDI, and Instrument Tracks

As you probably noticed, there are three other kinds of tracks listed in the Track Type drop-down menu—Master Fader, MIDI, and Instrument tracks. Although you might not use these kinds of tracks in every session you create, they'll come in very useful when you need them.

If you've ever worked with a traditional mixing board, you know what a Master Fader does. These are the faders that control the overall volume of your entire mix after you have blended all the individual tracks. A Master Fader in Pro Tools does pretty much the same thing. Simply put, it's a fader that controls the overall volume of a given output path. It will also allow you to add plug-in effects to the entire mix at once. You'll learn about Master Fader tracks in Chapter 9, "Finishing Touches."

When it comes to MIDI tracks, there's one thing to keep in mind—MIDI is *not* audio. Rather, it is a digital language that allows different musical devices to communicate, something like a network. You can record (and then edit) MIDI data on a MIDI track in Pro Tools. When combined with Pro Tools' powerful set of virtual instruments, this can open all sorts of creative doors!

There's another MIDI-related track, called an *Instrument track,* which can allow you to use MIDI and virtual instruments together in one convenient track. You'll learn about MIDI and Instrument tracks in Chapter 7, "Using MIDI."

The method of creating a Master Fader, MIDI, or Instrument track is almost identical to creating any other kind of track. The only difference is that you'll choose your type of track accordingly. Just for practice, try creating one new stereo Master Fader, using the steps outlined earlier. (Refer to the preceding image for your reference.)

 WHY CAN'T I CHOOSE A STEREO OR MONO MIDI TRACK?

When you choose to create a MIDI track, you'll notice that there is no stereo or mono option available. Don't worry, it's not a malfunction of Pro Tools—it's because MIDI isn't audio, so the terms *stereo* and *mono* don't really apply in this case.

## Managing Your Tracks

This section contains a few techniques you can use to make the creation of tracks even easier and to set tracks up for efficient use after they've been created.

## Creating Multiple Tracks

In the previous sections of this chapter, you created different kinds of tracks one type at a time (mono Audio tracks, then stereo Audio, Aux tracks, and so on). If you want to create different kinds of tracks in one smooth operation, here's a neat little timesaver. Take a look:

❄ You can continue creating different kinds of tracks by repeatedly clicking the plus sign, as shown here.

❄ Did you go one step too far, and do you now want to remove one of the rows? It's easy—just click the minus (–) sign to the right of the row you want to delete.

❄ The tracks shown here will be created in your session from top to bottom, just as shown in this dialog box. If you want to reorder the tracks, just click and hold the double-arrow icon at the far right of the row that you want to move. A blue box will appear around that row (the Master Fader, in this case), indicating that it's ready to be moved. Still holding your mouse button down, drag the row up or down. A line will appear, displaying where the track will be deposited when the mouse is released.

❄ **MORE SHORTCUTS!**

There's also a shortcut to create or delete rows in the New Tracks dialog box. If you're a Windows user, you can press Ctrl+Plus/Minus(+/-) keys or Ctrl+Shift+Up/Down Arrow keys. If you're a Mac user, you can use Command+Plus/Minus(+/-) keys or Command+Shift+Up/Down Arrow keys.

## Naming Your Tracks

One of the most important aspects of working in a DAW is documentation. (It may be *the* most important, depending on who you talk to.) Keeping track of your sessions, files, tracks, patches, and so on is absolutely critical, especially as your sessions become more complex.

When Pro Tools creates a new track, it assigns a generic name (such as Audio 1) as a default. Descriptively naming your tracks is a big part of session documentation—and the good news is, it's easy.

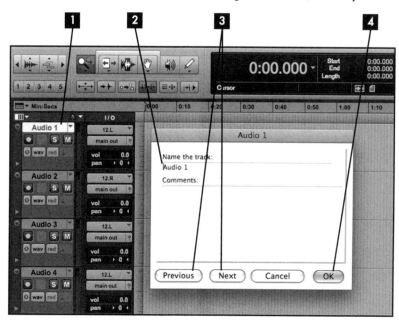

**1** Double-click on the **nameplate** of the track you want to rename. A dialog box will open.

**2** Type a **name** for the track in the Name the Track field.

**3** If you want to continue naming tracks, click on **Next** to name the track below the current track or click on **Previous** to name the track above the current track.

**4** When you're finished naming tracks, click on **OK**. The dialog box will close.

❄ NAMING YOUR TRACKS FOR THE TUTORIAL SESSION

If you've been following along with this chapter's examples, you should have four mono Audio tracks, two stereo Audio tracks, two stereo Aux tracks, and one stereo Master Fader. To keep the ball rolling, name each of the tracks as follows: Bass, Guitar, Vocal, Sax, Drums, Keyboard, Vocal Reverb Aux, Drum Reverb Aux, and Master Volume.

## Moving Tracks

After you've assigned names to all your tracks, you might want to reorganize them so that related tracks are near each other. Although moving tracks around in the Edit or Mix window won't change how they play back in any way, a logical arrangement of tracks can make the entire production process much easier. There aren't any hard-and-fast organizational rules—each session is unique, and you'll have to decide how to arrange your tracks so they make sense to *you*.

In this example, I want to move my Drums track to just below my Bass track:

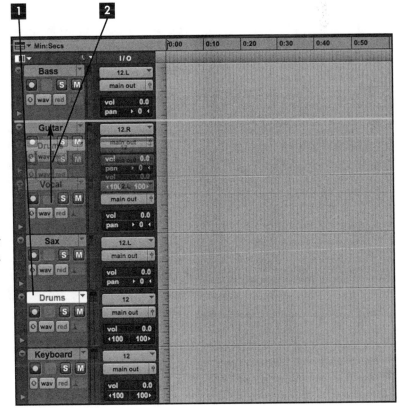

1 Click and hold on a track nameplate. The track will be selected.

2 Drag the track up or down to the desired location. As you drag the track, a gold line will appear, indicating the position the track would assume if the mouse button were released.

3 Release the mouse button when you have the gold line at the desired position. The tracks in your session will be reorganized.

ANOTHER WAY TO MOVE TRACKS

Here's another way to do it: Click and hold the track name in the Track Show/Hide list. Drag the track up or down to the desired position. (A thin line will indicate where the track will be moved.) When you release the mouse button, your tracks will be reordered.

THE "GOLD LINE"

As I mentioned earlier, you'll see a gold line that will indicate where your track would be deposited if you were to release the mouse button. This is new in Pro Tools 8, and it's a welcome addition for longtime Pro Tools users. You'll see similar lines and use of the gold color elsewhere in Pro Tools, to bring important elements to your attention.

In the Mix window, as in the Edit window, you can click and hold to drag any track to a new location. Of course, instead of dragging up or down, you drag left or right.

**1** Click and hold on a track nameplate. The track will be selected.

**2** Drag the track left or right to the desired location. As you drag the track, a gold line will appear, indicating the position the track will assume when it is dropped in its new location.

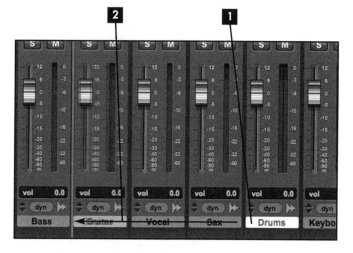

**3** Release the mouse button when you have the track at the desired location. The tracks in your session will be reorganized.

The Mix window reflects any rearrangement of tracks you make in the Edit window and vice versa. Tracks are listed in the Edit window from top to bottom; in the Mix window, they're displayed from left to right.

## Duplicating Tracks

From time to time, you might want to do a little more than simply create a new blank track. In some cases, you might want to "clone" your track, making an exact copy (including any regions that are on the track). Here's how it's done.

**1** Select the track(s) you want to duplicate by clicking the track nameplate(s).

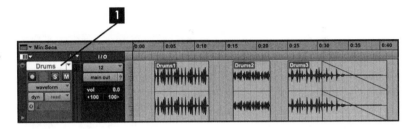

**2** Click on Track. The Track menu will appear.

**3** Click on Duplicate. The Duplicate Tracks dialog box will open.

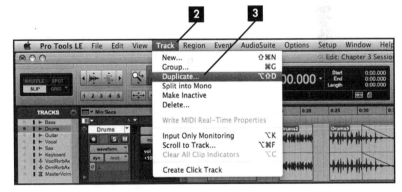

**4** In the Number of Duplicates field, **type** the **number of duplicates** you want to make.

**5** In the Data to Duplicate section, **choose** the **aspects** of the track that you want to copy. Right now, these terms might have little meaning to you, but don't fret—we'll explore their meanings in later chapters. To make a complete duplicate of the selected track(s), check *all* the boxes in the Data to Duplicate section.

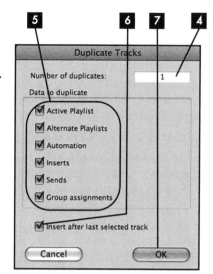

**6** Check the **Insert after Last Selected Track check box** if you want to have your duplicate tracks created directly adjacent to your selected tracks. If you leave this box unchecked, your new tracks will be created at the bottom of your Tracks list.

**7** When you're finished, **click OK**. The duplicate track(s) will be created.

## Deleting Tracks

Also, from time to time, you'll want to delete tracks that you've created but are not using for some reason. Suppose you've created a duplicate track (as you have just done), and then you decide it was a bad idea. No worries—deleting tracks is nearly as easy as creating tracks.

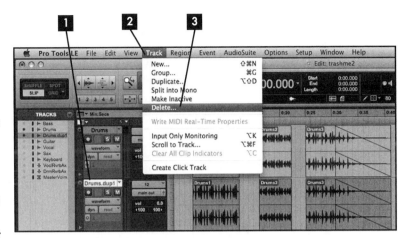

1. **Select** the **track(s)** you want to delete by clicking the track nameplates(s).

2. **Click** on **Track**. The Track menu will appear.

3. **Click** on **Delete**. The track(s) will be deleted. Note that there's no shortcut for deleting tracks, as there is for creating them. This is deliberate, so that you don't accidentally delete tracks.

## ❄ RIGHT-CLICK POWER

If you have a mouse that has a right-click button (which is virtually all PC mice and quite a few Mac mice as well), I've got some great news for you. Pro Tools has incorporated many common operations into right-click commands. This makes already easy jobs even easier.

Track functions are a great example of right-click functionality. Simply right-click on the desired track's name, and you'll see the list shown here. This list of common track-related operations includes many of the operations we just covered, plus some that we'll cover in chapters to come.

# Importing Audio

Although you can certainly record live audio into Pro Tools (it wouldn't be much of an audio workstation if you couldn't!), that's not the only way to get sounds into your session. Indeed, one of the big advantages of a computer-based DAW is that you can import digital audio files into a preexisting project, bypassing the recording process entirely.

Importing files into Pro Tools is a quick and easy way to get started, and as with so many of Pro Tools' operations, there are a number of ways to get the job done. In this section, we'll explore the two basic methods: using the File menu, and using the Workspace Browser.

> ❋ **USING YOUR TUTORIAL SESSIONS**
>
> The examples shown in the remainder of this chapter are using the Chapter 3 import materials. You'll find the files for this next section on your book's CD, in the Chapter 03 Import Materials/Source Audio for Import folder.

## Importing from the File Menu

Importing audio using the File menu is a method that has existed in Pro Tools for quite some time, and it's an easy and direct way to get the files you want into your session. The first thing you need to do is locate the file you want to import into Pro Tools.

### Choosing Where to Import From

Though you can use the File menu while viewing either the Mix window or the Edit window, it's typically done while working in the Edit window. For the purposes of this demonstration, if you're currently looking at the Mix window in Pro Tools, switch to the Edit window. (From the Window menu, choose Edit, and the Edit window will appear.)

**1** **Click** on **File**. The File menu
will appear.

**2** **Choose Import**. The Import
submenu will appear.

**3** **Choose Audio**. The Import
Audio dialog box will open.

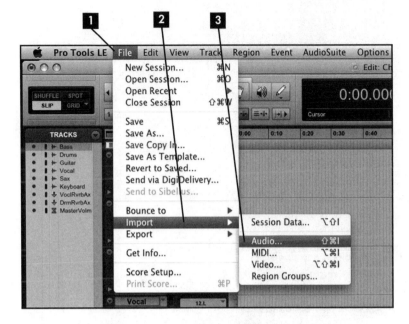

**4** According to the conventions
of your operating system,
**navigate** to the **folder** that
contains the audio you want to
import. (If you're using the
disc that came with your book,
find the Chapter 03 Import
Materials/Source Audio for
Import folder.)

**5** **Click** on the **audio file(s)** you
want to import into your Pro
Tools session. The file(s) will
be selected. If you're working
with the materials set up for
this book, select the two Synth
Only Mix files.

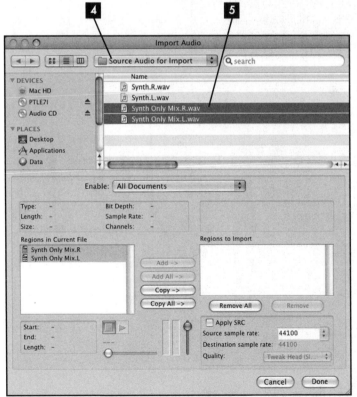

**6** The box on the left shows regions in the audio files you've selected, but those regions haven't actually been incorporated into your session yet. To do that, you'll need to add those regions to the box on the right (called Regions to Import). **Click** the **Copy button**. The regions will be added to the right box, as shown here.

**7** To audition any single file before importing, **select** the desired **audio file** and then **click** the **Play button** to preview your selected file. The file will begin to play.

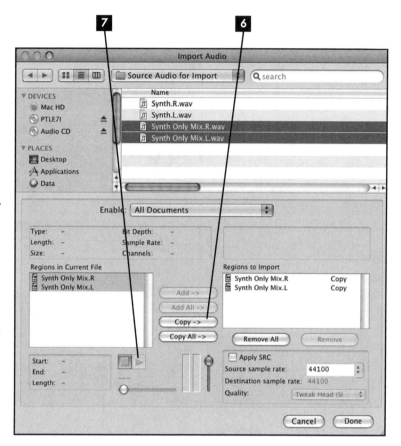

### ✽ ADDING FILES VERSUS COPYING FILES

You'll notice that there are Add buttons and Copy buttons in the bottom-center section of the Import Audio window. Clicking the Add button will simply add regions to your Pro Tools session, and Pro Tools will play the audio file from its original location on your hard drive, wherever that may be.

Clicking Copy, on the other hand, will actually make copies of those files and place the copies in your session's own Audio Files folder.

You'll notice that sometimes the Add buttons are grayed out and not clickable. Whenever any sort of conversion must happen (when importing audio files with different sample rates or bit depths than that of your session), those files must be copied (and converted). Also, as in the case of this example, Pro Tools will have to make copies whenever importing from CD discs.

Before you proceed, let's take a look at a couple of things:

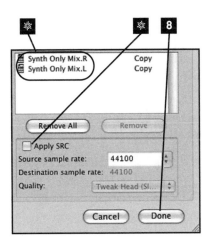

❋ You'll notice that one file has an .R listed before the file extension (in this case, it's a .wav file), and the other file has an .L in the file name. This indicates to Pro Tools that these files are two halves of a stereo region. (The L is for left, and the R is for right.) When these files are imported, they'll be listed in your Regions list as a single stereo audio region.

❋ Though Pro Tools will automatically convert sample rates and bit depths when necessary, checking the Apply SRC box will allow you to manually specify the source file's sample rate (even if it's different than the reported sample rate shown in the lower-left corner). You can also specify a conversion quality setting, which will override the Pro Tools default setting. Manual sample rate conversions like this are commonly done when converting between NTSC, Pal, and Film video sessions.

**8** Click on **Done** when you're finished. The audio will be immediately added to your session.

## Choosing Where to Import To

If you clicked the Copy button (as opposed to the Add button), you'll need to specify a location for your new files.

**1** By default, Pro Tools will choose to copy the audio files to your session's own Audio Files subfolder, as shown here, but you can choose to place them anywhere on your hard drive. If you want to change the location of the copies, simply **navigate** to the desired **location** according to the conventions of your operating system.

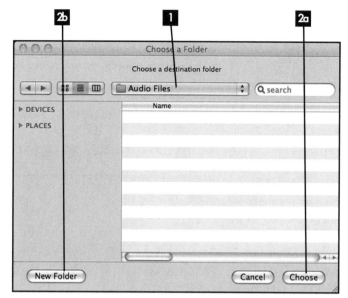

**2a** Click on **Choose**. The audio files will be copied to the folder and imported into your session.

OR

**2b** If you want to create a new subfolder for your audio, **click** on **New Folder**. You'll be prompted to name your new folder, and you'll be moved into it. Once you've reached your desired location, **click** the **Choose button**, and you're finished.

## Importing to the Regions List

Regardless of whether you chose to copy audio files or simply add regions to your session, the next window will allow you to add regions to the Regions list or create a brand-new Audio track. For starters, let's run through the steps involved in importing to the Regions list only.

**1** In the Audio Import Options dialog box, **click** the **Region List radio button**.

**2** **Click OK**, and the region(s) will be created in your session.

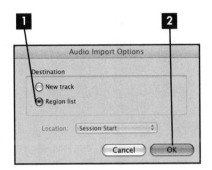

You'll notice that although the audio region is added to the Regions list, it hasn't been added to any of the Audio tracks you've created. Don't worry—that's the way this method of importing is supposed to function. Later, you'll drag this audio file onto an Audio track and use it as an element of your session.

❋ STEREO REGIONS IN THE REGIONS LIST

For every stereo region in your Regions list, you'll see a side-facing triangle by the region name. Actually, every stereo region is made up of two mono regions (one for the left side and one for the right). You can click on that triangle to reveal a list of the component mono audio regions that make up that stereo audio region.

## Importing Audio to a Track

Sometimes, instead of importing an audio region to the Regions list and using it later, you'll want to import the region onto the track directly. Just for practice, let's import the synth audio into a brand-new Synth track. The steps for importing audio to a track are, for the most part, the same as importing to the Regions list.

**1** **Click** on **File**. The File menu will appear.

**2** **Choose Import**. The Import submenu will appear.

**3** **Choose Audio**. The Import Audio dialog box will open, just as you've seen before.

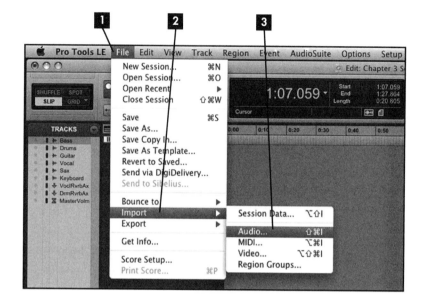

**4** **Select** the **audio file(s)** to import into your session. In this example, you'll want to choose Synth.L and Synth.R.

**5** For the purposes of this example, you can choose either to **Add** (if that's an option for you) or **Copy** your **audio**. If you choose to copy files, you will see the Choose a Destination Folder dialog box before you see the Audio Import Options dialog box.

**6** **Click** on **Done** when you're finished making your choices. The Audio Import Options dialog box will open.

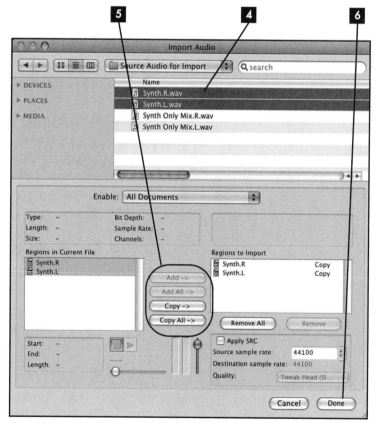

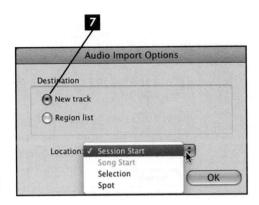

**7** In the Audio Import Options dialog box, **choose** the **New Track radio button**. When you select this button, the Location drop-down menu will become available, and clicking the button to the right of the menu (as shown in the graphic here) will give you a number of placement options.

❋ **Session Start.** This will place the audio region at the very beginning of the new track.

❋ **Song Start.** You can set your song to start at a place other than the beginning of your session (something we'll explore in Chapter 6, "And More Editing"). If your song start is anywhere other than the beginning of your session, the option to place your audio at the song start will become available.

❋ **Selection.** Choosing this option will place your audio at the beginning of any selected area. (You'll learn more about making selections in your session later in this chapter.)

❋ **Spot.** The term "spot" (usually used in a video context) is used to describe the placement of audio at a specific point in time. Choosing this option will open the Spot dialog box, where you can type a specific time location for your audio. You'll learn more about using the Spot window in Chapter 5, "Editing."

**8** For the purposes of this exercise, **choose** the **Session Start option**.

**9** **Click OK.** The dialog box will close, and your track will be created.

You'll notice that Pro Tools has done a couple of significant things with the click of a single button.

✳ Pro Tools has imported the desired region (in this case, Synth) into the Regions list. This means that you can use this region in your session.

✳ Pro Tools has *also* created a brand-new track, named Synth (named for the audio file being imported), and automatically placed the imported region at the beginning of that track. Since the imported regions had an L and an R after them, Pro Tools recognized them as being left and right channels, and so incorporated them into a single stereo Audio track. Pretty cool, don't you think?

### ✳ NEW IN PRO TOOLS 8: MIXED FILE FORMATS

In previous versions of Pro Tools, audio used in your session needed to be all of one type. (For example, in a session set up to use .wav files, any non-.wav file needed to be converted to .wav when it was imported.) Those days are over, and .wav, .aiff, and .sd2 files can peacefully coexist within a single session. That means you can import any of these types without having to convert them on the basis of their file format.

However, it's important to remember that Pro Tools sessions still need to use a single bit depth and sample rate. That means if you import audio of a different sample rate or bit depth than the one you chose when you created your session, that audio will be converted and copied into your Audio Files folder.

## Importing Tracks

Importing audio to a track is certainly an easy way to get started, but there is a limitation—the region that you import will simply be placed at some point on your track's timeline, with no specific editing or mixing. But what if you want to import a fully tweaked-out track that you created in *another* session? No problem—Pro Tools can import tracks from other sessions, including all edits, volume, panning, and so on, for you to use in your current session!

**1** **Click** on **File**. The File menu will appear.

**2** **Choose Import**. The Import submenu will appear.

**3** **Choose Session Data**. The Choose a File to Import Session Data From dialog box will open.

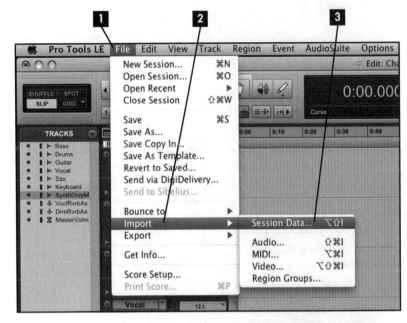

**4** According to the conventions of your computer's operating system, **navigate** to the **session file** from which you want to import. Remember, you're not importing just audio anymore, but rather an entire track. That track exists in the session file, which is why you're selecting a session file, and not an audio file. If you're following the example shown here, you'll find a folder named Source Session for Import within the Import Materials folder on the disc that was included in your book. Select the session named Source Session for Import.

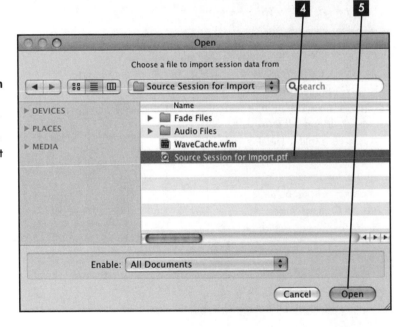

**5** **Click** on **Open**. The Import Session Data dialog box will open.

The Source Properties section (in the upper-left corner) of the Import Session Data dialog box provides a wealth of specific information regarding the session from which you'll be importing. The bottom of the dialog box contains a list of all tracks in this session, and that's where we'll pick our tracks.

**6** Click on the **Drums 1 (Stereo Audio) bar**. The Import menu will appear.

**7** **Choose New Track** to create a new track in your session without overwriting any preexisting tracks.

**8** It's possible to import more than one track at a time. **Click on the Drums 2 (Stereo Audio) bar** and select New Track here also.

**9** Before you leave this window, you can choose whether to simply add the tracks' audio regions to your session or copy their audio files to your Audio Files folder (similar to what we did in the Import Audio window earlier in this chapter). **Click the Audio Media Options button**. A drop-down menu will appear.

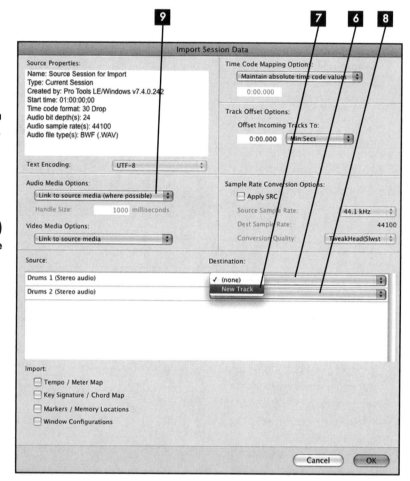

**10** The Link to Source Media
(Where Possible) and Copy
from Source Media options are
the most commonly used.
Linking to source media will not
make a copy of any audio files,
but rather will direct the session
to refer to the audio files in
their original location. Copying
from source media, on the
other hand, will copy any
audio files used in the imported
tracks into the session's Audio
Files folder. For the purposes of
this example, **choose Copy
from Source Media**.

**11** When you're finished, **click OK**.

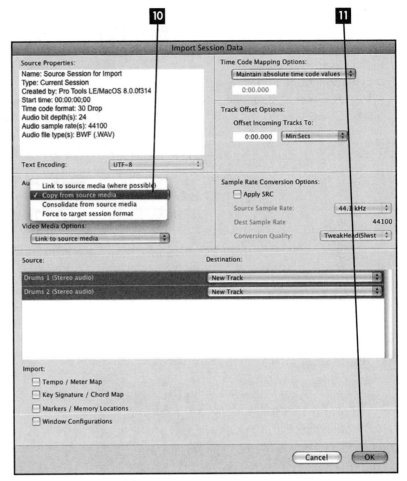

Again, you'll see that Pro Tools has done a number of operations
with one user command.

❋ Two new tracks will be created in your session. The interesting thing about both tracks is that you've imported a number of audio regions, and they are already arranged at specific times in your session.

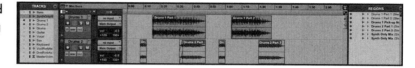

❋ Note also that each separate region in each of the tracks is listed individually in the Regions list to the right.

## The Workspace Browser

A powerful new window called the *Workspace Browser* was added to Pro Tools in version 6, and it has gotten even better in more recent versions of Pro Tools. Think of the Workspace Browser as being similar to the Mac Finder or Windows Explorer window, but with added features specifically for Pro Tools. In this section, you'll see how the Workspace Browser provides you with yet another way to import audio into your session, and more!

**1** Click on **Window**. The Window menu will appear.

**2** Click on **Workspace**. The Workspace Browser will appear.

## Searching for Audio Using the Workspace

Finding the file you want is easy, and it's one of the Workspace Browser's special advantages.

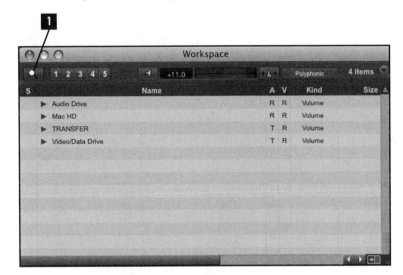

**1** Click on the **magnifying glass button**. The Find section of the Workspace Browser will appear.

**2** Click the appropriate **check boxes** to select the drives you want to search.

**3** Type the **name** of the file (or keyword) you want to search in the text box.

**4** You can further refine your search by specifying the *kind* of file you're searching for (audio files, video files, session files, and so on) from the Kind drop-down menu. For the purposes of this exercise, **choose Audio File** from the list.

**5** Click on the **Search button**. Matching results will appear in the bottom section of the Workspace Browser.

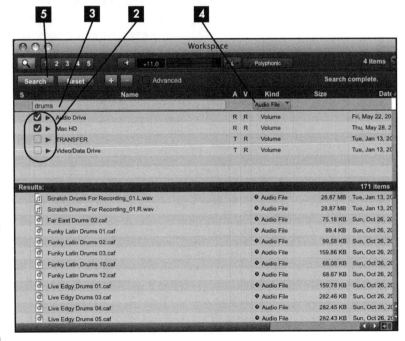

You can also navigate in a more traditional way, if you know where to look for a specific file.

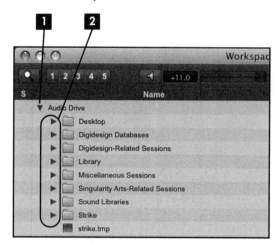

**1** Click the side-facing **triangle** next to the drive you want to search. The triangle will immediately point downward, and the folders within that drive will be revealed.

**2** In a similar manner, **navigate** through the **folders and subfolders** until you locate the file you want.

❄ THE VOLUME BROWSER

If you've used the Mac Finder or Windows Explorer, you should find the behavior of the Workspace Browser fairly straightforward. Also, like typical file browsers, you can view the contents of a specific drive (or folder) by double-clicking the drive's or folder's name. The browser that will open will have the location name in the title bar and will allow you to easily navigate through only the files in that drive or folder. The proper name for this type of browser is the *Volume Browser*.

The Workspace Browser has a few more nifty features:

❋ Click the Show/Hide button in the bottom right of the window to reveal (or conceal) a second pane in the Workspace Browser. This second pane contains a wealth of information about the files displayed in the main pane, such as sample rate, duration, and even comments about the files.

❋ In either pane, you can scroll through the different columns easily by using the appropriate scroll bar at the bottom of the browser.

❋ In this case, I'd like to move the Waveform column from the secondary pane to the primary pane. That's easy—just click on the column heading (the cursor will turn into a hand) and drag it to the desired location. You can drag columns not only to different panes, but also to different locations within a single pane.

❋ You can audition each audio file by clicking the speaker icon to the right of the desired file name. The waveform displayed to the right of the speaker icon will give an indication of the file's characteristics. To stop playback, simply click on the speaker icon again.

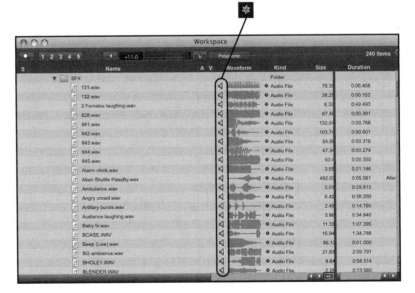

> **❋ A TIP WHEN AUDITIONING LONG FILES**
>
> If you're auditioning a particularly lengthy audio file, you can click at any point within the blue audio waveform to begin playback from that point.

❋ If you click the Browser Menu button, you'll find a list of useful options. Let's take a look at some that are specifically relevant to auditioning audio:

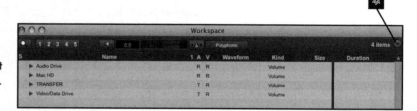

❋ **Loop Preview.** Selecting this option (which is indicated by a check mark, as shown here) will automatically repeat the file when you preview it. This is especially useful when you are previewing drum beats and other kinds of files that are typically repeated in a mix.

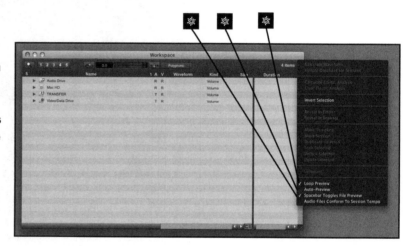

❋ **Auto-Preview.** The Auto-Preview option will set up the Browser to automatically play an audio file as soon as it has been selected in the Workspace Browser. This means you won't have to click the speaker icon to hear it, but it also means that files will always start playing as soon as you select them, which can be distracting to some users.

❋ **Spacebar Toggles File Preview.** In the normal Pro Tools environment, pressing the spacebar will start or stop playback in your session. It's one of Pro Tools' most fundamental shortcuts (and one we'll cover later in this chapter). If you enable this option, the spacebar will have a similar behavior in the Workspace Browser. Just select a file and press the spacebar to start or stop playback of the audio.

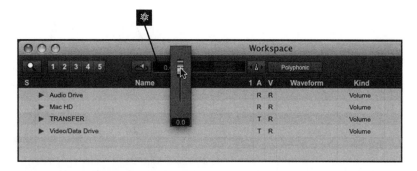

❄ **Preview Volume Control.** Longtime users are painfully aware that in previous versions of Pro Tools, previewed files would play at their full volume. This was often a shock to the ears and could potentially even damage speakers! Thankfully, those days are over. Simply click and hold on the volume field (indicated here), and a volume slider will be revealed. Just drag the slider up or down to increase or decrease the volume of the previewed audio.

❄ PREVIEW AND PLAYBACK

Another nice addition to the Workspace Browser is the ability to preview audio while your session is playing. Doing this in conjunction with adjusting the preview volume control can give you a great sense of how the audio works with your session before you commit to importing it.

The process is easy—just start playback of your session, open the Workspace Browser, and preview to your heart's content!

## Importing Audio Using the Workspace

Once you've located the audio you want to use in your session, the Workspace Browser will give you a few options for importing.

**1** Click and hold the file you want to import into your session. Your next step will be to drag and drop the file into your session, but *where* you drag it will affect *how* it will be imported.

✳ If you drop the file into the session's Regions list, a new region will appear in the Regions list. When you move your mouse into the Regions list, the list will be outlined in gray, indicating that you can release the mouse button.

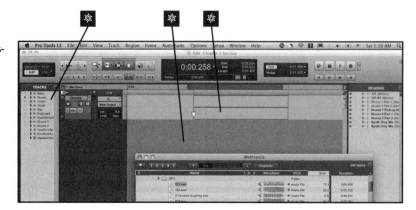

✳ If you drop the file onto an existing track, a new region will appear on that track. As shown here, a rectangle will indicate where the region will be placed when you release your mouse button. The region will also appear in the Regions list.

✳ If you drop the file into an area with no track, a new track will be created, and a region will be placed on that new track. The region will also appear in the Regions list.

✳ IMPORTING AND EDIT MODES

When you drag a file onto either an existing track or a blank area where there is no track, the placement of the region will depend on the Edit mode you're currently using. You'll learn more about the edit modes in Chapter 5.

✳ If you drop the file into the Tracks list, a new track will be created, and a region will be placed at the beginning of that track (regardless of the edit mode you're using). The region will also appear in the Regions list.

**2** Once you've dragged your mouse to the desired location, just **release** the **mouse button** to complete the importing process—easy!

✳ FILE CONVERSION

Did you notice that you didn't have to do any sample rate or bit depth conversion? Pro Tools automatically converts the file if it's necessary!

## Preference: Automatically Copy Files on Import

Importing audio from the Workspace Browser is certainly very convenient, but there's one thing that you should be aware of when you do it. By default, Pro Tools will refer to audio files dragged from the Workspace Browser, which means that the audio will not automatically be copied into your Audio Files folder. Instead, Pro Tools will access the audio from its original location (unless sample rate or bit depth conversion is needed— in those cases, files are always copied into your Audio Files folder). Sometimes, especially for new Pro Tools users, this can lead to confusion about where your audio files actually are!

This leads you to a very important window in Pro Tools, called the Preferences window, which allows you to decide how Pro Tools will behave in a wide range of situations. Let's take a quick first look at this window and a preference that will allow you to always copy files when you import them.

1 **Click Setup**. The Setup menu will appear.

2 **Choose** the **Preferences** menu item. The Pro Tools LE Preferences window will open.

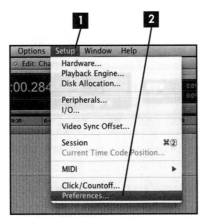

**3** Click the **Processing tab**. The Processing preferences will be revealed.

**4** Click the **Automatically Copy Files on Import option**. It's that simple—now your dragged and dropped files will always be copied to your Audio Files folder, even if no file conversion is required.

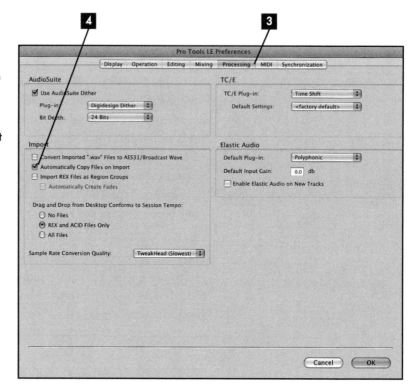

# Working with Tracks

This next section will take some things that we discussed in the first chapter and put them into a more practical situation.

## Selecting and Moving Tracks

Let's start by moving your newly created tracks to the top of the Edit window.

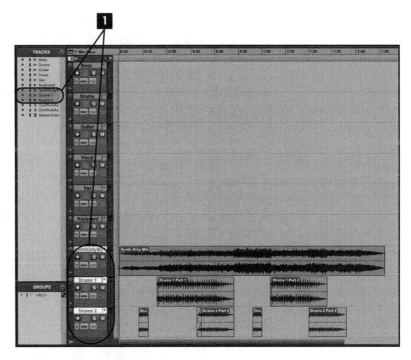

**1** To select a range of tracks, **hold down** the **Shift key** and click the **track names** of the tracks you want to select. You can make this selection either in the main Edit window area (also known as the Playlist area) or in the Tracks list. In this case, I've selected the Synth Only Mix, Drums 1, and Drums 2 tracks.

❄ **SELECTING NONADJACENT TRACKS**

The Shift key is handy for selecting a range of adjacent tracks, but what if the tracks you want to select aren't next to each other? No problem—just hold down the Ctrl key (on a PC) or the Command key (on a Mac) and click the individual track names that you want to select.

**2** Just as you did when you moved a single track, **click and drag** the **group of tracks** to the desired location in your Edit window.

If you drag the tracks to the top of the window, your Edit window should look something like this.

## Deleting Tracks

If you've been following the steps throughout this chapter, you'll notice that you have two imported drum tracks, plus the Drums track that you originally created. We don't really need that original Drums track—let's delete it.

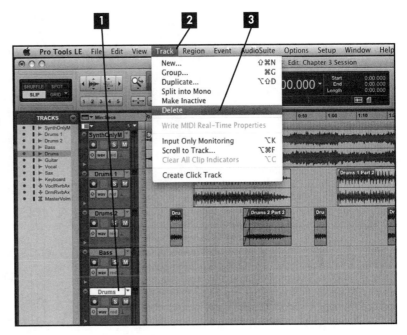

**1** Click the **track name** of the track that you want to delete (in this case, the Drums track).

**2** Click on **Track**. The Track menu will appear.

**3** Click on **Delete**. The track will be removed permanently.

If you have a mouse with a right-click button, you can easily delete any track from that track's individual menu. (If you don't have a right-click button on a Mac mouse, you can reveal the menu by Control-clicking the track name.)

**1** **Right-click** the **track name** of the track you want to delete in either the Playlist area or the Tracks list. The track name menu will appear.

**2** **Click** on **Delete**. The track will be removed permanently.

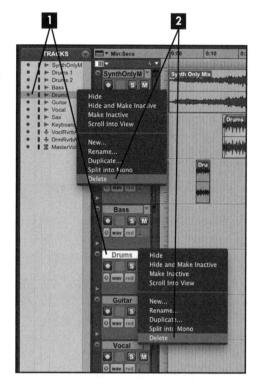

## Muting and Soloing Tracks

Mute and Solo are two of the most traditional functions in audio production, and they are used in a variety of situations (some of which we'll explore as this book progresses). Many readers already know what these terms mean, but here are some definitions for those who don't know what exactly *mute* and *solo* mean.

* **Mute.** Tracks that are muted will be inaudible.

* **Solo.** Tracks that are soloed will be heard, and any non-soloed tracks will be inaudible.

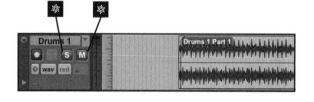

❋ **MUTE AND SOLO ON MULTIPLE TRACKS**

Clicking the M (Mute) or S (Solo) button on multiple tracks will allow you to mute or solo more than one track at a time.

✳ NEW IN PRO TOOLS 8: MUTE AND SOLO SHORTCUTS

Pro Tools users have been waiting a long time for shortcuts for Mute and Solo—and with Pro Tools 8, they get their wish! Shift+M will mute, and Shift+S will solo, any tracks that contain a timeline insertion (the vertical "play" line, which indicates your current location).

# Making Selections and Playing Audio

Being able to play your session in a few different ways (in addition to being able to play it from the beginning) will allow you to be flexible in your work. In this section, we'll take a look at the two primary variations—playing a selection and loop playback.

## Playing a Selection

Playing a selection may just be the easiest process we'll discuss in this chapter, but being able to do it correctly is an absolutely essential skill. First, start with a basic playback scenario.

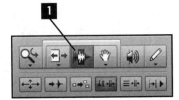

**1** Click on the **Selector Tool** button.

**2** In this case, we just want to operate in a basic playback mode, so let's make sure that Loop Playback (which we'll talk about in just a bit) is disabled. In the Options menu, **uncheck** the **Loop Playback menu item** if it is selected.

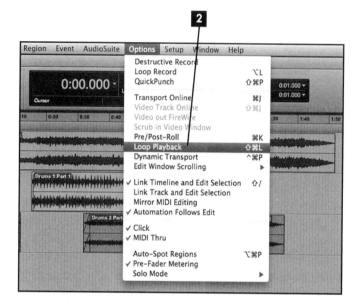

**3** With the Selector tool chosen, **click and drag** over any **section** in your session. (This can be done in the main Playlist area or in the ruler section.) To select an entire region, as shown here, just double-click the desired region. The area you select will appear dark.

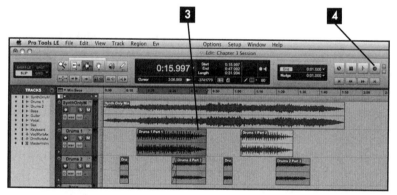

### EDIT AND TIMELINE SELECTIONS

Note that any selection you make in the Playlist area (this is called your *edit selection*) is mirrored in your rulers (this is called your *timeline selection*), and vice versa. This is a default setting for Pro Tools, and it is useful in the vast majority of cases. If you find that this is *not* the case in your session, please refer to the section in Chapter 10 called "Edit versus Timeline Selection."

**4** **Click** on the **Play button**. The selected area will play back one time and then stop.

**WHERE'S MY PLAY BUTTON? (ANOTHER USEFUL SHORTCUT)**

In Pro Tools 8, the transport section at the top of your Edit window can be moved or hidden completely! No worries—you can press the spacebar instead of clicking on the Play button to play the selection.

## Loop Playback

*Loop playback* does just what it says—it will loop, or repeat, any selected area of your session until you stop playback.

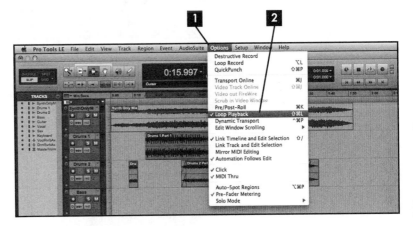

**1** Click on **Options**. The Options menu will appear.

**2** Select **Loop Playback**. The option will be checked, and a curving arrow will be shown on the Play button of your transport controls.

**ANOTHER QUICK WAY TO ACTIVATE LOOP PLAYBACK**

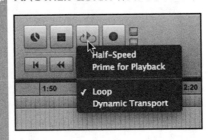

In the transport control section of the Edit window (or in the Transport window), right-click on the Play button and choose Loop from the list shown.

**3** Click on the **Play button** (or **press** the **spacebar**) to begin loop playback of your selection. The selection will repeat until you press the Stop button (or until you press the spacebar again).

## ❈ NEW IN PRO TOOLS 8: RESTORE LAST SELECTION

Before we close out this chapter, here's a useful new feature in Pro Tools, called *Restore Last Selection*. This feature, like Loop Playback, does just what it says—it will re-select the previous selection you made.

You can find this useful little option in the Edit menu. The shortcut is Ctrl+Alt+Z (PC) or Option+Command+Z (Mac).

Good work! Next up...recording!

# 4 } Recording Audio

The things you've learned in the previous chapters are some of the most important parts of being a strong Pro Tools user. Sooner or later, though, you'll want to move beyond simply importing audio and actually record an audio performance. The ability to *record* quickly and easily is a key area where Pro Tools really shines, and the flexibility this software offers has helped it earn its place as a leader in the field. In this chapter, you'll learn how to:

* Set up a click track
* Make your first recording
* Use punch-in/punch-out recording and other recording options
* Make the most of your monitoring options

# Getting Started: Signal Flow 101

We took a good first look at the Edit window in the first few chapters. Now it's time to dig deeper. First, though, you'll need to create a new blank session. (See Chapter 1 for a complete rundown of this process.)

If you don't have any musicians on hand to record, don't worry—I've got you covered. The CD that's included with your book is actually a *hybrid* disc, which means that it is a data disc *and* an audio CD. Just pop the CD in a regular CD player, and you'll hear the following tracks:

**1** Kick

**2** Snare

**3** Hi Hat 1

**4** Hi Hat 2

**5** Drum Stem

**6** Bass

**7** Blorp

**8** Synth Pad 1

**9** Synth Pad 2

**10** Synth Pad 3

You can connect the line outputs of your CD player to line inputs of your Pro Tools interface. It's imperfect, but it'll simulate a live musician well enough to suit our purposes.

**1** **Create** a **new session**. (From the File menu, choose New.)

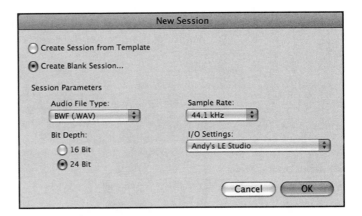

**2** Create a new blank session with the settings shown here.

> ❈ SHOULD I USE THE LAST USED I/O SETTINGS?
>
> By default, Pro Tools' New Session dialog box opens with Last Used as an I/O setting. These are the settings that were last used by Pro Tools on this system. Especially in cases of multi-user facilities, users might not know just what they'll get with Last Used, so it's a good general practice to specify an I/O setting of your own (like the I/O settings you created in Chapter 3).

**3** **Choose** your new session's **name and location** and then **click** the **Save button**.

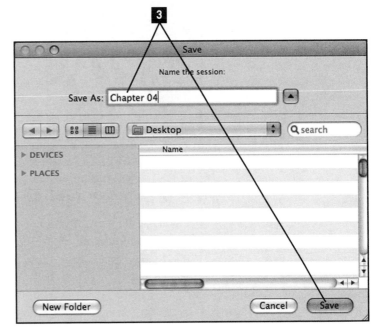

Since we're going to be recording audio, you need to create an Audio track upon which to record.

**1** From the Track drop-down menu, **choose New**. The New Tracks dialog box will open.

**2** **Click** the **Create button**. A single mono Audio track will be created.

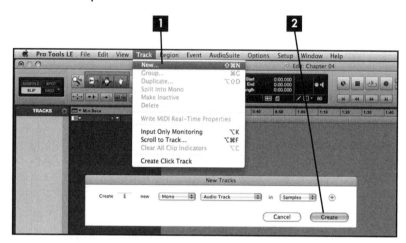

**3** **Double-click** on the **track name** and type a descriptive **name** for the track in the Name the Track text box.

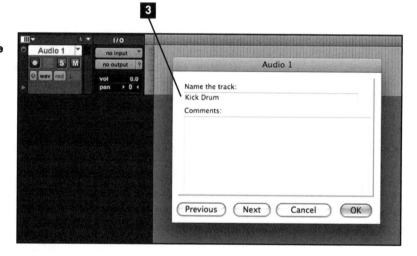

## How I/O Settings Affect Your Session

It's time for the work you put into your I/O settings to start paying off. Your configuration of the I/O Setup will determine how your tracks receive and output audio.

## Setting Up the Output

There is an output assignment button in the I/O column of each track. By default, each track will be assigned according to the Default Output setting in the I/O Setup dialog box. In a typical studio setup, this output will be connected to your studio monitors. If you want to change the output assignments, however, changing the output is easy—just follow these steps.

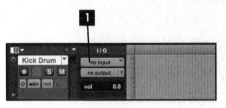

**1** Click on the **Output button** for the track you want to change. An Output drop-down menu will appear.

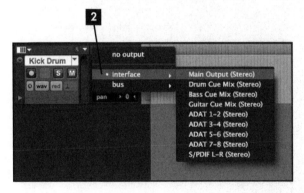

**2** Click on **Interface**. A submenu will appear, from which you can select any output path or sub-path that you created earlier in your I/O setup. In the case of recording sessions, you can change the output of any given track to be routed to your musicians' individual (or cue) mixes.

## Setting Up the Input

The top button in the I/O column of each track shows the *input* of that track. From here, you can select the desired input for your track.

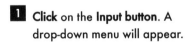

**1** Click on the **Input button**. A drop-down menu will appear.

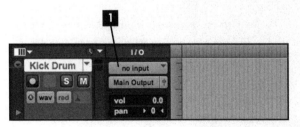

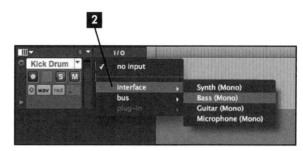

**2** Click on the **physical input or bus** that your audio will be coming from (as specified in your I/O settings). The input will be selected. If you're recording a live musician, the input that you choose for a track in a typical recording session should match the physical input on your audio interface to which his or her instrument or microphone is connected.

❄ INPUT OPTIONS

Since the track in this example is a mono track, only mono input paths (and sub-paths) will be displayed.

❄ RIGHT-CLICK RENAMING

Here's another recent addition to Pro Tools—the ability to rename inputs, outputs, and busses *without* having to go into the I/O setup window. Simply right-click on either the Input or the Output button (depending upon which one you want to rename), and you'll see the drop-down menu shown here. Choose Rename from the list. The Rename I/O window will appear (where you'll type a new name and click the OK button), and the changes you make there will be reflected in the I/O window.

## Setting the Output Volume

Right below the Output selector button, you'll see a display showing you the output volume of the track. You can easily adjust the volume by clicking in this field.

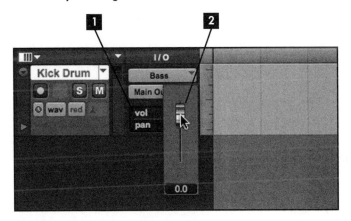

**1** Click and hold in the **Volume field**. A volume fader will appear.

**2** Still holding down your mouse button, **drag** the **fader** to the volume level you desire and then **release** the **mouse button**. The volume will be changed.

## Setting the Output Pan

Just below the Volume field, you'll find a display showing you the pan value (the placement of the audio between the left and right speakers) for the track. You can adjust the pan setting by clicking in the field.

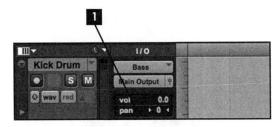

**1** Click and hold in the **Pan field**. A horizontal slider will appear.

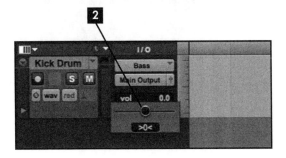

**2** Still holding down your mouse button, **drag** the **slider bar** to the pan you desire and then **release** the **mouse button**. The output pan will be set.

❄ IMPORTANT: RECORDING LEVELS VERSUS TRACK OUTPUT LEVELS

The changes you make to the output volume and output pan controls will affect the track's output only, not the input level. This means that if you're recording an especially loud signal that is clipping your input, you'll need to bring down the level of your sound source (instrument, microphone, and so on) rather than the volume fader on the track.

## Using an Output Window

There's another way that you can view and manipulate essential track-related data. A track's Output window (also commonly called a *tear-away strip*) can allow you to adjust many of your track's parameters through a single mixer-like interface.

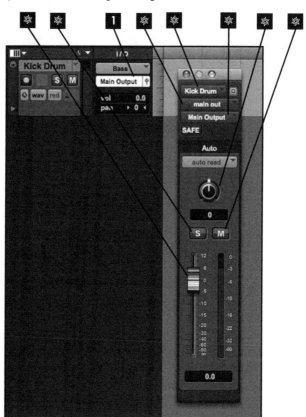

**1** Click on the **icon** at the right of the output selector. (The icon looks like a tiny fader.) The track's Output window will appear. Note that much of the track-related data you set up earlier in this chapter is shown here as well.

❄ Track name

❄ Output View selector (which will allow you to quickly switch over to one of that track's sends—something we'll discuss in Chapter 8, "Basic Mixing")

❄ Output Path selector

❄ Pan knob

❄ Solo button

❄ Mute button

❄ Volume fader, with a volume meter to its right

> ❀ **QUICK RESET SHORTCUT**
>
> You can quickly reset your volume to unity (0.0) or your pan to center (0) by holding the Alt key (PC) or the Option key (Mac) while you click on the volume or pan controls in either the track's display fields or the tear-away strip.

# Synchronization

In many recording scenarios, you'll have to make sure that the timing of your musicians—and sometimes even the timing of other machines—lines up with the timing of your Pro Tools session. This is an essential skill for all sorts of work and is generally referred to as *synchronization*. In this section, we'll examine a number of ways to get everything in sync.

## Setting Up a Click Track

You might be wondering just what a click track is. Fair question—even though it's a common term, it's surprising how many musicians don't know what a click track is or what it's used for. The answer is pretty straightforward: A *click track* is an audible track in a multi-track environment that indicates the tempo of a song through a series of short tones (usually click sounds, hence the name). This is similar to what a metronome does when it helps a musician keep tempo in the practice room.

This feature is not specific to Pro Tools. Indeed, click tracks have been used for decades, dating back to the earliest analog recording studios, when multiple musicians would all listen to the same click track in their headphones as they played, in order to stay in time with each other.

Although you certainly won't need a click track every time you work with Pro Tools, you'll find that they're a convenient way to keep everything in sync as you add track upon track to a complex session. Especially suited to music-oriented work, click tracks are very common in studios worldwide, and the ability to work with them is considered an essential skill.

Creating a click track is very simple:

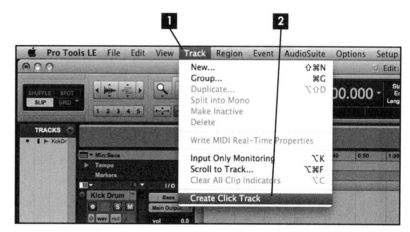

**1** Click on **Track**.

**2** Choose **Create Click Track**. A click track will be created.

Just in case you're curious, here's what you've created: a mono Auxiliary Input track.

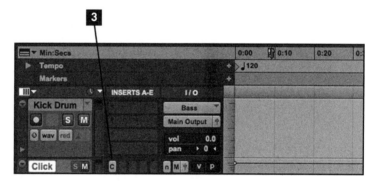

**3** On this track, you'll see a small box in the Inserts column. This is a very simple virtual instrument plug-in called Click. This primitive instrument has one simple job—to make clicks that follow the session's tempo. Despite its simplicity, you do have a few options at your disposal—just **click** the **Insert button** (on this track, it is the small box with the C on it, for Click). The Click plug-in window will open.

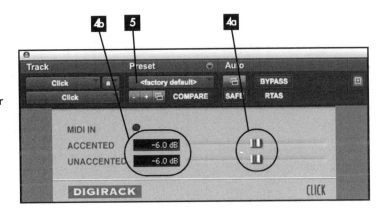

**4a** You can **adjust** the **Accented** (for each measure's Beat 1) **and Unaccented** (for the other beats) **sliders** to get the best overall volume. You can change these values at any time in your session.

OR

**4b** **Type** a **value** in the Accented or Unaccented field to adjust the values manually. **Press Enter** when you're finished to confirm your entry.

**5** If you want a different sound for your metronome, **click** on the **plug-in preset name**. A preset drop-down menu will appear, from which you can choose the best tone for your click.

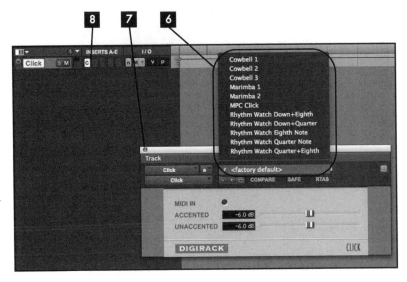

**6** **Choose** a **tone** for your click track. The sound of your click track will change to reflect your selection.

**7** When you're finished, **click** on **Close**. The Click plug-in window will close.

**8** If you want to change your settings at some later point, **click** on the **Insert button** to reopen the Click plug-in window.

The next thing you'll need to do is set up how your click track will behave.

**1** Click on **Setup**.

**2** Choose **Click/Countoff**. The Click/Countoff Options dialog box will open.

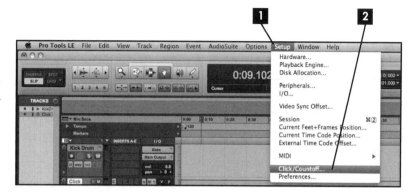

✳ ANOTHER WAY TO THE CLICK/COUNTOFF OPTIONS DIALOG BOX

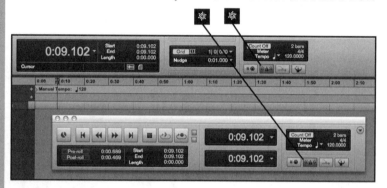

Another way to access the Click/Countoff Options dialog box is to double-click on the Metronome icon in the MIDI controls section of either the Edit window or the Transport window.

❄ You'll see that the Only During Record radio button is selected by default. This means that you'll hear the click when you're *recording* audio, but not when you're only playing back. This is the most common way to use a click, so we'll leave this button selected.

❄ You have the option of sending click information to a MIDI synthesizer (something we'll discuss in greater depth in Chapter 7). In the case of using a MIDI synth for a click, you can enter specific notes, velocities, and durations for the accented and unaccented click sounds, according to the layout of your specific MIDI device.

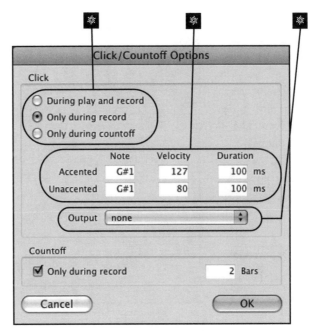

❄ Again, if you're using a MIDI synthesizer for your click source, you'll need to click on the Output menu and select a MIDI output port for your click information.

### ❄ CLICK PLUG-IN CONVENIENCE!

If you're using the Click plug-in (which is probably the most common way of working these days), you don't need to worry about assigning specific MIDI notes, velocities, durations, or MIDI output ports, since the Click plug-in is not a MIDI synthesizer in the traditional sense. If you followed the steps earlier in this chapter and created a click track from the Track menu, settings in the Accented, Unaccented, and Output rows of the Click/Countoff Options dialog box won't affect your click track one way or the other.

※ Select the Only During Record check box to ensure that your countoff will only be heard before recording. During regular playback, you won't be bothered with the countoff.

※ Enter the number of bars you want for your countoff in the Bars field. Two measures is a common setting.

**3** Click on OK. The Click/Countoff Options dialog box will close.

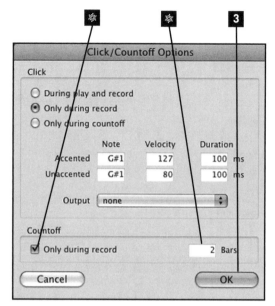

Now that the parameters of the click have been set up, the last step is to make sure that the click is actually enabled. The Options menu is a good place to check on the status of your click (and many other features in Pro Tools as well).

**1** Click on **Options**. The Options menu will appear.

**2** If your click is enabled, you'll see a check mark next to the Click menu item. If there's no check mark shown, just **click** the **menu item** to turn it on.

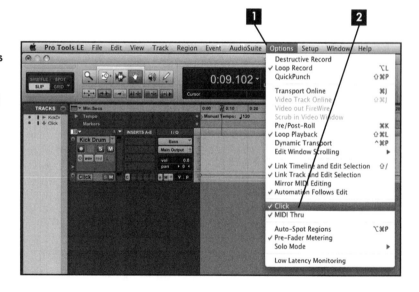

If you've followed the steps in this chapter so far, you're all set—but as with many things in Pro Tools, there's more than one way to get the job done. You can also enable the click (and the countoff) from the MIDI controls section of the Edit or Transport window.

**1** Click on the **Metronome icon** in the MIDI controls section to activate the click, if it isn't already selected. When enabled, the button will have a blue color.

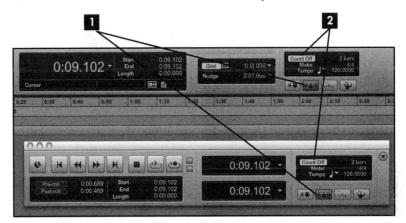

**2** To activate or deactivate your countoff, **click** on the **Count Off indicator** in the MIDI controls section. An active countoff (shown here) will be displayed in black text with a green background, and an inactive countoff will be indicated by green text with a black background.

## Tempo and Meter

Now that you have your click track set up, you'll need to choose the tempo and meter of your song—the two main factors controlling your session's metronome.

### Basic Tempo Setup

A Pro Tools session's tempo can operate one of two ways: Either the session will follow a single tempo value (giving you a static tempo), or it will follow the tempo ruler (which will allow you to have your song speed up and/or slow down as it plays). In this chapter, let's choose to use a static tempo. (You'll learn how to use the tempo ruler in Chapter 7.)

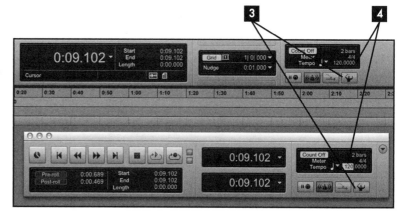

**3** If the Conductor Track button is highlighted in blue, **click** the **button** to deselect the Conductor. With the Conductor deselected, a numeric tempo display will be shown in green.

**4** Click the **Tempo value area**, which will highlight the tempo number. At this point, you have a number of options as to how to set your session's tempo.

**5a** Type a **tempo** in the numeric Tempo value field.

OR

**5b** Click and drag your **mouse** up or down to increase or decrease the tempo value.

OR

**5c** Press the **T key** on your computer keyboard in tempo. The numeric display will change to reflect the tempo of your taps.

### Basic Meter Setup

Just as with tempo, you can have a constant meter (time signature) throughout your session, or you can make metric changes during the course of your song—something we'll discuss in Chapter 7. For now, though, let's set a single meter for our session. There are two ways to get the ball rolling.

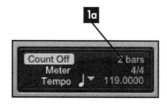

**1a** In the MIDI controls section of either the Edit window or the Transport window, **double-click** on the **Meter display**. The Meter Change dialog box will open.

OR

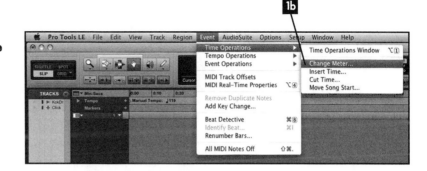

**1b** From the Event menu, **choose Time Operations** and then **Change Meter**. The Time Operations window will appear.

Though the Meter Change and Time Operations windows appear to be quite different, they do the same thing. Depending on which window you're looking at in your session, setting your meter is a straightforward process.

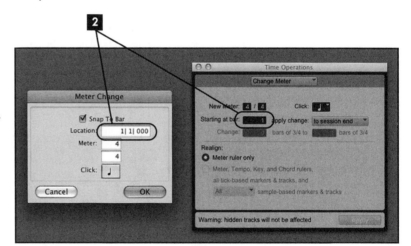

**2** **Type a location value** to indicate where the meter change should take place. In the Meter Change dialog box, the value is displayed in bars|beats|ticks. For this example, we want our meter to start at the beginning of the song, so enter a value of 1|1|000 in the Meter Change dialog box or simply 1 in the Time Operations window.

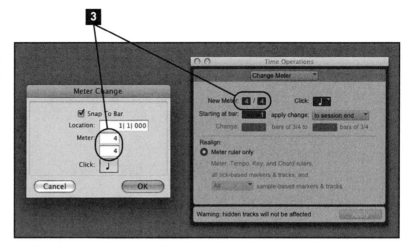

**3** **Type** a **value** in the Meter field to select the meter you want to use.

> ❄ **SNAP TO BAR**
>
> When dealing with meter changes, it's very unusual to have a metric change at any point other than the beginning (Beat 1) of a bar. In the Meter Change dialog box, checking the Snap to Bar box will place the meter change at the beginning of the bar indicated in the Location field.

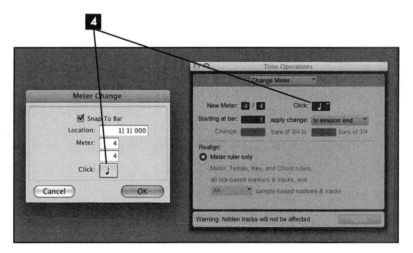

**4** Though a quarter note is most commonly used in click tracks, you can choose any note value for your click. **Click** on the **Click button** (or in the Click field if you're working in the Time Operations window). The click resolution menu will appear.

**5** Click on the **note value** that matches the desired value of your click.

**6** Additionally, you can **click** on the **dot** if you want to use a dotted-note value for your click.

**7** Once you're satisfied with your settings, **click** on **OK** in the Meter Change dialog box or **click** on **Apply** in the Time Operations window. Your meter changes will be applied.

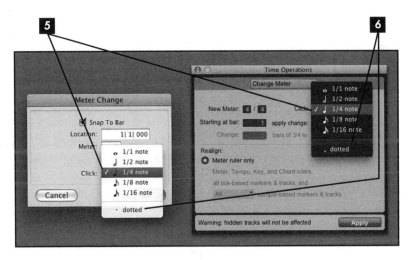

## Online Mode

In some more complex recording scenarios, Pro Tools must operate in concert with other hardware systems. Commonly, this means that Pro Tools must be set up to work with tape-based devices (video or audio) in such a way that all devices start, stop, and play together. For this sort of arrangement to work, they must be *synchronized*—in other words, when a master device starts and stops, the slave devices will follow.

Though the complexity of such setups is beyond the scope of this book, enabling Pro Tools to operate as a synchronization slave device is an easy matter—it's called *Online mode*.

❅ You'll find the Online button in your Transport window or in the Synchronization tool cluster of the Edit window. When active, the button will appear blue. With this option enabled, Pro Tools will follow the master device (which you can determine from Setup > Peripherals > Machine Control).

❅ ❅ ❅

Once Pro Tools is put online, all transport operations will be carried out remotely—you won't need to touch the transport controls.

## Generating MIDI Time Code (MTC)

Pro Tools can also operate as a synchronization master device, and one of the most common ways for Pro Tools LE to control a complex setup is through the use of *MIDI Time Code*, also known as *MTC*. For those more technical readers, MTC is a digital form of SMPTE time code and is transmitted to slave devices via MIDI (which you'll learn more about in Chapter 7).

 You'll find the Generate MTC button in the Synchronization tool cluster of the Edit or Transport window. When active, the button will appear blue. When Pro Tools is acting as an MTC master device, all devices configured to follow MIDI Time Code will follow your Pro Tools session. (You can configure this from Setup > MIDI > MIDI Studio.)

 FOLLOWING MTC

Setting up an external device to follow MIDI Time Code is a very straightforward process, and one we'll go through in Chapter 7.

WHAT ABOUT MIDI BEAT CLOCK?

There are two kinds of MIDI synchronization that Pro Tools can use: MIDI Time Code, which we've just touched on here, and another type of synchronization called MIDI Beat Clock. Beat Clock is used to keep different MIDI musical devices working at the same tempo, which is a bit different than MTC (which deals with synchronization in terms of hours, minutes, seconds, and divisions of seconds called frames). You'll learn more about Beat Clock and how to use it in Chapter 7.

# Basic Recording

You're all set—let's go! Now you're ready to record some audio from the outside world into the Pro Tools environment.

❄ TRACKS FOR RECORDING PRACTICE

Here's where the included disc's audio CD tracks can help out. If you don't have a live musician on hand, just play the audio CD, and you can record the individual tracks through available inputs on your audio interface. (Just make sure you're familiar with the input assignments in your I/O Settings window.)

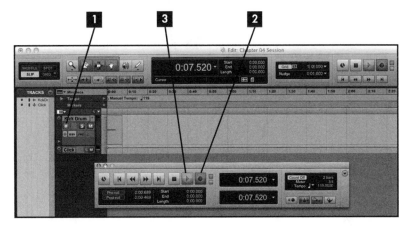

**1** Click on the **R button** to arm the desired track for recording.

**2** Click on the **Record button** in the Transport window (or the Edit window's Transport controls section). The Record button will begin to flash.

**3** Click on the **Play** button. Recording will begin.

❄ RECORDING SHORTCUT

The shortcut for record/play is Command+spacebar (Mac) or Ctrl+spacebar (PC).

**4** Click on the **Stop button** when you want to stop your recording. A new region will be shown in the track and will also be listed in the Regions list.

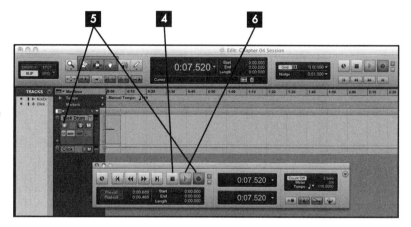

**5** Before you listen to your track, **click** the **R button** (to disarm the track), and **make sure** the **Record button** is not highlighted.

**6** Click on the **Play button**. You will hear your newly created track. Woo hoo!

# Other Recording Options

Congratulations! You've taken another important step down the Pro Tools road. Now let's explore some different ways to record audio that can come in useful in specific situations.

## Punching In and Punching Out

Let's suppose you recorded a perfect take, except for just one problem section. Don't worry—it's a situation that comes up in recording sessions again and again. With Pro Tools, you can specify a section of your track and redo it, a technique commonly called *punching in*. Remember, too, that Pro Tools generally operates *nondestructively*, so you don't have to worry about losing any of your original take!

**1** **Click** on the **Selector tool**. The tool will be highlighted (in blue).

**2** **Mark** the **area of audio** that you want to re-record by clicking and dragging with your mouse.

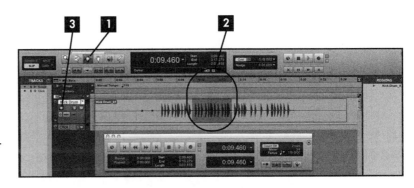

❊ **ANOTHER WAY TO MAKE A SELECTION**

You can also make a selection during playback: Just press the Down Arrow key to begin your selection and the Up Arrow key to end your selection.

**3** If your track isn't record armed already (signified by a red R button), **click** the **R button** on the track you want to redo. The track will be armed for recording. Note that the selected area in the Ruler area, which is usually bordered by blue arrows, is now bordered by red arrows (indicating that there is a track in your session that is record armed).

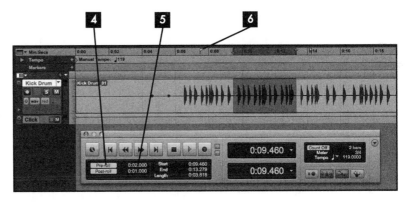

**4** If you want to hear a little bit of your original track before you start recording (before you "punch in"), you'll want to set up some pre-roll. **Click** on the **Pre-Roll** indicator. When active, it will be shown as black text against a green background (as shown here).

**5** **Click** inside the **numeric display** to the right of the Pre-Roll button and **type** the **length** of your pre-roll. Bear in mind that the scale of this value follows the Main Counter display.

**6** **Press Enter** to confirm your entry. A small gold flag in the Ruler area will represent your enabled pre-roll.

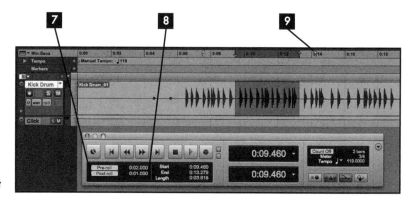

**7** If you want to hear a little bit of your original track *after* your recorded section is finished (after you "punch out"), you'll want to set up some *post*-roll. **Click** on the **Post-Roll indicator**. When active, it will be shown as black text against a green background (as shown here).

**8** **Click** inside the **numeric display** to the right of the Post-Roll button and **type** the **length** of your post-roll. Bear in mind that the scale of this value follows the Main Counter display.

**9** **Press Enter** to confirm your entry. A small gold flag in the Ruler area will represent your enabled post-roll.

**❋ MAKING CHANGES**

You can click and drag the arrows and flags on the Ruler timeline to change your selection, pre-roll time, or post-roll time. You can also hold the Alt (PC) or Option (Mac) key and click before or after a selection to instantly move your pre- or post-roll to that location.

**10** **Click** on **Record**.

**11** **Click** on **Play**. If you've selected a pre-roll value, your session will begin playback from the pre-roll position. If no pre-roll is selected, recording will begin immediately at the selected area.

If you've set up a pre-roll, Pro Tools will automatically start recording when the timeline insertion reaches the selected area. Pro Tools will continue recording until the end of the selection and then switch back to normal playback and continue playing for the post-roll duration (if any). When the timeline insertion reaches the end of the post-roll duration, playback will stop.

Here's what you'll end up with:

❋ Two new regions will be created, representing the "good" parts of the original take.

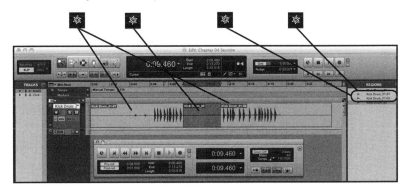

❋ Both of these new regions also appear in the Regions list. However, these regions are not shown in bold text because they are only incomplete parts of a whole file. Note that the original take is still in the Regions list as well, and it is displayed in bold type (since it does represent a whole file).

❋ Your punch has been recorded as a new region. For this example, I've recorded silence for visual effect.

❋ Your punch region appears in bold text because it is a whole-file region, which means that it represents an entire file in your Audio Files folder.

❄ WHOLE-FILE REGIONS VERSUS SUBSET REGIONS

When using Pro Tools, audio files fall into one of two categories—*whole-file* regions and *subset* regions. This is a simple but important distinction.

❄ Whole-file regions are regions that represent entire audio files. In other words, the region begins at the very beginning of an audio file and ends at the very end of that file. Whole-file regions are most commonly created during the recording process and are displayed in bold text in your Regions list.

❄ Any time a region has been created that represents anything *other* than an entire audio file, that region is called a subset region. Subset regions are commonly created during the editing process, when unwanted sections are trimmed from a region. Subset regions are also automatically created when punching in and out, as shown in the preceding example.

## QuickPunch Recording

The main limitation of the basic punch-in and punch-out workflow is that it's a one-time thing—you punch in, you punch out, and you're done. So what if you want to punch in and out more than once in a single pass? Rejoice—QuickPunch mode is for you!

**1** **Click** on **Options**. The Options menu will appear.

**2** **Click** on **QuickPunch**. QuickPunch record mode will be enabled, indicated by a letter P displayed inside the Record button.

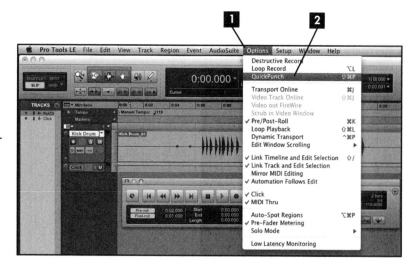

❄ QUICKPUNCH SHORTCUT

Here's another way to access QuickPunch mode: Right-click on the Record button to reveal a list of the various recording modes. Just select QuickPunch from that list.

❄ ❄ ❄

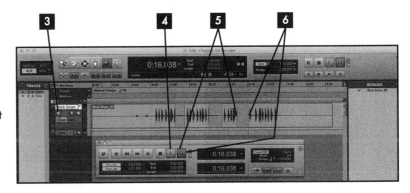

**3** If your track isn't record armed already (signified by a red R button), **click** the **R button** on the track you want to redo. The track will be armed for recording.

**4** **Click** on **Play** at any point prior to when you want to record new audio. (In this case, I'll start from the beginning of the session.) Your session will play as normal.

**5** When you want to begin recording, **click** on **Record**. Recording will start.

**6** **Click** on **Record** again when you want to *stop* recording. Recording will stop, and playback will continue. To start recording again, simply click the Record button when you wish to resume recording.

❊ ANOTHER QUICKPUNCH SHORTCUT

Here's another way to start or stop recording in QuickPunch mode: During playback, press Ctrl+spacebar (PC) or Command+spacebar (Mac).

Here's what you'll end up with:

❊ New regions will be created in your track to reflect each time you engaged and disengaged recording.

❊ As you might expect, new regions will also be added to the Regions list. The regions created in the track are not whole-file regions, though a whole-file region is also created in your Regions list. We'll discuss whole-file regions in the next section.

## Loop Recording

Suppose you want to record several passes of a certain section (a guitar solo, for example) and then pick the best one. In cases like this, you'll want to use Pro Tools' Loop Record function. Loop recording will essentially record a selected area over and over, allowing the artist to create as many takes as desired without stopping. When you're finished, you can choose the best take or even combine takes (a process called *comping* a track, which we'll discuss in Chapter 5, "Editing").

While loop recording has existed in Pro Tools for quite some time, the way that you work with loop-recorded tracks—especially in the editing phase of a project—has changed massively. We'll go through these new features and workflows in depth in Chapter 5, but for now, let's lay the foundation for those workflows by setting a few preferences *before* we start loop recording.

**1** Click on **Setup**.

**2** Choose **Preferences**.

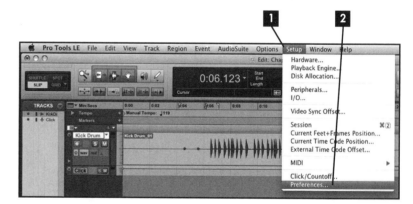

**3** In the Preferences window, **click** the **Operation tab**.

**4** In the right-hand area of the Preferences window, you'll find a check box named Automatically Create New Playlists When Loop Recording. **Click** this **box** to enable it. (When it is enabled, a check mark will appear in the box.) You'll learn more about the effect of this preference in Chapter 5.

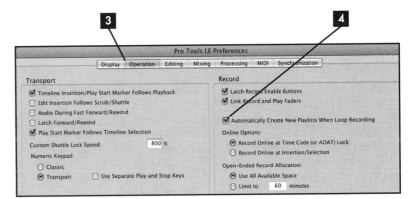

Now that you've laid the groundwork for more effective editing later on, you're all set to go through the normal process of loop recording.

**1** Click on **Options**.

**2** Click on **Loop Record**. The Loop Record feature will be enabled (as indicated by a looped arrow around the Record button icon).

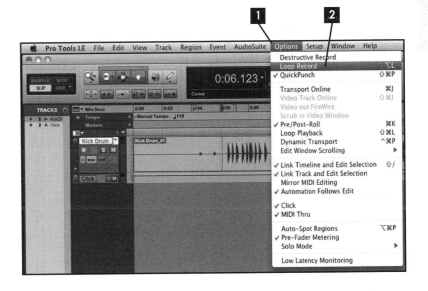

**3** Use the **Selector tool** to click and drag over the section you want to loop.

**4** If your track isn't record armed already (signified by a red R button), **click** the **R button** on the track on which you want to loop record. The track will be armed for recording.

**5** Click on **Record**.

**6** Click on **Play**. Playback will begin at the pre-roll position (if pre-roll is enabled). When the selected area is reached, Pro Tools will begin recording. At the end of the selection, recording will immediately begin again from the beginning of the selection (even if pre-roll is enabled).

**7** When you have enough takes, **click** on **Stop**. The last take will appear in the selected area.

After your loop-record passes, you might want to check your takes to see whether you captured a good one.

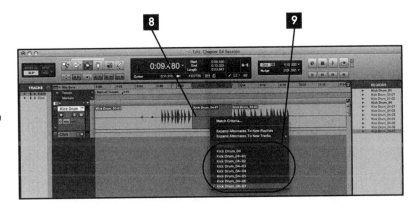

**8** With the Selector tool chosen, **Control-click (PC)** or **Command-click (Mac)** on the **loop-recorded region**. A menu of alternate takes will appear.

**9** **Click** on the **take** you want to use. The take will be selected, and the region will be replaced. This is a great way to audition different takes to find just the right one.

✵ **RIGHT-CLICK FOR MATCHING TAKES**

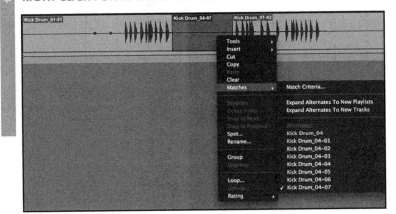

Just when you thought there couldn't *possibly* be more uses for that right mouse button, here's another one: If you right-click on your loop-recorded region, you'll see a menu of common region-related functions (many of which we'll get into later in this book). If you choose Matches, as shown here, you will see the matching takes list, and you can choose your favorite take from here. This method has the advantage of not being shortcut-dependent, and it works with any of the edit tools chosen. (The previously discussed method of auditioning different takes works only with the Selector tool chosen.)

## For the Brave: Destructive Recording

Thus far, you've only seen nondestructive recording modes, meaning that you never actually erase any audio in the process of punching in, punching out, or looping, and you can always recover your original recording pass with no loss. This is a huge advantage over working with tape, and it was one of the initial attractions to DAWs in general. With Destructive Record mode, however, you can record directly—and permanently—onto a preexisting audio file. Be careful, though; there's no way to undo what you've done if you make a mistake!

**1** Click on **Options**.

**2** Click on **Destructive Record**. Destructive Record mode will be enabled (indicated by a check mark by the menu item and a letter D inside the Record button).

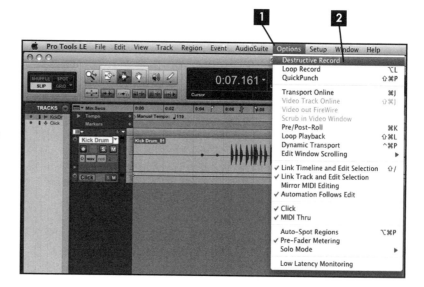

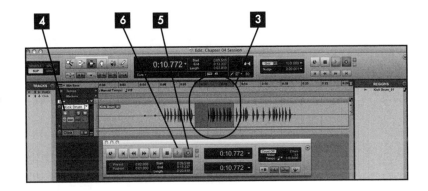

**3** Use the Selector tool to **choose** the **section** of the Audio track that you want to overwrite.

**4** If your track isn't record armed already (signified by a red R button), **click** the **R button** on the track on which you want to record. The track will be armed for recording.

**5** Click on **Record**.

**6** Click on **Play**.

At this point, the process works much the same as basic punch-in and punch-out recording—with one important difference. Just as you saw when you did basic punch-in/punch-out, your session will begin playing at the pre-roll position (if you've enabled pre-roll), and then it will automatically begin recording at your selected area. It will stop recording at the end of your selection and play for the post-roll amount (if post-roll has been enabled).

The important distinction between Destructive Record mode and the other modes becomes apparent when the recording pass has finished.

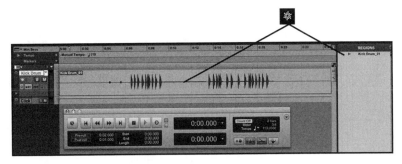

❋ Unlike the other record modes in Pro Tools, with Destructive mode *no new regions* have been created—in the track itself or in the Regions list. What you've done is permanently change the file you originally recorded!

❄ NEW IN PRO TOOLS 8: RECORD ARMING SHORTCUT

If you've gone through the previous chapter, you'll have learned that Pro Tools 8 now includes shortcuts for Mute and Solo—Shift+M and Shift+S, respectively—for any tracks that contain a timeline insertion (the vertical "play" line that indicates your current location). Well, you can add another shortcut to that list—Shift+R will record arm any tracks that contain a timeline insertion.

❄ NEW IN PRO TOOLS 8: LARGER FILE SIZES

This might be a little technical for most users, but it bears mentioning: Prior to version 8, Pro Tools only supported audio file sizes up to 2 gigabytes (admittedly, a very long audio file!). In Pro Tools 8, however, single file sizes up to 3.4 gigabytes are supported.

In a typical studio situation, you're not likely to run into either of these file-size ceilings. However, if you're recording a lengthy live performance, this might become an issue. It's an easy fix: At some point before you reach the maximum file size (at about 7.66 hours if you're recording at 44.1 kHz sample rate and 24-bit depth), just quickly stop and restart recording. This will automatically create a new file (unless you're in Destructive Record mode).

# Tips, Tricks, and Troubleshooting

Fantastic! You're on your way to running a great recording session! Before we close this chapter, here are a few tidbits to call on when you need them.

## Naming Regions and Files

When it comes to good file management practices, remember this: The names of regions and files that you create during recording will follow the names of the tracks upon which they're being recorded. For example, a track named Drums will yield recording passes named Drums_01, Drums_02, and so on.

Bottom line: The best work habit is to name your tracks *before* you start recording. However, if you ever forget to do this, or if you ever want to change the name of a region after that region has been created, it's easy to do.

**1** **Double-click** on the **region** you want to rename (either in the Regions list or in a track with the Grabber tool selected). The Name dialog box will open.

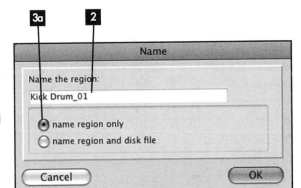

**2** **Type** a new **name** for the region in the Name the Region text box.

**3a** To rename the region only and leave the audio file's name unchanged, **click** the **Name Region Only radio button**.

OR

**3b** To rename the region in the session *and* the audio file's name, **click** the **Name Region and Disk File radio button**. Note that this option will only be available if the region you are renaming is a whole-file region.

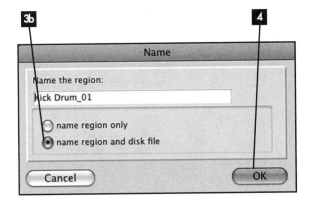

**4** **Click OK**. The Name dialog box will close, and the region will be renamed.

## Understanding the Monitor Modes

In addition to all the different record modes you've learned about, there are two monitor modes that affect how you hear your audio during the recording process. The two modes, called Auto Input Monitoring and Input Only Monitoring, will be useful in different situations.

**1** Click on **Track**. The Track menu will appear.

❈ This next bit might seem a tad unusual: The monitor mode that you're not in will be shown as an option in this menu. In the case of the image shown here, the menu item reads Input Only Monitoring, which indicates that the *current* monitoring mode is Auto Input Monitoring.

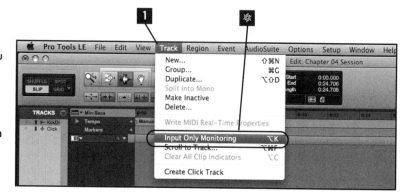

**2a** Choose **Auto Input Monitoring mode** if you want to hear what was previously recorded right up to your punch-in point. Pro Tools will behave as if it is in playback mode during any pre-roll and post-roll and will automatically switch over to monitoring your live input in the selected area only. Though both monitoring modes are useful, Auto Input Monitoring mode is more frequently used for many users.

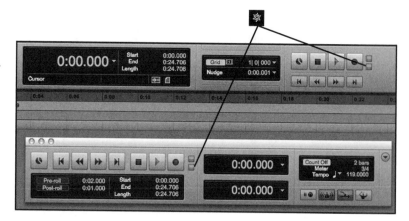

❈ To the right of the transport controls (in the Edit window or the Transport window), the Input Status LED will be off (the box will be gray) when you're in Auto Input Monitoring mode.

OR

**2b** Choose **Input Only Monitoring mode** if you *don't* want to hear what you've already recorded during a punch-in/punch-out situation. Pro Tools will still only record during the selected area, but for the pre-roll and post-roll durations, you'll hear live input rather than the previously recorded track.

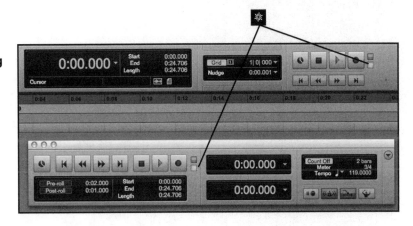

❄ With Input Only Monitoring enabled, the Input Status LED will be on (the box will be green) to indicate that you're in Input Only Monitoring mode.

## Low Latency Monitoring

Sometimes when you're recording, you might notice a bit of delay between the time a note is played and the time it is heard through your monitor speakers or headphones. This is called *latency*, and it's an unavoidable part of host-based DAWs in general—a byproduct of the conversion of analog and digital audio. The good news is that there's a way to minimize this delay in Pro Tools, called *low latency monitoring*. This monitoring mode minimizes the process of running audio through the host computer's CPU, reducing the delay you hear.

Low latency monitoring is only available in Pro Tools software running in conjunction with Digi 002 or 003 hardware or with the Mbox2 Pro. For Mbox 2 and Mbox 2 Mini users, there's a different solution, which we'll discuss in the next section.

**1** Click on **Options**. The Options menu will appear.

**2** Click on **Low Latency Monitoring**. That's it!

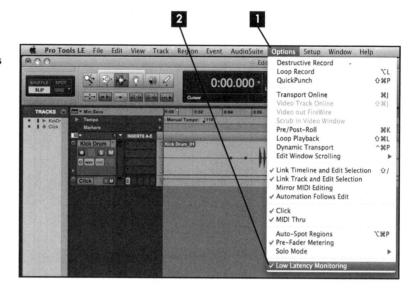

The good news is that your latency situation just got a lot better, but there's a small price to pay for low latency recording in Pro Tools LE. All inserts on any record-enabled tracks will be bypassed. (For example, if you need to have an EQ plug-in on the track's insert while you're recording, low latency monitoring isn't for you.) Fortunately, having inserts on your recorded tracks is fairly rare in normal situations.

### LATENCY AND HD

Recording latency is an issue that must be dealt with in all LE systems. As we discussed in Chapter 3, you can minimize recording latency to some degree by reducing the hardware buffer size (from the Setup menu, go to the Playback Engine window), or you can use Low Latency Monitoring mode if your interface supports it, but there are disadvantages to both techniques.

One of the advantages of Pro Tools|HD systems is that the business of recording isn't managed by your computer's CPU, but rather by dedicated processors that reside on cards that are added to the host computer. The result is that latency is typically not an issue when recording audio, with no need for low hardware buffer settings or low latency modes.

## Mbox 2 and MBox 2 Mini "No Latency" Operation

If you're working with an Mbox 2 or Mbox 2 Mini audio interface, you'll notice that the Pro Tools software doesn't give you a low latency monitoring option. Does that mean you're out of luck? No way! The solution lies in the Mbox 2's Mix knob, which is on the front panel of your Mbox 2 interface. When the knob is all the way to the input side (fully counterclockwise), you'll be monitoring signals coming directly into the interface *only*, and you won't hear the Pro Tools software play back at all. When the Mix knob is set all the way to playback (fully clockwise), you'll *only* hear audio coming from the Pro Tools software. Here's how to eliminate the latency problem using the Mbox 2's Mix knob.

1. **Set** the **Mix knob** to twelve o'clock as a starting point, giving you an even balance between input and playback.

2. **Record arm** the **Audio track** upon which you wish to record. If you play now, you should hear a doubled signal. The earlier signal is from the input side of the mix; the latent (delayed) signal is coming from the Pro Tools software, routed through the playback side of the Mix knob.

3. **Mute** the **track** upon which you wish to record. You can still record onto the track, but you won't hear that annoying delayed signal.

4. **Adjust** the **Mix knob** to get the desired balance between your live input and the Pro Tools software playback.

5. **Record** as normal.

6. When you're finished recording, you can **change** your **mix** fully to play back (clockwise) so you won't be distracted by any audio going into your Mbox or Mbox 2.

❄ RECORDING WITH BUSSES

So far, we've only dealt with physical inputs as being sources for audio recordings, but what about busses? Actually, using a bus as an input is done all the time, especially when working with virtual instrument plug-ins—we'll explore that scenario in Chapter 7, "Using MIDI." Don't worry if you're not a MIDI whiz—the section entitled "Recording Virtual Instruments to Audio Tracks" shows a classic bus recording scenario.

## ✳ A SETUP FOR RECORDING PRACTICE

In this chapter, we've been working with only a single track, recorded from the first track of the audio CD portion of your book's disc. There are nine more tracks that you can practice with. Try recording Tracks 1, 2, 3, 4, 6, and 7 to mono audio tracks and Tracks 5, 8, 9, and 10 to stereo audio tracks. If you want to check your work, you'll find a session named "Chapter 04 Session – Finished" in the data portion of your book's disc to give you an idea of what your recording session might look like when you're finished.

Next step—editing!

# 5 } Editing

Audio production can be broken down into a number of phases—recording (or tracking), editing, mixing, and mastering to name but a few. Like many DAWs, Pro Tools perhaps shines brightest in the editing phase. In its nonlinear environment, you can accomplish in seconds what used to take minutes or hours with tape-based systems. And of course, there is always the Undo function if you make a mistake.

Even among DAWs, Pro Tools has led the pack in the world of editing, and Pro Tools 8 introduces some particularly useful editing features. In this chapter, you'll learn how to:

❋ Take full advantage of the Pro Tools Edit window

❋ Use edit modes to their greatest advantage

❋ Work with Pro Tools' basic editing features

❋ Use processes such as cut, copy, and paste to create your own arrangements

❋ Use Pro Tools 8's new playlist lanes to work with loop-recorded tracks

> ❋ **TUTORIAL NOTE**
>
> For the purposes of this chapter, I'll be reconstructing a song from rough elements, so if you want to follow the screenshots, just copy the Chapter 05 Session folder from the included disc and launch the Chapter 05 Session session file.

# Understanding the Edit Window

We took a good first look at the Edit window in Chapter 2, and now it's time for a closer examination of this powerful editing environment.

## Using the Tools of the Trade

Some of Pro Tools' most useful tools are located in the top row of the Edit window. Let's start with the tool clusters included with the minimal tool set.

The four edit modes—Shuffle, Spot, Slip, and Grid—are at the heart of the editing process. The mode you choose will determine the way regions can be moved in time within your session. You'll learn more about these modes in the section "Moving Regions on the Timeline: The Edit Modes," later in this chapter.

The Edit tool cluster includes the most popular editing tools in the Pro Tools arsenal. From left to right on the top row, the tools are Zoom, Trim, Selector, Grabber, Scrub, and Pencil. These tools can operate directly on specific regions within your session. The bottom row of the Edit tool cluster includes different features that can be enabled or disabled; these are Zoom Toggle, Tab to Transient, Mirrored MIDI Editing, Link Timeline and Edit Selection, Link Track and Edit Selection, and Insertion Follows Playback. You'll learn more about these in the section "Basic Tool Functions" later in this chapter.

The Location Display cluster will give you a variety of information about your session and where you are within it. On the left side, you'll see your session's Main Counter, which will show you exactly where you are in your session. To the right are the Start, End, and Length displays, which show you the beginning, end, and duration of any selected area. Other displays in this cluster are related to session status.

I've already mentioned the Grid edit mode. Here's where you can choose the size of the grid. (Don't worry if this doesn't make sense now—we'll go through this later in this chapter.) There's also a feature that allows you to move regions by very small amounts, called *nudging*, and you can choose your nudge amount right below the grid amount. We'll talk about nudging regions in Chapter 6, "And More Editing."

Though they're not part of the minimal tool set, I personally find the Zoom Controls particularly useful. The Zoom Controls cluster will allow you to quickly zero in on a very brief section of your session (useful for fine editing) or zoom out to view longer sections in your project. The numbered buttons on the bottom of the Zoom Controls cluster will allow you to save your favorite zoom settings as zoom presets.

You can also zoom in or out using other methods, which will enable you to view your regions in different ways, which we'll discuss later in this chapter.

## Navigating Your Session

Before you can do anything else, you need to know the basics of how to get around. You'll find that the Selector tool is well suited to this task. Along with this tool, you want to use the location displays to their best advantage.

**1** Click on the **Selector tool**.

**2** Right now, the Main Counter scale is set to view time in terms of minutes and seconds, but you can view time in a number of ways. **Click** on the **arrow** to the right of the Main Counter display. A drop-down menu will appear.

**3** Choose the desired **scale** with which you wish to navigate through your session. For this example, choose Bars|Beats. The time scale of the Main Counter display will change to reflect your selection.

The scale of the Edit Selection display (to the right of the Main Counter display) will change to match the Main Counter's scale. For example, if you change the Main Counter's scale to Bars|Beats, any selections you make will also be shown in bars and beats in the Edit Selection display area.

In many cases, you might want to see the passage of time in a number of ways simultaneously. In the case of a music song, you might be working in terms of bars and beats, but you might also want to see where you are in the real-time scale of minutes and seconds. That's where the Sub Counter can help.

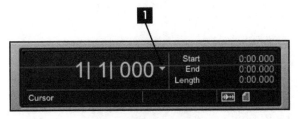

**1** **Click** on the **arrow** to the right of the Main Counter display. A drop-down menu will appear.

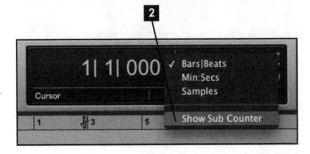

**2** **Choose Show Sub Counter.** The Sub Counter display will appear in the Counter display.

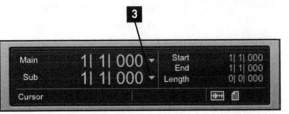

**3** In this case, my Sub Counter is showing exactly the same value as my Main Counter—that doesn't help at all, so I'll need to change the Sub Counter's time scale. **Click** on the **arrow** to the right of the Sub Counter display. A drop-down menu will appear.

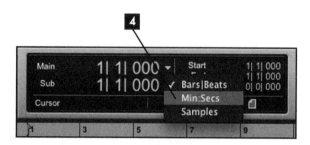

**4** **Choose** the desired **scale** for your Sub Counter. In this case, I'll choose Minutes and Seconds (displayed as Min:Secs), so that I can view my position in terms of not only bars and beats (in my Main Counter), but in real time as well.

Now that you've got your counters set up, you're all set to roam your session!

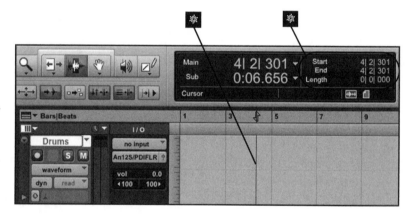

✳ Click anywhere in the session's Edit area. A small line (called the *timeline insertion*) will appear where you clicked. In the Main and Sub time displays, your timeline insertion's location is precisely displayed.

✳ The Edit Selection display will show the timeline insertion location. Because you've selected only a single location, the Start and End values are identical, and the Length value is zero.

Now, try to make a different kind of selection.

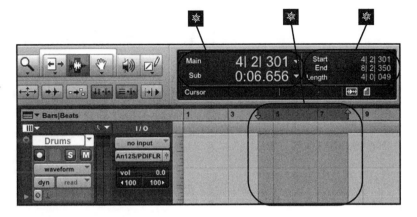

❄ Click and drag (to the left or right) in the track to make a selection with a length greater than zero. The selection you make in the track is mirrored in the Ruler area. A down arrow indicates the beginning of the selection, and an up arrow indicates the end.

❄ The Main and Sub Counters will show the start of your selection.

❄ The Edit Selection display will show the start, end, and length of your selection.

## Navigating with the Tab Key

The Selector tool is one way to get around your session, but it's not the *only* way. For example, the Universe section of the Edit window (which we explored back in Chapter 2) is a way to navigate as well. There's also the Tab key (on your computer's keyboard), which can really be useful in a number of different ways. Let's take a look.

The Tab key can be set up to operate in one of two different modes. We'll take a look at the most basic mode first, so we need to make sure that the Tab to Transients mode is *disabled*.

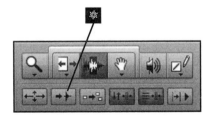

❄ Immediately below the Trim tool in the Edit tools cluster, you'll find the Tab to Transients button. When enabled, this button will be colored blue. Since we want this mode to be disabled for the time being, make sure the button is toggled off and is shown in a basic gray color.

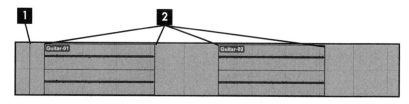

**1** Still using the Selector tool, **click** on a **track** with a number of regions, before any (or all) of the regions. The timeline insertion line will appear wherever you click.

**2** **Press** the **Tab key**. The timeline insertion will move to the next region boundary (the start or end of a region). Each additional time you press the Tab key, the timeline insertion will move to the next region boundary (moving from left to right as you continue to press the Tab key).

❊ **MODIFYING THE TAB KEY BEHAVIOR**

Here's a twist on using the Tab key: Hold the Alt key (PC) or the Option key (Mac) while you press the Tab key to move the timeline insertion to the previous region boundary (moving right to left).

With Tab to Transient enabled, the Tab key will continue to jump to region boundaries, but it will also stop at each *transient*. The first step in the process is to turn Tab to Transients mode on.

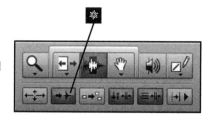

❊ The Tab to Transients button will let you know if it's enabled or disabled. When enabled, this button will be colored blue. If the button is disabled (the color will be a basic gray), just click it to turn Tab to Transients mode on.

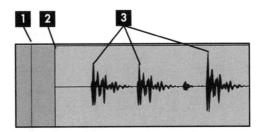

**1** Still using the Selector tool, **click** on a **track** with at least one region, and before a region, as shown here.

**2** **Press** the **Tab key**. The timeline insertion will immediately jump to the beginning of the region. Regardless of whether Tab to Transients is enabled or disabled, the Tab key can always be used to quickly move to region boundaries (start or end).

**3** **Press** the **Tab key** again. Here's where Tab to Transients differs in its behavior: This time, instead of moving directly to the next region boundary, the timeline insertion line will jump from transient to transient as well. This is a fantastic way to locate drum hits and other transient-based audio.

### ❋ MODIFYING TAB TO TRANSIENTS

Again, the Alt key (PC) or the Option key (Mac) will move the timeline insertion *backward* in time, this time to the *previous* transient peak.

### ❋ ONE MORE MODIFIER

If you want to make a selection while you're moving with the Tab key, just hold down the Shift key as you tab. This is particularly useful in combination with Tab to Transients and is a quick and effective way to select transient-heavy phrases (such as drum beats, for example).

※ SO WHAT THE HECK *IS* A TRANSIENT, ANYWAY?

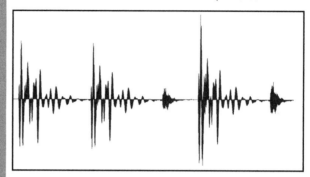

Simply put, a transient is a rapid change in amplitude (loudness) and is commonly found at the beginning of a percussive waveform, such as a pick or a hammer hitting a string or a drumstick hitting the head of a drum. Different types of instruments have different kinds of transients, but they tend to be good visual cues when editing, indicating the beginnings of notes (or words, in the case of a vocal track).

※ MOUSE-BASED SCROLLING

If you have a mouse equipped with a scroll wheel, you've got some additional navigational power at your disposal. You'll find that your scroll wheel will move you up and down through your shown tracks. (This will only work when you have more shown tracks than can be seen at once in your Edit window.) Holding down the Shift key as you use the scroll wheel will allow you to scroll horizontally along the timeline. Bear in mind that this horizontal scrolling will not move the timeline insertion.

## Zooming

Sometimes when you're editing a specific section (such as when you're working with transients, for example), you'll want to get a close look at your audio. When you're finished, you might want to take a step back and get an overview of your entire session. To do either of these things, you'll need to know how to use the Zoom tools.

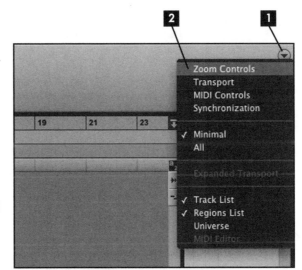

**1** If your Zoom cluster isn't showing, **click** the **Edit Window Toolbar Menu button** (in the upper-right corner of the Edit window). The Edit Window Toolbar menu will appear.

**2** **Choose Zoom Controls.** The tools that are currently being shown in your Edit window will be indicated by a check mark.

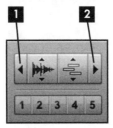

**1** Click on the **left zoom arrow** to zoom out. Each time you click on this button, the Edit window will show you a greater span of time.

**2** Click on the **right zoom arrow** to zoom in. Each time you click on this button, you will gain a finer view of your session's timeline.

❋ ZOOMING BEHAVIOR

Note that your zooming centers on your timeline insertion's location.

❋ ZOOMING SHORTCUTS

You might use these shortcuts more than any others covered in this book: On PCs, it's Ctrl+] (right bracket) to zoom in and Ctrl+[ (left bracket) to zoom out. On Macs, Command+] will zoom in and Command+[ will zoom out. You can also use the T key to zoom out and the R key to zoom in.

### ❄ SCROLL WHEEL ZOOMING

Here's even more scroll wheel power: If you hold down the Alt key (PC) or the Option key (Mac), you'll be able to smoothly zoom in and out, centered on the timeline insertion point. Scrolling up will zoom you in, and scrolling down will zoom you out. This is a very handy new addition, and you'll find that this new mouse power will speed up your editing processes!

Even if you don't have the Zoom controls shown at the top of the Edit window, you still have access to zoom buttons. You'll find them in the lower-right corner of the Playlist area of the Edit window.

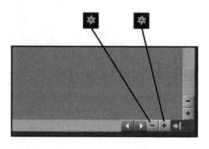

❄ Click the Minus (–) button to zoom out.

❄ Click the Plus (+) button to zoom in.

### ❄ CONTINUOUS ZOOMING

Clicking any of these zoom buttons (either at the top or the bottom of the Edit window) will incrementally zoom in or out, but you can also smoothly zoom by clicking and holding on any horizontal zoom button and dragging your mouse to the left or right.

Here's another way to zoom in on a specific section.

**1** Click on the **Zoom tool**.

**2** Click and drag horizontally on a track to select an area.

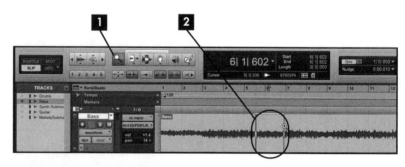

**3** Release the mouse button. The view will zoom in on the selected area.

# Moving Regions on the Timeline: The Edit Modes

Pro Tools has four basic edit modes that determine how regions can be moved in your session. Each mode is unique, and as you gain experience with each of them, you'll get a feeling for which mode is best suited to any given task. To demonstrate how each mode works, we'll work with the drum track of the Chapter 5 tutorial session.

## Using Slip Mode

When you need flexibility, Slip mode gives you the most freedom of region movement.

**1** Click on the **Slip Mode button**. The mode will be selected (indicated by the word "Slip" being shown in black text against a green background).

**2** Click and hold a **region** in the Regions list. (In this case, I've chosen the Drums region.)

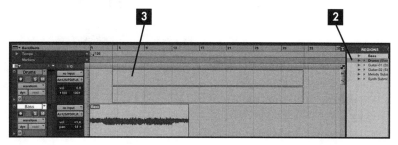

**3** Drag the **region** onto a track. You will see an outline of the region, indicating where it will be placed when you release the mouse button.

> ❋ SOME RULES ON MOVING REGIONS
>
> It's important to remember that when you're working with mono regions, you can only drop them onto mono tracks. However, when you drag stereo regions onto the timeline, they can occupy a single stereo track (as in the example just shown) or two mono tracks.

## Using Grid Mode

Sometimes it's convenient to have your regions snap to predetermined increments or *grids*. This can be particularly useful when you're working on a music-based project, when it's often helpful to have your regions align themselves to bars and beats. Pro Tools actually gives you two ways of doing this sort of grid-based work, which we'll cover here.

### Absolute Grid Mode

First, let's take a look at Grid mode in a typical music context.

> ❋ IF YOU'RE USING THE TUTORIAL SESSION
>
> If you're following along with the steps so far in this chapter, you should have a selected region on your drum track that you just deposited using Slip mode. Let's get that region out of there before we move on. Because the region is probably still selected, all you have to do is press the Delete key to remove it. If the region is not selected, just double-click with the Selector tool or single-click with the Grabber tool to select the region and then hit the Delete key. (Note that the region is still present in the Regions list, so you're not losing anything.)

**1** You'll want to make sure that your Main Counter is showing you the kind of information you need. In this example, we'll want to view our location in terms of bars and beats. If that's not what you're seeing in your Main Counter, just **click** on the **Main Counter down arrow** and **change** the **display** to Bars|Beats. The scale will be shown in Bars|Beats|Ticks. Note that the Edit Selection display will also change scale.

**2** The next thing you need to do is check your grid value to make sure that it's what you want, and make the appropriate changes if needed. **Click** on the **Grid Value arrow**. The Grid Value menu will appear.

**3** Select the desired **scale** for your grid. Because we're working with music in this case, Bars|Beats is a good fit. The scale will be selected, indicated by a check mark.

**4** Choose the desired **resolution** for your grid. For the purposes of this example, 1 bar will do the trick.

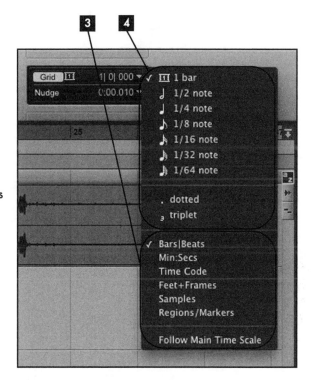

### FOLLOW MAIN TIME SCALE

At the very bottom of the Grid Value menu, you'll find an item called Follow Main Time Scale. When this is chosen (indicated by a check mark), the grid scale will automatically change whenever you change the Main Counter's scale. For many users, it's a very convenient way to work.

### BARS|BEATS GRID INCREMENTS

Because this scale is musical, you will see grid resolutions such as bars, half notes, quarter notes, and so on. At the bottom of the resolution section of the menu, you'll also see options for dotted-note and triplet-based grids.

### HEY, WHERE ARE MY GRID LINES?!?

Normally, when you're in Grid mode, you'll see a series of vertical lines to indicate your grid positions. If you're not seeing them, just click the word "Grid" in the Grid Value display. When grid lines are being shown, the word "Grid" will be shown in black text against a green background. On the other hand, if you ever want to hide your grid lines for any reason, you can click the word "Grid" to toggle the lines off. (When the grid lines are hidden, the word "Grid" appears in green text against a black background.)

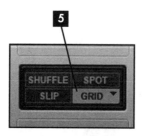

**5** **Click** on **Grid**. When Absolute Grid mode is active, the word "Grid" will appear in black text against a blue background.

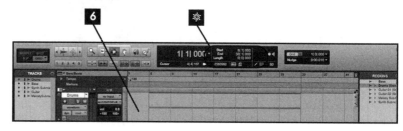

**6** Just as you did before, **drag** a **region** from the Regions list onto the Track area. With Absolute Grid mode, however, the region will snap to the nearest bar as you drag it.

❈ It might seem unusual, but your Main Counter will not be much help while you're moving regions—it will continue to show your current timeline insertion position. However, note that the Edit Selection display will reflect the beginning, end, and duration of the dragged region as you move it, helping you get it to the desired position. Because you're in Grid mode and your grid resolution is 1 bar, the Start value will always change in one-measure increments.

The essence of Absolute Grid mode is simple—regions will strictly align themselves with the grid values. In this case, with our grid value being 1 bar, any region moved from the Regions list (or even regions moved within your Playlist area) will always jump to the beginning of a bar. (In this case, the start of the region will be x|1|000, with x representing a bar number.)

## Relative Grid Mode

There's a second Grid mode available to you, called *Relative Grid mode*. This mode won't move regions to the nearest grid line, but rather it will move regions by the grid value that you set. Here's a hypothetical situation that shows the operation of Relative Grid mode.

❊ TAKING A BREAK FROM THE TUTORIAL SESSION FILE

The demonstration of Relative Grid mode that follows isn't based upon the Chapter 05 session that you've been working with up to now. If you'd like to follow along with the steps here, close (and save) the Chapter 05 Session and open up the session named Chapter 05 – Relative Grid Mode Session, which is included on your disc.

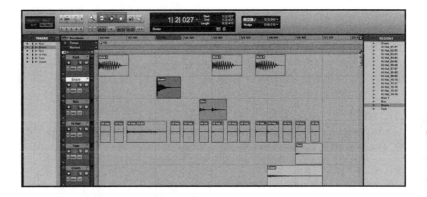

In this example, we've got a number of drum tracks. On the Snare track, we have a single snare drum hit. Using Slip mode, I've dragged a single snare region onto the track and placed it a little to the right of the Beat 2 grid line (if you look at the Main Time Counter on the following graphic, you'll see that the region has been placed at 1|2|078) to "lay back" and give the beat a bit of a groove.

We want to move that snare region to the fourth beat, but we don't want to lose that laidback feel. Relative Grid mode will allow you to do just that—move the region and maintain a consistent distance from the grid line.

**1** Click and hold the **Grid Mode button**. The Grid Mode menu will appear.

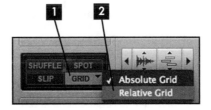

**2** Choose **Relative Grid** from the menu shown. The Grid Mode button will now be shown in purple and will read Rel Grid.

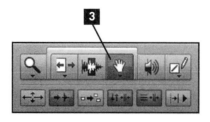

**3** Since we're going to move a region within a track, **choose** the **Grabber tool** from the Edit Tool cluster at the top of the window.

**4** With Relative Grid mode selected, **click and drag** the **region** to its new position. (In this case, I've dragged it to just after the fourth beat.) You'll see that as you drag your region, it maintains a uniform distance from the grid lines.

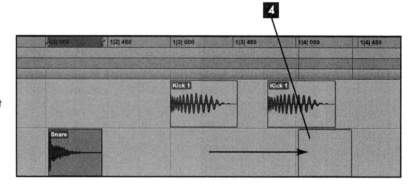

 COPYING WHILE DRAGGING: A NEW KEY COMMAND

We'll talk more about editing in the next two chapters, but there's one you might like to try with this example. Hold the Option (Mac) or Alt (PC) key as you drag a region with the Grabber tool to make a copy of the region as you drag it.

## Using Shuffle Mode

Shuffle mode operates in a much different way than either Slip or Grid mode. In this mode, regions move end to end with each other. When you see how this mode works, you'll see how it can be useful for stitching together verses, choruses, and so on into a seamless final product!

 SETTING THINGS UP

Again, you should go ahead and delete the region that you've dragged onto the drum track while you worked with Grid mode—just hit the Delete key (assuming that the region is still selected). Also, you might want to zoom out a bit to see this mode in its best light..

**1** Click on **Shuffle**. The mode will be selected.

**2** One by one, **drag and drop** various **regions** from the Regions list onto a single track. For the purposes of this example, try dragging Synth Submix, then Melody Submix, and finally Synth Submix again. Wherever you drop these regions, they will snap end to end with the previous region, starting with the first region, which automatically snaps to the beginning of your track.

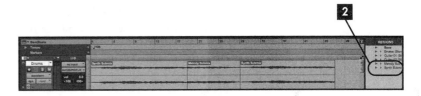

**3** Now let's actually "shuffle" the regions a bit. **Click** on the **Grabber tool**.

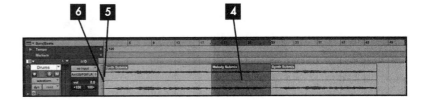

**4** Click and hold on a **region** that you want to move.

**5** **Drag** the **region** over another region on the track. A light-colored line will appear at region boundaries, indicating where the region would be repositioned if the mouse were released.

**6** **Release** the **mouse button** when the region is at the desired location. The regions will be reorganized.

Note that all regions are still adjacent to each other, despite the fact that their order has been changed. Of course, you can move more than one region at a time. In fact, you can shuffle regions forward and backward at will and create new arrangements of these regions, while keeping all the regions snugly end to end.

### SHUFFLE LOCK

In some cases, users want to make sure that they can't enter Shuffle mode inadvertently. (This is most common in audio post-production situations, where Shuffle mode is rarely used.) If that fits with your workflow, it's easy to lock yourself out of Shuffle mode: While you're in any mode *other* than Shuffle mode, Command-click (Mac) or Ctrl-click (PC) on the Shuffle Mode button. A small lock icon will appear in the lower-left corner of the Shuffle Mode button. To unlock Shuffle mode, simply Ctrl-click (PC) or Command-click (Mac) on the Shuffle Mode button again.

## Using Spot Mode

Spot mode is very popular in audio post-production situations, where users commonly want to assign a region to a specific place in time. For example, if a producer wants a specific sound effect to occur at a specific point, with Spot mode, you can just type in the location for your region.

### SETTING THINGS UP (AGAIN)

Once more, you'll want to clear the drum track for this next section. Here's a quick way to do it: With the Selector tool, triple-click anywhere in the track you want to clear. All the regions in that track will be selected, and you can now remove them by pressing the Delete key.

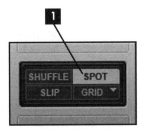

**1** Click on the **Spot button**.

**2** Select a **region** and **drag it** onto an appropriate track.

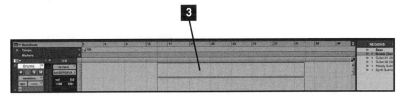

**3** **Release** the **mouse button** to drop the region on the track. The Spot Dialog box will open.

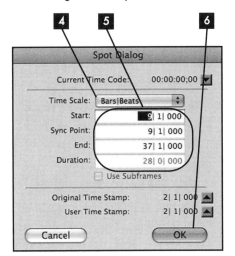

**4** Click on the **Time Scale menu button** and **select** the **time scale** you want to use in positioning your region. (You can choose Bars|Beats, Min:Secs, or Samples.)

**5** You can choose to place your region's start, end, or sync point (something we'll discuss in Chapter 10, "Moving to the Next Level: Tips and Tricks") to a position that you type into the appropriate field. Very often, users are most concerned about the placement of the start of the region, so let's try moving the region's beginning to a specific point in time. **Type** exactly **where you want your region to begin** in the Start field.

**6** Click on OK. The region will be placed on the track at the specified location.

❄ NEW IN PRO TOOLS 8: MULTIPLE EDIT MODES

The idea of having more than one edit mode active at a time might seem a bit strange to longtime users of Pro Tools, but it's a new feature that is actually quite useful and straightforward.

You can combine either Shuffle, Slip, or Spot mode with Grid mode. (In the case of this image, Shuffle mode and Grid mode are simultaneously active.) Setting this up is easy—simply select your primary mode (Shuffle, Slip, or Spot) and then hold the Shift key as you click the Grid Mode button.

Once you've set up your two modes, how will your tools behave? It's actually pretty simple: The Selector and Trim tools will operate in Grid mode, and your Grabber tool will work according to the rules of the other mode. For example, if you choose both Shuffle and Grid, you can select an area of a large region according to a grid and then separate the region (something you'll learn more about later in this chapter) and move the region in Shuffle mode.

# Basic Tool Functions

The three main edit tools you'll use are the Trim, Selector, and Grabber tools. We've touched on some of their functions already, but let's go just a bit deeper so that you can make the most of them.

## Understanding the Trim Tool

The first tool we'll look at is the Trim tool. Its basic function is to change the left or right boundary of a region.

❄ MAKING THINGS GO A BIT MORE SMOOTHLY

This tool can get a little tricky when you're working in Spot mode. Just for simplicity's sake, change your edit mode to Slip mode.

**1** Click on the **Trim tool**.

**2** **Position** your **cursor** at the beginning or end of a region that you wish to change. The cursor will take on the appearance of a bracket, indicating that the Trim tool is ready to be used.

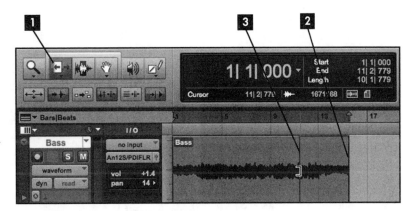

**3** **Click and drag** the **region boundary** horizontally. You will see a graphic representation of how your region will be altered as you drag.

**4** When you have reached the desired position, **release** the **mouse button**. The region will be changed accordingly.

❋ SOME NOTES ON THE TRIM TOOL

There are a few things to keep in mind when you're using the Trim tool:

❋ Trimming a region is nondestructive—it only changes the part of the audio file you are choosing to hear in your session.

❋ When you use the Trim tool, new regions will be created in the Regions list.

❋ When you're in Grid mode, your trimming will snap to the current grid values. This is particularly useful when you're editing drum beats and other musical material.

## Understanding the Selector Tool

You've already used the Selector tool to choose a section of your session to play. You can do other things with the Selector tool as well. For example, let's try removing several regions over a number of tracks all at once.

**1** Click on the **Selector tool**.

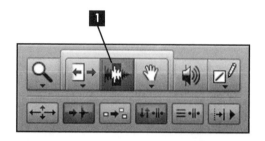

**2** Starting in one corner, **click and drag** a **square area** that includes the elements you wish to remove from your session. A gray box will indicate what you've selected.

**3** **Press** the **Delete key**. The regions (or portions of regions) will be removed from your tracks.

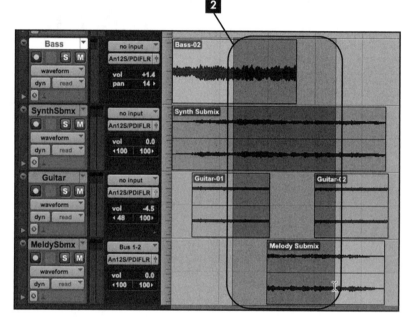

> ❋ THE POWER OF A NONDESTRUCTIVE ENVIRONMENT
>
> Remember that Pro Tools is (for the most part) a nondestructive DAW. The regions you clear from your tracks won't be removed from the Regions list or your hard drive. Nondestructive also means that you can easily undo what you've done (by choosing Undo from the Edit menu), which you should do right now, to set up the next section.

## Link Track and Edit Selection

There's another way to easily make selections over a number of tracks or to move a selected area from one track to another. It's a feature called Link Track and Edit Selection, which allows you to assign edit selections based upon track selections and vice versa. In a nutshell, here's how it works:

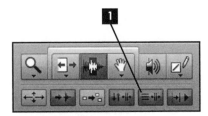

**1** The first thing to do is to enable this feature. The Link Track and Edit Selection button is just below the Scrub tool. Just **click** this **button** to enable or disable the feature. (When enabled, the button will appear blue.)

❋ Note that any track that has a selected area is also selected.

**2** To move the selected area to another track, simply **click** the target track's **nameplate**.

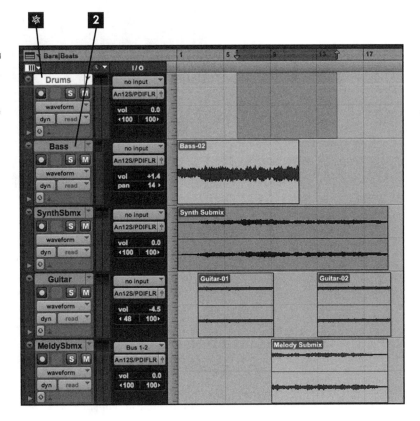

❋ Here's what you'll get: The selection will migrate immediately to the newly selected track.

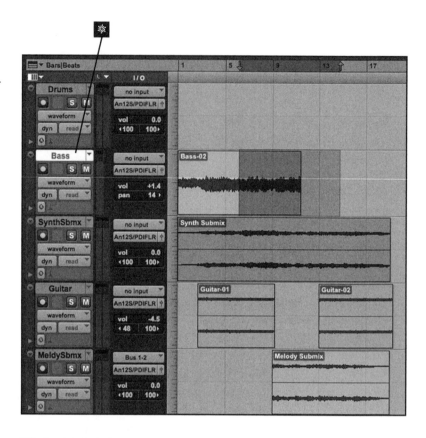

❋ **SELECTING A BLOCK OF TRACKS**

If you want to select a consecutive block of tracks (and hence a selected area that spans those tracks), just hold down the Shift key when you click the tracks' names. If you want to add or remove track selections individually, just hold the Ctrl (PC) or Command (Mac) key while you click the desired track name(s).

## Understanding the Grabber Tool

Last but not least, you have the Grabber tool. We've used it before, but this section will show you how to move more than one region at a time.

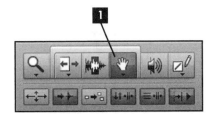

**1** Click on the **Grabber tool**.

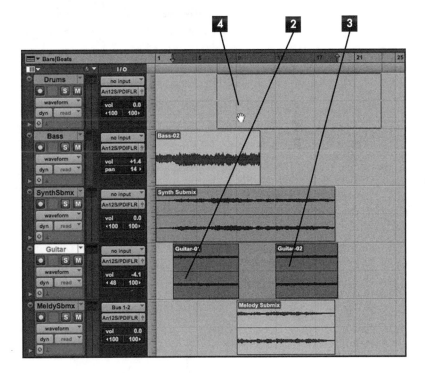

**2** Click on a **single region** that you wish to move. The region will be highlighted.

**3** Press and hold the **Shift key** and **click** on **additional regions**. The regions will be highlighted.

❉ GRABBING A BLOCK OF TIME

As you grab additional regions using the Grabber tool, a shaded area will appear. This area will include not only all the regions you directly selected, but also all regions that fall within that shaded area. This is the normal operation of the basic Grabber tool, which is more accurately known as the Time Grabber. There's a variation of the Grabber tool, called the Object Grabber, which we'll explore in Chapter 6.

**4** Drag and drop the **regions** you selected. As you drag, a box will show you where your regions are going to be deposited.

> ❋ SETTING THINGS UP FOR THE NEXT SECTION
>
> Once more, please undo any changes you've made before progressing to the next section.

# Assembling a Track

Now we're going to combine a number of tools you've already worked with, plus a few editing tricks, and re-create the bass line from the Chapter 1 session. In addition to tools from this chapter, you'll be drawing on some knowledge you picked up in earlier chapters as well. When you're finished, you'll have a good idea of how you can put together tracks of your own!

## Creating Regions

We've already created regions through the process of importing and recording audio, but that's only the beginning of the story. In this section, you'll create new regions for your track based upon preexisting regions.

### Capturing a Selection

Here's the mission: In this example, you have a reference track named Bass, which simply contains a single region. The task at hand is to reconstruct the Bass track from this single region.

**1** Click on **Grid**. The Grid mode will be selected.

**2** Click on the **Selector tool**.

**3** **Double-check** the **grid resolution** to make sure it is 1 bar.

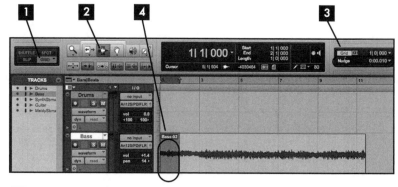

**4** Using the Selector tool, **select** the **first measure** on the Virus Bass Audio track. When you've selected the right amount, your Edit Selection display will show a start time of 1|1|000, an end time of 2|1|000, and a length of 1|0|000.

**5** Click on **Region**. The Region menu will appear.

**6** Click on **Capture**. The Name dialog box will open.

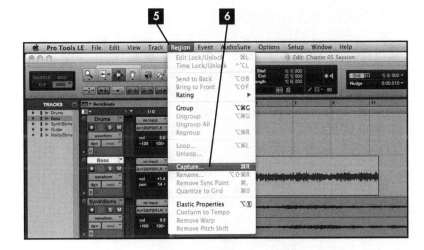

**7** **Type** a descriptive **name** for your new region in the Name the Region text box.

**8** Click on **OK**. The Name dialog box will close, and the new region—a copy (or capture) of the area you selected—will be created. You can see your newly created region in the Regions list.

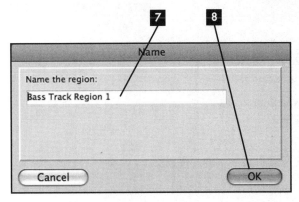

## Separating a Region

Here's another way to create a region from a selected area. This time, instead of *capturing* a selection, you're simply going to start chopping up your big region into smaller, more manageable bits. Visually, these two methods might appear quite similar, but by separating a region, you'll be creating a new region in the Regions list *and* in your track simultaneously. (Capturing will only create a new region in the Regions list.)

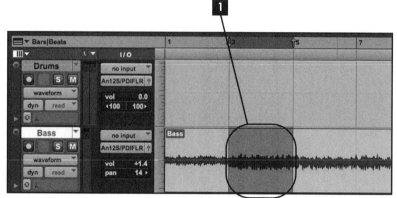

**1** Still using the Selector tool, **select Measures 3 through 5** on the Bass track. It's easy when you're in Grid mode with a whole-measure grid!

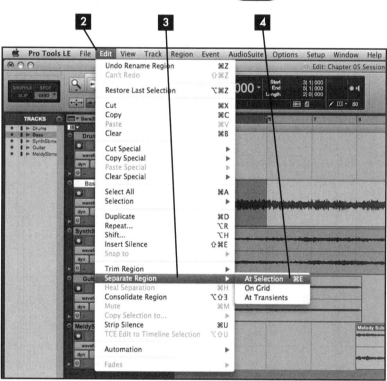

**2** **Click** on **Edit**. The Edit menu will appear.

**3** **Click** on **Separate Region**. A submenu will appear.

**4** **Choose At Selection**. A new region will be created.

## ❄ AUTO-NAMING REGIONS

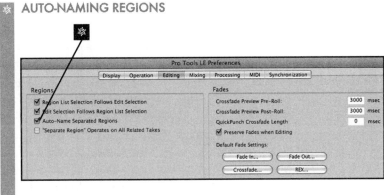

❄ You can select or deselect the Auto-Name Separated Regions field to enable or disable this feature, respectively.

At this point, Pro Tools *might* ask you to name your new region—a feature called *Auto-Name*. You can disable or enable the Auto-Name feature by selecting the Setup menu, choosing Preferences, and then clicking on the Editing tab.

Your original region has been separated into three smaller regions. The region that matches your selection will be in the middle.

❄ **CONSTRUCTING THE BASS TRACK: STEP ONE**

If you've been working with the Chapter 5 session and following the steps in this chapter, you're well on your way to building this bass part from scratch. Good for you! Now you're ready to do some work on your own.

To get to the next step, you need to use either the Capture Region or the Separate Region function—in addition to using your ears—to create the next three regions. The next steps will be a rough guide for you:

**1** Import the Reference Bass track from the Reference Bass Track Session (in the Session 05 Import Materials subfolder on the disc included with your book). This will be your guide in rebuilding the bass track. Please refer to the "Importing Tracks" section in Chapter 3 for directions on importing session data.

**2** Listen to the region beginning at Measure 9 on the Reference Bass track. Select a section on the Bass track that matches it and then capture or separate a region. Name this region Bass Part Reassembly 3 (if prompted for a name).

**3** Listen to the region beginning at Measure 12 on the Reference Bass track. Select a section on the Bass track that matches it and then capture or separate a region. Name this region Bass Part Reassembly 4 (if prompted for a name).

**4** Finally, create a region that matches the region on the reference track that starts at Measure 15 and ends at Measure 20. (Keep in mind that this section is five measures long.) Name this region Bass Part Reassembly 5 (again, if prompted).

One thing to keep in mind: Although either capturing or separating will do the job as far as this example is concerned, there are differences in the way each method works. Capturing will leave the original region intact on the timeline and will only create a new region in the Regions list. Separating a region will alter the region in your track, in addition to creating new regions in the Regions list.

## Cropping a Region

You've got nearly all the regions you'll need to assemble the Bass track. To finish the job, we'll be trimming a region, but in a new way.

The last thing we need to do is to create a region based on Measure 14 on the Bass track. You know by now that there are a number of ways that you could create this region—capturing, separating, or trimming with the Trim tool. In this section we'll trim the region, but in a different way.

1. Click on the **Selector tool**.

2. **Select** the **area** of the audio region that you want to retain. (In this case, it will span from 14|1|000 to 15|1|000.)

3. Click on **Edit**. The Edit menu will appear.

4. Click on **Trim Region**. A sub-menu will appear.

5. **Choose** the **To Selection menu item**. The region will be trimmed to your selection on the track, and a new region will be created in your Regions list.

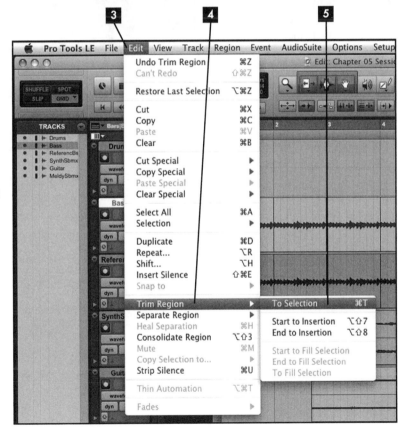

### Renaming a Region

At any time in the editing process, you might want to rename a region in your session. Here's how to do it.

1. Click on the **Grabber tool**.

2. **Double-click** on the **region** you want to rename. The Name dialog box will open.

3. **Type** the **name** you want for the region in the Name the Region text box.

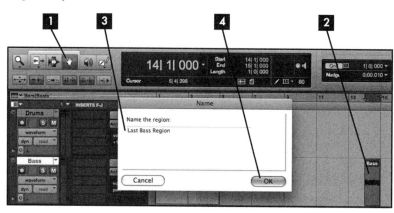

4. Click on OK. The Name dialog box will close, and the region will be renamed.

## Arranging Regions

Now that we've created the regions we need, the next step in the process is to organize them on the track. In this part of the process, what you've already learned about the edit modes will serve you well, and a couple additional tricks will make the process even easier!

❄ CONSTRUCTING THE BASS TRACK: STEP TWO

If you're following the steps so far in this chapter, the next step is to select all remaining regions on the Bass track and press the Delete key, leaving a blank track on which to assemble your newly created regions.

Working in Shuffle mode makes the job easy!

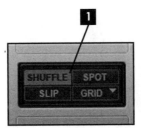

**1** Click on **Shuffle** if you're not already in Shuffle mode.

**2** One by one, **drag regions** onto the desired track in the order that you want them to be played back.

❊ CONSTRUCTING THE BASS TRACK: STEP THREE

If you're following the example in this chapter, drag Bass Track Region 1 onto the track six times and then find the region that sounds like the region on the Reference Bass track at Measure 7 (you'll have to use your ears, and you may find that the region lengths aren't the same!) and drag it onto the Bass track twice. Last but not least, find the region that sounds like the Reference Bass Track at Measure 9 and drag it to the Bass track once.

Remember that in Shuffle mode, it doesn't matter where you drop your regions—they'll automatically move to the edge of the preceding region.

## Duplicating Regions

Of course, you *could* just drag the same region onto a track over and over to create a looping phrase, but that can get really boring very quickly. Here's another way to make a copy of a region or selection and place it immediately after the original.

1 **Select** the **region** you want to duplicate (either by single-clicking with the Grabber tool or by double-clicking with the Selector tool).

2 **Click** on **Edit**. The Edit menu will appear.

3 **Click** on **Duplicate**. A duplicate of the selected region will appear immediately after the selection.

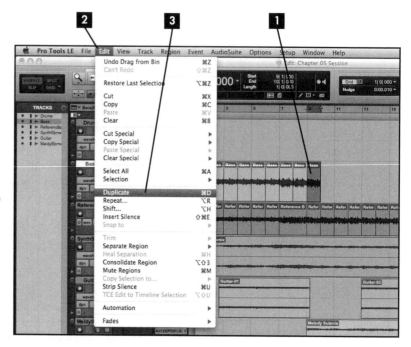

❈ **DUPLICATE SHORTCUT**

The shortcut for the Duplicate function is Command+D (Mac) or Ctrl+D (PC).

❈ **FINISHING UP THE BASS TRACK**

If you've been following the steps in this chapter, you'll want to duplicate the region named Bass Part Reassembly 3 (if you've named your regions manually) two times and then add the Bass Part Reassembly 4 region at Bar 12. After that, you'll add the Bass Part Reassembly 3 region another two times.

When that's done, add the region named Bass Part Reassembly 5 at Measure 15. Last but not least, add the region named Last Bass Region at Measure 20, and you're ready to continue on to the next section.

If you have Auto-Naming enabled, you might find that some of the region names I've listed here don't match the regions in your Regions list. In that case, you'll want to audition the regions in the Regions list. You can do this by holding down the Option key (Mac) or the Alt key (PC) and clicking and holding on the desired region's name. You'll be able to hear the highlighted region and use your ears to find the right ones (which is a great practice for beginning editors).

## Repeating Regions

Repeating regions is similar to duplicating regions, but with a twist. Instead of repeating the process for each additional loop, you can create multiple loops in one quick process.

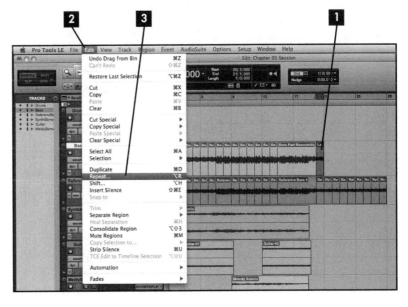

**1** **Select** the **region** you want to repeat (either by single-clicking with the Grabber tool or by double-clicking with the Selector tool). In this case, you should select the region named Last Bass Region.

**2** **Click** on **Edit**. The Edit menu will appear.

**3** **Click** on **Repeat**. The Repeat dialog box will open.

**4** **Type** the **number** of **times** that you want the region to repeat in the Number of Repeats text box. (In this case, type 8.)

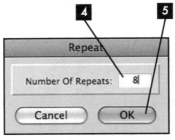

**5** **Click** on **OK**. The selected region will be repeated the specified number of times, just as if you had used the Duplicate command multiple times.

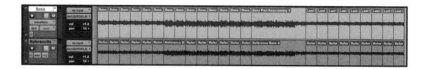

Solo both bass tracks (if you haven't already) and play them together. They should sound identical. If they do, then you're finished! If they don't, then it's time to take a closer look at the Reference Bass track and the Bass track you just created, find where they disagree, and then make the necessary changes.

## Working with Grids

By now you're getting a good sense of the usefulness of working in Grid mode. However, using a grid value as large as a whole measure might not work for you in all situations. Changing the grid value will open new possibilities.

If you've listened closely to the melody track, the timing should seem a bit off. The good news is that the tempo isn't the problem—the entire melody is just an eighth-note too late. You can still use Grid mode to fix the problem, but we'll need to make a finer adjustment than a whole-measure grid can provide. Read on . . .

1 Click on the **arrow** next to the Grid value. The Grid Value menu will appear.

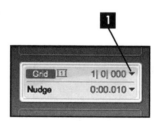

**2** Select the **scale** (for example, Bars | Beats or Min:Secs) if you want to change the scale of your grid. If you want to continue in the same scale, just **click** on the **Grid value** you want. In this case, choose an eighth-note value. The grid will immediately change in the Edit window.

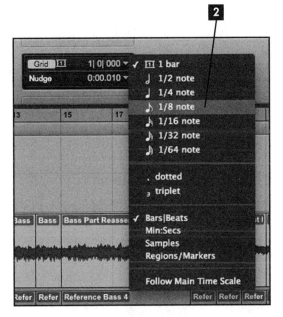

**3** If you're not in Grid mode already, **click** the **Grid Mode button**.

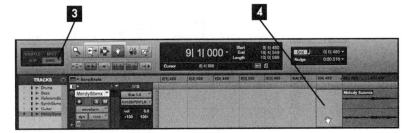

**4** Drag the **Melody Submix region** one eighth note earlier. (You may want to zoom in a bit so that you can see the individual grid line clearly.) As you drag the region in the track, a box will show you where your region will be deposited when you release the mouse button (moving in eighth-note increments). This region will sound a *lot* better if it begins at 8 | 4 | 480.

**5** Drop the **region** at the desired location.

## Cutting, Copying, and Pasting

Cut, copy, and paste are tried-and-true staples of many kinds of software, and Pro Tools is no exception. These processes are very straightforward and easy to use.

## Copying a Region

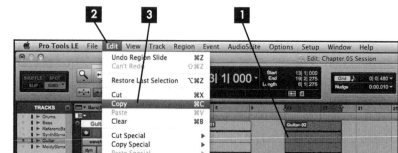

**1** Select the **region** you want to copy.

**2** Click on **Edit**. The Edit menu will appear.

**3** Click on **Copy**. The region will be copied to the Pro Tools clipboard, ready to be pasted.

 **COPY SHORTCUT**

The shortcut for the Copy command is Command+C on a Mac or Ctrl+C on a PC.

## Pasting a Region

A copied region means nothing until it's pasted to a new location. Here's how to do it:

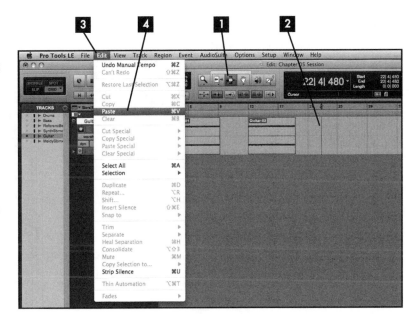

**1** Click on the **Selector tool** if it's not already selected.

**2** Click in a **track** at the location where you want the pasted region to begin.

**3** Click on **Edit**. The Edit menu will appear.

**4** Click on **Paste**. The region will be pasted at the location you selected.

❊ **PASTE SHORTCUT**

The shortcut for the Paste command is Command+V (Mac) or Ctrl+V (PC).

## Cutting a Region

Because you're not going to use that region you just pasted, let's go ahead and cut it.

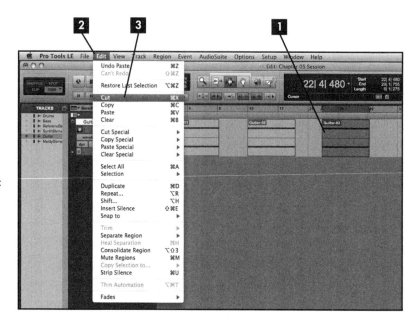

**1** Select the **region** you want to cut.

**2** Click on Edit. The Edit menu will appear.

**3** Click on **Cut**. The region will be cut and placed on the Pro Tools clipboard (for pasting, if desired).

❄ CUT SHORTCUT

The shortcut for the Cut command is Command+X (Mac) or Ctrl+X (PC).

## Working with Overlapping Regions

From time to time, you'll want to move one region so that it partially overlaps another region. This is absolutely not a problem—it happens all the time—but there are some things you should be aware of. First of all, you will only ever hear the region that's "in front," meaning that you won't hear both audio regions play together. Second, this sort of action is nondestructive, meaning that when you overlap regions, no audio is being removed from your audio files.

Let's take a look at how you can view and manipulate overlapped regions.

❄ NOW'S A GOOD TIME TO SAVE YOUR WORK

We're going to work with the Guitar track a little bit to show how overlapped regions work, but you won't want to keep this work. If your session sounds good (and it shouldn't sound too bad if you've been following the steps in this chapter), you should save your work before moving on.

First, let's take a look at the normal behavior of overlapped regions:

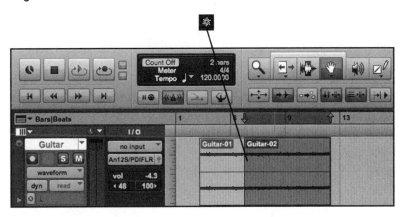

❊ Drag a region over another region using the Grabber tool (in this case, the second region on the Guitar track is dragged over the first), and you'll notice that when you play back the track, only the region (or portions of a region) that is immediately visible will be heard.

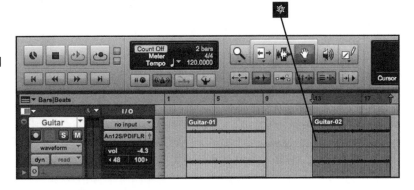

❊ Move the region that was "on top" out of the way, and you'll see that the region that was partially blocked hasn't changed at all!

❊ OVERLAPPING REGIONS' BEHAVIOR

If only one region boundary overlaps another region, then you'll see the same nondestructive behavior that you've just seen here. If, however, a smaller region is dragged completely over a larger region and dropped (in other words, both region boundaries are overlapping), a hole will be left when that smaller region is moved away again. This is still fundamentally nondestructive, because you can use the Trim tool to reveal any material that is taken off the timeline.

Sometimes it's hard to visually determine when regions are overlapping versus when they are simply next to each other. It would sure be easier if there were some sort of visual cue to show an overlapped arrangement. No sooner said than done!

**1** Click on **View**. The View menu will appear.

**2** Click on **Region**. The Region submenu will appear.

**3** This submenu is a checklist of region-related attributes that can be shown or not shown. **Click** on **Overlap**. (It will appear checked when activated.)

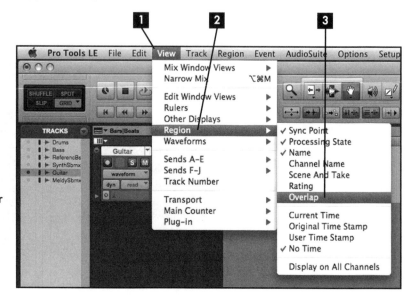

❋ Note that now you'll see a small bevel in the overlapping upper corner of a region that is covering another region.

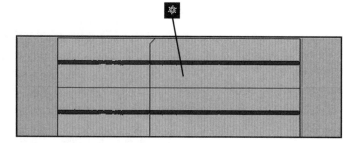

But wait, there's more! What if you want to reverse the way the regions are overlapped *without* moving either of the regions?

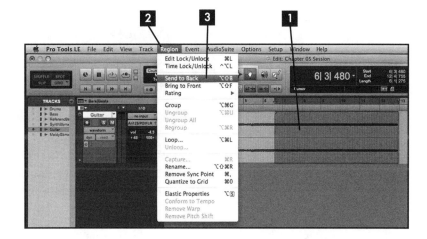

**1** **Select** the **region** in front.

**2** **Click** on **Region**. The Region menu will appear.

**3** **Click** on **Send to Back**. The selected region will be moved *behind* the first region and will now be partially covered by it. Here again, there will be a beveled upper corner to indicate the overlap (though now it is in the first region, indicating that *it* is covering another region).

You can similarly choose a region that is in back and choose Bring to Front from the same menu. Again, the relationship between these two overlapping regions has been reversed, while leaving their timing untouched.

# Edit Playlists

An Edit Playlist is perhaps best defined as a sequence of regions on a track. For example, any given mono audio track may have regions that sound like a bassist or a saxophonist. The track is the same—only the Edit Playlist is different.

Though Edit Playlists are among the most unsung of Pro Tools' features, they're easy to use. Better still, there's no limit to the number of Edit Playlists, so you've got a whole new dimension of editing flexibility to work with.

Here's an example of how Edit Playlists can be used.

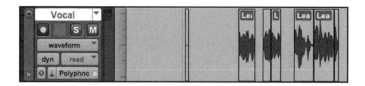

The track shown here is a mono audio track with a number of vocal regions on it. Normally, we would say that the track name is Vocal, but that's not 100-percent accurate. It is actually more technically accurate to say that the Edit Playlist name is Vocal and describes the sequence of audio regions on this track.

Suppose we want to make a few changes on this track but keep the original version as well. No problem—that's just what Edit Playlists are good at!

**1** Click the **Playlist Selector** on the track you want to change. A menu will appear.

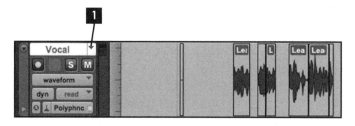

**2** Because in this case we want to make a change on an existing playlist, **choose** the **Duplicate menu item**. Effectively, what you'll be doing is copying this sequence of regions. A dialog box in which you can name your duplicated playlist will appear.

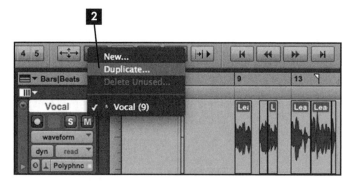

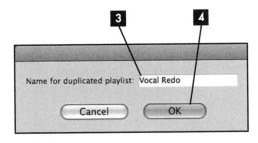

**3** **Type** a descriptive **name** for your new playlist.

**4** **Click** on **OK**. The window will close, and your new playlist will be created.

✳ Note that your "track name" (which you now know is actually the Edit Playlist name) has changed to match your new Edit Playlist.

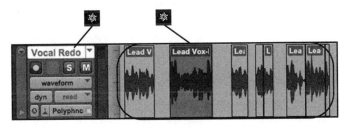

✳ Now you're free to make whatever changes you like to your regions.

Here's the coolest part—you can change between playlists anytime and compare the two different edits!

✳ Now, if you click the Playlist Selector button, you'll see both of the Edit Playlists that you've created, and you can choose the desired one at any time—even during playback! Edit Playlists are a great way to explore different creative directions and compare multiple versions.

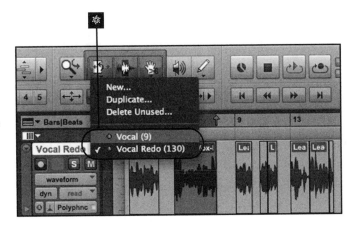

Of course, you can use Edit Playlists for more than just creating multiple versions of a given track. If you like, you can create entirely different playlists on a given track.

Again, we have a mono Audio track, with one bass solo region on it. The Edit Playlists name (which we commonly would refer to as the track name) is Bass Solo. What if we wanted to try something completely different on this track?

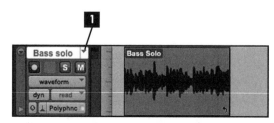

**1** Click the **Playlist Selector button**. The Edit Playlist menu will appear.

**2** In this case, we want to create a blank playlist—one with no regions on it—so that we can do something completely different. **Click** on **New** to do this. A dialog box in which you can name your new playlist will open.

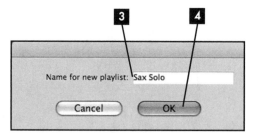

**3** Type a descriptive **name** for your new playlist. (In this case, I want to try a sax solo instead.)

**4** Click on **OK**. The window will close, and your new playlist will be created.

We still have our mono Audio track, but now we have one with a brand-new Edit Playlist—a blank track ready for us to work with. In this particular case, I would record my saxophone solo on this track.

❋ Once you've recorded your sax solo, you can switch between the different Edit Playlists by clicking on the Edit Playlist selector button.

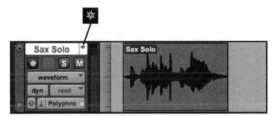

❋ You can change between the two Edit Playlists at any time, even during playback, so that you can determine which fits best.

# New in Pro Tools 8: More Track Comping Tools

Let's say that you've just gotten finished with multiple takes of a section (either by recording a number of times or though loop recording). In most cases, the next step is to compile a final track that includes the best parts of each take. This process is called *comping* a track, and it is one of the cornerstones of professional editing. Prior to Pro Tools 8, there have been a number of ways to comp a track, with a variety of methods appropriate to different situations. Now, with the advent of Pro Tools 8, there are some fantastic new comping tools that have radically changed the way we comp tracks.

This new workflow relies heavily on the knowledge you've just gained about Edit Playlists. Essentially, what we'll be doing is taking the best parts of the different takes, each of which will reside on individual Edit Playlists, to a "blank track" (which you now know is simply an Edit Playlist with no regions on it). How you record your individual takes is important, and it will allow you to utilize these new track comping tools during the editing phase of your process, so let's start there.

If you're recording multiple takes *without* loop recording:

1 Record the **first take** normally.

2 Before recording the second take, **create** a **new Edit Playlist** (using the steps outlined in the previous section of this chapter). The track will now be "empty," since the first take's region resides on a different Edit Playlist.

3 Record the **second take** normally.

4 For each additional take, **create** a **new Edit Playlist** before recording. This will ensure that each recording pass will be represented individually on its own Edit Playlist.

After recording, you can access each individual take by clicking the Playlist Selector button (again, as discussed in the previous section) and choosing the desired take from the list of Edit Playlists.

If you are recording multiple takes *with* loop recording:

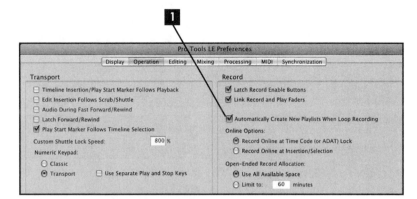

**1** In the Preferences window (which you can find in the Setup menu), **go to** the **Operation tab** and **check** the **Automatically Create New Playlists When Loop Recording box.**

**2** Loop record normally.

Here again, you'll wind up with a dedicated Edit Playlist for each time the section was recorded. In this case, though, each new playlist has been automatically created and named.

## Viewing Playlists in the Edit Window

Now that you've got all your takes separated into individual playlists, you can get down to some serious comping.

❈ COMPING PRACTICE

If you don't have any material of your own for track comping practice, don't worry—just open the session named Chapter 05 – Track Comping Session, which you'll find on your book's disc.

In this example, we have a single mono audio track, upon which was recorded four different takes of a keyboard solo. In this case it doesn't matter whether we recorded the solo using Loop Record or not—our job is to pull out the best parts of each take and make a final comped track.

**1** Click the **Playlist Selector button** to reveal a menu of Edit Playlists.

As you've done before, you can choose the take you want to view. Once you see a take you like, you can select an area, copy it, change playlists, and paste the section to the new playlist. Although that's an effective way of editing, it's not the most efficient way of working.

**2** It would be great if we could see *all* the Edit Playlists for a given track at one time and create our comped track without having to switch playlists all the time. That's exactly what Pro Tools 8 allows you to do. **Click** the **Track View selector** (which reads Waveform in this example) on the desired track. A menu will appear.

**3** Click the **Playlists menu item**.

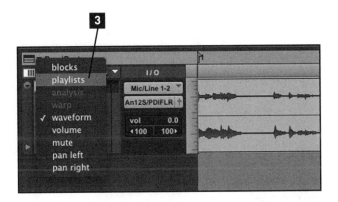

❉ In Playlists view, you'll see all the Edit Playlists associated with a given track, displayed as different "lanes."

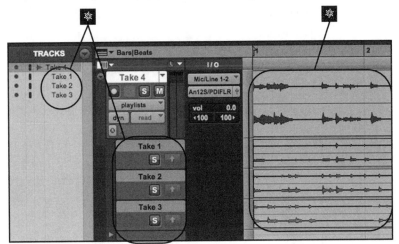

❉ Working in Playlists view—especially when you're using this view with multiple tracks simultaneously—can result in a pretty complicated-looking Edit window. To let you know which lanes are associated with which tracks, alternate playlists lanes are indented (both in the Playlist area and in the Tracks list).

## Basic Track Comping

Now the fun starts. The first thing to do is to create a new playlist, giving you a "blank" track to comp to. Playlists view makes this easy!

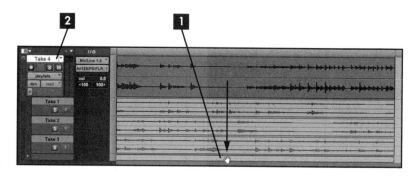

**1** Using the Grabber tool, **drag** the desired **region(s)** to the empty lane at the bottom of the track. When the region has been dragged to the proper place, you'll see an empty box displayed. **Release** the **mouse**, and the region will be moved to a new playlist, leaving a blank area at the top for comping.

**2** You can **double-click** on the track's **nameplate** to rename the main playlist if you wish. Similarly, you can **click** on the **alternate playlists' names** to name individual takes.

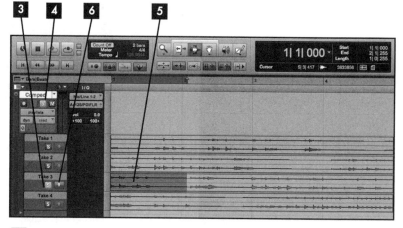

**3** To preview alternate playlists, **click** the **Solo button** for the desired playlist lane. The soloed playlist will be heard instead of the active Edit Playlist.

**4** If you **click** the track's main **Solo button**, all the other non-soloed tracks in your session will be muted.

**5** With the Selector tool, **mark** an **area** that you wish to use in your comped track.

**6** **Click** the **Copy Selection to Main Playlist button.**

Here's what you'll get:

As you can see here, the selected area has been copied from the original playlist and automatically pasted to the main playlist. At this point, you can audition other sections, pick your favorites, and send them from the alternate playlist to the comped track playlist as well, creating a new track that represents the best parts of each take. Because this is all nondestructive, you can still adjust boundaries with the Trim tool or move segments around with the Grabber tool. If a particular transition from one region to another is abrupt, you can use crossfades to smooth things out. (You'll learn more about crossfades in the next chapter.)

❋ COMPING SHORTCUT

Instead of clicking the Copy Selection to Main Playlist arrow button, you can press Control+Option+V (Mac) or Start+Alt+V (PC) after selecting an area on a playlist lane to paste the selected area up to the main Edit Playlist.

## Beyond the Basics

As if this radical improvement in the editing process wasn't enough, Pro Tools also has more ways to organize and view your takes!

### Region Ratings

In the preceding example, we had four takes. In a normal comping situation, you might have dozens! It might be hard to believe, but the mere act of separating the good takes and sections is often an important step in the process. With the new comping tools, Pro Tools 8 has some important improvements to this as well, in the form of Region Rating.

The first thing to do is make sure you can see the ratings of regions.

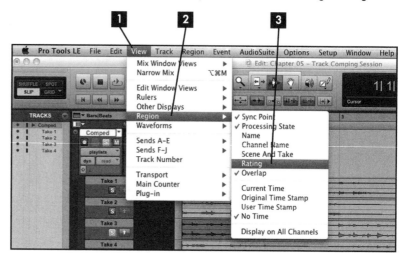

**1** Click on **View**. The View menu will appear.

**2** Click on Region. The Region submenu will appear, showing different display options for regions.

**3** As with other menus you've seen so far, aspects that are shown are indicated with a check mark. Because we want to see regions' ratings, **click** the **Rating menu item** to check it (assuming that it's not already checked).

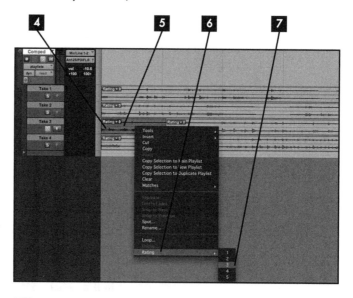

You'll see that all the regions on your track show an initial ranking of zero.

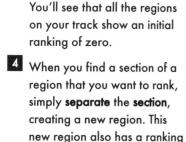

**4** When you find a section of a region that you want to rank, simply **separate** the **section**, creating a new region. This new region also has a ranking of zero.

**5** Right-click the **region** you want to rank. A menu will appear.

**6** Choose the **Rating menu item**. The Rating submenu will appear.

**7** Choose the desired **ranking** for the region. You can have the ranking either ascending or descending, but it's important to be consistent with your method.

RATING SHORTCUT

Instead of right-clicking the region to rank it, you can press Control+Option+ Command+[number from 1–5] (Mac) or Ctrl+Start+Alt+[number from 1-5] (PC) after selecting a region.

## Filtering Lanes

When you've picked out the best takes, you can show only the lanes containing good takes and hide the lanes that you don't want to include in the comping process.

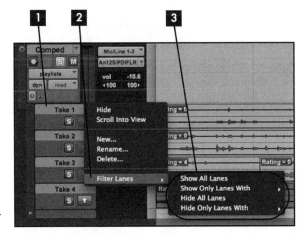

**1** Right-click the **nameplate** of any lane. A menu will appear.

**2** Choose the **Filter Lanes menu item**. The Filter Lanes submenu will appear.

**3** In this menu, you can show or hide all lanes or show/hide lanes based on their ranking. Here's where your ranking system will make a difference.

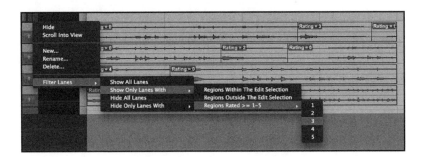

❋ If your ranking system is set up so that your best takes are ranked higher (the best being ranked a 5), you'll want to choose Show Only Lanes With and then choose Regions Rated >= 1–5. In this case, I've chosen 3, which means only lanes with regions ranked 3, 4, or 5 will be shown.

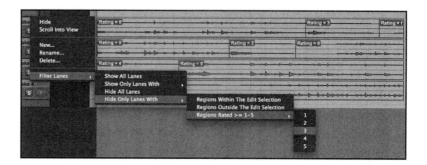

* If your ranking system is set up so that your best takes are ranked
  lower (the best being ranked a 1), you'll want to choose Hide Only
  Lanes With and then choose Regions Rated >= 1–5. In this case, I've
  chosen 3, which means only lanes with regions ranked 3, 2, or 1 will
  be shown.

That's it for beginning editing! Now on to some of the more
"tweaky" features!

# 6 } And More Editing

Although the editing power of a DAW like Pro Tools is impressive indeed, the editing process in and of itself is rarely glamorous. A good editor knows that the job of editing essentially boils down to a few simple functions done many, many times. In the editor's world, patience is a virtue, and it is put to the test when you cut and paste, drag and drop, and switch editing tools time and time again. Indeed, it's not uncommon for a professional editing session to involve thousands of individual editing operations!

The good news is that you already learned the basics of editing in Chapter 5. The next step is to expand upon the basic editing tools you've already begun to use and learn more flexible and efficient ways to work. The idea behind these techniques is that the time you'll save with each editing function will accumulate, saving you a sizable amount of time by the end of the day. Better yet, you'll not only save time, but you'll also become a better and more creative editor in the process! In this chapter, you'll learn how to:

* Navigate your session with greater ease
* Use and customize the Zoom tools for maximum efficiency
* Use variations of the Trim and Grabber tools
* Boost your editing power by using the Smart tool
* Put new region-based features (region looping, region groups) to use in your session
* Protect your regions from accidental change by *locking* them

# More Organization: Memory Locations

As your session gets more complex, organizing and navigating through the maze of regions and tracks can become a real issue. This is not only true of the editing phase, but in the mixing stage as well, when you're mainly working in the Mix window, and you don't have the convenience of clicking on a specific time on a track (although you will still have the Transport window when you want it). The good news is that you can make navigation significantly easier by setting up a few memory locations.

*Memory locations* are user-defined presets that allow you to recall a variety of settings with a single click of a button. Not only will you be able to instantly jump to important places in time, but you can also change zoom settings, track visibility, track height, and more!

> ❋ **USING THE TUTORIAL SESSION**
>
> For this section, please use the session named Chapter 06 Session - Part 1 included on the disc that came with your book. Remember, you'll want to copy the folder to a location on your computer's hard drive before working on it.

## Creating a Memory Location

Before you can use memory locations, you have to create them!

Typically, the first step is to set up the Edit window in a way that you would like to be able to recall. In this case (and this is something I commonly do), I want to set up the window in a sort of default state. Here's what I do:

❋ Set the timeline insertion cursor to the beginning of the session (1|1|000).

❋ Show all of the tracks in the session.

❋ Zoom out horizontally so that I can see the entire length of the session.

❋ Set the track heights so that I can see all the tracks in the session.

**1** Click on the **Window menu**.

**2** Click on **Memory Locations**. The Memory Locations window will appear.

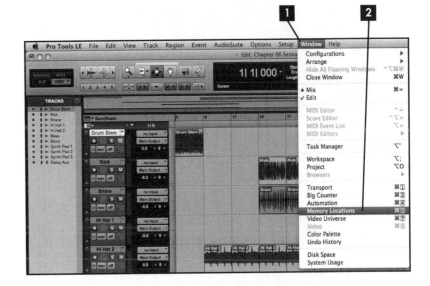

**3** Click on the **Memory Locations Menu button** in the upper-right corner of the Memory Locations window. A menu will appear.

**4** Click on **New Memory Location**. The New Memory Location dialog box will open.

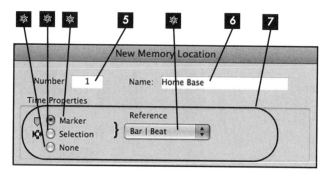

**5** Though Pro Tools will automatically assign a memory location number when you create a new memory location, you can **type** a different **number** in the Number field. This number will determine the ranking of the new memory location and the shortcut you will use to recall it (which we'll cover later in this section).

**6** **Type** a descriptive name for your new memory location in the Name text box. In this case, I'm calling my memory location Home Base, because it recalls some basic settings for my session.

**7** **Select** the **time property** that you want this memory location to recall. The choices are:

❄ **Marker.** The timeline insertion cursor will jump to a specific location when the memory location is chosen. (In this case, it will go to the beginning of my session.) This is the kind of memory location I want for this example.

❄ **Selection.** A selected area will be recalled when the memory location is chosen.

❄ **None.** The timeline insertion/selection will not change when the memory location is chosen.

❄ **Reference button.** Clicking the Reference menu button will reveal two basic modes for your time properties:

　 ❄ If you choose Bar|Beat, your memory location's position on the timeline will be anchored to a specific bar and beat position and will move on the timeline if the tempo is changed. This is most useful in musical situations.

　 ❄ If you choose Absolute, your memory location will be anchored to a sample-based location and will not move if your session's tempo changes. This is most commonly used when working with video soundtracks (since video typically doesn't deal with musical tempo).

**8** **Check** the **General Properties boxes** that match the settings you want to recall with this memory location. In this example, when the Home Base memory location is chosen, the current zoom settings, track show/hide, and track heights will be restored. Other characteristics, such as pre-/post-roll and group enables, will not change when you recall this memory location.

**9** **Type** a descriptive **comment** in the Comments field to describe the memory location.

**10** **Click** on **OK**. Your memory location will be saved, and the New Memory Location dialog box will close.

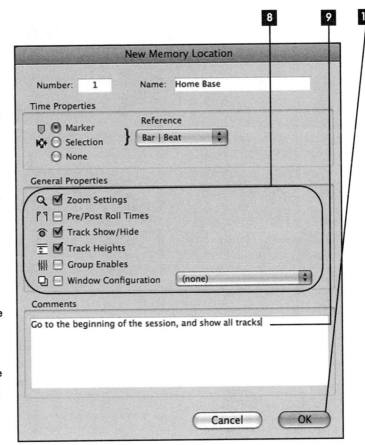

249

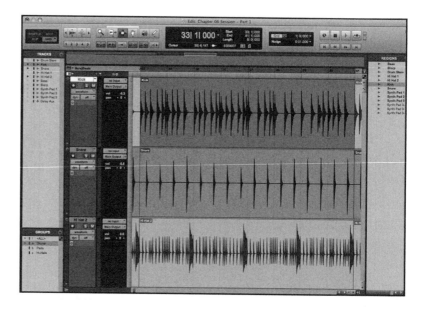

**11** Now let's try setting up a different memory location. Select a different **area** (in this case I selected from Bar 33 to Bar 41), different **zoom settings, track heights, and track show/hides.** (In this case, I am showing only the Kick, Snare, and Hi Hat 2 tracks.) And this time, enable a group. (I've enabled the Drums group by clicking the word Drums in the lower-left area of the Edit window.)

**12** Create a new **memory location** by repeating Steps 3 and 4. If you're following this example, name the new memory location Breakdown Drums and choose the following settings in the New Memory Location dialog box.

❄ Choose the Selection option in the Time Properties section. When this memory location is recalled, the selection will be as well.

❄ Select Zoom Settings.

❄ Select Track Show/Hide.

❄ Select Track Heights.

❄ Select Group Enables. This will activate the currently active groups (in this case, the Drums group) when this memory location is recalled.

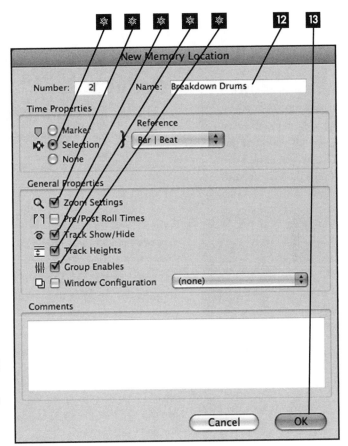

**13** Click on **OK** when you're finished.

If you're following along with the steps so far in this chapter, your session will now have two different memory locations, and you can begin to get a sense of their usefulness.

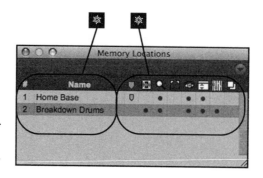

❉ By clicking on the desired memory location name, you will instantly recall all of the aspects associated with that memory location. In this example, you will not only change position instantly, but also radically change the view in your Edit window.

❉ If you're ever unclear as to what parameters are stored in a specific memory location, you can find out just by noting the icons that are shown to the right of the memory location name. From left to right, the icons are Marker, Selection, Zoom, Pre-/Post-Roll, Track Show/Hide, Track Heights, Group Enables, and Window Configurations (something we'll talk about in just a few pages).

❉ MEMORY LOCATION SHORTCUT

You can recall a memory location from your keyboard easily—just press the period (.) key on your keyboard's numeric keypad, then the number of the memory location you want to recall (again, on your computer's numeric keypad), and then the period key again. This works identically for both Mac and PC systems.

❉ ANOTHER WAY TO CREATE MEMORY LOCATIONS

You can also create memory locations by pressing the Enter key on your computer keyboard's numeric keypad. You can even do this on the fly as your session is playing. After creating the memory locations, you can then go back and edit them by right-clicking the desired memory location or double-clicking the memory location that you want to change.

## Using Memory Locations

There's no big mystery to creating and using memory locations, but before we delve into the next section, let's take a quick look at some of the various options available to you.

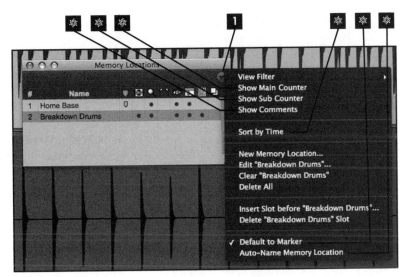

**1** Click on the **Memory Locations Menu** button.

✳ When you select the Show Main Counter option, the location of each memory location in relation to the Main Counter scale will be shown in a column in the Memory Locations window.

✳ When you select the Show Sub Counter option, the location of each memory location in relation to the Sub Counter scale will be displayed.

✳ When you select the Show Comments option, any comments you've entered for your memory locations will be shown.

✳ When you select the Sort by Time option, your memory locations will be sorted depending on how early or late they are in your session rather than by the order in which they were created or their numeric ranking.

✳ When you select the Default to Marker option, the Memory Locations dialog box will open the marker option chosen by default. This is particularly useful when you're creating memory locations while your session is playing. (See the earlier note.)

✳ The Auto-Name Memory Location option is also very handy when you're creating memory locations on the fly, and it will remove the need to type in a name for your memory location.

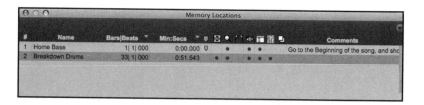

Here's what the window will look like when the Main Counter and Sub Counter are shown, as well as the comments. Note the two new columns created, and that their time scales reflect the currently selected Main and Sub Counter scales. Either (or both) of these columns can come in mighty handy, particularly when you're working in the Mix window, where it's harder to visualize your time position in your session.

## Inserting a Memory Location Slot

For those of you who have been using memory locations for some time already, you'll appreciate a relatively new bit of functionality to the Memory Locations window. The Insert Slot feature will allow you to create a new memory location *between* two existing memory locations. Here's how it's done.

**1** **Select** the **memory location** that you want to be *after* the new memory location. In this case, I've selected memory location #2, because I want to create a *new* slot #2 and shift the existing slot to position #3.

**2** After you set up your desired memory location settings (selections, zoom settings, track show/hide, and so on), **click** on the **Memory Locations Menu button**. The menu will appear.

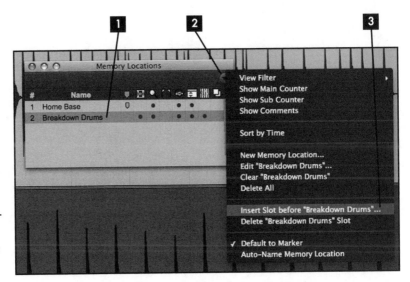

**3** **Select Insert Slot before "[memory location name]"**. Once you click this menu item, the New Memory Location dialog box will open, and you'll be able to create the new memory location as usual. When you're finished, this new memory location will be inserted in the desired slot, and the appropriate existing memory locations will be moved to later slots.

# Window Configurations

In our discussion of memory locations, you may have noticed a property called Window Configuration and wondered what the heck it was. Well, it's just what it sounds like—a recallable arrangement of windows that you can create to make your editing work go even more smoothly.

## Creating a Window Configuration

Creating a recallable *Window Configuration* is even easier than creating memory locations. Here are the steps.

**1** **Arrange** your **windows** as desired, including any columns, rulers, and lists that you want shown in the Edit and Mix windows. For this example, let's set up a basic Edit window layout. (If you're using the tutorial session, the Edit window is already set up this way.)

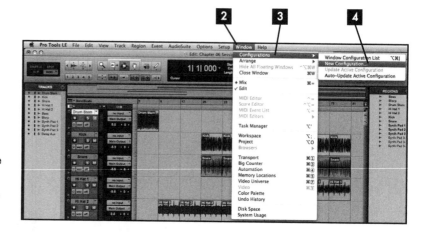

**2** Click the **Window menu**.

**3** Click on **Configurations**. The Configurations submenu will appear.

**4** Because you want to create a *new* Window Configuration, **click** on **New Configuration**. The Edit Window Configuration dialog box will open.

Now, you've got to choose what aspects of your layout you want to be able to recall. The two radio buttons will allow you to choose what aspects of your desktop will be incorporated into the Window Configuration (similar to the General Properties section of the New Memory Location dialog box). The choices are pretty simple:

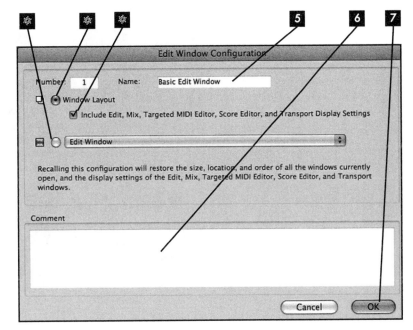

❋ Clicking the Window Layout radio button will set up your Window Configuration to recall all the windows you see on your desktop, sized and positioned as they are right now. In this example, since I want to recall the entire desktop, I'll choose this option.

❋ If you additionally check the Include Edit, Mix, Targeted MIDI Editor, Score Editor, and Transport Display Settings option, the view settings that you've chosen for these windows (things such as column show/hide settings) will also be recalled.

❋ The second main radio button is for more specific control and will allow you to recall settings for *only* the Edit, Mix, Score Editor, Targeted MIDI Editor, or Transport windows. For example, if you only want to recall your ruler settings for the Edit window, you would click this radio button and then select Edit Window Display Settings from the drop-down menu. (Click on the menu button to reveal the options.) The Edit window would be changed, but any other active windows would be unaffected.

**5** Type a **name** for your Window Configuration in the Name text box.

**6** This is an optional step, but a useful one: Type a **description** for your Window Configuration in the Comment section.

**7** That's it—just **click OK**, and you're finished!

Now that you've created a basic Edit window Window Configuration, let's set up a basic Mix window view (like the one shown here) and create a second Window Configuration by repeating the previous steps. (Name the new Window Configuration Basic Mix Window.) For a refresher on how to customize the Mix window, you can refer to Chapter 2.

Window Configurations aren't limited to single-window views only—in fact, the ability to arrange multiple windows as you please and save that arrangement is where Window Configurations really shine. Try this: Create a layout that has the Edit window across the top of your monitor and a minimal Mix window along the bottom. (This is a personal favorite desktop arrangement of mine.) Once that's done, create another new Window Configuration and call it Edit/Mix Split.

## Recalling Window Configurations

Now that you've created a few Window Configurations, you can recall them easily, much as you did with memory locations. There are three main ways that you can do it.

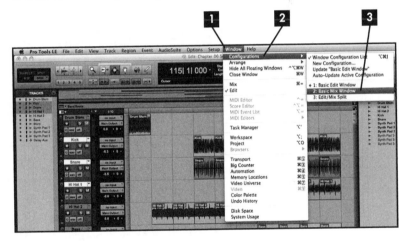

**1** Click the **Window menu**.

**2** Choose **Configurations**. The Configurations submenu will appear.

**3** At the bottom of the submenu, you'll see a list of all the session's window locations. (The currently targeted one will be indicated with a diamond to the left of the name.) Just **click** the **Window Configuration** that you want to recall, and your desktop will be instantly rearranged.

Here's another way:

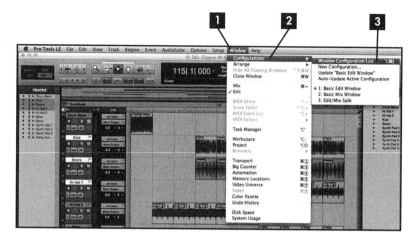

1 Click the **Window menu**.

2 **Choose Configurations**.

3 **Choose Window Configuration List**. The Window Configurations window will appear.

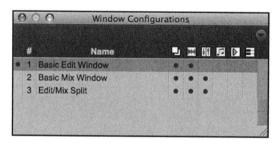

The Window Configurations window not only looks like the Memory Locations window, but it acts like it as well. Just click the Window Configuration that you want to recall. The dots to the right of the Window Configuration name will let you know what settings have been stored in it (window layout, Edit window settings, Mix window settings, Score Editor settings, Transport window settings, and targeted MIDI Editor settings).

In addition to these two methods, you can also recall a Window Configuration as a property of a memory location. Basically, this means that you can associate a Window Configuration with a memory location and change not only your desktop's layout, but any memory location property as well, all in one click! Here's how:

**1** In the Edit Memory Location window, in the General Properties area, just **click** the **Window Configuration check box**. This will configure the memory location to recall a Window Configuration along with any other properties that you've chosen to associate with that memory location.

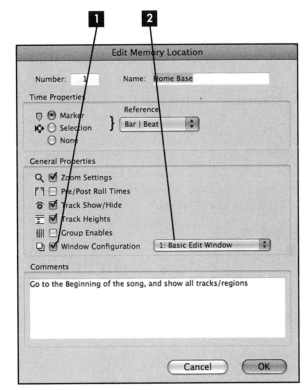

**2** Once the Window Configuration check box is marked, the next step is to **choose** which **Window Configuration** will be recalled with that memory location. Just select the desired Window Configuration from the drop-down list to the right of the words Window Configuration. (Click on the menu button to reveal a list of all the Window Configurations that you have created in the session.)

❊ WINDOW CONFIGURATION SHORTCUT

Here's yet another way to recall a Window Configuration—just press the period (.) key on your keyboard's numeric keypad, then the number of the memory location you want to recall (again, on your computer's numeric keypad), and then press the asterisk (*) key. This works identically for both Mac and PC systems.

# Zoom

Zooming is not only one of the most basic of operations; it's also one of the most frequent things you'll do in any editing session. In Chapter 5, you learned the basics of zooming. The following sections will discuss other ways to zoom and how to use them.

> ❄ **TIME TO CHANGE TUTORIAL SESSIONS!**
>
> For the next section of this chapter, we'll take advantage of what you just learned about memory locations. Please copy the folder named Chapter 06 Session – Part 2 to your audio hard drive and launch the session. Once it's launched, go to memory location #1, named Selections.

## More Zoom Tools

Let's start from what you already know and work from there.

❄ Click on the Zoom Out button of the Zoom cluster. As you've seen before, your view of your session's timeline will expand, and a longer duration will be shown in your Edit window. Note that this horizontal zooming affects all tracks in your session.

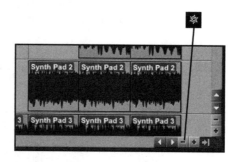

❄ Even if your zoom cluster isn't being displayed in the top row of the Edit window, you still have access to zoom controls in Pro Tools 8. In the lower-right corner of the Edit window, you'll see a group of buttons. Click the minus sign on the bottom of the Edit window to zoom out.

❄ Click on the Zoom In button. Again, you'll see that Audio and MIDI tracks are zoomed at the same rate. The Zoom In and Zoom Out buttons will allow you to zoom in on the time scale, and although they won't affect the speed at which your session will play back, they will allow you to view your regions and data differently to suit different kinds of editing.

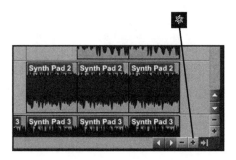

❄ Once more, the cluster of buttons in the lower corner of your Edit window's Playlist area will give you zoom control, even if the Zoom cluster isn't being displayed in the top row of the Edit window. In the lower-right corner of the Edit window, you'll see a group of buttons. Click the plus sign on the bottom of the Edit window to zoom in.

In addition to these basic horizontal Zoom controls, you have the ability to zoom in and out *vertically* as well.

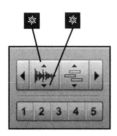

* Click on the top half of the Audio Zoom button. With each click, your audio data will zoom up vertically, allowing you to more clearly see low-level signals.

* Click on the bottom half of the Audio Zoom button. The height of your audio waveforms will be reduced with each click of this button.

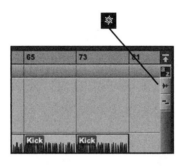

* The Zoom cluster's Audio Zoom button is duplicated in miniature in the upper-right corner of your Edit window's Playlist area. Click on the top or bottom half of this button to zoom up or down on your audio regions.

### VERTICAL ZOOM (AUDIO) SHORTCUT

Although vertical zooming is not quite as common as horizontal zooming, the shortcut keys are still useful to know. On a Mac, the shortcut is Command+Option+] (right bracket) to zoom up and Command+Option+[ (left bracket) to zoom down. On a PC, it's Ctrl+Alt+] (right bracket) to zoom up and Ctrl+Alt+[ (left bracket) to zoom down.

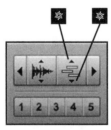

* Click on the top half of the MIDI Zoom button. With each click, your MIDI data will zoom up, allowing you to more clearly see individual notes. Note that all your MIDI regions have zoomed up at the same time, but audio regions are left unchanged.

* Click on the bottom half of the MIDI Zoom button. Your MIDI data will zoom down, allowing you to see a greater range of notes at one time in the Edit window.

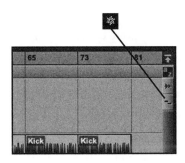

❋ You'll also find a MIDI Zoom button in the upper-right corner of your Edit window's Playlist area, just below the small Audio Zoom button. Click on the top or bottom half of this button to zoom up or down on your MIDI regions.

As you zoom up or down, you will see less or more of the keyboard graphic on the left edge of each MIDI track. You can use this display as a reference point to see how broad (or narrow) of a tonal range you're viewing. Low pitches are displayed toward the bottom of each MIDI track, and high notes are toward the top. You can scroll up and down the MIDI note range by clicking on the up and down arrows at each end of the keyboard graphic.

### ❋ VERTICAL ZOOM (MIDI) SHORTCUT

Here are the shortcuts for vertical zooming for MIDI data: On a Mac, the shortcut is Command+Shift+] (right bracket) to zoom up and Command+Shift+[ (left bracket) to zoom down. On a PC, it's Ctrl+Shift+] (right bracket) to zoom up and Ctrl+Shift+[ (left bracket) to zoom down.

### ❋ ZOOM DRAGGING

In the previous section, you zoomed incrementally by clicking on the appropriate button, but there's also a very easy way to zoom smoothly. Just click and hold on any of the zoom buttons and drag your mouse (left or right if you're horizontally zooming and up or down if you're vertically zooming) to smoothly change the view.

## Zoom Presets

Okay, I'm going to go out on a limb with this comparison, but bear with me. Take the average car radio. If you're a music lover, you probably use it quite a bit. On most car radios, there are a number of buttons (usually below the main display) that you can use to quickly get to the stations you listen to most often. Once you set up these presets, you can simply press an individual button and immediately jump to your favorite channel.

Many Pro Tools users find that, although they use all the zoom tools a *lot*, they tend to use certain zoom settings more frequently than others. Like on a car radio, you can set up your most common zoom presets and recall them with the click of a button. In fact, setting these zoom presets is pretty similar to setting the presets on your car radio!

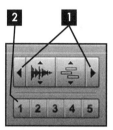

**1** Using the horizontal zoom tools, **adjust** your **zoom level** until you arrive at a setting that you want to be able to recall.

**2** **Hold down** the **Command key (Mac) or Ctrl key (PC)** and **click** on the **Zoom Preset button** that you want to assign to the current zoom level. The button will flash briefly to let you know that the preset has been stored.

From this point on, it's easy. Simply set the five presets for the five zoom settings you use the most. To recall any preset, you can click on the desired Zoom Preset button.

 **WILL ZOOM PRESETS RECALL BOTH HORIZONTAL AND VERTICAL ZOOM SETTINGS?**

The Zoom Preset buttons will recall only the horizontal (time) zoom amount, not the vertical zoom levels for Audio and MIDI tracks.

**ZOOM PRESET SHORTCUTS**

The shortcuts to switch between your presets are pretty straightforward. Just press 1, 2, 3, 4, or 5 on your computer's keyboard (above the alphabet section).

## Zoom Toggle

Over the last few versions of Pro Tools, Digidesign has added some new functionality to a feature called *zoom toggle*. Zoom toggle does just what its name would suggest—it allows you to quickly take a close-up look at a section and then get back out to the previous zoom level. In truth, this feature has been a part of Pro Tools for some time, but with the new power that's behind it, it's become even more useful!

Actually, using zoom toggle is very easy when you use the Zoom Toggle button.

**1** Make a **selection** of the area on which you want to zoom in.

**2** Click the **Zoom Toggle button**. The selection will zoom in according to the zoom toggle settings (which we will talk about in just a moment). When active, the Zoom Toggle button will be colored blue to show that you are indeed zoomed in.

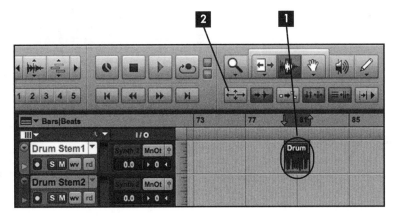

**3** To zoom back out to your previous zoom level, just **click** the **Zoom Toggle button** again. You'll be zoomed back out, and the Zoom Toggle button will be displayed in its inactive gray color.

> **ZOOM TOGGLE SHORTCUT**
>
> There is also a shortcut for zoom toggling: Just press Command+E (Mac) or Ctrl+E (PC).

What makes the zoom toggle function particularly useful is the customization you can get through the setting of preferences. Here's how.

**1** Click the **Setup menu**.

**2** **Choose Preferences**. The Preferences window will appear.

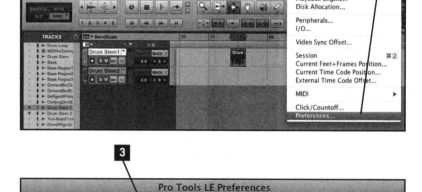

**3** If your Preferences window isn't already showing the Editing page, **click** the **Editing tab** at the top of the Preferences window.

You'll find the Zoom Toggle section in the lower-right corner of the Preferences window's Editing page. The settings that you make here will determine how the zoom toggle feature will behave when you engage it. The first set of choices you need to make covers just how much you want to zoom in!

✳ MIDI is a topic we'll tackle later (in Chapter 7, "Using MIDI"), but for now it's sufficient to know that you can view MIDI data in fundamentally different ways than you view audio. If you click the Vertical MIDI Zoom dropdown menu, you can control zoom toggle behavior when MIDI data is selected. You have two options in this list.

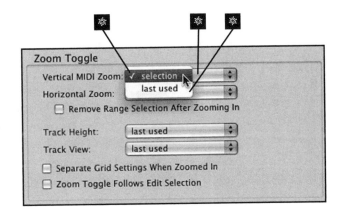

☼ **Selection.** This option will allow you to zoom into only the note range that is currently selected in the Edit window.

☼ **Last Used.** This option will recall the MIDI vertical zoom level that you used last time zoom toggle was engaged. Practically speaking, this means that if you zoom toggle in, change your MIDI vertical zoom level, and then toggle out, the next time you engage zoom toggle, you will recall those last-used vertical zoom settings.

✳ The Horizontal Zoom setting that you choose will control how the Zoom Toggle tool deals with zooming in on the time axis. Again, there are two options.

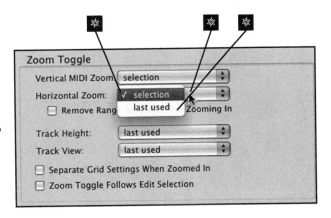

☼ **Selection.** With this option selected, the selected area will be zoomed in so that the selected area spans from the left edge to the right edge of the Playlist area.

☼ **Last Used.** This option will recall the horizontal zoom level that was used when zoom toggle was last engaged.

✻ When the Remove Range Selection After Zooming In box is checked, as soon as you engage zoom toggle, your selected area will be deselected, so that you can quickly make a different selection.

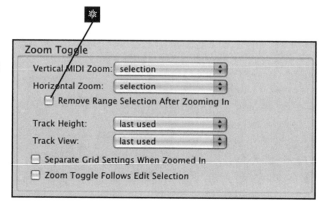

But wait—there's more!

✻ The Track Height drop-down menu will allow you to choose the track height that will be recalled when zoom toggle is engaged. Here's a tip: The Fit to Window setting works particularly well for this sort of work.

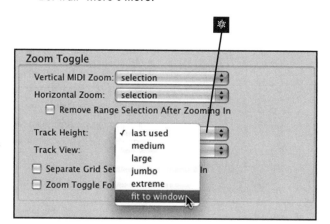

❄ The Track View drop-down menu can allow you to change your Track view to a desired view when zoom toggle is engaged. Here are your options:

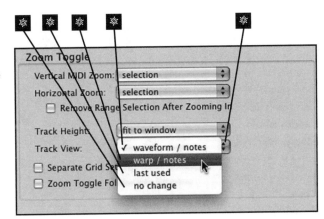

☆ Waveform/Notes (waveform for Audio track, Notes view for MIDI tracks)

☆ Warp/Notes (Warp mode for Audio tracks, Notes mode for MIDI tracks)

☆ Last Used (which will recall the format view that you used when you used zoom toggle last on that track)

☆ No Change (which will make no view format change when you zoom toggle)

※ If you check the Separate Grid Settings When Zoomed In box, it will allow you to choose two different zoom resolutions—one that you see when you're toggled in and one when you're in your normal mode. To set the zoom toggle zoom resolution, just activate zoom toggle and then select the grid resolution that you want to use. It's really that easy! When you zoom back out, you'll see the grid resolution change back.

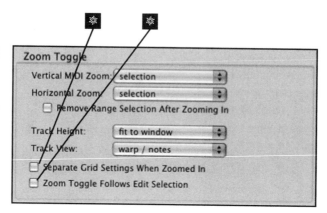

※ This last check box—Zoom Toggle Follows Edit Selection—is an option that requires a bit of explanation, With this option selected, aspects such as track height and horizontal zoom settings will continually follow any tracks or regions that you have selected. For example, suppose you select a region on the top track in your session and then turn on zoom toggle—your chosen zoom toggle settings will be recalled. Now, suppose you click a region on *another* track. With Zoom Toggle Follows Edit Selection checked, *that* track will immediately change its track height to the zoom toggle level. (Admittedly, this can be a little distracting from time to time!)

**4** Once you've made your desired selections, just **click** the **OK** button, and you're ready to rock!

# More Ways to Work with Selections

Now that you're comfortable with these more flexible ways of zooming, let's take a look at some different ways of making selections.

## Making Selections Using the Arrow Keys

In Chapter 3, you learned that the boundaries of a selected area are represented in the Ruler area (above the tracks) by a down arrow and an up arrow, representing punch-in and punch-out points, respectively. Using the arrow keys on your computer's keyboard is an easy way to make a selection as your session plays.

**1** Choose a **starting point** for playback, making sure that it is *before* the spot where you want your selection to start.

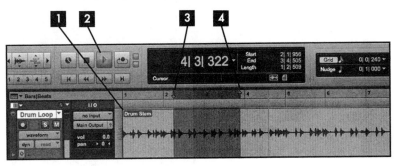

**2** Start playback. (Remember, you can use the Start button on the transport controls, or you can press the spacebar.)

**3** As your session continues playing, **press** the **Down Arrow key** on your keyboard at the point where you want to begin your selected area.

**4** With your session still playing, **press** the **Up Arrow key** on your keyboard when you want your selection to end.

❄ TWEAKING YOUR SELECTION

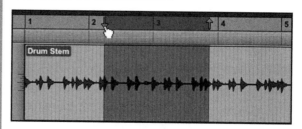

If your timing is a little off on a punch-in or a punch-out, don't worry. You can adjust your selection by clicking and dragging either of the arrows in your ruler.

❄ HEY—I JUST STOPPED PLAYBACK, AND MY SELECTION DISAPPEARED!

If you find that you lose your selection when you stop playback, don't worry—it's not a malfunction of Pro Tools. Here's a quick fix (which we'll talk more about later in this section): Deactivate the Insertion Follows Playback button.

❄ You'll find the Insertion Follows Playback button immediately below the Pencil tool button in the Edit tool cluster. When inactive, the button will be colored gray.

## Making Selections Using the Return Key

You've already learned that pressing the Return key (on a Mac) or the Enter key (on a PC) will send the timeline insertion back to the beginning of the session. Here's a useful variation, which will allow you to make a selection from the beginning of your session to a specified point.

**1** Choose the **Selector tool**.

**2** **Click** on the **point** on a desired track (or ruler) at which you want your selection to end. A flashing timeline insertion will appear where you clicked.

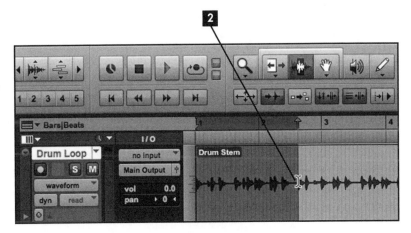

**3** **Press and hold** the **Shift key** and then **press** the **Return key (Mac) or Enter key (PC)**. A selection will be made from the timeline insertion back to the beginning of your session.

Here's a variation of the same technique that will allow you to make a selection from a specified point to the end of your session.

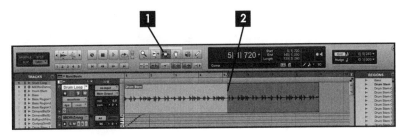

**1** **Click** on the **Selector tool** if it is not already selected.

**2** **Click** on the **point** on a desired track at which you want your selection to start.

**3** **Press and hold** Option+Shift (Mac) or Ctrl+Shift (PC), and **press** the **Return key (Mac) or Enter key (PC)**. A selection will be made from the timeline insertion to the end of your session.

## Making Selections Using Tab to Transient

The Tab to Transients feature is a great way to make selections with transient-based audio, particularly for those of us who enjoy chopping up beats into loopable segments.

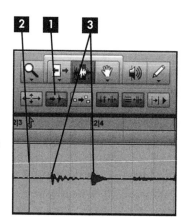

1 **Click** on the **Tab** to **Transients tool**. When active, it will be colored blue.

2 **Use** the **Selector tool** to set a timeline insertion a little before the transient with which you want to start your selection.

3 **Press and hold** the **Shift key** and **press** the **Tab key**. As you've seen before, the timeline insertion will jump from transient to transient each time you hit the Tab key, but the addition of the Shift key will cause a selection to be made in the process.

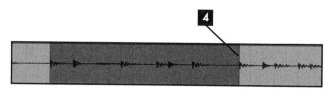

4 When you reach the end of your desired selection, **stop pressing** the **Tab key**. You've now made a selection based upon Pro Tools' analysis of the transients, which can help you find the right start and end points quickly and accurately!

## Timeline Insertion Follows Playback

Consider this scenario: You've selected a nice loopable selection. You wisely put yourself into Loop Playback mode to hear your selection in the proper context. Sounds great, doesn't it? Then you hit Stop, and the selection goes away! Is this a bug within Pro Tools? Nope—it's the effect of a mode of operation called *Timeline Insertion Follows Playback*, which you can set in the software in a number of ways. You can either enable or disable this mode to fit your circumstance, but it's important to understand how it works so you'll know when to use it and when not to!

One of the ways to enable or disable this mode of operation is from the Preferences window. Let's take a look at that method first.

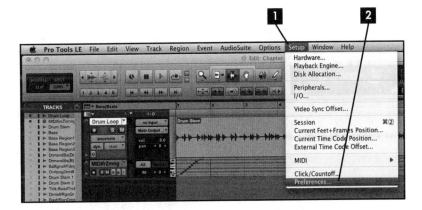

**1** Click on the **Setup menu**.

**2** Click on **Preferences**. The Pro Tools LE Preferences window will open.

**3** Click on the **Operation tab**.

You'll find the preference you're looking for in the Transport section, located in the upper-left corner of the Operations page.

**4** Select or deselect the **Timeline Insertion/Play Start Marker Follows Playback** check box. Here's what the options mean:

**Transport**

☐ Timeline Insertion/Play Start Marker Follows Playback
☐ Edit Insertion Follows Scrub/Shuttle
☐ Audio During Fast Forward/Rewind
☐ Latch Forward/Rewind
☑ Play Start Marker Follows Timeline Selection

Custom Shuttle Lock Speed: [800] %
Numeric Keypad:
○ Classic
◉ Transport      ☐ Use Separate Play and Stop Keys

❋ **Checked (enabled).** Playback will begin wherever the timeline insertion is set. When playback is stopped, the timeline insertion will jump to the point where playback ended. When you start again, playback will pick up where you left off. If you have a selected area in your timeline, that selection will be lost when you hit Stop.

❋ **Unchecked (disabled).** Playback will begin wherever the timeline insertion is set. When playback stops in this mode, the timeline insertion will stay where it was originally set. When you start playback again, it will start from this original position. If you have a selected area in your timeline, that selection will be maintained when you hit Stop, making this the ideal mode for editing loopable selections.

## New in Pro Tools 8: Insertion Follows Playback Button

Prior to Pro Tools 8, there was no way to visually check to see whether Timeline Insertion/Play Start Marker Follow Playback was enabled or disabled—until you stopped playback and observed Pro Tools' behavior. With Pro Tools 8, we not only have a visual cue to find out the mode we're working in, but we have a quick and easy way to enable or disable this feature.

❋ ❋ ❋

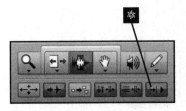

❄ You'll find the Insertion Follows Playback button immediately below the Pencil tool. When the mode is active, the button will be colored blue. You can toggle the mode on and off simply by clicking the button.

## Separate Regions Options

Once you've made a selection within a region, you can separate your regions based upon that selection, as you've done already in Chapter 5. Let's take a quick look at two more new ways to use your selected area to separate your region.

 SETTING THINGS UP

For the purposes of this example, select the entire Drum Stem region shown in Memory Location 1.

### Separate Region on Grid

As the name might suggest, Separate Region on Grid will chop up your region on every grid point. In the case of the tutorial session, our grid value is sixteenth notes, so this will create new regions in sixteenth-note increments.

**1** Click on the **Edit menu**.

**2** Click on **Separate Region**. The Separate Region submenu will appear.

**3** Click the **On Grid menu item**. The Pre-Separate Amount dialog box will open.

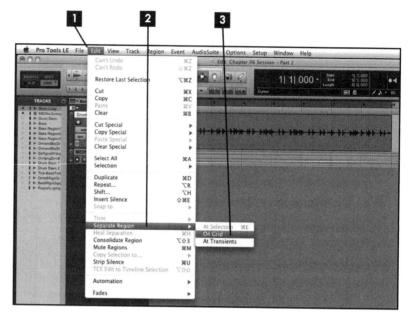

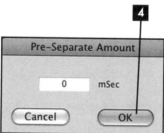

**4** Setting any value above zero in the Pre-Separate Amount dialog box will shift the created region boundaries earlier. The greater the value, the farther ahead of the grid the separations will be. To separate regions exactly on the grid lines, **choose 0**. When you're finished, **click OK**.

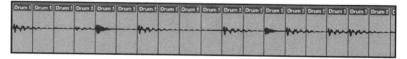

The result is immediate: Your region will be separated regularly according to the grid value you've got and any Pre-Separate amount you've entered. If you look at your Regions list, you'll see that you've created new regions as well (in the case of the tutorial session, lots of them).

## Separate Region at Transients

A variation on the theme, this is a handy little feature that creates a new region boundary at each detected transient. Take a look.

**1** Click on the **Edit menu**.

**2** Click on **Separate Region**. The Separate Region submenu will appear.

**3** Click the **At Transients menu item**. The Pre-Separate Amount dialog box will open.

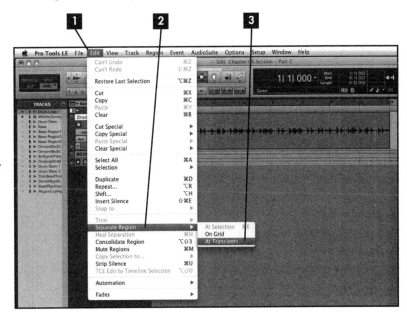

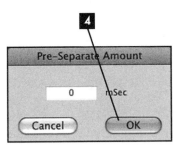

**4** Setting any value above zero in the Pre-Separate Amount dialog box will shift the created region boundaries earlier. The greater the value, the farther ahead of each transient the separations will be. To separate regions exactly at the beginning of each transient, **choose 0**. When you're finished, **click OK**.

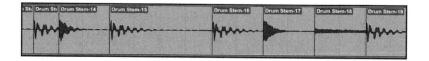

Again, you'll see your region immediately separated into a number of regions, with each new region being represented in the Regions list, but the placement of the region boundaries will be a little different from when you separated at each grid line. This time, you'll see that your region has been separated at each transient (and shifted earlier if you entered a Pre-Separate amount).

## Navigating and Auditioning a Selection

Usually when making a selection, the most important parts to get right are the beginning and the end. You'll listen to the boundaries of your selections many times, just to make sure you've got everything you want and nothing you don't.

❉ SETTING THINGS UP

For this section, go to the second memory location of the tutorial session named "Navigating a Selection."

❉ Press the Left Arrow key. The Edit window's focus will move to the beginning of the selection, as shown in this image.

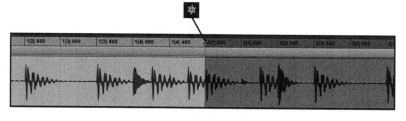

❉ Press the Right Arrow key. The Edit window's focus will move to the end of the selection and center that boundary in your Edit window.

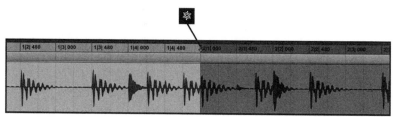

The next shortcuts depend upon the value entered for your pre-roll and post-roll. As you learned in Chapter 3, you can set the values for both of these by typing the desired number in the appropriate fields in the lower-left corner of the Transport window. You don't have to enable pre-roll or post-roll—just set a value.

❋ Now it's time to audition the boundaries of your selection. Press and hold the Option key (Mac) or the Alt key (PC) and press the Left Arrow key. Your audio will play up to the beginning of your selection by the pre-roll amount. Since the pre-roll amount is set as one measure in this example, playback will start one measure before the beginning of the selection and stop when the selection begins.

❋ Press and hold the Option key (Mac) or the Alt key (PC) and press the Right Arrow key. Your audio will play up to the end of your selection by the pre-roll amount.

❋ Press and hold the Command key (Mac) or the Ctrl key (PC) and press the Left Arrow key. Your audio will play from the beginning of your selection by the post-roll amount.

❋ Press and hold the Command key (Mac) or the Ctrl key (PC) and press the Right Arrow key. Your audio will play from the end of your selection by the post-roll amount.

# Beyond the Basics

You've already worked with the basic editing tools, and things such as trimming, selecting, and grabbing are starting to become familiar by now. Some of these tools have secondary layers to them, giving them added functionality. And then there's the Smart tool....

## The TCE Trim Tool

First on the list is the TCE (Time Compress/Expand) Trim tool. This useful variation of the standard Trim tool allows you to stretch or compress the duration of an audio region without changing the pitch!

To follow with this demonstration, go to Memory Location #3—TCE Trim Tool.

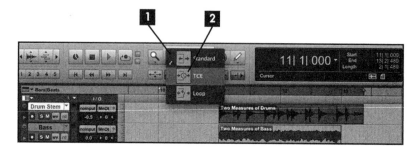

**1** **Click and hold** the **Trim tool button** until the Trim tool Options menu appears. The currently selected version of the Trim tool will be indicated by a check mark.

**2** **Click** on **TCE** to change to the TCE Trim tool. The icon for the Trim tool will change to reflect the currently active version of the tool.

**3** **Click and hold** the **boundary** that you want to adjust. In this example, I want to time-compress the end of the upper region so that it matches the bottom one, so I'm clicking on its right boundary.

**4** **Drag** the **boundary** left or right, just as if you were using the standard Trim tool. When you release the mouse button, a new audio region will be created with a different duration than the original region, but without a different pitch.

❄ TRIM TOOL TIP

The TCE Trim tool is really useful in Grid mode. Suppose you've imported a drum loop that doesn't match the tempo of the rest of your session. Just make sure your grids are a musical unit (such as quarter notes, for example) and use the TCE Trim tool. The edges of the region will snap to the nearest grid point when released, and you'll be perfectly in tempo!

# The Object Grabber Tool

Up to this point, you've used the Grabber tool to move a block of time (and all the regions that are contained within that block); hence the tool's name, *Time Grabber*. But what if you want to select more than one region without selecting all the regions between them? That's where the Object Grabber tool comes into play!

❄ **SETTING THINGS UP**

For this section, go to Memory Location #4—Grabbers.

**1** Click and hold the **Grabber tool button** until the Grabber tool Options menu appears. The currently selected version of the Grabber tool will be indicated by a check mark.

**2** **Click** on **Object** to change to the Object Grabber tool. The icon for the Grabber tool will change to reflect the currently active version of the tool.

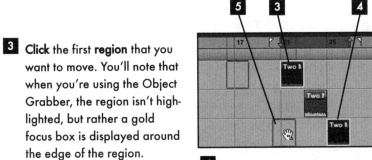

**3** **Click** the first **region** that you want to move. You'll note that when you're using the Object Grabber, the region isn't highlighted, but rather a gold focus box is displayed around the edge of the region.

**4** Hold the **Shift key** and **click** additional **regions** that you want to move. Note that only the regions ("objects") that you click are selected, and not a rectangular block of time between them (as would be the case if you were using the Time Grabber).

**5** **Drag and drop** the **regions** that you want to move to the desired location. As you drag, you'll see an outline indicating where the regions would be placed if you were to release your mouse button.

## The Separation Grabber Tool

Either the Time Grabber or the Object Grabber tool will allow you to move regions around in your session, albeit in different ways. The Separation Grabber tool goes a step further, allowing you to take a selection from within a single region and move just that selected area. This is a cool trick (and a real timesaver as well), but there are a few steps in using this tool most effectively.

**1** Click on the **Selector tool**. (Have faith—we're going somewhere with this.)

**2** **Select** the **section** of a region that you want to separate and move.

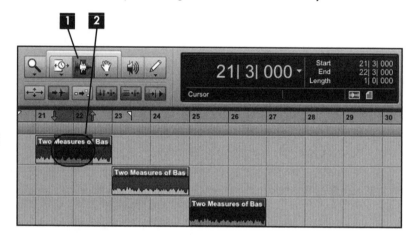

**3** **Click and hold** the **Grabber tool button** until the Grabber tool Options menu appears. The currently selected version of the Grabber tool will be indicated with a check mark.

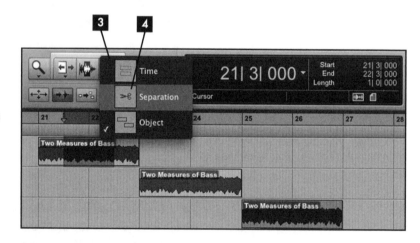

**4** Click on **Separation** to change to the Separation Grabber tool. The icon for the Grabber tool will change to reflect the currently active version of the tool.

**5** With the Separation Grabber tool selected, **click and hold anywhere** in the selected area.

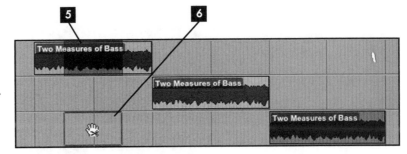

**6** **Drag and drop** the **selection** to the desired destination. As you've seen with other variations of the Grabber tool, you'll see an outline indicating where the selected area will be placed when you release your mouse button.

The selection will be removed from the original region and will become its own region, represented on the track and in the Regions list.

❋ **A TWIST ON THE SEPARATION GRABBER**

If you want to drag out a selection of a region but leave your source region unchanged, hold down the Option key (Mac) or the Alt key (PC) as you drag.

## The Smart Tool

The Smart tool is a real timesaver, combining the editing power of the Trim, Selector, and Grabber tools and adding some extra functionality for good measure. It might take you a while to get used to using the Smart tool, but once you've got it under your belt, you'll be able to work more efficiently.

★ SETTING THINGS UP

For this section, go to Memory Location #5—Smart Tool.

**1** **Click** on the **Smart Tool bracket,** which arches over the Trim, Selector, and Grabber tool buttons. The button will be highlighted (blue) when the Smart tool is active, as will the three tools below it.

The concept behind using the Smart tool is simple—your cursor will take on different tool behaviors based upon its location within a track.

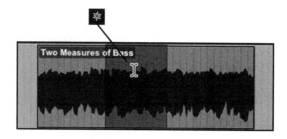

※ When your cursor is in the *upper* half of a track, it will take on the function of the Selector tool.

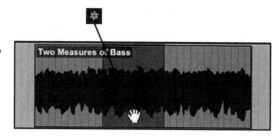

※ When you move your cursor to the *lower* half of a track, the cursor will take on the behavior of the currently active version of the Grabber tool (in this case, the Time Grabber).

※ THE SMART TOOL AND THE SEPARATION GRABBER

The Smart tool works particularly well when you have the Separation Grabber tool selected. Just move your cursor to the top half of a track to make your selection, and then move your cursor to the bottom half of the track to drag the selection to its new location. Easy!

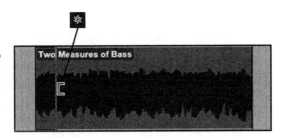

❋ When you move your cursor to either end of a region, the cursor will change its function to that of the currently active version of the Trim tool (in this case, the Standard Trim tool).

### MORE SMART TOOL FEATURES

You might have discovered that if you move your cursor to the corner of a region, it takes on a different function, beyond that of the Trim, Selector, or Grabber tool. Be patient—we'll get to that in a couple of pages!

### THE SMART TOOL AND TRACK HEIGHTS

Because the position of the cursor within a track is so critical when you're using the Smart tool, shorter track heights can be a little tricky to work with at first. As you get used to using the Smart tool, medium track height (or greater) is a good way to practice.

## Edit Groups

Hopefully, you've found the edit tools you've learned to be powerful and easy to use. Now let's boost your effectiveness by enabling you to edit a number of tracks at the same time. To do this, we'll create an edit group.

### SETTING THINGS UP

For a simple run-through of how to use an edit group, go to Memory Location #6—Edit Groups.

### GROUPS AND MIXING

You'll notice that there are some features we'll pass over in this section. Not to worry—these are features more relevant to the process of mixing, so we'll cover them in Chapter 8, "Basic Mixing."

**1** Click the **Groups list menu button**. A menu will appear.

**2** Choose the **New Group menu item**. The Create Group dialog box will open.

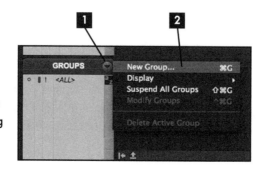

**3** Type a descriptive **name** for your group in the Name text box at the top of the Create Group dialog box.

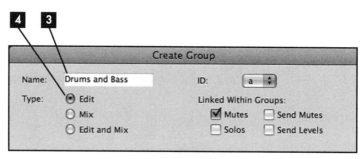

**4** You can choose to have your selected tracks available as an edit group (active only in the Edit window), as a mix group (active only in the Mix window), or as an edit and mix group (active in both windows). In this case, we'll only be using these tracks as an editing exercise, so **choose Edit** in the Type section.

**5** Initially, any currently selected tracks will be placed in the Currently in Group area. If you want to add more tracks to your group, just **select** the desired **tracks** in the Available area and then **click** the **Add button**. Conversely, if you want to remove a track from the group, just **select** the **track** in the Currently in Group area and then **click** the **Remove button**.

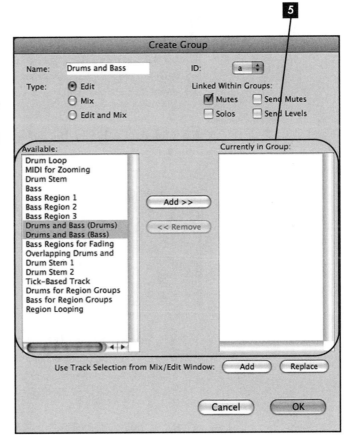

## FOLLOWING ALONG?

If you're following the steps with the book's tutorial session, make sure that the Drums and Bass (Drums) and Drums and Bass (Bass) tracks are the only tracks shown in the Currently in Group area.

## A TRADITIONAL TECHNIQUE

In some previous versions of Pro Tools, group membership was solely determined by the tracks that were selected *prior* to creating a new group. (Once the Create Group dialog box was open, group membership couldn't be changed.) Even now, the Currently in Group area is determined by the currently selected tracks. As a result, many longtime users of Pro Tools make it a point to select the tracks they want to use in their group before creating the group, often saving themselves a few steps in the process.

**6** **Click** the **OK button**. The dialog box will close.

※ Your new edit group has been added to the Edit Groups list. By default, a newly created group is immediately made active, indicated by a gray highlight around the group name. To make the group *in*active, just click the group name to un-highlight it.

When you apply any edit tool to a member of an active edit group, you'll see that the effect of the tool is mirrored on all members of that group. This is particularly handy when you are assembling or tweaking tracks together (commonly done for drum kits, string or horn sections, and multiple vocal tracks). Shown here, I've made a selection on one of the tracks in a group, and that selection is mirrored on all members of this active edit group (named Drums and Bass).

# Creating and Customizing Fades

Fade-ins and fade-outs are used to gradually transition into or out of a region. Additionally, you can create *crossfades* between regions to make a smooth transition from one region into another. Of course, this is nothing new in the world of DAWs, but Pro Tools makes fades easy to create and tweak. You can even use the Smart tool to create them!

 **SETTING THINGS UP**

For our discussion of fades, go to Memory Location #7—Fades.

## Creating a Fade-In

Everybody has heard fade-ins used on a mix, as when a song starts from a silent beginning and gradually gets louder until it reaches its running volume. In Pro Tools, however, you can create a fade-in for an individual region *within* a mix. Here's how:

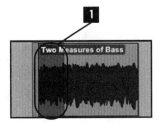

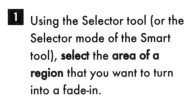 Using the Selector tool (or the Selector mode of the Smart tool), **select** the **area of a region** that you want to turn into a fade-in.

 **ABOUT YOUR SELECTION**

It's important to make sure that your selection starts at or before the region begins and ends where you want the fade-in to end.

2 **Click** on the **Edit menu**.

3 **Click** on **Fades**. The Fades sub-menu will appear.

4 **Click** on **Create**. The Fades dialog box will open.

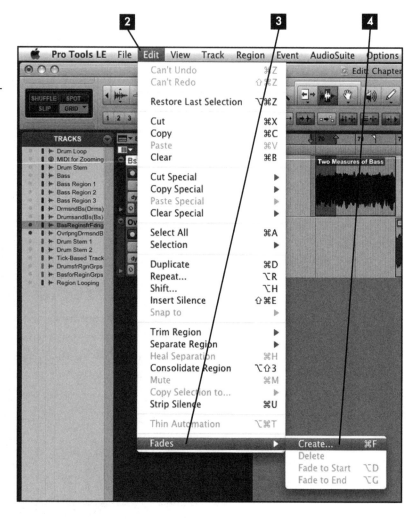

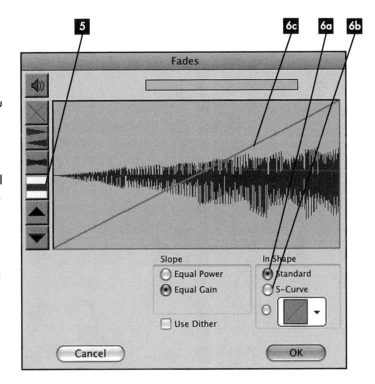

**5** Click on the **Waveform Display button** to show a graphic view of the audio you will be fading in.

The next step is to choose the contour (often referred to as the *curve*) of the fade you will be creating. There are a number of ways to get the shape you want.

**6a** Click on the **Standard radio button** in the In Shape section to select a basic exponential or logarithmic curve for the new fade.

OR

**6b** Click on the **S-Curve radio button** in the In Shape section to select an S curve for the new fade.

**6c** Once you've chosen either the Standard or S-Curve radio button, click on the fade curve and drag horizontally with your mouse to change its shape.

OR

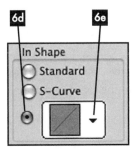

**6d** Click the **Preset Curve radio button** to use a standard fade curve.

**6e** Click on the **Preset Curve Selection down arrow**. A menu of fade-in curve presets will appear.

**295**
❊ ❊ ❊

**6f** Click on the desired **fade-in curve preset** from the menu.

**7** Once you've got the fade curve you want, **click** on **OK**. The Fades dialog box will close.

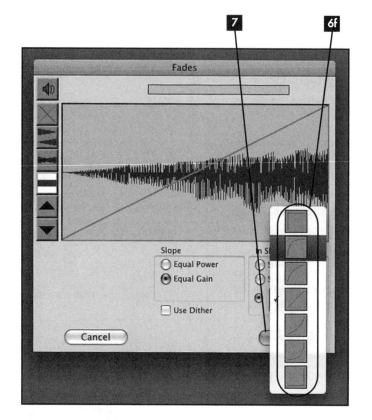

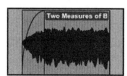

At the beginning of the region, you'll now see a new fade region. This region is shown with an ascending line, indicating that it is a fade-in, as well as indicating the curve of the fade-in. This fade region represents a fade file located in the Fade Files subfolder on your hard drive. Although this is certainly a region and an audio file, it will not be displayed in the Regions list.

❄ AUDITIONING FADES

Often, when creating a fade, it's useful to preview the sound of the fade before you've created it. In the Fades dialog box, you'll see a small button in the upper-left corner (shown here) that will do just that. Click the preview button to hear the effect of the fade curve on the audio region.

## Creating a Fade-Out

After you've created a fade-in, creating a fade-out will be easy. As you might expect, it's essentially a mirror image of the fade-in process.

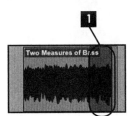

**1** **Select** the **area of a region** that you want to become a fade-out. Make sure your selection starts at the point that you want your fade-out to begin and ends *at or after* the region boundary.

**2** Click on the **Edit menu**.

**3** Click on **Fades**. The Fades sub-menu will appear.

**4** Click on **Create**. The Fades dialog box will open.

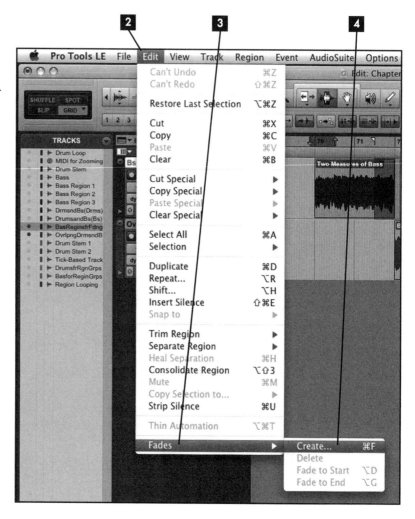

**5** Use the **shaping options** of the Fades dialog box to customize your fade-out curve, just as you did when you created your fade-in. The tools still operate the same, just in the opposite direction!

**6** Click the **OK button** when you're finished. The Fades dialog box will close.

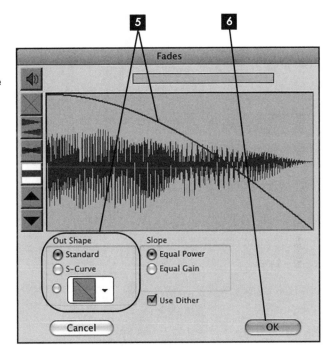

❄ **FADE-IN OR FADE-OUT?**

Here's something to be careful about when creating fades: If you don't select to the end (or beginning) of a region, Pro Tools will get confused about what you want to do. Even if you go to the Edit menu and select Fades, the Create option will be grayed out and unavailable.

## Crossfades

For readers who are unfamiliar with the term *crossfade*, it's a simultaneous fading out of one sound while another sound fades in, creating a smooth transition from one sound to the other. Here's how to create a crossfade between two overlapping regions.

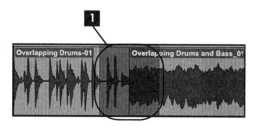

1. **Select** an **area** of two overlapping regions that you want to become a crossfade. (If you're following the tutorial session, I've created a track of alternating bass and drum regions so that you can easily hear the transition from one region to another.)

2. **Click** on the **Edit menu**.

3. **Click** on **Fades**. The Fades submenu will appear.

4. **Click** on **Create**. The Fades dialog box will open.

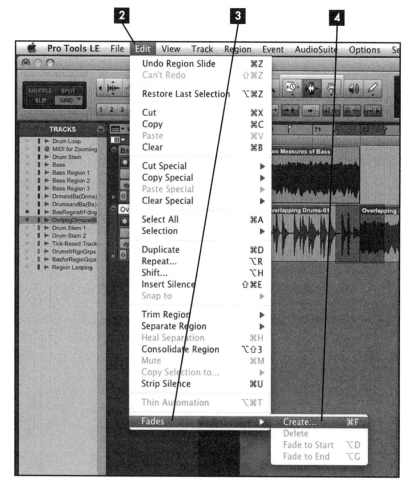

**5** Set up the **fade-in portion** of your crossfade the same way you would a standalone fade-in.

**6** Set up the **fade-out portion** of the crossfade in the same way.

**7** Drag the **crossing point** of your crossfade earlier or later, depending on your preference for this particular crossfade.

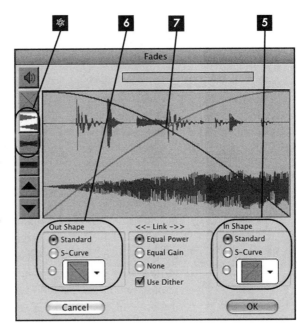

You'll notice that the fade-in and fade-out curves are linked—changes made to either curve will affect the other. Let's take a look at the different fade linking options.

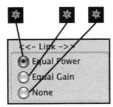

❈ **Equal Power**. This linking option will compensate for the volume drop that can sometimes occur when significantly different waveforms are combined, and it is usually heard as a smooth transition between dissimilar regions.

❈ **Equal Gain**. When you select this as a linking option, the midpoint of the crossfade will not be boosted in any way. When you are crossfading identical or similar audio, this linking will often give you the desired smooth transition from region to region.

❈ **None**. This will allow you to change one half of a crossfade without changing the other half. Though it's the least commonly used of all the linking options, it will give you a degree of flexibility that the other linking options don't provide. Let's take a look at how to use this linking option.

❈ ❈ ❈

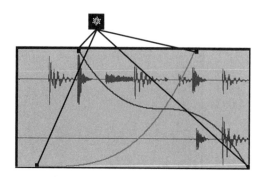

※ With linking set to None, you have the ability to move the beginning or end of either curve independently. Just click on the small black handle at the beginning or end of a fade curve and drag it to the desired position. These handles are small and can be a little difficult to click on with your mouse, but once you do get them, you'll be able to drag and drop them anywhere you want, with all other aspects of the crossfade remaining unchanged.

> ※ THE ADVANTAGE OF "NONE" LINKING
>
> Although the None link mode might not be the most commonly used mode of crossfading, it is often the mode of choice if you need a specific nonlinear transition.

## Creating Fades Using the Smart Tool

In addition to the triple benefit of Trim, Select, and Grabber tools that you get with the Smart tool, you can also quickly create fade-ins, fade-outs, and even crossfades!

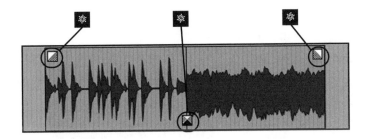

❋ **Fade-in.** If you move your cursor to the upper-left corner of an audio region, the cursor will change to a small square with an ascending diagonal line through it (looking something like a fade-in region). Just click and drag your cursor to the right to quickly create a fade-in region. Release the mouse button at the point where you want your fade-in to end, and the region will be created.

❋ **Fade-out.** If you move your cursor to the upper-right corner of a region, the cursor will change to a small square with a descending diagonal line through it. Just click and drag your cursor to the left to quickly create a fade-out region. Release the mouse button at the point where you want your fade-out to begin.

❋ **Crossfade.** If you move your cursor to the bottom corners of two adjacent regions, the cursor will change to a small square with two diagonal lines through it (looking like a crossfade region). Just click and drag your cursor to the left or right to quickly create a crossfade region. Release the mouse button at the point where you want your crossfade to begin or end. Your crossfade will be created and centered on the regions' boundaries.

You'll notice that when you create a fade or crossfade using the Smart tool, the Fades dialog box does not appear. The shape of the fade is automatically determined by the default fade setting. Customizing this default is easy to do and will allow the Smart tool to be even more useful!

**1** Click on the **Setup menu**.

**2** Click on **Preferences**. The Pro Tools LE Preferences window will open.

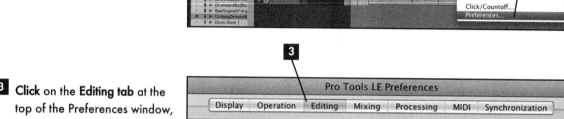

**3** Click on the **Editing tab** at the top of the Preferences window, if it's not already selected. The editing preferences will be displayed.

The Fades section is located in the upper-right corner of the Editing page, and it's in this section that you can set up your default fade settings (the ones that the Smart tool will apply when creating a fade or crossfade). The process of setting up default fade settings is identical to the process of creating fades themselves.

**4** Click on the **Fade In button** to open the (by now familiar) Fades dialog box. From here you can configure your default fade-in curve. **Click** the **OK button** to close the Fades dialog box.

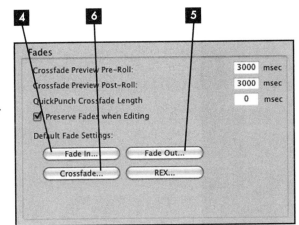

**5** Click on the **Fade Out button** to open the Fades dialog box again, and **choose** your **default fade-out curve**. **Click** the **OK button** to close the Fades dialog box.

**6** Click on the **Crossfade button** to open the Fades dialog box and **set up** your default **crossfade settings**. Once more, **click** the **OK button** to close the Fades dialog box.

**7** Once you've set up your default fade settings, just **click** on the **OK button** at the lower-right corner of the Preferences window. Your settings will be saved, and the window will close.

## ❄ CHANGING FADE REGIONS

If you create a fade and decide later that you want to change its contour, just double-click on the fade region with the Grabber tool. The Fades dialog box will open again so you can adjust the individual fade. Note that any changes you make in this dialog box will not affect the defaults you've set in the Preferences window.

## ❄ TOOLS AND FADES

Longtime users of Pro Tools will recall that there have been some things that you simply couldn't do with fades or with regions that contain fades. With Pro Tools version 7.4 and later, all the basic editing tools are fully functional with fade regions, except the Trim tool variations (the TCE Trim tool and the Loop Trim tool).

# Getting Specific: Nudging Regions

Using the Nudge function, you can move regions (or region boundaries) by incremental amounts, allowing you to get very specific with your timing. First, though, you'll have to choose a Nudge amount.

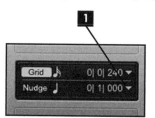

**1** Click on the **downward-facing triangle** to the right of the Nudge value. The Nudge menu will appear.

**2** Select the **scale** with which you want to nudge your region. The currently chosen scale will be indicated by a check mark. (In this case, Bars|Beats is chosen, which is well-suited for music sessions.) Based upon the scale you choose, the options at the top of the list will change.

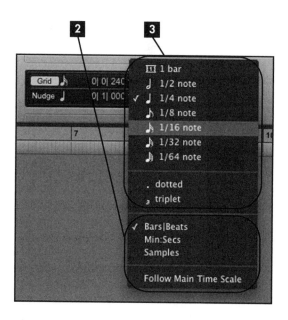

**3** Select the **increment** by which you want to nudge your region. The currently chosen increment will be indicated by a check mark.

Once you've got the Nudge value you want, using the feature is very straightforward.

**1** **Select** the **region(s)** you want to move.

**2a** **Press** the **+ (plus) key** to move your selected region(s) *later* in time (to the right) by the Nudge amount.

OR

**2b** **Press** the **– (minus) key** to move your selected region(s) *earlier* in time (to the left) by the Nudge amount.

❄ NUDGING SHORTCUTS

Holding Option (Mac) or Alt (PC) while pressing the plus or minus key will nudge only the left boundary of a region. Holding Command (Mac) or Ctrl (PC) while pressing the plus or minus key will nudge only the right boundary. Holding the Shift key while pressing the plus or minus key will move only the selected area and will leave the selected region in its original position.

# Cool Editing Tools

Before we move on, let's take a look at some features that can kick your editing up a notch!

## Tick-Based Audio Tracks

In most cases, you'll want your audio regions securely anchored to an absolute time location, right down to the sample. In this kind of scenario, audio regions' timing will not change if you change your session's tempo. MIDI notes and regions (which we'll talk about in the next chapter), on the other hand, typically *do* change along with tempo, their position being locked to your session's bars, beats, and ticks. With Pro Tools, you have the option of breaking away from this default behavior, setting up an Audio track's regions to be locked to a tick-based location. In this sort of tick-based Audio track, when you change your tempo, your regions will move accordingly.

❄ SETTING THINGS UP

If you go to Memory Location #9—Tick-Based Audio, you'll see a familiar-sounding drum part, separated at each transient.

**1** Click the **Timebase Selector button**. A menu will appear.

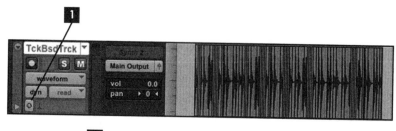

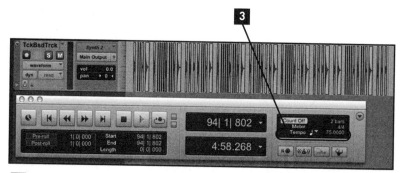

**2** In this menu, you choose between having a sample-based or a tick-based timebase for your track. The currently selected timebase is marked with a check mark. In this case, the Audio track shown is currently set to Samples, meaning that the placement of regions on the track is based upon a real-time location and won't move if the tempo (which is tick-based) is changed. To change the track to be tick-based, **click** the **Ticks menu item**.

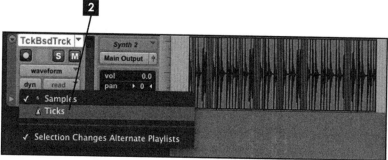

**3** Now that you have a tick-based Audio track, all the regions on this track are locked to bar|beat|tick-based locations, which means if you change the tempo in your session, each individual region (in this case, each individual transient) will move accordingly. In this example, I've reduced the tempo from 150 beats per minute down to 75 beats per minute. The regions have moved, and the drum beat now plays at half-tempo.

If you're following the steps using the tutorial session, you'll notice that you might be hearing clicks and pops when you change the tempo (especially if you slow the tempo down, as I have here). This is not uncommon in this sort of situation. The cause of the problem is that some regions have been separated at a point *other* than the zero crossing. Let me explain.

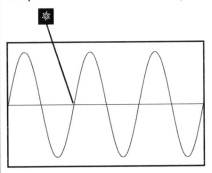

❄ As your audio waveform oscillates, it intersects the line in the center of the Waveform view. This line, commonly called the *zero* line, represents no voltage being sent to a speaker—a speaker at rest.

When a region begins and ends with the waveform at the zero line, there will be no unwanted clicks and pops. If, however, the waveform has been cut at a point other than the zero volt line, clicks and pops may be heard (as a result of the speaker suddenly receiving a radical change in voltage).

You can use the Trim tool to change a region's boundary so that it begins and ends on the zero line, but this is sometimes prohibitively time-consuming. Not to worry—you can also treat the problem by creating fade-ins or fade-outs for the regions, which will create a zero crossing at the beginning or end of the region.

# Link Edit and Track Selection

This is a simple enough feature, but it's definitely worth taking a look at! When it's active, any edit selection will follow the selected tracks in your session. Let's take a look:

For the purposes of this demonstration, show all the tracks of your session.

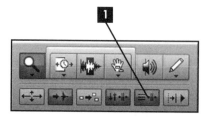

**1** Click the **Link Track and Edit Selection button**, located just below the Scrub tool button in the Edit tool cluster.

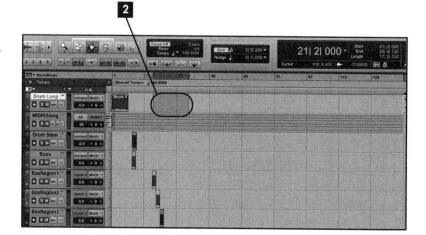

**2** Using the Selector tool, **make a selection** on any track you like. Note that as soon as a selection is made on that track, the track name is highlighted, indicating that the track itself is also selected.

**3** Now, **select a different track** in your session. (This can be done by clicking the track name or pressing the appropriate select button on a control surface.) Note how the selection moves with your track selection.

❊ SELECTING A BLOCK OF TRACKS

If you want to select a block of adjacent tracks and have your selected area mirrored on each track, just hold down the Shift key as you select tracks. To select multiple nonadjacent tracks, hold down the Command key (on a Mac) or the Ctrl key (on a PC) as you select additional tracks.

# Region Groups

Region groups are a way to link regions together so that they move and behave as a single unit, even though they may span multiple tracks. Similar to edit groups, region groups give you the power to have a single edit applied to multiple tracks, but with even more individual control.

❊ SETTING THINGS UP

For this section, go to Memory Location #10—Region Groups.

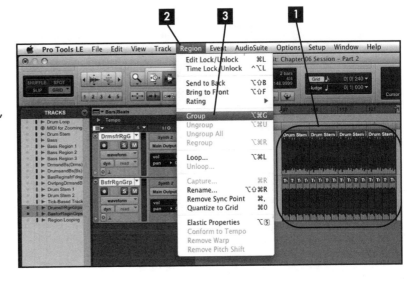

**1** Select the **regions** that you want to assign to your region group. It's worth mentioning that any type of region (audio, MIDI, and even video) can be part of a region group. If you're following the tutorial session, your regions have been selected for you.

**2** Click the **Region menu**.

**3** Click on **Group**.

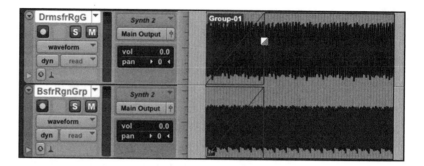

The region group is a single object that contains all of the regions you've selected. It will have its own name and will appear in the Regions list at the right edge of your Edit window. Even though it may span many regions and tracks, you can edit the region group as a single object, such as creating a long fade, as shown here.

## Region Looping

The ability to loop regions is a very useful feature when you're working with repetitious material, such as drum beats. Here's how it works.

 SETTING THINGS UP

For this section of the chapter, recall Memory Location #11—Region Looping.

**1** **Select** the **region** you want to loop. If you're following the tutorial session, your region has been selected for you.

**2** Click the **Region menu**.

**3** Click on **Loop**. The Region Looping dialog box will open.

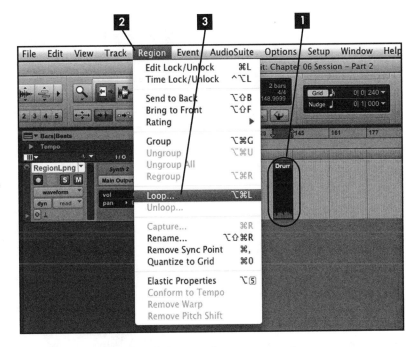

You have a number of choices when it comes to how you want your region to loop. You can:

❄ Choose the number of repetitions you want your region to have.

❄ Specify a length of time (based upon the Main time scale) that you want to fill with these loops.

❄ Loop until the end of the session or until the next region (whichever comes first).

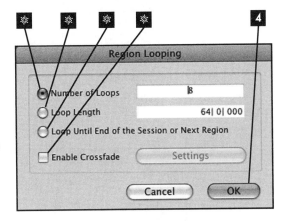

❄ Check the Enable Crossfade box to create crossfades between each loop iteration. When this box is checked, you can adjust the crossfade curve by clicking the Settings button (which will open the same kind of Crossfades dialog box that you worked with earlier in this chapter).

**4** Once you've chosen how you want your region to loop, just **click** on **OK**. The dialog box will close, and your region will be looped.

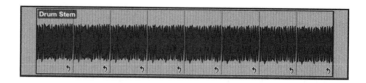

In this example, I've chosen to repeat this region eight times, and here's the result. This series of looped regions, like region groups, functions in many ways like a single unit and can be moved and edited with great flexibility.

## The Loop Trim Tool

As if region looping wasn't easy enough already, the Loop Trim tool will give you even more functionality. For example, you can use the Loop Trim tool to quickly create just the right amount of looping.

**1** Click and hold the **Trim tool button** until the Trim tool Options menu appears. The currently selected version of the Trim tool will be indicated with a check mark.

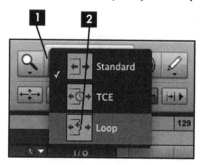

**2** Click on **Loop** to change to the Loop Trim tool. The icon for the Trim tool will change to reflect the currently active version of the tool.

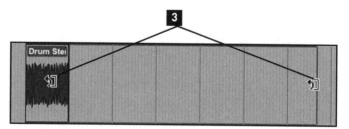

**3** The rest is pretty simple. When you see the Trim tool with the curved arrow icon (as shown in this image), just **click and drag** the desired **region boundary**. (You can drag either the left or the right boundary to loop forward or backward.) As with other versions of the Trim tool, all you have to do is **release** the **mouse**, and you'll have your new looped region.

There's another side of region looping that's particularly interesting: Using the Trim tool with a looped region object, you can change the length of the member regions without changing the total length of the looped region object. Sound confusing? Take a look, and I think it'll become clear.

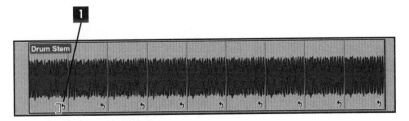

**1** With the Trim tool selected (actually, any version of the Trim tool will do the trick), **move** your **cursor** to a lower corner of any member region of your region loop object. The Trim tool will be displayed as a basic Trim tool, as shown here.

**2** Click and drag your **mouse** horizontally to adjust the boundary of the member region, just as if you were trimming a normal region.

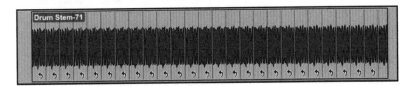

The difference becomes apparent when you release your mouse button. You'll notice that the overall length of the looped region object is the same, but the length of member regions within it has changed! This technique can be particularly useful when you are dealing with drum beats, and it can often yield interesting results!

## New in Pro Tools 8: Region Locking Improvements

When you're finished editing a section of a project, you might want to make sure that your regions don't inadvertently move or change. Region locking will do just that, and it's been a fixture in Pro Tools for quite some time. With the advent of Pro Tools 8, however, the usefulness of region locking has improved, and it's worth mentioning before we close this chapter.

### Edit Lock

The first kind of region locking to look at is called edit lock, and it will prevent your locked regions from being moved or edited accidentally.

**1** Select the region(s) you want to lock.

**2** Click the Region menu.

**3** Choose Edit Lock/Unlock. The region will be locked.

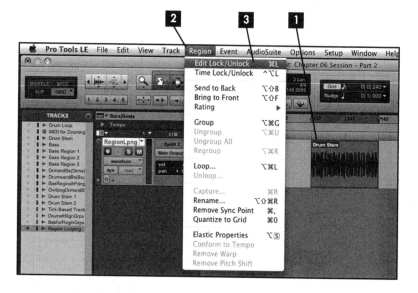

An edit locked region will be indicated by a small lock icon in the bottom-left corner of the region.

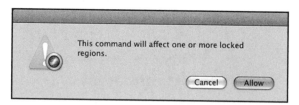

This command will affect one or more locked regions.

Cancel    Allow

If you attempt to change the region in any way (including moving the region to another location), you will see a window that will allow you to apply this change or leave the locked region unchanged.

## Time Lock

When a region is time locked, it can be freely edited in all ways
other than moving the region to a different location.

**1** Select the **region(s)** you want
to lock.

**2** Click the **Region menu**.

**3** Choose **Time Lock/Unlock**. The
region will be locked.

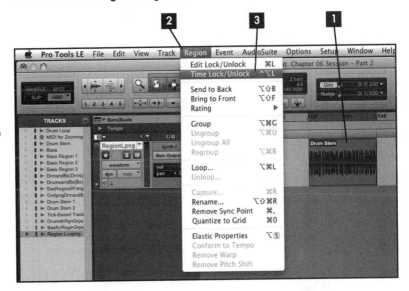

A time locked region will be indicated by a small lock icon in the
bottom-left corner of the region. Notice that the edit lock icon is
solid-colored, whereas the time lock icon is an outline of a lock.

When a region is time locked, all editing processes can be applied
normally, *except* moving the region. This new variation of region
locking is particularly useful, allowing a region to be tweaked and
faded, but maintaining the position of the region.

That's all for now. Next...MIDI!

# 7 } Using MIDI

**MIDI** (which stands for *Musical Instrument Digital Interface*) is a language that allows keyboards, synthesizers, and other musical devices to interact with one another. Since its inception in the early 1980s, MIDI has proved to be an invaluable creative tool to musicians of all kinds, and it has changed the face of the music industry.

Not too long ago, music software worked with *either* audio *or* MIDI, but typically not both. Thankfully, those days have changed, and there are a number of DAW products, including Pro Tools, that incorporate the creative power of MIDI and the advantages of digital audio. Pro Tools LE 8, in particular, has made impressive gains in its MIDI power functionality, while remaining a solid audio workstation. In this chapter, you'll learn how to:

* Set up your MIDI studio
* Route MIDI and audio signals so you can work with synthesizers in Pro Tools
* Record and edit MIDI data
* Work with your MIDI data intelligently, including importing to and exporting from Pro Tools
* Use Pro Tools 8's new MIDI Editor and Score Editor windows

※ MIDI RESOURCES

A mastery of MIDI is a study in and of itself, upon which volumes of information have been written. For the purposes of this chapter, a fundamental understanding of MIDI will necessarily be assumed, and we'll focus on how to use MIDI in the Pro Tools environment, rather than on the underlying principles of MIDI itself. For a good book on the subject of MIDI, check out *MIDI Power! Second Edition: The Comprehensive Guide* (Thomson Course Technology PTR, 2005).

※ VIRTUAL INSTRUMENTS

For the purposes of this chapter, you'll be dealing with *virtual* instruments—in other words, instruments that are software-based, rather than physical devices. Pro Tools 8 has really increased its offerings with regard to virtual instruments, and we'll be taking advantage of many of them in this chapter's tutorial sessions.

The list of free instruments included with Pro Tools 8 is impressive:

- ※ **Boom:** Vintage drum machine emulation
- ※ **DB-33:** Tonewheel organ emulation
- ※ **Mini Grand:** Acoustic piano emulation, featuring a number of different piano models and ambient effects
- ※ **Vacuum:** Vintage monophonic tube synthesizer emulation
- ※ **Xpand2!:** Workstation synthesizer, featuring a wide variety of useful sounds
- ※ **Structure Free:** Sample playback instrument

Again, these instruments are free, and installation files are included on your Pro Tools 8 LE installation disc (bundled as the Pro Tools Creative Collection). If you haven't installed them already, now would be an excellent time to do so!

# Setting Up Your MIDI Studio

When we were working with audio, one of our first steps was to configure inputs and outputs (in the I/O setup window). You'll want to do this with MIDI as well, using the MIDI Studio Setup window, identifying your MIDI devices before proceeding. Don't worry; it's easy!

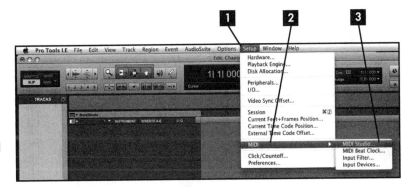

**1** Click on the **Setup menu**.

**2** Click on **MIDI**. The MIDI sub-menu will be displayed.

**3** Choose **MIDI Studio**. The Audio MIDI Setup window will appear.

❋ **PC AND MAC MIDI SETUPS**

The process of configuring your MIDI studio varies a bit between Mac systems and PCs, though the basic process is largely similar. Where appropriate, both Mac and PC screenshots will be shown.

## Adding a MIDI Device

Before you can record any MIDI data, you'll need to physically attach your external MIDI device(s) to your system's MIDI interface. (Refer to the documentation that came with your MIDI gear for more information.) Let's assume that you've physically connected your MIDI gear in a traditional configuration—in other words, you've connected the output of your MIDI interface to the MIDI input of your device and then connected the MIDI output (*not* the Thru) of your device into an input on your MIDI interface. Once that's done, you'll need to set up Pro Tools to recognize that connection.

### MIDI Studio Setup on a Mac

The Audio MIDI Setup window will give you an overview of the devices attached to your system. Initially, it might show you only your MIDI interface (the device to which you'll attach any external MIDI devices). The next step is to add a device to your system.

**1** Click the **Add Device button**. A New External Device icon will appear.

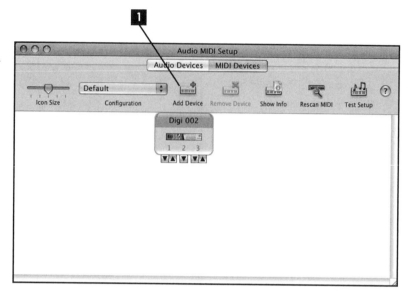

**2** Click and hold on the **MIDI OUT port** of the MIDI interface that is connected to your external device.

**3** Drag with your mouse to the **MIDI IN port** of your external device. You'll see a line connecting the MIDI interface icon and the New External Device icon.

**4** Repeat Steps 2 and 3 for the connection from the MIDI OUT port of your external device to the MIDI IN port of your interface, if applicable.

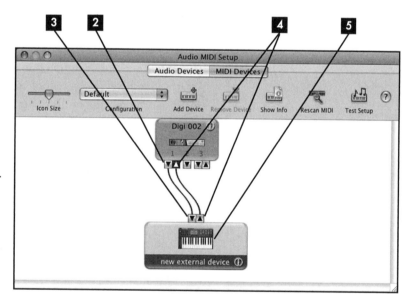

**5** Double-click the New External Device icon. The New External Device Properties dialog box will appear, allowing you to customize the connection.

✳ The top section will allow you to type a descriptive name for your device, plus choose the manufacturer and model that match your gear. If you don't see your manufacturer or model, don't worry—just leave the fields blank.

✳ Click the Transmits channels that you want to make available to your device. (Enabled channels will be colored blue.) You can also choose to enable the device to be able to transmit MIDI Beat Clock and/or MIDI Time Code. (Enabled options will be indicated with a check mark.)

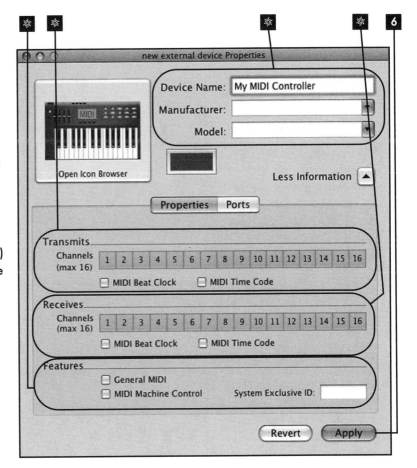

✳ Click the Receives channels that you want to make available to your device. (Enabled channels will be colored blue.) You can also choose to enable the device to be able to receive MIDI Beat Clock and/or MIDI Time Code. (Enabled options will be indicated with a check mark.)

✳ Finally, you can enable your device to operate as a General MIDI device or a MIDI Machine Control device (to control transport of Pro Tools), or you can assign a System Exclusive ID number (if you have multiple devices of the same model).

**6** When you've set up your device, click the Apply button. The dialog box will close. When you've created and configured all your external gear, just close the Audio MIDI Setup window.

## MIDI Studio Setup on a PC

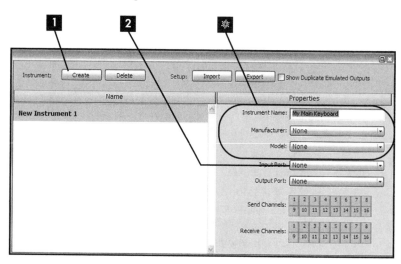

**1** Click the **Create button**. A new device, initially named New Instrument 1, will be created.

❄ The top section will allow you to type a descriptive name for your device, plus choose the manufacturer and model that match your gear. If you don't see your manufacturer or model, don't worry—just leave the fields blank.

**2** Click the **Input Port button**. A menu will appear.

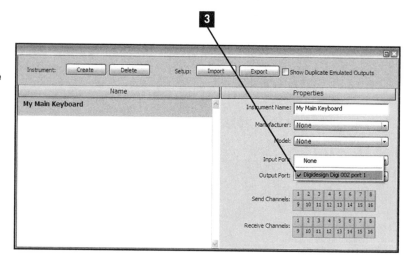

**3** Choose the appropriate **MIDI IN port** on your MIDI interface (the MIDI IN port that is connected to your external device).

**4** Now it's time to choose how your system will send MIDI information to the device. **Click** the **Output Port button.** A menu will appear.

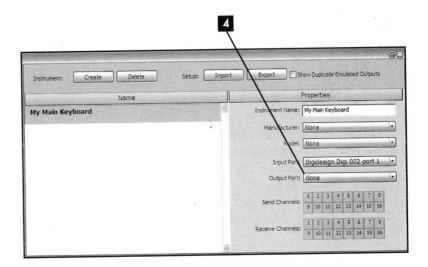

**5** **Choose** the appropriate **MIDI OUT port** on your MIDI interface (the MIDI OUT port that is connected to your external device).

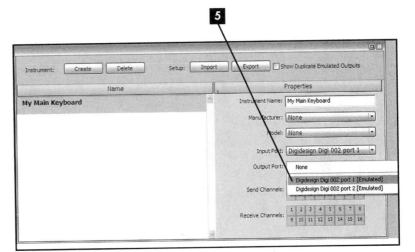

* Click the send channels that you want to make available to your device. (Enabled channels will be colored blue.)

* Click the receive channels that you want to make available to your device. (Enabled channels will be colored blue.)

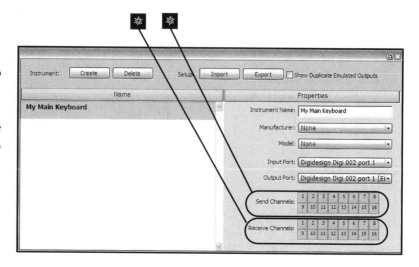

You can repeat this process for each of the external MIDI devices in your system. Before we leave this window, though, let's take a look at some of its other features:

* The Import button will allow you to open any MIDI setup file (stored with a *.dms file extension) that has been previously created. Be careful, though—this will overwrite your current settings.

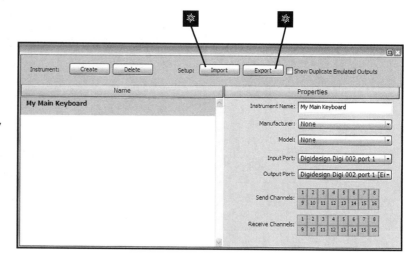

* Want to store the setup you've got now for future use or to transplant to another system? Just click the Export button. You will be prompted to save your settings as a *.dms file.

* When you're finished, just **close** the **window**, and your settings will be applied to your system.

# Signal Flow 201: MIDI versus Audio

If there's one important thing to remember about MIDI, it's this: MIDI is *not* audio. MIDI isn't even audible—it's a digital language that allows musical devices to communicate with each other on a fundamental level. It's a common (and dangerous) misconception that MIDI and audio are somehow related, and this probably stems from the fact that the use of MIDI allows musical gear to make sound.

Given that MIDI and digital audio are fundamentally different, it should come as no surprise that MIDI has its own rules for signal flow. The good news is that if you know the rules, setting up your instruments is easy, and you can manage MIDI signal paths and audio signal paths simultaneously in one Pro Tools session.

## Managing the MIDI Signal Path

We've already gone through the process of basic audio signal routing. You'll find that managing your MIDI tracks has a familiar look and feel.

**1** **Create** a **MIDI track** and **name it** descriptively. (See Chapter 3 if you need a refresher on how to do this.)

You'll notice that the overall layout of a MIDI track is consistent with other tracks you've seen so far:

❋ Track name

❋ Record, Solo, and Mute buttons

❋ Input selector

❋ Output selector

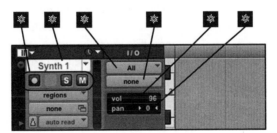

❋ Volume control

❋ Pan control

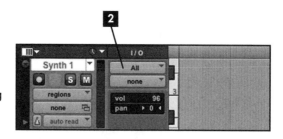

**2** **Click** on the **Input Selector button**. The Input menu will appear, including the following options:

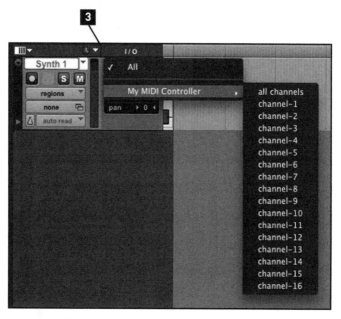

✳ By default, a new MIDI track will have All set as the input and will allow the track to accept MIDI data from any port and on any channel. This is a particularly convenient way to work if you're a single user in a multi-keyboard studio. With All selected as an input, you can play any MIDI device in your studio and have it recorded to the track, without having to change your input selection.

✳ Additionally, each input device you've specified in your MIDI setup will appear as an input option. You can choose a single device or even a specific MIDI channel as an input for your track. This is useful in multi-keyboard setups in which you have multiple musicians playing simultaneously. You can assign multiple tracks to accept input from specific MIDI sources, isolating each musician's performance to separate tracks.

**3** **Select** the **input** that suits your situation.

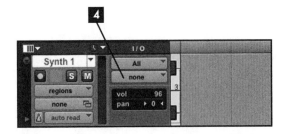

**4** Click on the **Output Selector button**. The Output menu will appear.

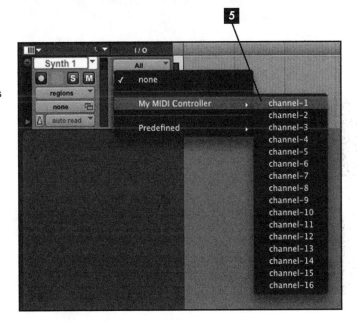

**5** Select the **device and MIDI channel** that are routed to the device you want to use for this track.

❄ **USING MIDI CONTROLLERS**

With MIDI, the device you physically play does not necessarily have to be the device that you hear. In these cases, the device you actually play is called a MIDI controller.

Now your MIDI track is set up to route MIDI data from a source (for example, a MIDI controller) to a destination (for example, an external sound module). When you play your MIDI instrument, you should see an indication on the destination device that it is receiving MIDI data. At this point, that device should respond to the MIDI data by making sound.

Occasionally, you'll need to adjust your MIDI track's volume. This is also a straightforward process.

**1** Click and hold on the **Volume display area**. A small fader box will appear.

**2** Still holding down the mouse button, **drag** the **fader** on the fader box to adjust the volume to suit your session.

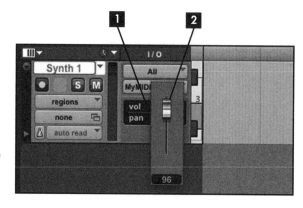

### MIDI VOLUME RESOLUTION

MIDI volume has a range of 128 steps, from 0–127.

Similarly, you can adjust a track's pan settings.

**1** Click and hold in the Pan display area. A small slider box will appear.

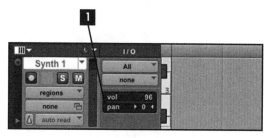

**2** Still holding down the mouse button, **drag** the **slider** to adjust the pan to suit your session.

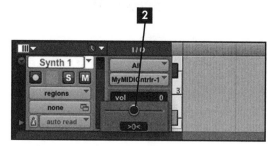

## Setting Up an Aux Track to Monitor Your MIDI Gear

We discussed the idea of *Aux tracks* (or more formally Auxiliary Input tracks) back in Chapter 3. Aux tracks are the track type of choice for when you need to manage an audio signal, but you don't need to record audio to your hard drive. In this example, we'll use an Aux track to hear an external MIDI sound module through Pro Tools.

> ❊ **AUX TRACKS VERSUS AUDIO TRACKS**
>
> Even though an Aux track is an *audible* track, it certainly isn't an *Audio* track. The main difference between the two is that an Audio track can play back regions in your session (as you've already seen), whereas an Aux track cannot.
>
> Though you technically *could* use an Audio track to monitor an external MIDI device's output, Aux tracks usually are more suited to the task, and using Aux tracks whenever possible will conserve resources so you can get the maximum performance out of your system.

Once you've connected the audio outputs of the MIDI sound module to the appropriate audio input(s) of your Pro Tools interface, follow these steps.

**1** Create a new **Aux track** and **name it** descriptively. (This is the track you'll use to hear your MIDI device.)

**2** Assign the **input** of this Aux track to match the *audio* inputs to which your external MIDI sound module is attached.

**3** Assign the **output** of this Aux track to the audio outputs to which your monitor speakers are attached.

**4** When an Aux track is created, its volume is set ∞ to prevent accidental feedback and damage to your ears and speakers. **Adjust** the **volume** of the Aux track to suit your session.

At this point, you've completely configured your MIDI signal flow, as well as the audio signal routing that will allow you to listen to your sound-producing device. When you play your controller device (with the MIDI track record armed), you will trigger your slave device (with MIDI data traveling through the MIDI track and recordable on that track) and listen to the audio output of your sound module through the Aux track.

## Using Virtual Instruments

A recent addition to the world of music creation, virtual instruments have really boosted the power of the modern DAW. Virtual instruments are real-time plug-ins, but whereas most plug-ins *process* sound, virtual instruments *make* sound! Think of them as the marriage between software plug-ins and MIDI synthesizers, giving you the best of both worlds. With virtual instruments, you not only have the power of a MIDI synth without the bulk of physical hardware, you also have the ability to automate its parameters just like any plug-in. (Don't worry; we'll talk more about that in the next chapter.)

The secret to using virtual instruments is in the setup, which is really just a variation of the traditional MIDI setup that you learned in the previous section. Here again, you can use two tracks to get MIDI and sound to work together within Pro Tools—a MIDI track (for the MIDI data) and an Aux track (for your virtual instrument).

**1** Create a new **stereo Aux track** and **assign** its **output** to your system's monitor speakers.

**2** Since we'll be using a plug-in and since plug-ins are used via inserts, you'll want to make sure that you can see an Inserts column in your Edit window. If you're not seeing an Inserts column, just **click** the **Edit Window View selector** and choose an Inserts view from the list. (In this case, I'm showing Inserts A-E.)

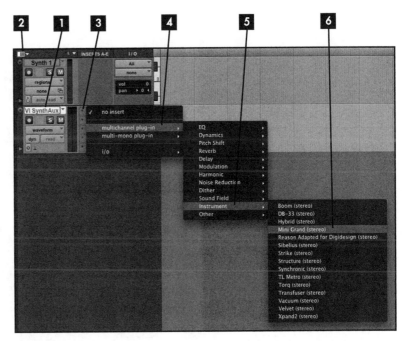

**3** **Click** on an **Insert Selector button**. A menu will appear.

**4** **Select** either a **multichannel or multi-mono plug-in** (based on the kind of instrument you want to use—I've chosen multichannel). A submenu will appear.

**5** **Click Instrument**. Yet another submenu will appear.

**6** **Choose** your desired **virtual instrument**. (In this case, I've chosen the Mini Grand plug-in.) The plug-in's window will appear.

### ✸ DON'T GET CAUGHT!

Remember, a newly created Aux track's volume is turned all the way down. If you created a new Aux for this virtual instrument, you'll need to bring the volume up on the track in order to hear your instrument.

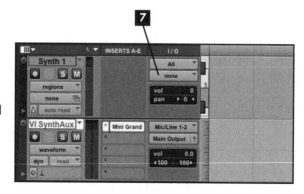

**7** Next, you'll need to create a MIDI track (if you haven't already) and set up the output to be routed to your new virtual instrument. **Click** on the **Output Selector button** of the MIDI track. A menu will appear.

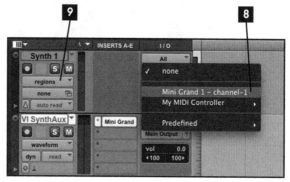

**8** You'll notice that, once you've launched a virtual instrument plug-in, it will appear as an output option for your MIDI track. **Select** the **instrument** you want to control from the Output drop-down menu.

**9** Now let's test your setup. **Click** the MIDI track's **Track View Selector** button (which will initially read "regions"). A menu will appear.

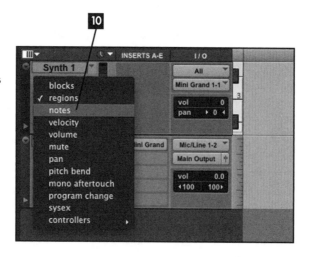

**10** The Track View list will show you the available view options for this track. (The currently active view will be indicated by a check mark.) **Choose Notes** from the list.

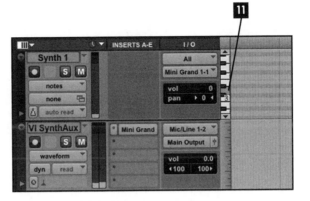

**11** Click on any **note** of the "mini keyboard" to the left of your MIDI track's Playlist area. If everything is set up properly, MIDI data will be created, the data will be sent to the virtual instrument, and the instrument will sound.

❋ MIDI METERING

As you play a session that contains MIDI, you will see activity in your MIDI track's level meters as notes are played. Remember that what you're seeing is *not* audio, but rather control data being sent to the virtual instrument on your Aux track. The levels you see on the Aux track are the audible signal being routed to your monitor speakers.

## Instrument Tracks

Instrument tracks are real timesavers for MIDI production, combining the power of a MIDI track *and* an Aux track in a single unit. Let's delete the two tracks you created in the previous virtual instrument scenario and redo the whole job with just one track.

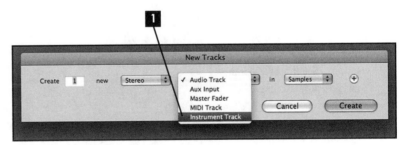

**1** Open the **New Tracks dialog box**. (See Chapter 3 if you need a refresher on how to do this.) From the Track Type menu, **select Instrument Track**. When you click Create, a new Instrument track will be created.

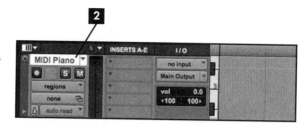

**2** **Name** your **track** descriptively.

Below the track name, you'll see some familiar-looking buttons.

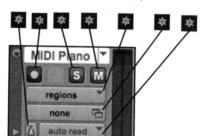

※ Track Record Enable.

※ Solo.

※ Mute.

※ Track View Selector.

※ Patch Select.

※ Timebase Selector.

※ Automation Mode Selectors. (We'll discuss this in the next chapter.)

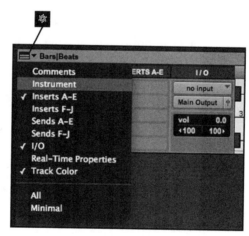

※ The Instrument column contains the functionality of a MIDI track's I/O column. If you're not seeing the Instrument column, just click the Edit Window View selector, and click the Instrument menu item. (Visible columns will be indicated by check marks.)

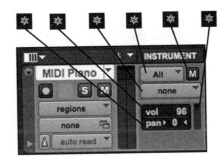

- ❋ MIDI Input Selector
- ❋ MIDI Mute
- ❋ MIDI Output Selector
- ❋ MIDI Volume
- ❋ MIDI Pan
- ❋ MIDI Level Meter

**3** The Inserts column of an Instrument track functions just like the Inserts column of an Aux track. Simply **choose** the desired **virtual instrument plug-in** on this track, just as you did before with an Aux track. Your plug-in will launch, and the plug-in window will be displayed.

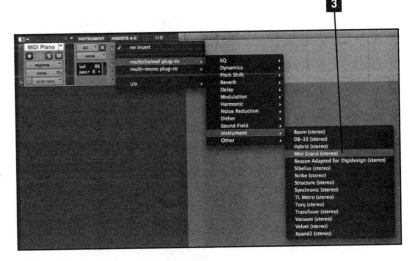

You'll notice that as soon as your virtual instrument launched, the MIDI Output button of the Instrument track automatically changes to match the plug-in, making an Instrument track even more convenient. If you need to change that MIDI output for any reason, you can do it easily by clicking the MIDI Output button.

**4** The I/O column of an Instrument track is identical to the I/O column of an Aux track, and you'll use it the same way. **Set** the **output** of the Instrument track.

**5** Last but certainly not least, **adjust** your track's **output level** as needed.

Now, your track should look something like the image shown here. Initially, the Instrument track view will be set to Regions (similar to the MIDI track you worked with earlier), but like a MIDI track, you can change the view to Notes and click your mini keyboard to test your setup, as you did in the previous section of this chapter.

## MIDI and Instrument Tracks in the Mix Window

The Mix window is well suited to the task of routing and combining individual signals in order to get a pleasing total mix. We'll take a closer look at mixing in the next chapter, but for now let's take a look at how MIDI and Instrument tracks appear in this environment.

**1** First, you need to make sure you're seeing the appropriate aspects of each track strip in the Mix window. **Click** the **View menu**.

**2** **Choose Mix Window Views**. A submenu will appear.

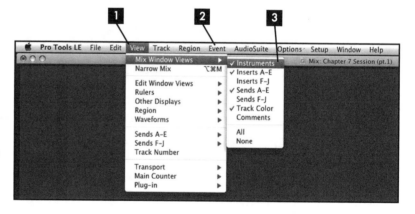

**3** Displayed elements of your session's tracks will be indicated by a check mark. If the Instruments menu item isn't checked, **click it** now.

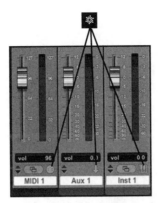

❄ The icons at the bottom-right corner of each channel strip indicate track type (a MIDI plug for a MIDI track, an arrow for an Aux track, and a keyboard for an Instrument track).

❄ The Instrument row (at the top of the channel strip) mirrors the functionality of the Instrument column that you saw earlier in the Edit window (MIDI input, output, volume, pan, and mute). Note that the area is blank in any track other than an Instrument track.

※ The I/O sections of an Aux track and an Instrument track are identical, and it is here where you will set up your audio ins, outs, and more (which we'll explore in greater depth in the next chapter). In a MIDI track, you can choose the MIDI input and output assignments.

※ The bottom section of each of these track types allows you to adjust positioning with pan controls and includes record (when applicable), solo, mute, and volume controls.

# Recording MIDI

Recording MIDI is similar to audio recording in many respects, but with some additional flexibility.

## Choosing a Sound

Usually, your first step is to pick a sound that you want to use. Doing this varies slightly depending on whether you're using an external MIDI device or a virtual instrument plug-in. Let's start with the external device.

## Choosing a Sound for an External Device

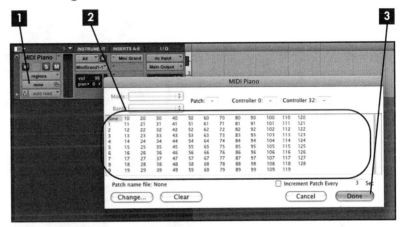

**1** Click on the **Patch Select button**. (Conveniently, it's in the same position on a MIDI or an Instrument track.) A dialog box containing a patch list for the MIDI device will open. Depending on the device that you configured in your MIDI setup, the patch list displayed will consist of numbers and/or text names.

**2** Click on the **patch** you want to use.

**3** Click on the **Done button**. The Patch Select dialog box will close, and the program number or name will appear on the Patch Select button.

## Choosing a Sound for a Virtual Instrument

If you're using a virtual instrument (such as Mini Grand), you'll need to choose a sound directly from the plug-in's window.

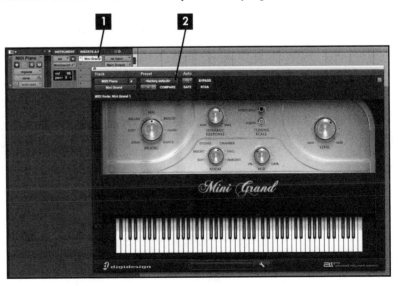

**1** If your plug-in window isn't open already, **click** on the virtual instrument's **Insert button**. The Insert button will be highlighted, and the plug-in window will open.

**2** Click the **Librarian Menu button** (which will be displaying the currently active sound). A menu of available sounds will appear.

❉ ❉ ❉

**3** **Choose** the desired **sound** from the menu. The menu will close, and your choice will be applied.

Here's an alternative method:

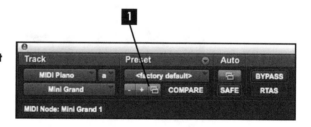

**1** **Click** the **Plug-In Settings Select button**. The plug-in settings window will open.

**2** If your plug-in presets are organized into submenus, **click** the **Folder menu**. The subfolder hierarchy will be displayed. Once shown, **select** the desired **subfolder** from the list that is displayed. When you make your selection, the programs in that subfolder will be displayed in the window.

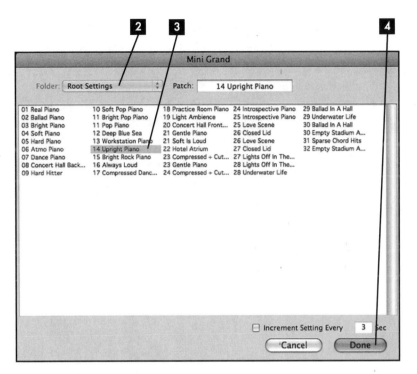

**3** **Select** the desired **sound**.

**4** When you've settled on the best sound, **click** the **Done button**.

❄ **INCREMENT PATCH**

If you're searching for just the right sound, the Increment Setting Every n Sec check box (at the bottom-right corner of the plug-in settings window) can come in handy. Just enable the feature to cycle through all the sounds in this window automatically, allowing you to keep playing while the patches change.

Before you start recording, you might want to set up a click track (which you learned about back in Chapter 4). Remember to click on the Metronome icon to enable your click. Now it's time to actually record the MIDI. The process of recording MIDI is nearly identical to recording audio.

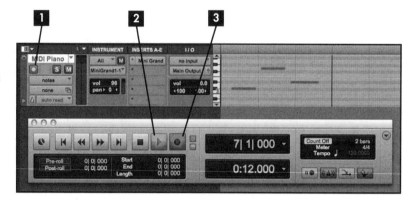

**1** Click on the **Track Record Enable button** to arm the track for recording.

**2** Click on the **Record Enable button** in the Transport window (or in the transport controls at the top of the Edit window).

**3** Click on the **Play button**. Recording will begin. It operates the same as when you record audio, with pre-rolls, post-rolls, and so on.

❋ There's a nifty feature called *MIDI Merge* that allows you to record on a MIDI track without overwriting any preexisting MIDI data. It's an especially useful feature when you're working in Loop Playback mode.

When you're finished, you'll have a region, as you did when you recorded audio. This time, however, you'll see MIDI note data within the region rather than audio waveforms!

## Using MIDI Beat Clock

MIDI Beat Clock is a continuous stream of tempo-based pulses (going faster with higher tempi, slower with lower tempi) that allows multiple tempo-based devices to stay in sync. For example, if you have a synthesizer that includes an arpeggiator, you'll want that device to not only play the notes that are sent to it, but also arpeggiate them in time with the Pro Tools session. That's where MIDI Beat Clock comes in. Beat Clock is also commonly used with external drum machines, ensuring that drum patterns not only start and stop at the right time, but play at the proper tempo as well.

These days, most virtual instruments that can follow MIDI Beat Clock automatically configure themselves to do so, and manual configuration is generally reserved for external hardware devices. Here's how to set them up.

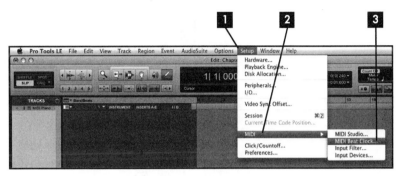

1 Click the **Setup menu**.

2 Choose the **MIDI menu item**. A second menu will **appear**.

3 Choose the **MIDI Beat Clock menu item**. The MIDI Beat Clock dialog box will appear.

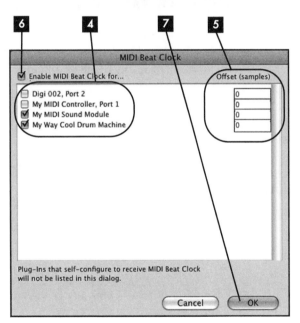

4 **Select** the specific **ports** through which you wish to send MIDI Beat Clock. Note that the ports are named according to the devices you set up in the MIDI Studio setup window. Selected devices will be indicated by a check mark.

5 Frequently, MIDI can include a significant amount of latency (a fact that experienced MIDI users are only too aware of). You can compensate for that latency by **typing** an **Offset value** on a port-by-port basis. This value can be either positive (offsetting the MIDI Beat Clock *later*) or negative (offsetting the MIDI Beat Clock earlier, to compensate for MIDI latency).

6 **Click** the **Enable MIDI Beat Clock For** check box to activate MIDI Beat Clock for the selected ports. When enabled, the box will be checked.

7 **Click OK**. The MIDI Beat Clock dialog box will close, and you're all set!

❄ HEY, I'M NOT SEEING MY VIRTUAL SYNTH!

It's not uncommon for virtual instruments to automatically enable themselves to receive MIDI Beat Clock as soon as they're launched. These devices will not be shown in the MIDI Beat Clock dialog box.

## Recording MIDI Instruments to Audio Tracks

Suppose you've created a killer track using your favorite MIDI hardware, and you want to send the session to a friend (so that your friend can lay down tracks of his or her own). There's a potential problem: If your friend doesn't have the same MIDI hardware (or virtual instrument) that you've got in your studio, he or she won't be able to hear your killer track the way it's meant to be heard. The solution is to record your MIDI instrument to an Audio track and then send your session out for collaboration.

The process is simple enough. You'll use a bus to connect the output of your MIDI instrument's Aux or Instrument track to the input of an Audio track to which you'll record.

**1** Assign the **output** of your instrument's Aux or Instrument track to an available bus. (In this case, I've chosen Bus 1-2.)

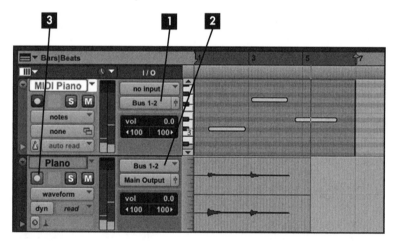

**2** After creating an Audio track to record to, **assign** the **input** of that track to the same bus that you chose for the output of the Aux or Instrument track (again, Bus 1-2 in this example).

**3** Now that you have your signals routed properly, you can **record** your **Audio track** normally (which we covered back in Chapter 4). You'll see that the level meters of the two tracks are identical.

# Editing MIDI

Editing operations that would be extremely difficult with audio,
such as fixing a single note in a chord, are easy with MIDI, if you
know how to use the tools available to you. That's what we'll discuss in this section.

## Editing with Tools

There are a number of ways to edit MIDI data, giving you a
greater degree of control over specific notes than you might have
when working with Audio tracks. Of course, you'll still have all the
region editing tools that you've come to know in the previous editing chapters—Selector, Grabber, and Trim (including the TCE Trim
tool) will still work with MIDI regions the same way that they've
worked with audio regions. In the interest of efficiency, I won't
rehash these basic (but powerful) ways of working in the Edit window, but do take some time to reacquaint yourself with these tools
when you get the opportunity.

The interesting thing about working with MIDI lies in the specificity
of control you have over your tracks. You can go beyond the relatively large region level and work with individual notes themselves,
and beyond. Even at these deeper levels, you still have use of the
editing tools that are already familiar to you, though their behavior
will be somewhat different. The first thing to do, though, is to
change your Edit window's view so that you can actually see what
you're working with.

**1** Click on the **Track View selector** on the desired track. (In this example, I've chosen the Bass track.) The Track View menu will appear.

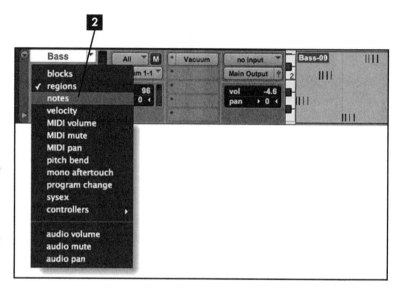

**2** The Track View menu allows you to choose the kind of data you will view and manipulate. Because this is an Instrument track and contains MIDI data, the menu will display all editable aspects of MIDI in Pro Tools, including controllers and system-exclusive data. You'll be working on note data first, so click on the **Notes** menu item.

※ The regions will fade out a bit, and a series of blocks will gain prominence. Each of these blocks represents a MIDI note.

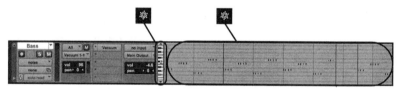

※ On the left edge of the MIDI track's Playlist area, you will notice an image of a piano keyboard. This side-facing keyboard indicates the pitches of the MIDI notes on the track.

Depending on the kind of track you're working with, your next step is to get your MIDI data into easy view. There are a few ways to do this, using some familiar tools.

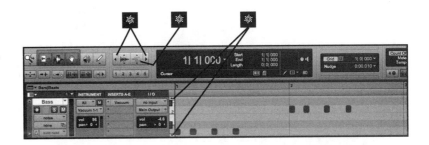

❊ Use the horizontal zoom buttons to see more or less of your timeline.

❊ Use the MIDI Zoom buttons to zoom *vertically* on your MIDI data. Note that the keyboard image to the left of the Playlist area will expand and contract accordingly.

❊ Click on the arrow at either end of the keyboard image to scroll the register of the track up or down.

## The Grabber Tool

The Grabber tool does just what it says—it allows you to grab objects in the Edit window and move them. Since we're working with a MIDI track in Notes view, your "objects" in this case are individual notes!

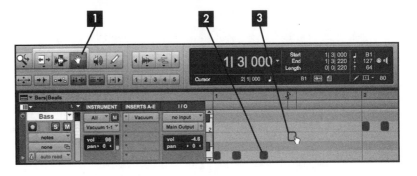

**1** If the Grabber tool isn't already selected, **click** the **Grabber tool** to activate it.

**2** **Click** on a **single note** in your track. The note will be highlighted, indicating that it has been selected and is ready to be moved.

**3** **Drag and drop** the **note** to a different pitch or timing, as desired.

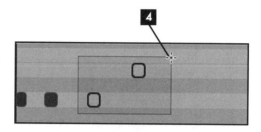

**4** If you want to move more than one note at a time, just **click and drag** a box around the **notes** you want to change. The group of notes will be highlighted, indicating that they are selected.

**5** **Drag and drop** the **group** of **notes** in the same manner that you moved a single note.

### ❊ SELECTIVE SELECTING

There's another way to move a group of notes: Just hold down the Shift key while clicking the notes you want to move. The selected notes will be highlighted.

### ❊ SELECTING A SINGLE PITCH

Here's a quick way to select *all* the notes of a given pitch on a MIDI or Instrument track: Just click on the desired note on the keyboard at the left of your track's Playlist area. All the notes of that pitch will be selected. This is particularly useful when you are dealing with MIDI drum tracks (which typically use repeated notes of identical pitch)!

## The Trim Tool

The Trim tool allows you to adjust the beginning and/or end of MIDI notes in much the same way you've changed region boundaries when working with Audio tracks.

### ❊ SETTING THINGS UP

If you're not in the Slip Edit mode, now would be a good time to switch to it, so that you can change your note lengths freely. Of course, you can use any of the edit modes depending on your work situation, but in this case, Slip will work the best.

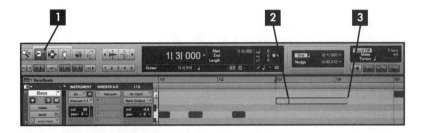

**1** If the Trim tool isn't already selected, **click** the **Trim tool** to activate it.

**2** **Click** on **either end** of a note in your track. The note will be highlighted, indicating that it is selected.

**3** **Drag** the **end** of the note as desired. The length of a note can be lengthened or shortened using the Trim tool.

## The Pencil Tool

The Pencil tool might just be the most useful of all the MIDI editing tools. Using the Pencil tool, you can create a MIDI note (or another type of MIDI data) and then modify it after the data is created.

> ✳ SETTING THINGS UP
>
> In the Slip Edit mode, you can create your data anywhere, but in this case, I want to create a quarter note right on Beat 4 of the first bar. To make the job easier, let's switch to Grid mode and set a grid value of 1/4 note. (For a review of this process, refer to Chapter 5.)

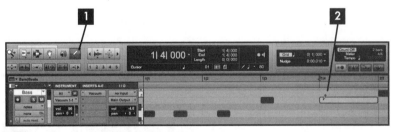

**1** If the Pencil tool isn't already selected, **click** the **Pencil tool** to activate it.

**2** **Click** on any **open area** of your track. Wherever you click, a MIDI note will be created. Since I've put myself in Grid mode with a grid value of 1/4 note, the note will be placed directly on the beat.

※ SETTING NOTE DURATION AND VELOCITY

With Pro Tools 8, you have new ways of setting default note durations and MIDI velocity values for notes created with the Pencil tool, making the Pencil tool even easier to use.

※ Click the Note Duration pop-up menu, located in the lower-left area of the Counters and Edit Selections section of the Edit window. The Note Duration menu will appear.

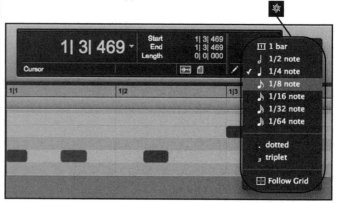

※ Choose the desired note duration from the list. (The currently selected duration will be indicated by a check mark.) Choosing the Follow Grid option will change your duration to continually match your grid settings (regardless of whether Grid mode is active).

※ Click the MIDI Velocity indicator (the value will be highlighted, as shown here) and type the desired default MIDI velocity. To confirm your value, press the Enter key.

## ❄ CREATING A SERIES OF NOTES WITH THE PENCIL TOOL

Creating a string of notes quickly can come in very handy, particularly when you're working with drum tracks. The Pencil tool makes it easy, if you use the Line version of the Pencil.

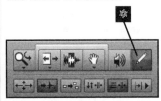

❄ Click and hold on the Pencil tool. A list of Pencil tool options will appear.

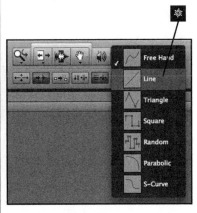

❄ This list of drawing shape variations will come in handy in a variety of situations (particularly when mixing, which we'll explore in the next chapter). In this instance, you'll want to use the Line variation of the tool, so select it from the list.

❄ Click and hold with your Pencil tool at the point where you want to *begin* entering new MIDI note data.

❄ Drag the Pencil cursor horizontally (left or right) to create a string of notes. Note that in this example, the duration of each note is an eighth note (based upon the note duration), and the spacing is every quarter note (based upon the grid value).

❄ **MORE POWER WITH THE PENCIL TOOL**

The Pencil tool is great for quick MIDI work—not only for its ability to create new notes, but also for its other functions. If you click in the body of an existing note, the Pencil tool will take on the function of a Grabber (allowing you to quickly move the note). If you move the Pencil tool to either end of an existing note, it will become a Trim tool (allowing you to adjust the beginning or end of the note).

❄ **PLAYING MIDI NOTES WHEN EDITING**

Sometimes it is very convenient to hear notes as you move or Tab through them, and sometimes it can be a distraction. Either way, Pro Tools makes it easy to work the way you want.

❄ Click the Play MIDI Notes When Editing indicator to toggle the feature on and off.

## The Event Menu

In addition to editing with tools, you can also transform your MIDI from the Event menu. Many of the features in this menu are commonly found in most MIDI sequencers and fall into the category of basic operations, but it is useful to know the layout of the menu and windows involved.

Here's how you start the process:

**1** Select the **group of notes** that you want to process.

**2** Click on the **Event menu**.

**3** Click on **Event Operations**. A second menu will appear.

**4** Choose the **process** you want to apply to the selection, and the appropriate window will open.

❋ GETTING AROUND IN THE EVENT OPERATIONS WINDOW

You can change MIDI processes without going back to the Event menu. Simply click on the menu at the top of the Event Operations dialog box to reveal the menu of Event Operations functions.

## Grid/Groove Quantize

At its most basic level, *quantize* is a MIDI function that aligns the timing of MIDI notes to a grid. It's commonly used to fix timing errors or to create mathematically "perfect" timing when the style of music calls for it. You'll find the Quantize function at the top of the Event Operations menu.

❋ The What to Quantize section allows you to choose individually which parts of your notes will be adjusted. (For example, if you wanted to have the beginning of your notes snap to the grid line but leave the end of the note unchanged, you'd check the Note On box only.)

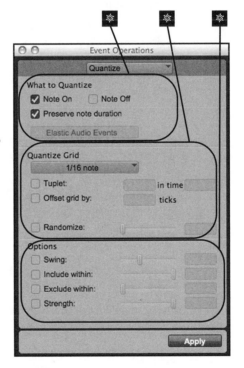

❋ The Quantize Grid section allows you to choose the resolution of your quantization. This includes Tuplet resolutions, commonly used to create a triplet-style feel, with three quantize points in the space where there would normally be only two. There's also a Randomize function, which will allow you to add a percentage of timing chaos. (See the note entitled "Advice on Randomizing" following this section.)

❋ The Options section will allow you to tweak your quantization and to choose how notes will be affected. Raising the Swing value will progressively add a triplet-style feel. The Include Within and Exclude Within parameters will allow you to choose how much of your data will be affected. (Including 100% and excluding 0% will ensure that all of your MIDI data is quantized.) Strength will allow you to choose how much to change your notes' original timing. For example, if your strength is set to 100%, your notes will be moved all the way to the nearest grid line, whereas at 50% strength they'll only be moved halfway to the nearest grid.

Beyond basic grid quantizing, there's Groove Quantize. When you use Groove Quantize, you won't be moving your notes' timing to your session's grid lines per se, but rather to a set of complex location points designed to emulate a certain musical feel. Fortunately, the process of groove quantizing is almost identical to regular grid quantizing. Here's how it works:

**1** Click the **Quantize Grid menu button**.

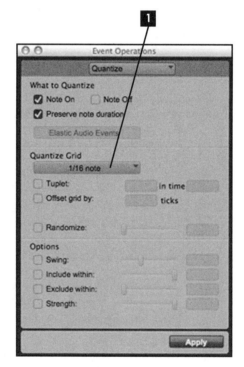

**2** The top part of this list is a selection of musical note grid values. **Choose** the desired **note value** to change your quantize resolution when you are quantizing to your session's grid.

**3** The bottom part of the list will present an assortment of musical grooves for you to use. **Choose** the desired **folder of grooves**, and from there a **specific groove**.

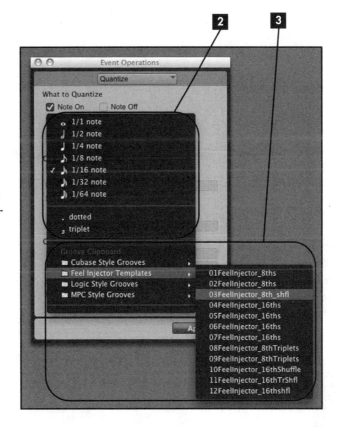

Users sometimes apply the Randomize feature to a MIDI drum track in the hopes that it will "humanize" the track, but this often has a negative effect upon the groove. (Remember, a live drummer, though mathematically imperfect, is not playing in a random fashion!) However, when used sparingly, the Randomize feature works very well with tracks that would normally be played by multiple musicians (string sections, brass sections, and so on), taking the edge off the mechanical accuracy sometimes associated with MIDI.

## Change Velocity

The Change Velocity window sports options with which you can manipulate MIDI velocity (how fast a key is pressed).

❋ The Set All To option allows you to assign a single velocity value to all selected notes.

❋ You can directly increase or decrease the velocity value by a set amount by using the Add or Subtract option.

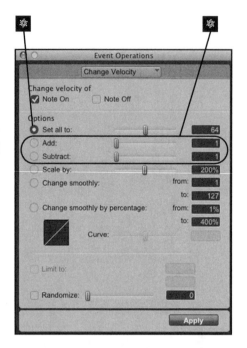

❋ You can scale, or proportionally change, the velocity of a set of notes using the Scale By option.

❋ You can use the Change Smoothly option to gradually change the velocity from the beginning of the selection to the end, resulting in an increase or decrease in intensity. By using the Change Smoothly by Percentage feature, you can even specify an exponential or logarithmic curve for the change.

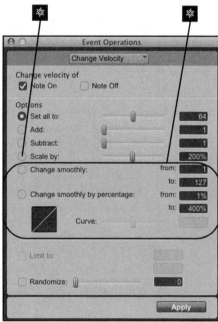

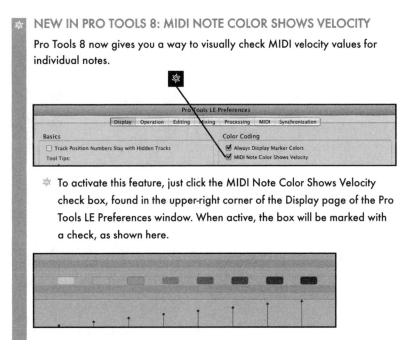

Pro Tools 8 now gives you a way to visually check MIDI velocity values for individual notes.

✳ To activate this feature, just click the MIDI Note Color Shows Velocity check box, found in the upper-right corner of the Display page of the Pro Tools LE Preferences window. When active, the box will be marked with a check, as shown here.

With the MIDI Note Color Shows Velocity preference checked, your MIDI notes will be lighter colored at lower velocities and darker at the higher velocities.

## Change Duration

The Change Duration window is similar to the Change Velocity window, but in this case, the parameters affect the length of the selected notes.

* The first radio button will enable you to set all durations to a single value or add or subtract a fixed value. (You can choose the desired behavior from the corresponding menu.)

* The Legato option will allow you to extend the duration of the selected notes. (The dropdown menu to the right of the radio button will allow you to specify either an overlap or a gap between notes.)

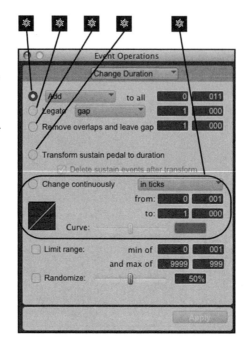

* The third radio button will allow you to remove overlaps (which can be problematic in some circumstances) and leave a specified gap between notes.

* The Transform Sustain Pedal to Duration radio button will detect pedal data and apply it to the durations of the affected notes.

* The Change Continuously option will allow durations to gradually change over time, similar to the Change Continuously feature of the Change Velocity window.

## Transpose

Transpose, a common MIDI operation, changes the note number of MIDI note data, effectively changing the pitch of your music. The options for Pro Tools' Transpose function are simple and straightforward.

❋ You can adjust pitch by octaves and/or semitones (half steps).

❋ You can transpose based upon relative pitches, selecting an original pitch and a destination pitch, to apply transposition to your selected notes.

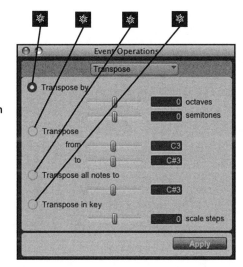

❋ You can change all pitches to a single pitch, regardless of their original pitch (which is particularly useful when you're working with drum tracks).

❋ You can move notes up or down by scale steps, based upon the active key in the key signatures ruler (which we'll discuss later in this chapter).

❋ BE CAREFUL WITH YOUR DRUM TRACKS!

Before you change the pitch of an entire section of a song, you might want to *exclude* your drum tracks from that transposition. Transposing drum kit patches tends to radically change the instrument assignments!

## Select/Split Notes

Once you've selected notes using the Selector or Grabber tool, you can further narrow down your selection by setting specific criteria. Once that's done, you can then transform them with another process or proceed to split the selected notes in a number of ways. Let's take a look:

**1** Whether you ultimately want to select or split the notes, you'll start by defining your selection based upon some sort of pitch value. You can **select all notes, set a range** (using the Notes Between function), or **pick out notes** starting from the top or bottom of each chord in the selected area.

**2** You can further **refine** your **selection** based upon velocity, duration, or even position (measured in beats|ticks) within the selected area.

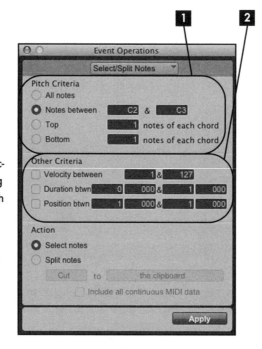

**3a** If you want to take your selected notes and process them further, **choose** the **Select Notes radio button, click** the **Apply button**, and **move on** to your **next step**.

OR

**3b** If your goal is to split the notes, **choose** the **Split Notes radio button**. You have a number of options in this case:

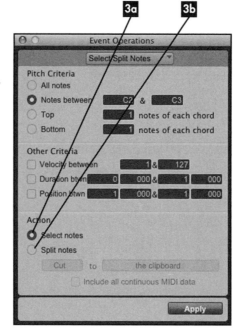

❋ Clicking the menu at the lower left of the window will give you the option of choosing whether the notes will be cut from the selected area or copied (leaving the original notes intact).

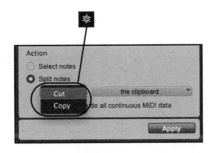

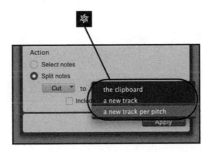

❋ The menu at the lower right of the window will allow you to choose your split notes' destination. You can send them to the clipboard (for pasting at a later time), to a new track (all the split notes will go to that track), or to a new track per pitch (for example, if you split up a four-note chord, you would create four separate tracks, each with one pitch).

## Input Quantize

The Input Quantize feature works just like the basic Quantize function with one important difference. Whereas Quantize is applied to MIDI data manually after it has been recorded, Input Quantize applies the change as soon as a record pass is finished. This feature is particularly nifty for technically challenged people like me, fixing my timing automatically!

❄ Select the Enable Input
Quantize check box to turn on
the Input Quantize feature.
Don't forget—Input Quantize
will stay enabled until you
manually turn it off!

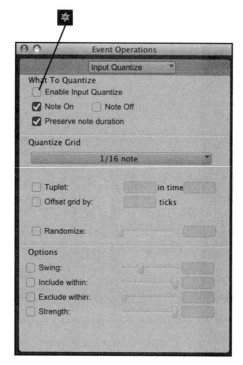

Just like regular quantize, Input Quantize can align notes to the grid or to a
groove template. You can choose the resolution and type of quantization from
the Quantize Grid pull-down menu.

## Step Input

It's been said that MIDI can lend a helping hand to pedagogically
challenged keyboardists (like yours truly), and Step Input is probably the ultimate expression of this aspect. Forget slowing down the
tempo so that you can play a difficult passage slowly; Step Input
allows you to play completely out of time—set a starting point and a
note value, and off you go! You can play as fast or slow as you
want, and notes will be sequentially created. Here's how:

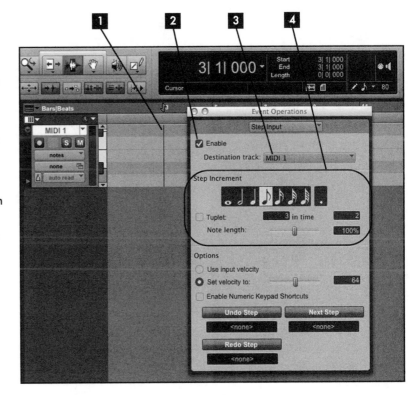

**1** Set the session's **timeline insertion** at the point at which you want to begin creating new notes.

**2** Click the **Enable check box** to activate Step Input.

**3** Choose the **track** you'll be writing to from the Destination Track menu. (Click the menu button to reveal a list of MIDI and instrument tracks in your session.)

**4** Choose the desired **note value** by clicking the appropriate Step Increment button. The Note Length slider will allow you to change the duration of the notes you create. (In this example, I've selected eighth notes as my step increment, and the 100% note duration means that each new note will be a full-length eighth note.)

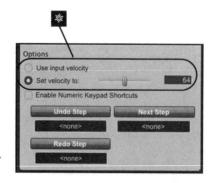

❋ You have a choice when it comes to note velocities: You can choose Use Input Velocity (each new note will be created at the velocity at which it was played) or Set Velocity To (which will assign a fixed velocity level to each note created).

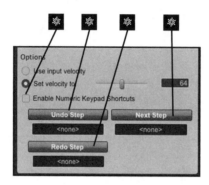

❋ Click the Enable Numeric Keypad Shortcuts box to enable your keyboard's numeric keypad to change the step increment settings. (Number 1 will change the value to a whole note, 2 will change the value to a half note, and so on.)

❋ Made a mistake? The Undo Step button will clear your last note entry.

❋ Next Step will skip the current step and move you to the next increment, leaving a silent step between notes (a rest).

❋ Finally, the Redo Step button will redo the most recently entered step, if it has been undone.

## Restore Performance

Pro Tools' Restore Performance feature is a simple enough operation, but it's invaluable when you need it. Think of the Restore Performance option as an improved version of the Undo operation. Consider this: When you save and close your session, the Pro Tools' undo history is cleared, which prohibits you from undoing things such as audio region edits and so on the next time the session is opened. What makes Restore Performance so special is that it extends beyond the last time you saved your session and the traditional levels of undo!

❋ Once you've selected the MIDI notes that you want to affect, you can selectively restore specific aspects of your MIDI data (timing, duration, velocity, or pitch)—it's up to you what to recover and what to keep current. When you restore any of these aspects, your MIDI data will revert to its original state (when it was recorded) or to the last time the performance was flattened (which we'll talk about next), whichever happened most recently.

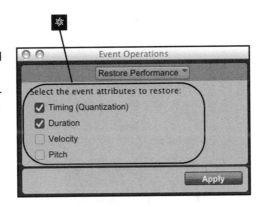

## Flatten Performance

Suppose you've perfected your MIDI data through meticulous editing, and you want to make sure you can easily recover this ideal state. That's the perfect time to flatten the data. When you choose to Flatten Performance, you "print" your MIDI data to your session and remove the option to undo any previous edits that you've performed. If, in the future, you choose to restore the performance, it will revert to this new flattened state.

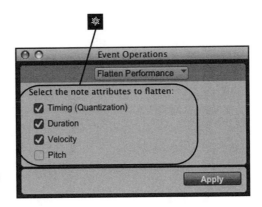

❋ Just as with the Restore Performance option, you can selectively flatten specific aspects of your MIDI data. When you flatten your performance, you will effectively set a new restore point (for any of the attribute boxes that you've checked) that you can recall at will, using the Restore Performance feature.

## Tempo Operations

As you learned in Chapter 6, your session's bars|beats time scale and your MIDI tempo settings are interrelated and form the timing basis for your tick-based tracks. You can control tempo quickly and easily from the tempo ruler or even enter values numerically.

&#10070; For your session to follow the tempo ruler (as opposed to a manually set static tempo), you'll need to have the Conductor Track button selected in the MIDI controls section of the Transport or Edit window.

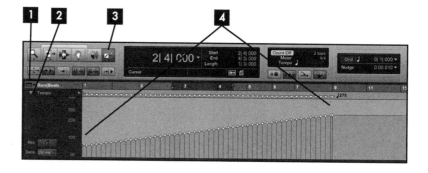

**1** If you're not seeing your tempo ruler, you'll need to reveal it in your Edit window now. **Go to** the **View menu**, **select** the **Rulers menu item**, and **choose Tempo**. You can also select it quickly by clicking the Ruler menu icon (indicated here) and choosing Tempo from the menu.

**2** Click on the **Tempo Editor Expand/Collapse triangle** to reveal the expanded tempo ruler.

**3** Click the **Pencil tool** (in this example, with the Line option selected).

**4** Changing tempo is very simple—just **click and drag** to create tempo change data.

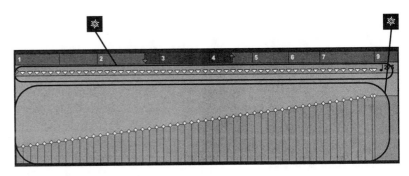

❋ The tempo change is represented as a straight ramp (because we were using the Pencil in Line mode), from 126 beats per minute up to 170 beats per minute. With the Pencil tool, you can write (and overwrite) tempo changes with the Freehand, Line, Parabolic, or S-Curve settings.

❋ The tempo changes that were created are also shown as a series of triangular value changes. These values can also be edited by clicking and dragging or even double-clicking and typing a specific tempo value, though the more graphic tempo display as described above is far easier for many Pro Tools LE users to work with.

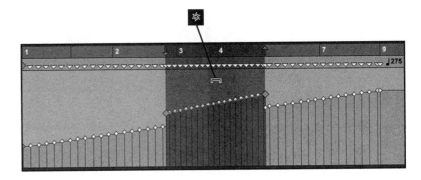

❋ Though changing tempo with the Pencil tool might be the easiest method, it's not the only way. By using the Trim tool (shown here), you can scale your automation up or down as desired. (Note that the Trim tool "points down" when editing tempo, as opposed to the normal horizontal facing of the tool when trimming region boundaries.)

You can also create a tempo change by choosing specific times and values.

**1** From the Event menu and then from the Tempo Operations submenu, you can choose to **create** a **tempo change** in a variety of shapes. The process is similar regardless of the shape you've chosen.

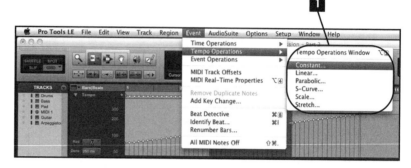

**2** Enter the **start and end points** for your tempo change.

**3** Select the **tempo value(s)**.

**4** When you're finished, **click** the **Apply button**, and your tempo change will be applied.

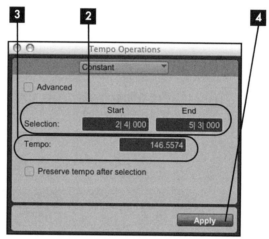

## Changing Meter and Renumbering Bars

In addition to changing your session's tempo, you can also change the meter upon which your measures (bars) are based and even shift the numbering of bars.

**1** From the Event menu and then from the Time Operations submenu, you'll find the Change Meter menu item. **Select** this **item** to reveal the Time Operations/Change Meter dialog box. Here are some key features:

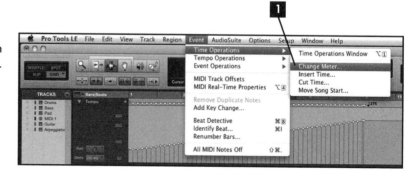

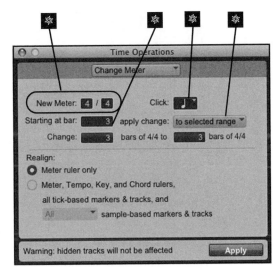

❅ Type the desired meter in the New Meter section.

❅ You can change the resolution of your click by clicking the Click display and then choosing the desired resolution from the subsequent drop-down menu. For example, if you change your meter to 6/8, you might want to set your click up as eighth notes or dotted quarter notes.

❅ Type the starting measure of your meter change.

❅ The Apply Change button will allow you to choose the duration of your meter change. Clicking this button will allow you to choose To Session End, To Selected Range, or Until Next Bar from a drop-down menu.

Renumbering bars is even easier. . . .

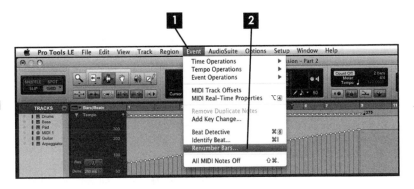

**1** Click on the **Event menu**.

**2** Click on **Renumber Bars**. The Renumber Bars dialog box will open.

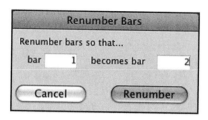

The use of the Renumber Bars dialog box is fairly self-explanatory—just enter the changes that you want to make and hit the Renumber button. This won't change the way your session sounds, but it will affect the numbering of your song's measures.

※ MAKING THE MOST OF THE RULERS

In the previous sections, you learned how to change tempo and meter from the Event menu. Although that's a great way to work, it's not the only way. You can also access the Tempo Change and Meter Change dialog boxes directly from the rulers. There are two basic methods.

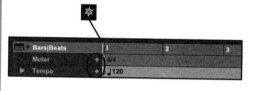

※ Click the Add Meter Change or Add Tempo Change button—indicated by a plus (+) sign—to open the appropriate dialog box. Once the box is open, just type in the desired location and value and click the OK button.

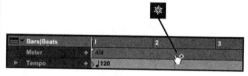

※ Here's a way to save a step. If you hold down the Control key (Mac) or Start key (PC) and move your mouse to the appropriate ruler, you'll note that your cursor will become a pointing hand with a plus (+) sign, as shown here. Just click at the position where you want to insert your change, and the Tempo Change or Meter Change window will appear, with the clicked location entered into the Location field.

## Changing the Song Start

Suppose you've written your song, only to find that you need to place some audio (or MIDI) *before* Bar 1. You could renumber the measures (which we just discussed), or you can take advantage of Pro Tools' Move Song Start feature. As with many aspects of Pro Tools, there are a number of ways to get the job done.

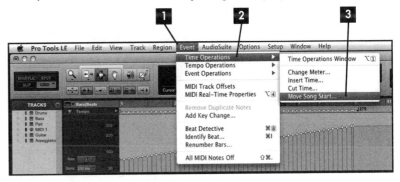

**1** Click on the **Event menu**.

**2** Click on Time **Operations**. A submenu will appear.

**3** Click on **Move Song Start**. The Time Operations/Move Song Start dialog box will open.

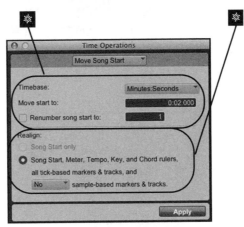

❋ The top section of the Move Song Start dialog box will allow you to enter a new location for your song start. The Timebase menu will allow you to choose different time scales for this choice. In this example, I've chosen Minutes:Seconds as my timebase and moved my song start later by two seconds.

❋ The bottom area will allow you to choose what aspects of your session are to be affected by the movement of the song start:

✧ Selecting the top radio button—Song Start Only—will only change your session's tempo ruler and will leave all regions where they are.

✧ The bottom radio button will move the song start; tempo, key, and chord rulers; and all tick-based tracks and markers. (By default, MIDI and Instrument track regions are tick-based.)

You further have the option of additionally affecting regions on sample-based markers and tracks (by default, Audio tracks are sample-based) by clicking the menu button. In this example, no sample-based markers or tracks will be changed. For more information on the distinction between tick-based and sample-based, refer to Chapter 6.

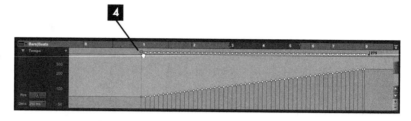

**4** Here's perhaps an easier way. Just **click and drag** the **song start marker** on your tempo ruler. (It will be slightly larger than the other tempo objects and is colored red.)

## Cutting and Inserting Time

Though the nonlinear nature of the modern DAW is an undeniable advantage, from time to time you may long for the simplicity of the old tape-based cut-and-splice method. Pro Tools has just what the doctor ordered, in the form of the Cut Time and Insert Time operations.

**1** Though not strictly necessary, **making** a **selection** of what you want to cut or insert will make the process easier.

**2** Click on the **Event menu**.

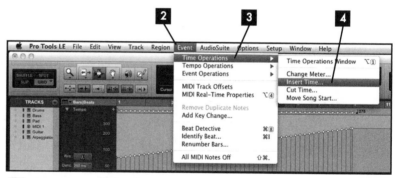

**3** Click on **Time Operations**. A submenu will appear.

**4** Click on **Insert Time** (shown here) or **Cut Time**. The appropriate Time Operations dialog box will open.

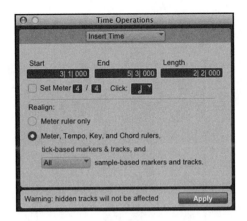

Whether you choose to insert or cut time, you'll notice that the dialog box bears great similarity to the Move Song Start window, with the main difference being that instead of shifting the timeline, you're either adding to it or taking away from it. If you've made a selection, you'll find these values reflected in the Start, End, and Length fields.

# More MIDI Tips

Before we finish our focus on the wonderful world of MIDI, there are a few more key features to explore.

## The Event List

Most longtime MIDI users are familiar with the traditional MIDI Event list, a simple yet powerful window in which you can type exact values for your MIDI data. Though it is among the oldest of all MIDI editing environments, it can come in very handy when you want to get specific with your MIDI. Here's how to use it in Pro Tools:

**1** **Click** on the **Window menu**.

**2** **Click** on **MIDI Event List**. The MIDI Event List window will appear.

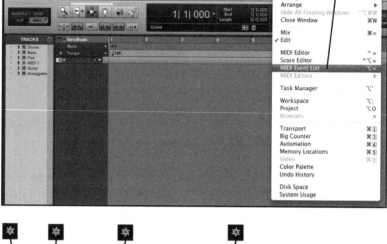

※ The button in the upper-left corner of the Event List window indicates the name of the MIDI track being viewed. Clicking this button will reveal a drop-down menu of all MIDI and Instrument tracks, where you can choose different tracks.

※ The Start column shows the beginning time for each event, listed sequentially.

※ The Event column indicates the type of individual events (note, pan, and so on), as well as their value.

※ The Length/Info column shows more specific information about each event.

✳ So how do you tweak this data? Easy—just double-click on the value you want to change, type the new value, and press the Enter key!

✳ Click the Event List pop-up menu button to reveal more event-related options.

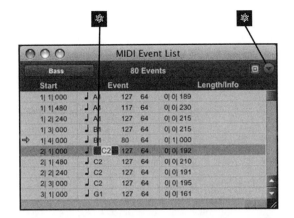

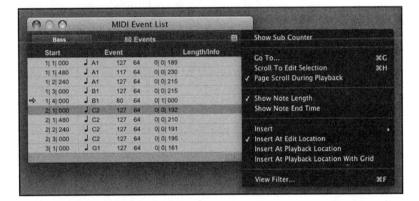

The Event List pop-up menu will give a variety of viewing options, as well as allow you to create new MIDI events (using the Insert function).

## Removing Duplicate MIDI Notes

From time to time, a MIDI note can be doubly triggered during the recording process. (In my personal experience, this has happened mostly with MIDI drum controllers.) Occasionally, these duplicate notes can result in erratic behavior from your MIDI devices (notes being cut off prematurely and so on), so Pro Tools includes a Remove Duplicate Notes operation.

**1** Select the **MIDI data** that you want to clean up through the removal of duplicate MIDI notes.

**2** Click on the **Event menu**.

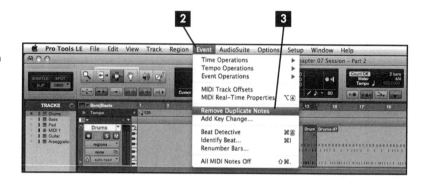

**3** Click on **Remove Duplicate Notes**. The duplicate MIDI notes will be removed—you're finished!

## Viewing and Editing Non-Note Data

Earlier in this chapter, you learned how to edit non-note data (such as volume, velocity, or pan) with the MIDI Event list, but in most cases it's more easily accomplished on the track itself. The process is a straightforward one, but you've got to know how to view it before you can work with it.

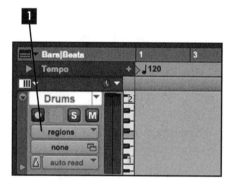

**1** In this example, we're looking at (and thus able to edit) regions, indicated by the label on the Track Display Format button. **Click** the **Track View Selector button**. A menu of other view options will appear.

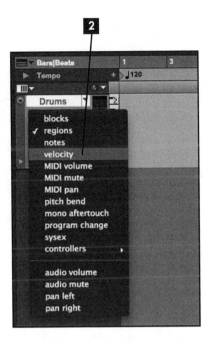

**2** **Select** the kind of **MIDI data** with which you want to work. The track to the right will change to show the kind of data you selected.

In this case, I've chosen to change my track's view to show velocity data. I can use the same tools I've used for the note data (such as the Grabber, Trim, Selector, and Pencil tools, and so on) to change these values.

We've talked about track "lanes" before (in Chapter 5), but now we'll use them in a different way. Through the use of track lanes, you can view not only non-note MIDI data, but also multiple types of non-note data simultaneously!

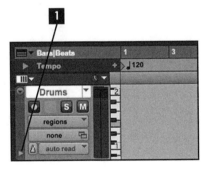

**1** **Click** the **Show/Hide Automation Lanes button** (the small triangle in the lower-left corner of the track row). An indented track lane will appear below the track's main Playlist area.

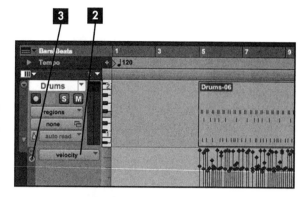

**2** **Click** the automation lane's **Lane View Selector button** to choose the desired view, just as you did with the Track View Selector earlier in this chapter.

**3** If you want to see more track lanes, just **click** the **Add Automation Lane button** (the small plus (+) button on the left margin of the lane). If you want to hide a lane, just click the minus (–) sign.

## MIDI Real-Time Properties

The MIDI Real-Time Properties feature is relatively new to Pro Tools (introduced in version 7), but it has already become one of my favorite additions to the DAW. What sets this feature apart from the MIDI processes we've discussed so far is that these Real-Time Properties, which are perhaps better described as real-time processes, only alter the data as it's being played back and don't alter the recorded data in any permanent way.

> **IF YOU'RE WORKING WITH THE TUTORIAL SESSION**
>
> If you're following the Chapter 07 Session – Part 2 tutorial session, let's solo the Drums track. If you select the first region on the track, you'll have a nice eight-measure selection to work with. Putting yourself into loop playback will let you hear the drum beat continually. To start off, we'll use MIDI Real-Time Properties to change the feel of the drums.

Though there are a couple of different ways to use MIDI Real-Time Properties, the most straightforward method is to use the Real-Time Properties Edit window column, so we'll begin there.

**1** If you're not currently seeing the Real-Time Properties column, you'll have to reveal it in your Edit window. From the View menu, **choose Edit Window Views**. A submenu will appear.

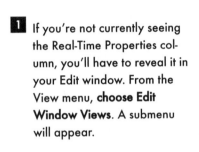

**2** This submenu is a list of columns available in your Edit window. (Shown columns are indicated by a check mark.) **Click** the **Real-Time Properties menu item** (if it isn't already checked), and the Real-Time Properties column will appear.

**3** Here's another way to show the Real-Time Properties column. **Click** the **Edit Window View Selector icon**, located in the upper-left corner of the Edit window's Track area. A list (identical to the Edit Window Views submenu) will appear, and you can make sure that the appropriate columns are being shown. (Again, shown columns are indicated by a check mark.)

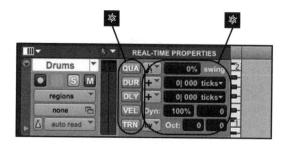

❄ In the Real-Time Properties column, you'll notice five enable buttons, which will allow you to adjust Quantize (QUA), Duration (DUR), Delay (DLY), Velocity (VEL), and Transpose (TRN). In the image shown here, all of the enable buttons are selected in order to show the complete layout of the column. Note that these buttons only appear on MIDI or Instrument tracks.

❄ Once a given enable button is clicked, you'll see a set of adjustable parameters displayed to the right of the enabled button. This is essentially a tiny version of the main parameter(s) that you would otherwise have chosen in the Event Operations dialog boxes.

**4** For this example, we'll try changing the timing of the drums track, so **click** the **Quantize button** (labeled QUA). You'll immediately see that the regions on your track are marked with a T (for Track-based Real-Time Processes) in the upper-right corner of each region, indicating that they are now being quantized in real time.

**5** Let's have some fun with some Groove Quantize. **Click** the **button** immediately to the right of the QUA button. A list will appear.

**6** Here's where it gets fun. **Choose** the **quantization** that you want to try out. For this particular example, I've chosen FeelInjector_8th_shfl from the Feel Injector Templates folder, since it's a very different feel than the original beat. If you feel that this difference is an improvement, you're finished. If you don't like it, no problem—you can choose any other kind of quantization you want, or you can choose not to quantize at all by clicking the QUA button and turning off Real-Time Properties. That's the beauty of this feature—nothing you've done is permanent!

❊ **TWEAKING ON THE FLY**

MIDI Real-Time Properties is great not only because it processes your MIDI as it plays, but because you can also change settings and immediately hear the result. In the case of quantization, you can change the feel during playback and listen to how your changes will affect the track and your entire song.

Although the Real-Time Properties Edit window column is the easiest way to access this feature, there is another method—through the use of the Real-Time Properties floating window—that will give you extra flexibility.

The fundamental difference between the Real-Time Properties column and the Real-Time Properties floating window is this: Changes made in a Real-Time Properties column will apply to an entire track, and any regions that you drag onto that track will reflect these real-time changes. The floating window, on the other hand, will allow you to modify any *selected regions* or *tracks*, and individual regions modified by this window will retain these changes, even if they're moved to another track.

Using the Real-Time Properties floating window may be a little more complex than using the Edit window column, but the flexibility that you gain is well worth the effort.

> ❄ **IF YOU'RE WORKING WITH THE TUTORIAL SESSION**
>
> If you listen to the tutorial session's Bass track, you'll hear that there's a problem with the pitch of the second region. (Soloing the track will help you to hear it.) In this section, we'll use the Real-Time Properties floating window to change this region (with transposition) but leave the rest of the track unchanged.

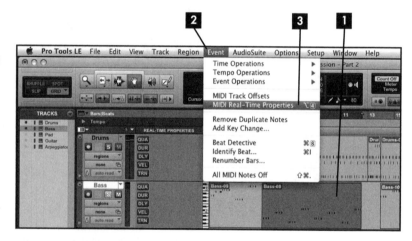

**1** Select the region(s) or track(s) that you want to change.

**2** Click the **Event menu.**

**3** Click the **MIDI Real-Time Properties menu item.** The Real-Time Properties floating window will appear.

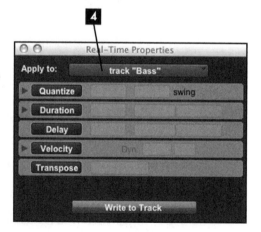

**4** The first order of business is to choose what selected elements you wish to affect. **Click** the **Apply To button.**

**5** The Apply To list will reflect any track(s) and region(s) that are currently selected. In this example, the Bass track is selected, as is the region Bass-08. Since we just want to change the selected region, **click** the **Bass-08 menu item**.

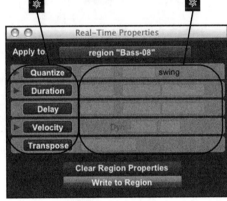

❄ As you've seen before with the Real-Time Properties Edit window column, you have the option of changing Quantize, Duration, Delay, Velocity, and Transpose.

❄ To the right of each Enable button is an area where you can adjust parameters and values as needed.

**6** Click the appropriate Enable button to affect the desired parameter. If you're following the tutorial session, you'll want to change the pitch of the selected region, so click the Transpose button. (You'll see that the area to the right of the button becomes active.)

**7** Enter the desired **values** in the appropriate fields. If you're using the tutorial session, the selected region can be easily fixed by transposing it up by one octave. (But don't take my word for it—use your ears!)

385
❄ ❄ ❄

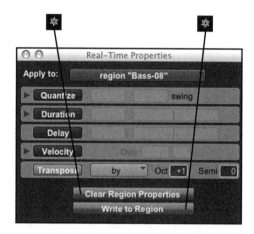

* Individual regions that are altered with the MIDI Real-Time Properties floating window are indicated by an R (for Region-based Real-Time Processes) in the upper-right corner of the region.

* Remember that when you're using MIDI Real-Time Properties (through either the column view or the floating window), you're working nondestructively. You can quickly remove any region-based changes by clicking the Clear Region Properties button.

* On the other hand, if you want to work destructively, you can apply your changes more permanently by clicking the Write to Region button. Your MIDI data will be changed (and the R will disappear from the region, since it's no longer being processed in real time).

## Key Signatures

Those of you who read traditional Western music notation (the notes, staffs, and other symbols that we commonly associate with written music) know that a *key signature* is a notational device that tells the reader what tonal structure, or key, the music is in. You'll typically find a key signature at the beginning of a piece of music, and additional key signatures may appear later in the piece to indicate a harmonic change (commonly referred to as a key change).

Pro Tools includes a key signature ruler to help you organize your music and keep track of what key you're in. In typical Pro Tools fashion, though, the functionality of key signatures goes beyond the basics. Let's take a quick look.

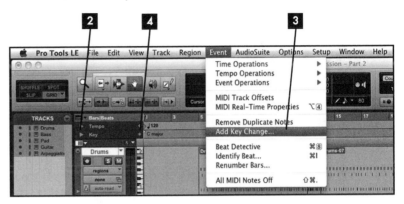

**1** The Key Signature ruler can be shown just like any other ruler. **Go to** the **View menu, choose** the **Rulers menu item,** and then **choose Key Signature** from the submenu. You can also choose to show the key signature ruler from the Ruler View icon (at the right-hand side of the main time scale), as we discussed back in Chapter 2.

**2** To see an expanded display of the key signature ruler, **click** the **triangle icon** to the left of the word Key.

**3** By default, the key signature of a Pro Tools session is the key of C major (no sharps or flats). To change that key signature or add a new key signature, **go to** the **Event menu** and **choose** the **Add Key Change menu item**. The Key Change dialog window will appear.

**4** If your key signature ruler is visible, you can also change or create a key signature by **clicking** the **Add Key Signature** button to the right of the word Key (indicated by a plus (+) sign). The Key Change dialog window will appear.

※ You can choose either major or minor key signatures by clicking the appropriate radio button in the upper-left corner of the Key Change window, and from there choose the specific key that you want to use. (Just click on the desired key signature.)

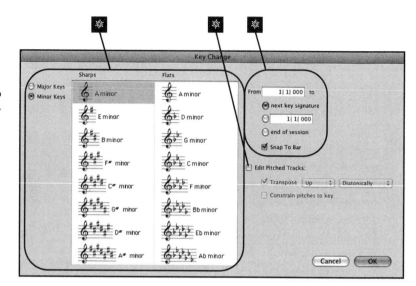

※ In the From field, you'll be able to choose where your key signature will be placed, and the radio buttons below this section will let you determine the duration of that key signature. (The default radio button is to next key signature, which works well in most situations.) Checking the Snap to Bar box will automatically set key changes to begin and end at the beginnings of bars (the most traditional way to use key signatures).

※ By default, a key signature is simply a visual marker for your convenience, but you can choose to have the key change your session's pitched tracks by clicking the Edit Pitched Tracks box.

※ **HUH?!?**

What the heck is a pitched track, you ask? Good question—we'll get to that in just a second.

❋ If you decide to edit your pitched tracks, you can change their tonality by clicking the Transpose check box. To the right of the Transpose check box are two drop-down menus:

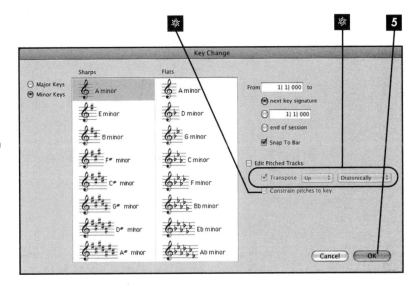

☼ The first menu will allow you to transpose your notes either up or down in pitch—pretty straightforward stuff.

☼ The second menu will allow you to transpose either chromatically or diatonically—and this can get a little tricky. Chromatic transposition (the simplest form) will merely move your existing notes up or down by a set number of half steps. Diatonic transposition will still move notes up or down, but will also automatically adjust notes to fit the new tonality (major or minor). "Blue" notes and other non-scale tones will retain their relationship to the tonic (the key letter) when transposing diatonically.

❋ Finally, the Constrain Pitches to Key check box will adjust all notes to fit the chosen key.

### ❋ IF YOU'RE WORKING WITH THE TUTORIAL SESSION

Many of you will quickly realize that this song isn't in C Major (the default key signature of Pro Tools), but rather in the key of A minor (which coincidentally also has no flats or sharps). Please change the key signature beginning at the start of Bar 1 to A minor, without editing any pitched tracks. (Refer to the image of the Key Change dialog window for the correct settings.)

**5** When you've made your choices, just **click OK**, and your new key signature will be created. You can create additional key signatures at any other point in your session.

## Editing Pitched Tracks

There's a concept closely related to key signatures, and that's the idea of pitched tracks. In Pro Tools, MIDI and Instrument tracks can either be pitched, in which case the notes are tonal in nature and should therefore follow key changes, or unpitched, in which case MIDI notes trigger non-tonal sounds. Drum kits are great examples of unpitched tracks. Here's how to change a drum track from being pitched (the default state for MIDI and Instrument tracks) to unpitched.

**※ IF YOU'RE WORKING WITH THE TUTORIAL SESSION**

Just to spice things up a bit, we'll add a key change to our song. Before we do that, though, we'll have to change the Drums track from pitched to unpitched, so that it doesn't change when the key change is applied.

**1** Click the **Playlist Selector button** of the desired track (in this example, the Drums track). A menu will appear.

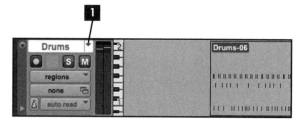

**2** By default, all MIDI and Instrument tracks are set to be pitched, indicated by a check mark next to the word Pitched. Just **click** the **Pitched menu item** to remove the check mark, and you're done—the track is now unpitched.

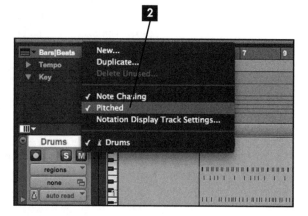

❅ Now, when you add a key change to your session, you can effectively use the Edit Pitched Tracks feature. With this box checked, the key changes you choose will affect all pitched MIDI and Instrument tracks (bass tracks, piano tracks, and so on) but leave your unpitched tracks (in this example, the drums) untouched.

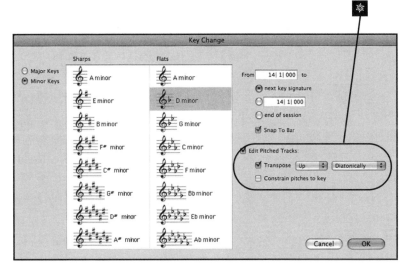

❅ IF YOU'RE WORKING WITH THE TUTORIAL SESSION

Try adding a key change to the key of D minor at Measure 14 (after the drum break), making sure to edit your pitched tracks. (Refer to the image of the Key Change dialog window for the correct settings.)

## Panic!

Reality check: Sometimes things go wrong. Worse yet, sometimes the things that go wrong can be audible, as in the case of a "stuck" MIDI note that never ends. When that happens, the most important thing to do is to stop the data and turn off those notes!

**1** Click on the **Event menu**.

**2** Click on the **All MIDI Notes Off menu item** (quickly!). A MIDI note-off command will be sent on all channels, on all ports of your MIDI interface, and through the four virtual MIDI connections.

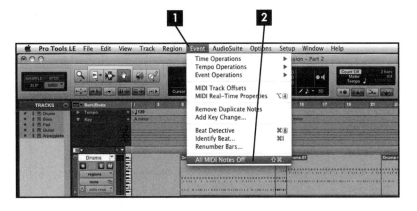

> ⁂ PANIC SHORTCUT
>
> The fastest way to trigger the All MIDI Notes Off function is to use the shortcut
> keys: Shift+Command+. (period key) will do it on the Mac, and Shift+Ctrl+.
> (period key) will do it on the PC.

## Importing and Exporting MIDI Data

One of MIDI's greatest advantages is its broad compatibility.
Nearly every MIDI application can utilize MIDI's SMF (*Standard
MIDI File*) format, and Pro Tools is no exception.

### Importing MIDI Data from the File Menu

Just as you can import an audio file to an Audio track, you can import
a standard MIDI file to one or more MIDI tracks in your session.

**1** Click on **File**.

**2** Select **Import**.

**3** Select **MIDI**. The Open dialog
box will appear.

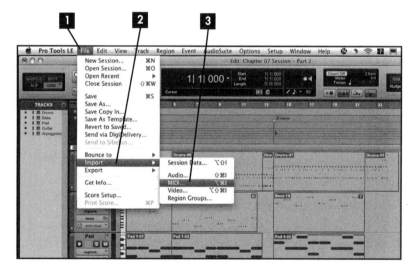

**4** In the Open dialog box, **select the MIDI file** you want to import.

**5** Click the **Open button**. The MIDI Import Options dialog box will open.

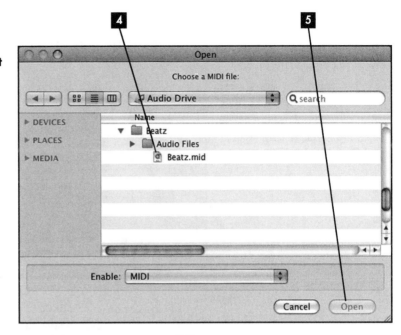

❀ The Destination section of the MIDI Import Options dialog box will allow you to choose whether the imported MIDI data will go to a new track (or tracks) or simply be added to the Regions list.

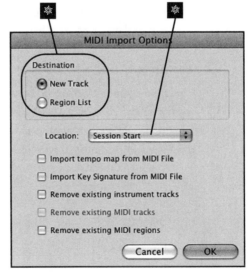

❀ The Location drop-down menu will let you choose where the region will be deposited on the timeline. In this image, the new MIDI data will begin at the session start, but you also have the option of choosing the song start (if it's different from the session start), the beginning of a selection, or a specific spot in your session. (The same Spot dialog box that you use in Spot mode will appear.)

❋ You have the option of also importing that MIDI file's tempo map or key signatures. Be careful, though—importing these will overwrite the preexisting tempo or key signature rulers in your session.

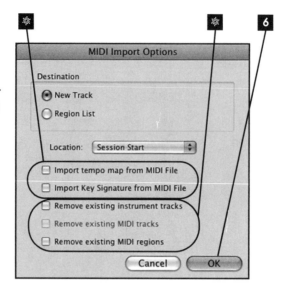

❋ Finally, you have the option of removing any preexisting Instrument tracks, MIDI tracks, or MIDI regions in your session.

**6** When you've chosen the options that work best, **click OK**. The MIDI will be immediately imported into your session according to your settings.

## Importing MIDI Data from the Workspace

Just as you can import audio from the Workspace window with ease, you can also import MIDI. When it comes to importing MIDI, though, the news gets even better, because you can import an entire song's worth of material with just a click and a drag. Here's how.

**1** Click **Window**.

**2** Click the **Workspace menu item**. The Workspace Browser will appear, as you've seen before in Chapter 3.

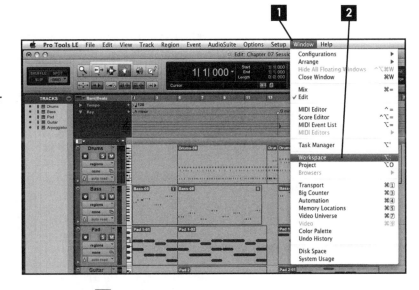

**3** Drag the desired **MIDI file** into your Edit window's Playlist area, just as you've done before with audio files. (You can also drag to the Regions or Tracks list if you like.) When applicable, the MIDI Import Options dialog box will appear, as you've seen earlier in this section.

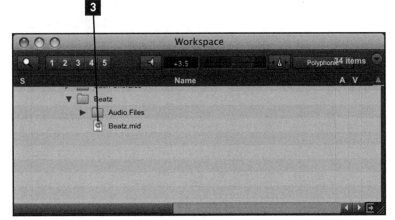

The individual MIDI tracks included in the SMF file will be created in your Edit window, and the appropriate regions will be created.

❋ AFTER YOU IMPORT

Keep in mind that even after you import your MIDI data, you'll still have to set your MIDI output and Aux track(s) before you can play and hear your MIDI data through the Pro Tools Mixer.

❋ ❋ ❋

## Exporting MIDI Data

When you save your session, your MIDI data will automatically be saved in that session file—there's usually no need to save your MIDI data as a separate file. However, from time to time you may need to save the MIDI portion of your session to a Standard MIDI file so that you can open it in a different program.

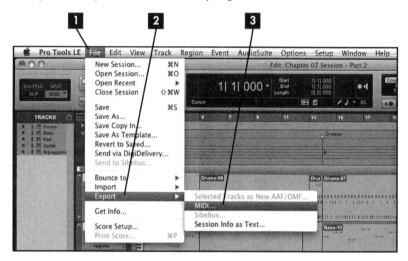

1 Click on **File**.

2 Click on **Export**.

3 Click on **MIDI**. The Export MIDI Settings dialog box will appear.

Before you can choose where you will save your SMF MIDI file, you'll need to make a few choices in the Export MIDI Settings dialog box.

**4** Click the **MIDI File Format button** to choose what kind of Standard MIDI File you'll be creating. You have two options.

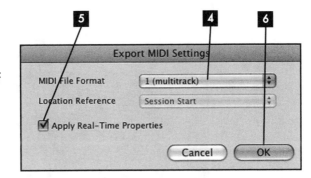

❋ Select the 0 (Single-Track) option to save all of your data as a single MIDI track, regardless of how many MIDI tracks you may have in your session. (This is commonly used in multimedia applications.)

❋ Select the 1 (Multitrack) option to preserve the multitrack organization of your MIDI data. This is the type of Standard MIDI file most commonly used in professional circles, allowing your tracks to be re-created in any program that supports Type 1 Standard MIDI files.

**5** Click the **Apply Real-Time Properties check box** to "print" any Real-Time Properties you may have in your session to your new Standard MIDI file.

**6** When you're finished, **click** on **OK**. A standard Save dialog box will appear, allowing you to choose the name and location for your new SMF.

Here's a way to export MIDI on a track-by-track basis.

**1** Right-click on the desired **track name** (in either the Playlist area or the Tracks list). A menu will appear.

**2** Choose the **Export MIDI menu item**. The Export MIDI Settings dialog box will appear, just as you've seen before. **Make** your **choices, click** the **OK** button, and **save** your **file**—easy!

# New in Pro Tools 8: MIDI Editor and Score Editor Windows

As I mentioned at the beginning of this chapter, Pro Tools 8 has made significant improvements over previous versions in the area of MIDI and music production. The addition of new virtual instruments (such as the DB-33 and Mini Grand) alone is a real leap forward, but the advancements don't end there.

At the heart of Pro Tools 8's new music production power are the MIDI Editor and Score Editor windows. These two new editing environments combine powerful new features with the tried-and-true editing tools that have made Pro Tools a leader in the audio editing world. What does this all mean? Basically this: With the MIDI Editor and Score Editors, you'll be able to apply the editing skills you've learned in previous chapters in a whole new way!

## The MIDI Editor

The MIDI Editor is the place to go if you want to get a close look at MIDI and Instrument tracks. There are two ways that you can access the MIDI Editor environment—with the Docked MIDI Editor (which is part of your Edit window) or through a stand-alone MIDI Editor window.

### The Docked MIDI Editor

The Docked MIDI Editor is a component of your Edit window, but one you might not have seen yet. Let's take a look.

**1** Click on **View**.

**2** Choose **Other Displays**.

**3** Choose the **MIDI Editor menu item**. (A check mark will appear next to displayed elements.) The Docked MIDI Editor will appear at the bottom of the Edit window.

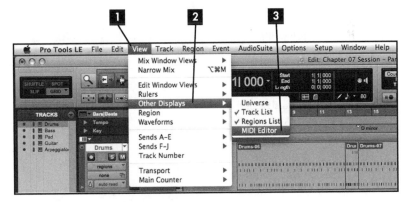

Here's another way to show the Docked MIDI Editor.

**1** Click the **Edit Window Pop-Up button** (located in the upper-right corner of the Edit window). A list will appear.

**2** Choose **MIDI Editor**. The Docked MIDI Editor will appear at the bottom of the Edit window.

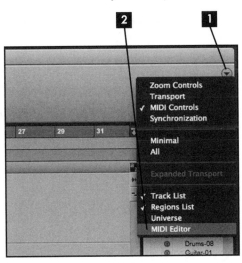

And yet *another* way!

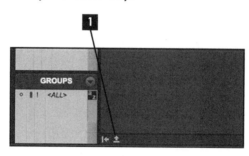

**1** In the bottom corner of the Edit window's Playlist area, you'll see a small upward-pointing arrow. It can be a little tricky to **click** on **it**, but if you do, the Docked MIDI Editor will appear.

✳ No matter which method you choose to reveal it, the Docked MIDI Editor will appear along the bottom of the Edit window. You can adjust the size of the MIDI Editor section of the Edit window by clicking and dragging the upper boundary of the Docked MIDI Editor. Note that the Docked MIDI Editor includes its own version of the Tracks list and edit tools—something we'll explore in just a bit.

## The MIDI Editor Window

Although the Docked MIDI Editor works well in combination with the Edit window, the window can get a little crowded—and remember, the bigger your MIDI Editor gets, the smaller the rest of the Edit window gets! For really serious MIDI editing, the MIDI Editor window is often the way to go.

**1** Click on **Window**.

**2** Choose **MIDI Editor**. The MIDI Editor window will appear.

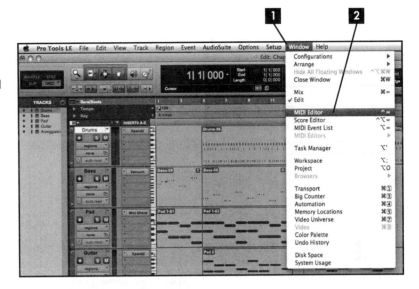

For those (like yours truly) who use the MIDI Editor window quite frequently, there's a quicker way to open the window. Simply by double-clicking a MIDI region, you can launch the window, if you set up your preferences properly.

**1** Open the **Pro Tools LE Preferences window** (from the Setup menu).

**2** Click the **MIDI tab**.

**3** Click the **Double-Clicking a MIDI Region Opens menu** to reveal a list of options.

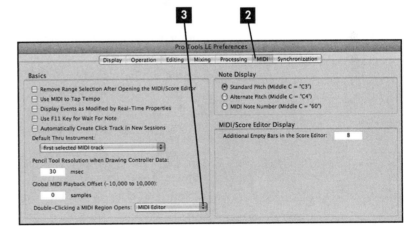

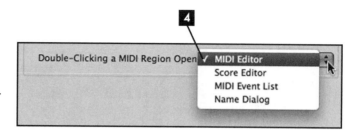

**4** This list will allow you to choose Pro Tools' behavior when a MIDI region is double-clicked. **Choose MIDI Editor**, and double-clicked regions will appear in the MIDI Editor window.

## Getting around the MIDI Editor

Regardless of whether you're using the Edit window's Docked MIDI Editor or the stand-alone MIDI Editor window, the tools and layout are the same.

On the left side of the MIDI Editor, you'll see a familiar-looking Tracks list, which will allow you not only to show and hide tracks (by clicking the dot to the left of the desired track name) but also to select tracks (by clicking the track name). In the image shown here, the Drums track is the only track being shown and is also the only track on this list that is selected.

The MIDI Editor's Tracks list will show you the session's MIDI, Instrument, and Aux Input tracks. This allows you not only to view and control MIDI data on MIDI and Instrument tracks, but also to control virtual instrument automation on Instrument and Aux Input tracks.

In this example, five tracks are being shown (if you're following along with the tutorial session, these are all Instrument tracks), and here we see one of the key advantages to the MIDI Editor: The MIDI notes of all of the shown tracks are displayed in a single environment, as opposed to being separated into track rows as they are in the normal Edit window. This allows you to work quickly and efficiently and see the relationships between multiple tracks clearly.

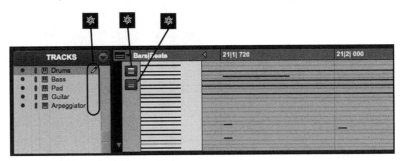

❄ In a situation like this, where you're viewing multiple tracks in a single environment, you might be wondering exactly which track you're working on. No problem—the Pencil icon to the right of the track name indicates the track(s) that are the target of your editing.

❄ By default, MIDI notes shown in the MIDI Editor window will follow the color of the region that they're in, which commonly means that you'll see a number of tracks' MIDI data all in the same color. You can make your editing easier by clicking the Color Code MIDI Notes by Track button, which will automatically assign a unique color for each track's notes.

❄ You can also color code MIDI notes by their velocity values by clicking the Color Code MIDI Notes by Velocity button. All notes, regardless of their track, will be shown with a red color, with darker colors indicating greater velocity values.

> ❋ **EDITING MULTIPLE TRACKS**
>
> You can easily edit multiple tracks simultaneously by placing Pencil icons to the right of multiple tracks. Hold down the Shift key as you click additional tracks to enable editing on a range of tracks. Hold down the Command key (on a Mac) or the Ctrl key (on a PC) to enable editing on multiple tracks on a track-by-track basis.

The top of the MIDI Editor features familiar-looking elements—things such as edit modes, editing tools, nudge and grid values, and so on. We covered most of these in Chapters 5 and 6, but there are a few things that bear mentioning before we move on.

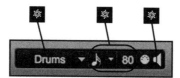

* ❋ You can choose which track you're editing by clicking the track name and choosing the desired track from a list that will appear. This will move the Pencil icon in the Tracks list and changes the focus of your editing.
* ❋ As with the Edit window, you can choose the default duration and velocity for notes entered using the Pencil tool.
* ❋ If you want to hear your MIDI data as you're editing it, make sure that the Play MIDI Notes When Editing indicator is illuminated. If it's not, just click it, and you're all set!

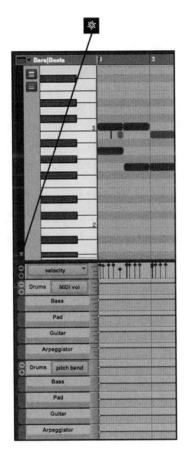

❋ If you click the small triangle icon at the lower-left corner of the Playlist area, you'll reveal the tracks' automation lanes, just as you've experienced in the Edit window. In the MIDI Editor, however, you'll be viewing automation lanes for all the visible tracks for a given automation type.

Editing notes in the MIDI Editor is largely identical to the editing workflows we covered earlier in this chapter, although in the context of the MIDI Editor they take on a new level of usefulness. There are a couple of techniques that come in particularly handy when editing notes.

❋ Double-clicking a note will delete it.

❋ If you're using the Grabber, Pencil, or Smart tool, you can adjust the velocity of a note by holding the Command key (on a Mac) or the Ctrl key (on a PC) and clicking and dragging vertically.

Perhaps the most engaging feature of Pro Tools 8 is the addition of traditional notation, and the MIDI Editor takes advantage of this addition by allowing you to view your note data either in the usual Piano Roll view or as notation. By clicking the Notation Display Enable button, you'll see your music in a brand-new way!

You'll note that your MIDI Editor stays essentially the same (whether you're dealing with the Docked MIDI Editor or the MIDI Editor window), but the format of your MIDI notes has changed. This view is especially useful when you want to tweak your MIDI data while looking at it in a way that makes rhythmic and harmonic structure a bit easier to determine (for those who read traditional notation). Bear in mind that you will still be able to view MIDI velocity and automation data via the track lanes.

Although this is an excellent environment for editing MIDI, it's not ideally suited to the creation of printable music parts. That's what the Score Editor is for, and it's what we'll look at next!

## The Score Editor Window

Suppose you've composed a great piece in Pro Tools, but what it *really* needs now is a live musician's touch. You'll probably want to create some sheet music for the musician to play, and the Score Editor is designed to help you do just that. Though this window shouldn't be confused with comprehensive notation software, it has what you need to get the job done quickly and easily.

### Getting around the Score Editor

Using the Score Editor window begins with learning how to show it!

**1** Click on **Window**.

**2** Choose **Score Editor**. The Score Editor window will appear.

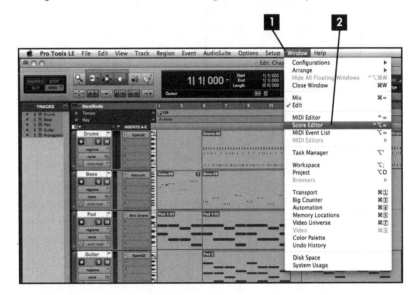

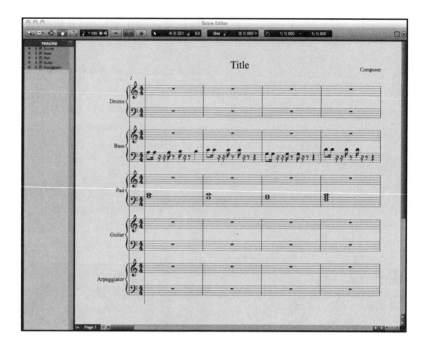

The Score Editor window, like the MIDI Editor, has a look and feel that is consistent with the main Edit window, but in the case of the Score Editor, the editing environment is even simpler and easier to use. By showing and hiding tracks in the Tracks list (this Tracks list will only include MIDI and Instrument tracks), you can show a single part or your song's entire score.

## Score and Track Layout

Though note editing can be done in the Score Editor window (something we'll touch on before we finish this chapter), the majority of your work here will involve the layout of your score and parts. Let's start by formatting the overall score.

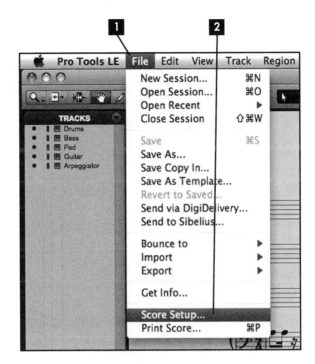

**1** Click on **File**.

**2** Choose **Score Setup**. The Score Setup dialog box will appear.

Here are some other ways to reveal the Score Setup dialog box:

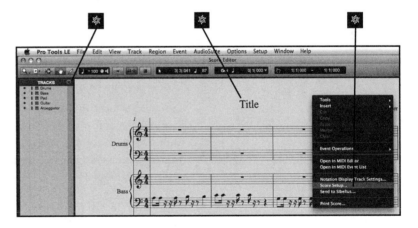

❋ Click the Tracks List Pop-Up button (a list will appear). Choose the Score Setup item from the menu, and the Score Setup dialog box will appear.

❋ Double-click on the score's title. The Score Setup dialog box will appear.

❋ Right-click in any blank area of the score. (A list will appear.) Choose the Score Setup item from the menu (indicated here), and the Score Setup dialog box will appear.

* In the Information section, you can type a title and composer for your song.

* The Display section will allow you to show or hide basic elements of your music. It's worth noting that you can show or hide chord symbols (the alphanumeric description of chords, such as CM7) independently from chord diagrams (also known as tablature, primarily for guitarists).

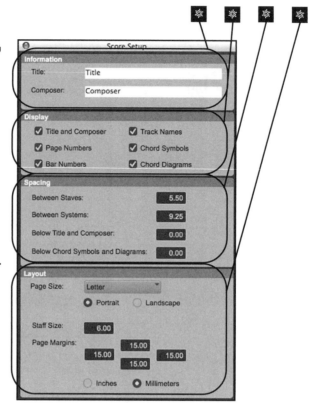

* The Spacing section of the Score Setup dialog box will allow you to type in values for the distance between various elements (or you can click in a value field and drag your mouse vertically).

* Last but not least, in the Layout section of the Score Setup dialog box, you can choose your paper size, orientation (portrait or landscape), staff size, and margins. A tip on changing staff sizes: When creating regular lead sheets, the default size is usually fine, but larger staff sizes can be excellent for music education worksheets!

Now that you've got the overall layout squared away, let's take a look at how to tweak individual parts with the Notation Display Track Settings dialog box.

❄ Click the Tracks List Pop-Up button. (A list will appear.) Choose the Notation Display Track Settings item from the menu, and the Notation Display Track Settings dialog box will appear.

❄ Double-click on any staff's clef symbol. The Notation Display Track Settings dialog box will appear.

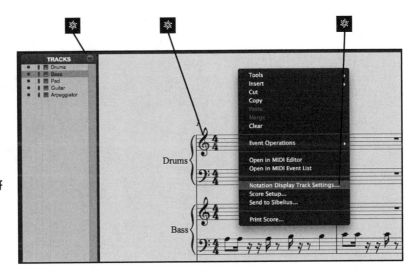

❄ Right-click in any blank area of the score. (A list will appear.) Choose the Notation Display Track Settings item from the menu (indicated here), and the Notation Display Track Settings dialog box will appear.

The important thing to bear in mind when working with the Notation Display Track Settings dialog box is that any changes you make here will affect the track's visual display only and won't change the way your track sounds.

※ The first thing to do is choose the track that you want to set up. Just click the Track menu button to reveal a list of all MIDI and Instrument tracks in your session and choose the desired track from the list.

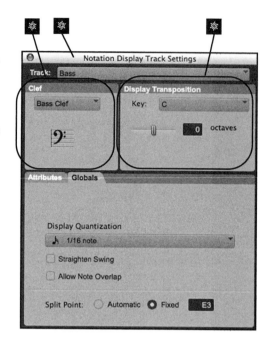

※ By default, tracks are created with a Grand Staff, which is the pairing of a Treble-clef staff and a Bass-clef staff. Although this works well in some situations (such as piano tracks, for example), it's not a good fit for other instruments (such as the Bass track shown here). You can choose the best clef for a track by clicking the Clef menu button to reveal a list of options (including Grand Staff, Treble Clef, Bass Clef, Alto Clef, and Tenor Clef). In this example, I've chosen to use the Bass Clef on my Bass track.

※ The idea of Display Transposition is a tricky one and only applies to certain instruments. When we say that an instrument is "in the key of C," we mean that all notes are played at the same pitch that they are displayed on the staff. Although it may sound strange to say it, not all instruments are like that! A trumpet, for example, is a B-flat instrument, and the pitches that a trumpeter plays are one step away from where they are written! This can get quite confusing, but the issue of transposing instruments arises frequently in the world of composing and arranging. Here's where you can set a track's transposition. Remember, this will affect the visual display of the pitches only, not the original sound of the track.

The bottom half of the Notation Display Track Settings dialog box is devoted to a track Attributes section, which deals with an assortment of general display preferences. You'll see that there are two tabs in this section—the Attributes tab and the Globals tab.

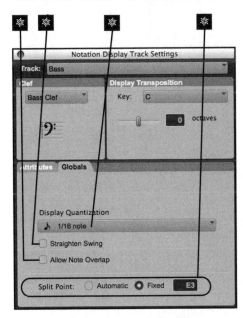

✳ Display quantization is a way for you to clean up the look of your parts. Though the written music's position and duration won't be exactly accurate in relation to the original MIDI data, the right quantization value can make the part much more readable for a musician. Again, your quantization here is only visual and won't alter the sound of the track at all.

✳ When music is "swung", eighth notes are played back with a degree of a triplet feel. If you have a swingin' MIDI part, swung eighth notes may therefore be visually represented as triplets, which can look a bit strange to the musician. By clicking the Straighten Swing check box, swung eighth notes will be represented as regular eighth notes, which is in line with what your musician would expect to see in this situation.

✳ Many instruments—such as saxophone, for example—are monophonic by nature and will play only one pitch at a time. For instruments like this, the Allow Note Overlap box should remain unchecked. For polyphonic instruments (such as piano or guitar), you will very often want to check this box.

✳ A split point refers to the point on a Grand Staff at which notes will be placed on either staff. (Pitches at or above the split point will be placed in the Treble-clef staff, and notes below the split point will be placed in the Bass-clef staff.) If you click the Automatic radio button, Pro Tools will determine the split point based upon the music on the track. You can, however, specify a fixed split point by clicking the Fixed radio button and typing a value in the field to the button's right.

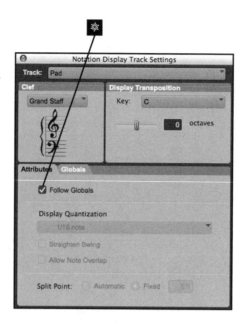

❊ Properly setting your Globals attributes is a good way to get your song in shape quickly, but you might run into a situation where you want to set up different attributes for a specific track. That's when you'll want to use the Attributes tab. Just click the Attributes tab and then uncheck the Follow Globals check box. Once the box is unchecked, you'll be able to set distinct settings for that specific track.

## Editing in the Score Editor

Given the massive power of the MIDI Editor (in either Piano Roll or Notation view), you might find yourself not doing too much editing in the Score Editor. When you do need to change a note, however, you'll find that the basic edit tools (Trimmer, Selector, and Grabber) do just what you would expect them to do. There are a couple of additional techniques worth pointing out, though.

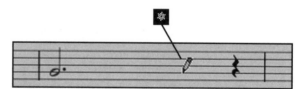

❊ As you might expect, the Pencil tool is great for creating notes. Just click at the desired location on the staff, and a note will appear at the default note duration and velocity. If you want to make the note longer in duration, then just hold down your mouse as you create a note and drag your mouse to the right.

If you want to add a key signature, meter change, or chord symbol, you can do it easily.

**1** Right-click at the **position** at which you want to insert your key, meter, or chord change. A list (shown here) will appear.

**2** Choose Insert.

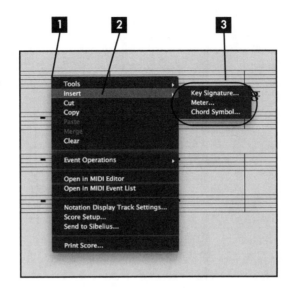

**3** Choose the **type** of **item** that you want to create. The appropriate dialog box (Key Change, Meter Change, or Chord Change) will appear, allowing you to set your values. When you're finished setting your values, **click** the **OK button**, and your change will be applied.

❋ SCORES AND RULERS

Any key, meter, or chord changes you apply in the Score Editor window will be reflected on the appropriate ruler in the main Edit window of Pro Tools.

## Printing Your Music

When you've gotten your music looking great in the Score Editor window, you'll want to print your parts. It's very straightforward and similar to the print process in many other applications.

**1** Make sure you're showing only the **part(s) that you want to print**.

**2** Click on **File**.

**3** Choose **Print Score**. The Print dialog box will appear.

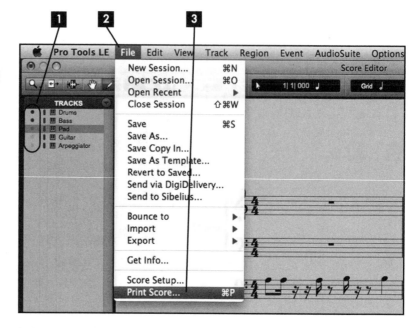

❋ Choose the printer and settings appropriate to your printer hardware.

❋ If you need to e-mail a part, saving it as a PDF file is a great way to do it. Click the PDF button, and a list of PDF-related options will appear. (I commonly choose to Save as PDF and attach it to an e-mail.)

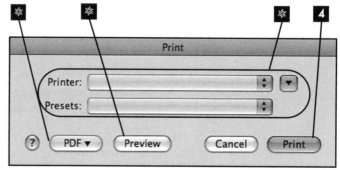

❋ Before printing, you might want to click the Preview button to get a sense of how the part will look when it's printed. Here's a tip: The resolution of the Preview window is fairly low, and when you're zoomed out, the part can look pretty bad. Don't worry—the final print of the parts will look just fine!

**4** When you've chosen your settings, just **click** the **Print button**, and your part will be printed.

### Send to Sibelius

For those of you who don't know the name Sibelius (other than the fact that Jean Sibelius was a famous Finnish composer), it's one of the leading notation programs on the market these days. Sibelius software is not only powerful and flexible, but it's also *fast*, which is making it an increasingly popular choice for musicians of all kinds.

If the Score Editor window is open, Pro Tools can export MIDI data as a Sibelius (.sib) file, allowing you to move your MIDI data from the Pro Tools production environment to a more full-featured notation software environment. It's easy.

**1** Make sure you're showing only the **part(s)** that you want to export.

**2** Click on **File**.

**3** Click on **Export**.

**4** Click on **Sibelius**. The familiar-looking Save dialog box will appear, allowing you to choose a name and location for your new .sib file.

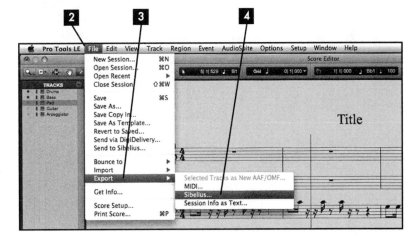

There's an easier way to get quickly into the Sibelius environment (assuming that you have Sibelius installed on your computer). By choosing the Send to Sibelius feature, you skip the steps of saving your Sibelius file.

**1** Make sure you're showing only the **part(s) that you want to send to Sibelius.**

**2** **Right-click** in any **blank area** of the score. A list will appear.

**3** Click on **Send to Sibelius.** Immediately, the Sibelius application will be launched, and your shown tracks will be exported to Sibelius, where you can work on them further.

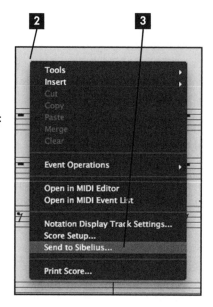

Next stop—mixing!

# 8 } Basic Mixing

When it comes to DAWs, there are two schools of thought on mixing—mixing "*inside* the box" or "*outside* the box." Mixing *inside* the box refers to making use of your DAW's virtual mixer and virtual effects entirely *within* the Pro Tools environment. At any given time, you will listen to a summed (for example, stereo) output of your mix from your Pro Tools interface, and all the required processing is performed by your computer (the "box"). Mixing *outside* the box refers to the practice of assigning individual tracks to individual outputs of your Pro Tools interface, and from there to individual channels on a separate physical mixing board. The mixing and automation are performed by this external mixer, and Pro Tools is reduced to a recording, editing, and playback device (still playing a critical role in any production workflow).

There is lively discussion (and I'm being polite here) within the professional community regarding the virtues of mixing outside the box versus inside the box. There are valid points on both sides of the debate, but for the end user, the debate boils down to an easy choice: Great work is being done using both methodologies, and individuals should follow the paths that best allow them to realize their creative vision.

For the purposes of this book, we'll be exploring the world of mixing "inside the box" (a method that has been used on countless professional projects). In this chapter, you'll learn how to:

* Work with the specific layout and function of the Mix window
* Use fader groups
* Use file-based and real-time effects
* Work with traditional mix routing
* Use basic automation techniques

> ❋ **ON MIXING**
>
> Those of you who have some experience mixing with Pro Tools will notice some differences between the way things used to be and the new world of mixing in Pro Tools. One of the most obvious that you'll find, as you go through this chapter, is that now you very rarely will have to stop playback to make changes to your Mixer (things such as adding tracks, sends, plug-ins, and so on). These sorts of things necessitated stopping of playback in the past—now you can go ahead and make these changes as you continue playback.
>
> There are two things to keep in mind, though: Depending upon what you're doing, you might hear a short gap of silence (as the mix engine reconfigures itself). Also, if you're recording audio, you will have to stop playback to make these sorts of changes (so that you don't interrupt the recorded audio).

# More Signal Flow

When you're talking about mixing, what you're really talking about is signal flow. The more complex your mix gets, the more complex the routing of those signals can be, but even the most complex mixes can be reduced to a few simple elements. The following list will go through the order of audio signal flow through those elements within a track.

**1 Input.** On an Audio or Aux track, input can be from an interface input, a bus, or in some cases a plug-in.

**2 Inserts.** Inserts are most commonly used as holders for effects. One-hundred percent of your signal passes through your insert.

**3 Sends (Pre-Fader).** A send makes a copy of the signal to be routed to another destination. A *pre-fader* send makes that copy before the signal hits your volume fader. The destination of this send can be an interface output or a bus.

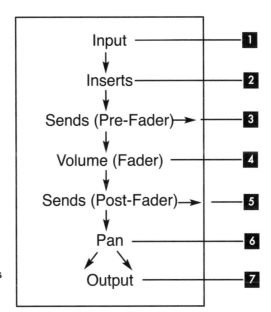

**4 Volume (Fader).** This is where you control the output volume of the track.

**5 Sends (Post-Fader).** This kind of send makes a copy after the signal has been altered by the volume fader. As with a pre-fader send, the destination can be an interface output or a bus.

**6 Pan.** Panning comes next and allows the level of the signal to be varied between a number of outputs (left and right, in the case of a stereo mix). This is how you will create a stereo mix of several mono or stereo tracks. If you route your track to a single output, no pan slider will be needed, and you won't see one in the channel strip.

**7 Output.** After all these stages are passed, the signal goes to the Pro Tools mix engine and out of an interface output.

## A WORD ABOUT FADERS

Remember that the volume fader on your track only controls the output of that track. That means that the fader has absolutely no effect on the input coming to the track. The net effect is this: If you're recording audio and you see your levels clipping, turn down the output of the instrument or microphone or change the gain on your interface. The fader in Pro Tools' Mix window cannot prevent clipping.

# Exploring the Mix Window

You've visited the Mix window before (way back in Chapter 2), but now it's time to dig deeper. If you're not looking at it already, the first thing to do is to switch over to the Mix window (which you also learned how to do in Chapter 2). Depending on how you left the Mix window last time, you might see the channel strips appearing rather narrow. Though the Narrow Mix view can certainly be useful in some situations, you'll be able to see more information with Narrow Mix view turned off. Here's how to check which view you're in and disable Narrow Mix if it's currently enabled.

## SETTING THINGS UP

For this chapter, please use the tutorial session named Chapter 08 Session, included on the disc that came with your book. Remember, you'll need to copy the session folder to a location on your computer's audio hard drive before working on it.

1 **Click** on the **View menu**. In this case, the Narrow Mix option is checked, indicating that Narrow Mix view is active.

2 **Click** on **Narrow Mix** to uncheck it. The channels will be shown in their normal mode.

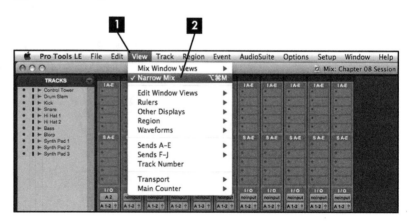

There are certainly times when the Narrow Mix view is desirable. For example, when your session contains too many tracks to be normally displayed at once in the Mix window, switching to Narrow Mix mode will allow you to view more of your mix at once.

## Basic Mixer Terminology

Before we progress further, let's review the basic layout of the Mix window.

- ❋ **Tracks list.** As in the Edit window, a dark dot will appear to the left of shown tracks, and highlighted track names indicate selected tracks.

- ❋ **Groups list.** Mix groups will be shown here. (You'll learn how to use them later in this chapter.)

- ❋ **Channel strips.** There is a separate vertical channel strip for each shown track.

Now take a look at the different sections of a basic Audio track's channel strip.

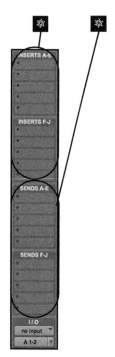

※ At the top of the channel strip are the Inserts sections. With the introduction of Pro Tools 8, there are now 10 inserts for you to use (previous versions had only five), divided into two sections of five inserts. All audio passing through a chan-nel strip will be routed through the inserts first, in descending order, and it is here that you will launch *plug-in* effects and virtual instruments.

※ Next are the sends. Like inserts, you have 10 sends, divided into two sections of five sends. You'll use sends to route a copy of your track's processed audio to another destination. Sends are commonly used in conjunction with other tracks to create more complex effect situations or to create cue mixes in recording situations. (We'll discuss this further in Chapter 10.)

 MIDI TRACK SIGNAL FLOW

MIDI tracks have no inserts or sends, as inserts and sends can route only audio data.

Moving down the channel strip, the next section looks and functions just like the I/O column of a track in the Edit window.

❄ Input Path Selector button

❄ Output Path Selector button

❄ Automation Mode Selector button (covered later in this chapter...finally!)

❄ Group ID indicator

❄ Pan knob

❄ Pan indicator

The bottom section of an Audio track's channel strip may look a bit different from what you've seen in the Edit window, but these buttons' functions should be old hat by now.

❄ Record Enable button

❄ Solo button

❄ Mute button

❄ Volume fader

❄ Volume Level meter

❄ Volume indicator

❄ Track Type icon

❄ Track name

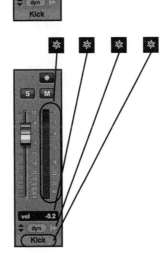

An icon at the bottom-right corner of each channel strip will indicate the type of track it is:

- ❄ A waveform indicates an Audio track.

- ❄ A MIDI plug indicates a MIDI track.

- ❄ An arrow signifies an Aux track.

- ❄ A small musical keyboard is shown on an Instrument track.

- ❄ A sigma marks a Master Fader.

The same icons can be found to the left of each track name in the Tracks list.

You can easily tell whether the track is stereo or mono by taking a look at the volume meters. One meter indicates a mono track, and a stereo track will have two volume meters.

## Improved in Pro Tools 8: Track Colors

If you take a look at the View menu, and from there to the Mix Window Views submenu, you'll see that you have the ability to show track colors—small colored tabs at the top and bottom of each channel strip. Though their function is purely visual, you'll find that using track colors is pretty handy—let's use track colors to differentiate between the different kinds of tracks.

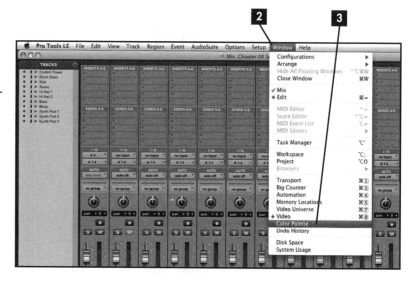

**1** Select the track(s) that you want to re-color by clicking on the track name(s). If you're following along with the tutorial session, let's select all the drum tracks (the Drum Stem, Kick, Snare, Hi Hat 1, and Hi Hat 2 tracks).

**2** Click the Window menu.

**3** Choose Color Palette. The Color Palette window will appear.

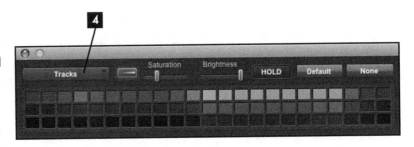

**4** The Apply to Selected menu will allow you to change the color of different parts of your session. In this image, the changes you make in this window will be applied to the selected tracks in your session. If the menu button does *not* read "Tracks," **click** the **button** now.

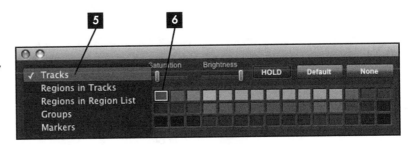

**5** In the Apply to Selected menu, the session element targeted for change will be indicated with a check mark. Since coloring our track is the job at hand, **make sure** that **Tracks** is checked.

**6** From this point, it's simple: **Click** the **color tile** that you want to assign to your selected tracks. In this example, I want my drum tracks to be re-colored red. Once you click the desired color, the tracks' color code will change accordingly.

Track coloring isn't limited to the small tabs at the top and bottom of each channel strip. You also have the ability to apply track colors to the entire channel strips, radically changing the look of your Mix window.

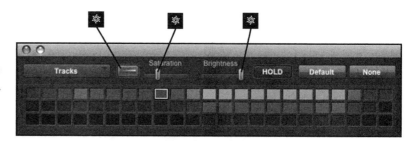

❄ You can toggle channel strip colors on or off by clicking the Apply to Channel Strip button. When active, the button will be colored blue, and you'll see the track color applied throughout the channel strip.

❄ Once you've activated your channel strip colors, you then have the ability to adjust the saturation, or intensity of the colors. The farther you move the slider to the right, the stronger your channel strip colors will become.

❄ Regardless of whether you're using channel strip coloring, you have the ability to adjust the brightness of your Mix window. Used in combination with the Saturation slider, you'll be able to tweak your Mix window to suit your taste.

Last but not least, here are also some useful options to assist in your track coloring:

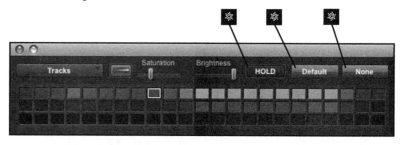

❄ If you ever want to assign the same color to multiple elements (such as multiple tracks or tracks and regions), the Hold button will come in handy. Just choose the color you want to use and then click the Hold button. The color will remain selected as you navigate different tracks and other session elements, until the Hold button is again clicked.

❄ Each track type has a default color code (for example, a new Audio track will be colored blue, a new Aux track will be green, and so on). If you want to set a track's color back to its default value, just click the Default button

❄ If you want to remove all color labeling from a selected track (or tracks), just click the None button.

# Mix Groups

One of the neatest things about mixing in Pro Tools is that you can link faders together, so that moving one fader will move all the faders in that linked *group*. This is particularly useful in cases where you have a good relative blend between a number of tracks (for example, a nice balance between all the individual drum tracks), and you want to change the volume of those tracks without changing the blend. By making a mix group, you can do precisely that!

To start off, let's get a feel for what a mix group can do. As luck would have it, Pro Tools automatically creates a group (named All), which always includes all the tracks in your session. Take a look at what it does:

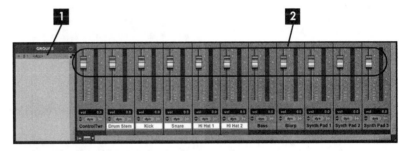

**1** Before you can use a mix group, that group must be active (indicated by the group's name being highlighted). If the All group name is not highlighted, **click** on **All**. The group name will be highlighted, and the group (which in this case includes all the tracks in your session) will be active.

**2** **Click** on any **volume fader** and **drag it** to change the volume of the track. Because the All group is currently active, all the tracks will move proportionally.

❋ GROUP ICONS

Above each track's Pan knob, the Group ID indicator indicates mix group activity on a track-by-track basis. When a group is activated, the group ID letter and name will be shown on the member tracks.

❋ ❋ ❋

## Creating a Mix Group

Of course, you can also create new mix groups of your own. For this section, I've set up a blend of my drum tracks (the same tracks that I re-colored red in the previous section), and I want to be able to link their volume faders.

Though it's not strictly necessary at this point, selecting the tracks that you want to group together will make the process easier. When that's done, you can open the Create Group dialog box in one of two different ways.

**1a** Click the **Track menu**.

**2a** **Select Group**. The Create Group dialog box will appear.

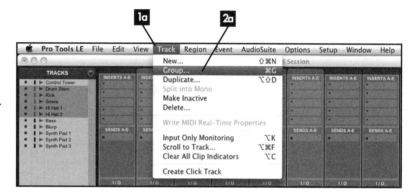

Here's another way to launch the Create Group dialog box:

**1b** Click the **Groups list pop-up button**. A list will appear.

**2b** **Select New Group**. The Create Group dialog box will appear.

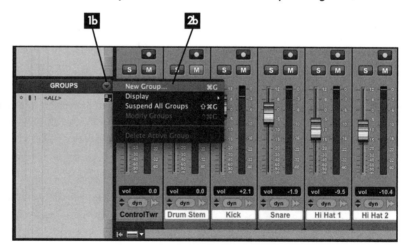

❀ NEW GROUP SHORTCUT

Here's an even quicker way to get to the Create Group dialog box: Press Command+G (Mac) or Ctrl+G (PC).

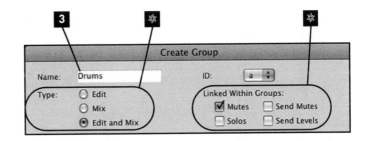

**3** **Type** a **name** for your new group in the Name field.

❀ By default, new groups are created as both edit and mix groups, meaning that the group will be accessible from both the Edit and Mix windows. (This default behavior works well in most situations.) If you choose, you can click on either the Edit or the Mix radio button to limit the group to a single window.

❀ Tracks that are grouped together are always grouped together as far as main volume faders are concerned, but you have the ability to group other aspects together as well. Commonly, I like to have my track mutes grouped together as well, so I've checked the appropriate box. Additionally, you can group solos, send levels, and send mutes.

❋ You can choose the members of your group by populating the Currently in Group area. Initially, your selected tracks will be placed in this area, but if you want to add more tracks to your group, just select the desired tracks in the Available field and then click the Add button. If you want to remove a track from the group, just select the track in the Currently in Group area and then click the Remove button.

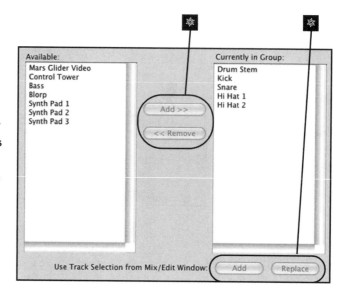

❋ If, after making changes to your group's membership, you want to once again add the selected tracks to the group, you can click either the Add button (to add the selected tracks to any tracks in the Currently in Group field) or the Replace button (which will clear the Currently in Group area and replace it with the selected tracks).

**4** Pro Tools will automatically assign a letter to your group for labeling purposes (in this case, it's currently assigned to group "a"), but let's change that group ID assignment. **Click** on the **ID button**. A list will appear.

**5** The Group ID list is divided into four banks of 26 group letters (for a grand total of 104 groups). **Choose** the desired **group letter** from this list. Since this is a group named Drums, I've chosen the "d" group letter from the first bank.

**6** **Click** on OK, and your group will be created.

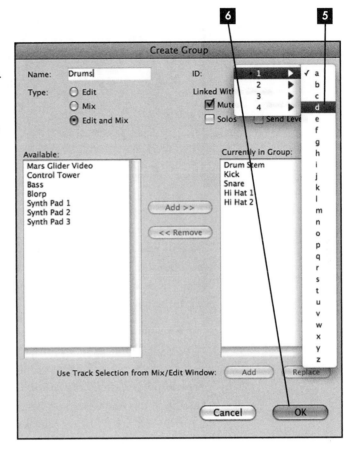

You can highlight more than one group at a time, making multiple groups simultaneously active within your session. Simply click on the name of the group you want to enable, and it will become active.

Using the tutorial session, I've created two more groups: a Bass group (which I've assigned to group letter "b" in the first bank) and a Synths group (assigned to letter "s"). Here's what I've ended up with:

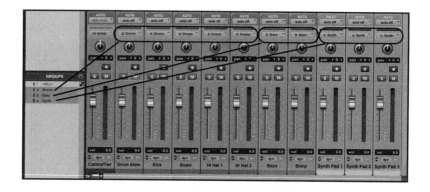

Active mix groups are shown by colored group indicators in member tracks' channel strips (showing the group ID letter and group name). You can activate or deactivate any group by clicking the group name in the Mix Groups list. When a group is deactivated, you will be able to change individual track settings without changing the other members of the group.

Here's where the care we took in choosing group ID letters is going to pay off: When you're in the Mix window, you can use your computer's keyboard to activate and deactivate groups by simply pressing the appropriate group ID letter. The way we've set up our session in this example, you can now toggle the Drums group by just pressing the d key on your keyboard. (Pressing b will toggle the Bass group, and pressing s will toggle the Synths group.) I think you'll find that these shortcuts greatly speed up your mixing!

> ❋ SHORTCUT SHORTCOMING
>
> One limitation of these shortcuts is that they only work for the first bank of group letters. Groups in the other three banks can only be activated or deactivated by clicking the group name in the Mix Groups list.

## Using Mix Groups

There's just a little more to learn about Mix Groups before we continue.

For this example, I've created a group of my two hi-hat tracks, which is a subset of the Drums group (referred to as a nested fader group). Let's take a look:

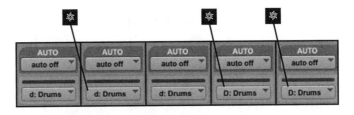

✳ A lowercase ID letter in the Group ID indicator indicates that the track is a member of only one active (highlighted) mix group.

✳ An uppercase ID letter means that the track is a member of more than one currently active group.

✳ You can click on a track's Group ID indicator button to reveal a menu of all the active groups of which that track is a member.

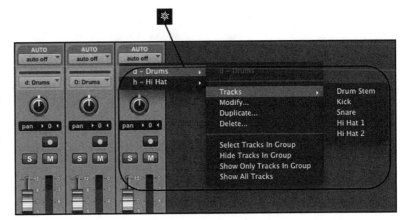

✳ In this example, the Hi Hat 2 track is a member of two active groups—the Drums group and the Hi Hat group. If you move your mouse over either group name, a submenu will be shown, including another submenu that lists all member tracks of that group (shown here).

This group options menu deserves a closer look. This list can be shown either by clicking on a track's Group ID indicator or by right-clicking a group's name in the Groups list. (This method works for both mix and edit groups.) Here's how the different options work:

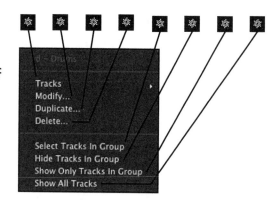

❄ Clicking Tracks will display a list of all the member tracks of the group.

❄ Clicking Modify will open the Modify Group dialog box (very similar to the Create Group dialog box). Here you can change any group attribute except the group ID assignment.

❄ The Duplicate menu item will open the Create Group dialog box, with initial settings identical to the selected group.

❄ The Delete menu item will remove the group.

❄ Clicking Select Tracks in Group instantly selects all the tracks in that group. Only the group's member tracks will be selected.

❄ Clicking Hide/Show Tracks in Group will hide the group's tracks if they are currently being shown. If the tracks are hidden, this menu item will show them.

❄ Clicking the Show Only Tracks in Group menu item will hide all non-member tracks.

❄ The Show All Tracks menu item will show all the tracks in your session.

❄ **SELECTING GROUP MEMBERS**

Another quick way to select all the members of a group is to click to the left of the group name in the Groups list.

There's one final list to take a look at before moving on. If you click on the Mix Groups list pop-up button, a menu will be shown, including:

❋ New Group, which launches the Create Group dialog box.

❋ Display, which shows a sub-menu (shown here), from which you can choose to see your session's mix groups, edit groups, or all groups in the groups area of your Mix window.

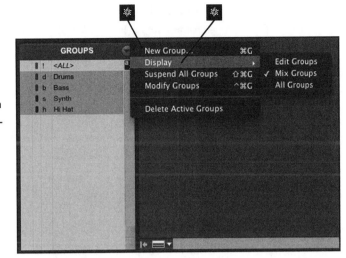

❋ Suspend All Groups, which renders all groups inactive. (The group names will be grayed out.)

❋ Modify Groups, which opens the Modify Group dialog box.

❋ Delete Active Groups, which removes all active groups from your session.

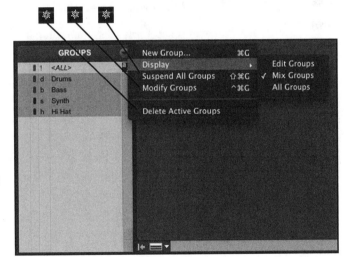

At this point, you've got a good sense of the Mix window's layout, and you know how to set up mix groups, which puts you in good shape to start doing a rough mix. Generally speaking, the first draft of a mix consists of simple volume and pan adjustments (which you'll tweak to perfection as your mix evolves). You'll find that the mix groups you've created will serve you well here, especially with larger, more complex sessions.

❋ ❋ ❋

If you're following along with the tutorial session, you should take some time to get a good rough mix. Once you've got a good blend of volume and pan, you'll probably want to add some effects. Read on!

# Using Effects

Many software applications use plug-ins—bits of programming that are designed to operate within a host program. With word processors, plug-ins can be editing tools or macros; graphics applications have visual effect plug-ins; and so on. Pro Tools is no exception, and Pro Tools plug-ins include all manner of effects processors and virtual instruments. Because they're software (and not hardware), they have great flexibility and can even save you money and rack space in your project studio!

In a Pro Tools LE system, plug-ins fall into two categories—file-based plug-ins (called *AudioSuite*) and real-time plug-ins (called *RTAS*, or *Real-Time AudioSuite*). First, let's tackle AudioSuite.

## AudioSuite

AudioSuite plug-ins, generally speaking, are the most basic of Pro Tools effects. They work directly on files, and this is *not* done in real time as your session plays. This means that AudioSuite plug-ins cannot be automated in your Pro Tools session. It also means that these plug-ins won't consume your session's valuable real-time resources, making AudioSuite plug-ins well worth knowing. Here's how they work.

**1** Select the region or area that you want to process.

**2** Click on the AudioSuite menu. A list of plug-in categories will appear.

**3** Click on the desired category of effect. A submenu will appear, showing all the specific plug-ins of that type.

**4** Click on the desired plug-in. The plug-in's window will appear.

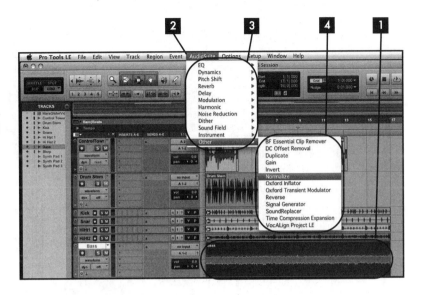

❄ NORMALIZE

The effect I've chosen for this section is a handy little process called *Normalize*. This process is a level adjuster that will bring up your entire selection so that the loudest part of the selection matches the value you set. The simplicity of the effect window makes it an obvious choice for tutorial demonstrations.

Normalize can be very useful in some circumstances, but beware of routinely using it to compensate for low recorded levels! Though the volume will be brought up, there can be minor damage done to the accuracy of your audio, and it will bring up ambient noise levels as well. The bottom line is to record at healthy levels, so you won't need to use normalization too often!

Although different effects will differ in appearance and parameters, they all share some common elements.

❄ GETTING AROUND IN THE AUDIOSUITE PLUG-IN WINDOW

When looking at an AudioSuite plug-in window, it's important to make a distinction between the *function* of some of the buttons and the *labels* they may display at any given time. The buttons at the top of every AudioSuite window show their currently selected settings (as opposed to their function) for quick visual reference.

**5** The Plug-In Selector button (which displays the name of the current plug-in, such as Normalize) will allow you to change effects without closing the window. Just **click** the **Plug-In Selector button**, and a list of AudioSuite plug-ins will appear, identical to the list you saw when you clicked the AudioSuite menu.

**6** **Click** on the **Selection Reference button** (which reads "Playlist" in this image) to determine what will be processed. A menu with two options will appear:

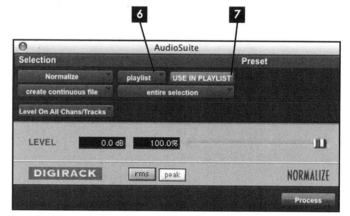

* **Playlist.** When Playlist is selected, the plug-in will process the selected area in your track(s).
* **Region List.** Choosing the Region List option directs the plug-in to process the currently selected regions in the Regions list.

**7** **Select Playlist** if you want the processed audio to appear in your tracks (and also in the Regions list). When activated, the button will be highlighted blue.

If the Use in Playlist button is not active, the processed audio will only appear in the Regions list, and the regions in your track will remain unchanged.

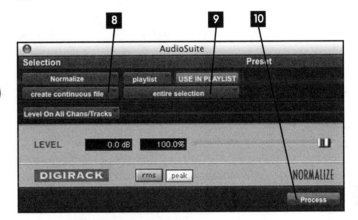

**8** Click the **File Mode button** (which reads "Create Continuous File" in this image) to determine how audio will be processed. A menu will appear, showing three different processing options:

❋ **Overwrite Files.** With this option chosen, the selected audio file(s) will be processed directly and *destructively*.

❋ **Create Individual Files.** This mode is *non*destructive and will create separate audio files for each selected region. If multiple regions are selected, multiple files will be created.

❋ **Create Continuous File.** This mode is also nondestructive, but in this case it will create a *single* new audio file regardless of the number of regions that are selected.

**9** Click on the **Process Mode button** (which reads "Entire Selection" in this image) to determine how your regions will be analyzed prior to processing. A menu will appear, showing two options:

❋ **Region by Region.** With this option chosen, each selected region will be individually analyzed and processed.

❋ **Entire Selection.** All selected regions will be analyzed prior to being processed.

❋ REGION BY REGION AND NORMALIZE

The Region by Region option is commonly used when normalizing multiple regions of different volumes (different sound effects, for example). With this mode selected, each selected region will be analyzed and processed individually, resulting in multiple regions that all have identical peak volume levels.

**10** Click the **Process button** to apply your effect.

Here's what you'll end with:

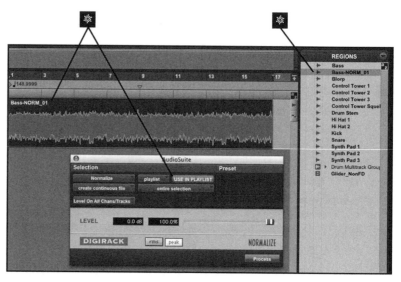

* Since the Use in Playlist button is enabled, a new region has been created to replace the selected region in the track.

* This new region has also been added to the Regions list and has been named Bass-NORM_01 to indicate that it was created by the Normalize AudioSuite plug-in.

* AUDIOSUITE VARIATIONS

The controls discussed here are basic AudioSuite options common to all AudioSuite plug-ins. Different kinds of effects may have additional features relating to their function.

* IMPROVED IN PRO TOOLS 8: AUDIOSUITE PREVIEW

Many AudioSuite plug-ins provide the option of previewing your changes prior to applying them. (These preview controls are located at the bottom of the AudioSuite window, as shown here.) In previous versions of Pro Tools, there was a significant gap between clicking the Preview button and hearing audio—this has been greatly reduced in Pro Tools 8. Additionally, there are level meters and volume control available. (Just click the volume level indicator to reveal a fader you can use to change your preview levels.)

# RTAS

The next evolutionary step in the world of Pro Tools' plug-in effects is RTAS (*Real-Time AudioSuite*). Instead of processing audio on a file basis (as is the case with AudioSuite), an RTAS plug-in resides on a track's insert and processes an incoming signal as the session is played (in real time).

There are two huge benefits that come from using RTAS plug-ins. First, because the audio is being processed in real time, the audio files on your hard drive won't be changed, which allows you to experiment freely with different plug-ins and settings without worrying about filling your hard drive with processed files. Also, as a result of RTAS's real-time operation, you can automate the parameters of your plug-in (something we'll cover later in this chapter), meaning that your effects can change dynamically over time.

✳ IF YOU'RE FOLLOWING ALONG WITH THIS EXAMPLE...

If you've been using the Chapter 8 Session file, you might notice that there's a Video track—in this section, we'll be doing a bit of sound design to make the audio work better with the scene. You can view your video by opening the Video window. (Go to the Window menu and choose Video—a Video window will appear.)

This short clip shows a space glider zooming over the Valles Marineris (a huge canyon on Mars). Thanks to Dave Oxenreider and Singularity Arts Inc. for creating this and allowing us to use it in this chapter!

## Launching RTAS Plug-Ins

Launching (or instantiating) an RTAS plug-in is easy once you know the steps. In this particular example, I'm going to add some equalization (EQ) to the Control Tower track to make it sound like the voice is going over a radio transmission.

1 Click on an unused **Insert button** on the track that you want to affect (in this case, the Control Tower track). A drop-down menu will appear.

**2** Click on **Plug-In**. A list of plug-in categories will appear.

**3** Click on the desired **category** of effect (in this case, let's choose EQ). A submenu will appear, showing all the specific plug-ins of that type.

**4** Click on the desired **plug-in**. The plug-in's window will appear (in this case, EQ3 7-Band).

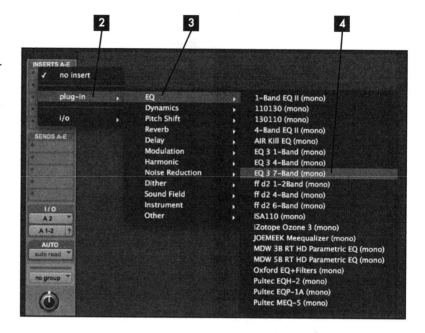

The RTAS plug-in window will vary depending upon the effect, but just as with AudioSuite plug-ins, there are some common buttons at the top of the plug-in window that you should understand.

**1** Click the **Track Selector button** (which shows you the track you're currently working with) to display a list of available tracks in your session. From this list you can select another track and instantly open an Insert window for that track.

**2** Click the **Insert Position Selector button** (a small lettered button to the right of the Track Selector button) to indicate the position of the insert on the track. If you click this button, a list of all 10 insert positions will appear—from this list, you can select any position and jump to that insert immediately.

**3** Finally, click the **Plug-In Selector button** (which currently shows you the plug-in you're using) to reveal the plug-in menu, from which you can select a different effect without closing the RTAS window.

❄ ADVICE ON INSERTS

Because inserts are processed in series from top to bottom, the order in which effects are placed in your tracks is significant. For example, a virtual amplifier placed before a reverb will sound a good deal different than an amplifier placed after a reverb. The good news is that it's easy to change the order (or even the track assignment) of an RTAS plug-in simply by dragging and dropping the insert icon to a new location in your Mixer.

## Recalling Settings

In addition to instantiating plug-ins with ease, you can also recall previously created settings (called *presets*). Here's how we'll recall a good preset for the EQ we just launched. (These steps also work with AudioSuite plug-ins.)

**1** Click the **Librarian Menu button**. A list of available presets will be displayed.

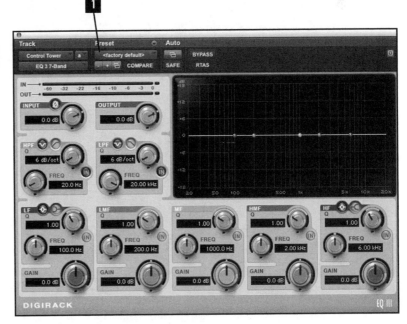

**2** Any factory presets for the plug-in will be shown in this menu, plus any presets that are saved in your session's Plug-In Settings folder (something you'll learn more about in Chapter 9). In this case, I've placed a good preset in your session's Plug-In Settings folder, so **click** the **Session's Settings Folder**. A list will appear.

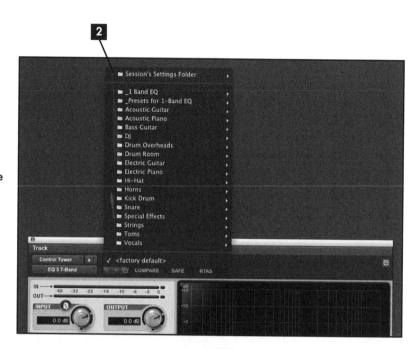

**3** If you're using the tutorial session, you'll see that there's only one preset in the Session's Settings Folder—appropriately named Control Tower Radio—created by yours truly. **Select** this **preset**, and the parameters will be applied to your plug-in.

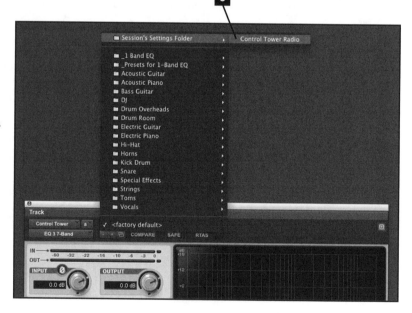

There are a couple other ways that presets can be accessed. (Again, this works for both AudioSuite and RTAS.)

❊ Use the plus (+) or minus (–) key to increment or decrement through the available presets.

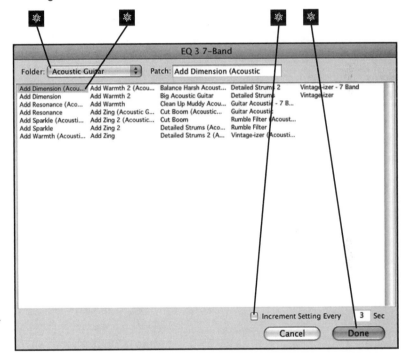

❊ Click the Plug-In Setting Select button to reveal the plug-in setting dialog box.

❊ Click the Folder button to reveal a list of all preset folders, and click the desired folder to display the presets in the dialog box's main area.

❊ Click the desired preset, and your settings will be immediately applied.

❊ Click the Increment Setting Every check box to automatically cycle through the available presets according to the value entered in the Sec field. (In this image, presets will change every three seconds.) This is a handy way to preview effects settings (especially when there is a large number of presets to choose from).

❊ When you settle upon the desired setting, click the Done button, and the plug-in setting dialog box will close.

### Digging Deeper into RTAS

Okay, so far it's been pretty straightforward, but things will get a little more complicated as we go on. For example, when you open a plug-in on a stereo track, you have the option of choosing between a multi*channel* and a multi-*mono* effect. For this example, let's set up a multi-mono delay on a stereo Aux track.

**❋ SETTING THINGS UP**

To follow along with these steps, create a stereo Aux Input track and name it Delay Aux.

**1** On a stereo track (in this case, a stereo Aux track named Delay Aux), **click** on an available **Insert button**.

Inserts on a multichannel track (such as the stereo track in this example) will give you the choice to use either multichannel or multi-mono plug-ins. Simply put, a multichannel plug-in is a single plug-in that is designed to process more than one audio stream. Choosing to use multi-*mono* will open multiple mono plug-ins in a single plug-in window. Confused? Read on!

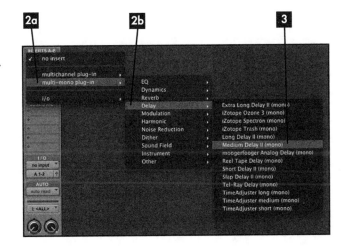

**2a** Click on **Multichannel Plug-In**. In the case of a stereo track (as shown here), a list of stereo plug-ins will appear.

OR

**2b** Click on **Multi-Mono Plug-In**. A list of mono plug-ins will appear.

**3** For the purposes of this example, **choose Medium Delay II** from the multi-mono plug-in family (shown here). The plug-in will be instantiated, and the plug-in window will open.

When you choose multi-mono on a stereo track, the mono plug-in you select will be opened twice, although only one plug-in window will be shown. A multi-mono plug-in window has several unique features.

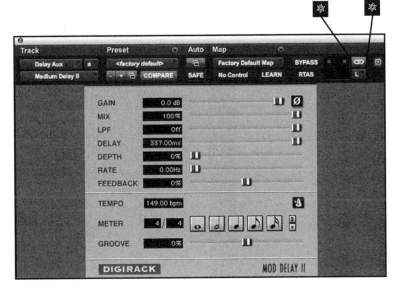

❄ The Channel Selector button will indicate the channel of the multi-mono plug-in you're presently viewing. Just click this button to reveal a list of available channels from which you can choose. (In this case, clicking the Channel Selector button will allow you to switch from the Left plug-in to the Right plug-in.)

❈ The Link button is unique to multi-mono plug-ins. When this button is highlighted, all channels of the multi-mono plug-in will share the same parameter settings. (In the image shown here, changes made to the left side will be mirrored in the right side.) When Link is disabled, both sides are independently configurable. (In this case, unlinking the plug-in will allow you to set different delay settings for the left and right sides.)

## RE-LINKING MULTI-MONO PLUG-INS

If you unlink a multi-mono effect and later choose to re-link, the Relink dialog box will appear. When re-linking a multi-mono plug-in, you will need to choose one channel's parameters to be applied to all channels.

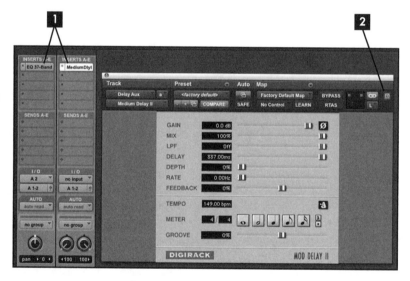

**1** Each plug-in that you launch (or instantiate) will appear as a rectangular button next to its corresponding insert. **Click** on the desired **button** to open or close the plug-in's window.

You'll notice that by default, only one plug-in window is shown at a time—clicking a plug-in button when a plug-in window is already open will change the plug-in displayed in that window. So what if you want to view more than one plug-in window at a time? That's when the Target button comes in handy.

❈ The rule for the Target button is simple: Only one plug-in window can be "targeted" at a time. If you **click** on the **Target button** of a plug-in window to deactivate the target (the button will turn gray), you'll be able to open another plug-in window. (The next plug-in window that you open will have an active Target button.)

❋ OPENING MULTIPLE PLUG-IN WINDOWS SHORTCUT

You can also open more than one plug-in window at a time by holding down the Shift key as you click on a plug-in button on an insert.

## Traditional Effects Techniques

The goal of the mixing process is to achieve the perfect blend of audio elements in your session. Over the years, certain conventions have evolved to help mixing engineers reach this goal, and these conventions have become something of a tradition. Before we leave our discussion of effects, let's take a look at some traditional ways to use them (though certainly not the *only* ways that they can be used!).

### Using Dynamic-Based Effects

Effects tend to fall into one of two categories—*dynamic*-based effects or *time*-based effects. Let's begin with dynamic effects. Dynamic-based effects change the volume level of the audio (or a portion of the audio) without changing its duration in any way. Some of the most common examples of dynamic effects are equalizers, compressors, and limiters.

Setting up dynamic-based effects is very easy—in fact, you've done it once already with the Control Tower track (if you've been using this chapter's tutorial session). Typically, you'll want dynamic effects to process 100 percent of the track's audio, so you'll simply place the effect on an insert of the track that you want to change.

1 Click on an **insert** on the desired track and select a **dynamic-based effect** (such as the EQ shown here). The plug-in window will appear.

2 Adjust the **parameters** of the effect to suit your mix's needs.

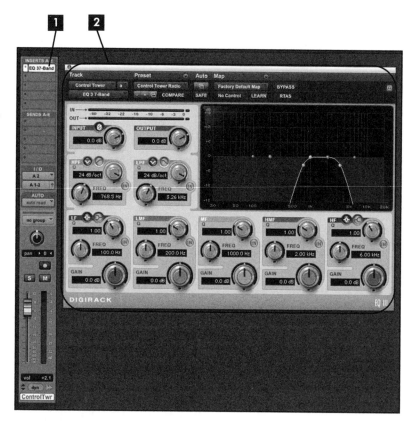

When you're finished tweaking the effect, you're done!

## Using Time-Based Effects

Time-based effects *do* affect the duration of the sound beyond that of its original waveform. Effects such as reverb, delay, and echo would fall under this classification. In these cases, you typically will want to have some sort of a wet/dry mixing scenario (*wet* meaning an affected signal and *dry* referring to an unaffected signal). The generally preferred way to mix these two signals is to use two separate tracks, so that you have the ability to adjust the wet/dry balance with faders in your Mix window. Let's go through this process and add a little delay to the Control Tower track.

**1** Create a stereo Aux track and instantiate the **time-based plug-in** that you want to use (in this case, a delay) on an available insert on that track. If you've been following the tutorial session so far in this chapter, you can use the stereo Aux track (named Delay Aux) that you created earlier in this chapter.

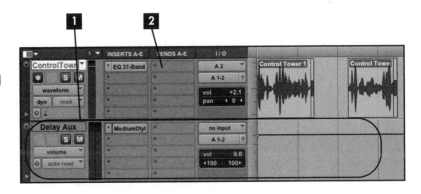

**2** Click on any available **Send Selector button** on the "dry" track (in this case, the Control Tower track). A list will appear.

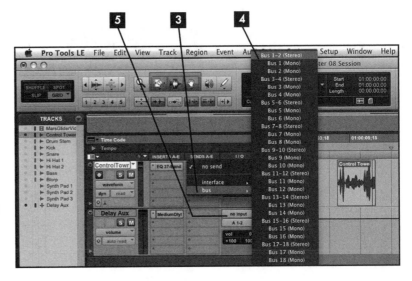

**3** Because you'll be routing audio from one track to another within the Pro Tools environment, you'll want to use a bus. **Click** on **Bus** from the list of output options.

**4** Select an unused stereo bus. (We're using stereo busses because the signal will be sent to a stereo track.) Busses already being used in the session will be shown in a bold amber font.

**5** To complete the signal routing process, you'll need to **set** the **input** of the Aux track to match the same stereo bus you chose for the Audio track's send.

**6** Drag the **volume fader** on the send's output window (if you're not seeing this window, just click on the send button to reveal it) and increase the volume to an appropriate level. At this point, it's a good idea to play your session to test your setup—if you've routed the audio signal correctly, it will appear in the send output window and the Aux track's main level meter.

**7** On the Aux track, **drag** the **volume fader** to achieve the desired blend of wet and dry sound. (The original Audio track is the dry part of the mix, and the Aux track is the wet part.) It's often useful to solo the tracks when adjusting this blend, at least in the initial stage.

### ❋ LEVEL SHORTCUT

Here's a quick way to move a volume fader (either the main fader or a send fader) to 0 dB (also called *unity*): Just hold the Option key (Mac) or Alt key (PC) and click the fader. The fader will immediately jump to the unity position.

❄ When the PRE button is highlighted on the send's output window (as shown here), the send is known as a *pre-fader send*, meaning that the output of the send will not be affected by the Audio track's main volume fader. When the PRE button is not highlighted (the default state of sends in Pro Tools), the send is a post-fader send, and the volume fader of the Audio track will affect the volume going out of the send.

❄ **PRE- VERSUS POST-FADER SENDS**

Although post-fader sends are generally more commonly used, both pre- and post-fader sends have their uses. It all depends on the results you want: Choose post-fader (the Pro Tools default) if you want to have your dry track's level affect the wet track's output. This way, when you raise and lower the volume fader on the dry track, you'll raise and lower the signal being routed to the Aux, maintaining a consistent blend of wet and dry. If, however, you want the wet and dry track levels to be completely independent, use a pre-fader send. Because signal will be routed to the Aux track before the dry track's fader, a full signal will be sent to both faders, allowing more flexibility with the wet and dry balance. Experiment!

❄ **THE MIX PARAMETER AND TRADITIONAL TIME-BASED ROUTING**

Most plug-in effects have a Mix parameter in the plug-in window that allows you to blend a dry and a wet signal. Usually this setting defaults to 100-percent wet, but not always. Be sure to check your plug-in's Mix parameter; in the traditional mixing workflow you just learned, you'll want that Mix parameter to be 100-percent wet.

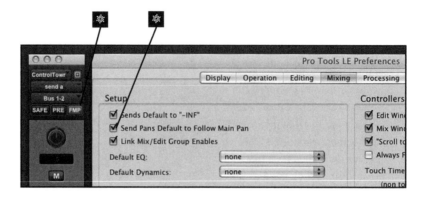

⁂ There's one more send button to talk about: The FMP button (which stands for *Follow Main Pan*) makes panning your sends much easier. Frequently, it's preferable to have the send's pan mirror the panning of the track as a whole. That's just what FMP does. Just click the FMP button in the send output window, and the send's pan will follow the panning that you choose for your track's output. You can tell whether your send is set to follow the main panner by the lit FMP button and the grayed-out panner in the send output window.

⁂ FMP can be automatically enabled on newly created sends. From the Preferences window, go to the Mixing tab, and from there check the Send Pans Default to Follow Main Pan check box.

Here's a variation on the traditional time-based effect workflow, and one that can make production much simpler and boost the performance of your DAW in the bargain!

**1** A bus can have multiple sources and destinations—that means that you can create sends on a number of tracks and assign them all to the same bus(ses). In this image, I've created sends on all of my individual drum tracks and assigned all of those sends to Busses 3 and 4.

**2** All of these signals can be combined and routed to a single Aux track, as shown here. Remember that you must set the input of the Aux track to match the busses you're using on your source tracks (in this case, Busses 3 and 4). The Aux track will contain the effect that you want to apply to your tracks (in this case, a reverb).

**3** It's worth noting that you can independently control the levels and panning of each of your sends, allowing you to individually set the level of each source track going to the effect. In the case of adding reverb to a drum kit, as shown here, I would typically have relatively little of my kick drum going to the reverb Aux track to maintain a crisp low end and send a bit more of my other tracks to the reverb.

That's it! Now you have dry faders (in this case, the Audio tracks) and a wet reverb track (the Aux track), and you can adjust the levels to suit your mix.

Want to move a plug-in or send from one track to another? No problem—just click on that plug-in or send button and drag it to any available track. To copy a plug-in or send, just hold down the Option key (Mac) or Alt key (PC) as you click and drag! There's only one limitation to this flexibility—multichannel plug-ins can only be moved to tracks of the same output format. (For example, you can drag a stereo plug-in to another stereo track, but not to a mono track.)

Remember, *all* of the static parameters that you've just set up (send levels, Aux levels, plug-in parameters, and so on) are just a starting point, setting the stage so that you can go on to tweak your mix further. That's where automation comes in...

# Automating Your Mix

Automation is one of the coolest things about mixing in a DAW, and in my opinion, nothing beats Pro Tools' automation features. If the term is new to you, *mix automation* refers to the ability to change aspects of your mix (such as volume, for example) over time and to have those changes "written" to your session. Once those changes have been written, they can be adjusted and played back automatically (hence the term automation), giving you the ability to control multiple parameters in real time as your session plays.

❋ RECORDING VERSUS WRITING

Before we start dealing with mix automation, we should cover some basic terminology. Audio and MIDI data are *recorded*, but automation is *written*. When your session plays back, the *written* automation can be *read*. This might seem like a matter of semantics at this point, but it'll help keep things clear as we work with automation (and these are the standard industry terms).

## The Automation Modes

There are five automation modes, which determine the way your fader, pan, and other parameters will be written. Understanding the distinction between these modes is the best way to start learning about automation.

**1** You can set the automation mode for any track, whether you're in the Mix window or the Edit window. **Click** on the **Automation Mode Selector button** on the track that you want to automate (which in this case reads Auto Read). A menu of the five automation modes of Pro Tools LE will appear.

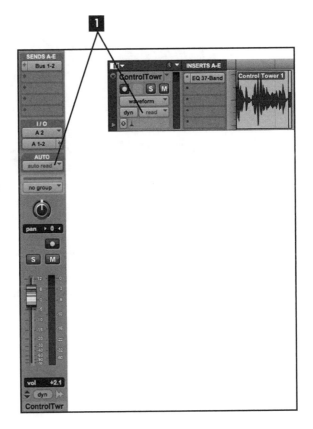

Each automation mode is unique, to fit a wide variety of mixing situations.

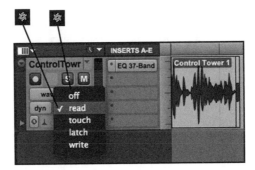

❊ **Auto Off.** Using this mode, automation will neither be written nor played back. This is a good way to suspend automation on a track that has automation.

❊ **Auto Read.** Automation cannot be written in this mode, but previously written automation will be played back. Use this mode to play back your automated tracks without running the risk of overwriting that automation.

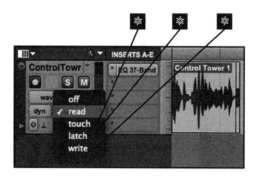

    ✻ **Auto Touch.** The track will read previously written automation, until a parameter is "touched" (by clicking with your mouse or using a control surface), at which time automation will be written for that parameter. When the parameter is released, it will return to its previously written automation.

    ✻ **Auto Latch.** This mode is similar to Auto Touch—only when a parameter that is "touched" will automation be written. When the parameter is released in Auto Latch mode, however, it will remain at the last value and continue to write automation at that position until you stop playback.

    ✻ **Auto Write.** In this mode, automation will be written on all enabled parameters, regardless of whether the parameter is being touched.

✻ **AUTOMATION ON A TRACK-BY-TRACK BASIS**

You can choose a different automation mode for each track.

✻ **A WORD ABOUT AUTOMATION WORKFLOW**

With the Auto Touch, Auto Latch, and Auto Write modes, automation will be written during playback, and writing will stop when playback is stopped (or in the case of Auto Touch, when you let go of the parameter that you're automating).

Let's start by using Auto Write mode to change the volume of the Synth Pad 3 track.

You can (and often will) do your automation work in the Mix window, but for purposes of visualization, the screenshots in this section will use the Edit window.

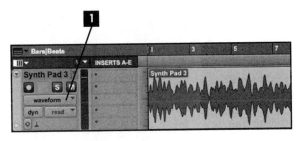

**1** Click the **Track View Selector button** to change to a graphical view of the parameter you want to automate.

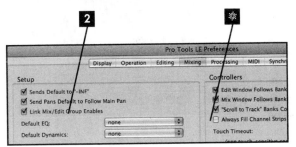

**2** Choose the **track parameter** that you want to view. In this case, I've chosen Volume.

✳ Note that automation parameters are displayed in the track's Playlist area as a horizontal line.

**3** If you're writing volume automation in the Edit window, you'll find that the Output window will help greatly. Just **click** the **Output Window button** to reveal the track's Output window.

**4** There is an Automation Mode Selector button on both the Edit window's track strip and the track's Output window. **Click** either **Automation Mode Selector button**.

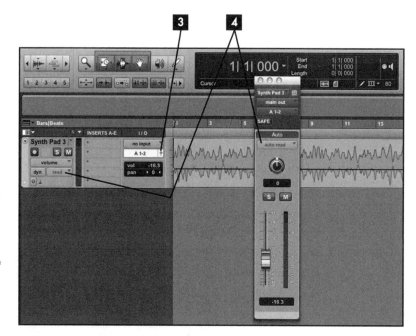

**5** For the purposes of this example, let's start by using Auto Write mode, which will create new automation data for all automatable parameters as soon as playback is started. **Choose** the **Auto Write automation mode** from the Automation Mode menu.

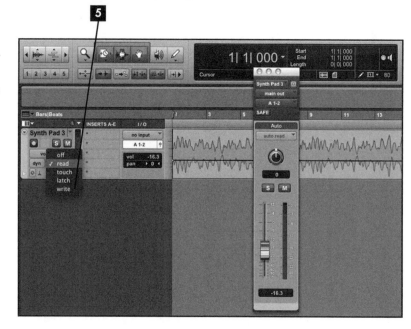

**6** Since Auto Write mode will begin writing automation as soon as playback begins, you should **set** your **initial levels**. (In this case, I want to do a fade-in from silence, so I've brought my fader all the way down.) Once you've done that, **move** your **timeline cursor** to the point at which you want to start writing automation (in this case, I've placed my time-line cursor at the beginning of the session) and **begin play-back** of your session.

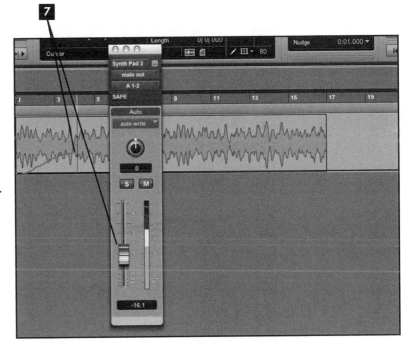

**7** **Click** on the desired **mix parameter** (in this case, volume) and **move it** to create automation data. As your automation is being written, you will see the data represented as a red line in the track's automation playlist.

**8** When you're finished writing automation, **stop** your session's **playback**.

❋ AUTO WRITE WARNING

Be careful of following an Auto Write pass with another Auto Write pass—this generally leads to problems. Auto Touch and Auto Latch, on the other hand, are common choices to follow an Auto Write pass (for reasons that will become apparent shortly).

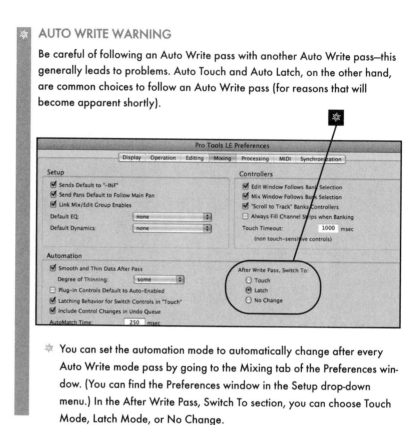

❋ You can set the automation mode to automatically change after every Auto Write mode pass by going to the Mixing tab of the Preferences window. (You can find the Preferences window in the Setup drop-down menu.) In the After Write Pass, Switch To section, you can choose Touch Mode, Latch Mode, or No Change.

You'll see that new automation data has been written, similar to the volume change that I created here. So what if you want to change things further, without losing the work you've already done? That's where the "update" modes—Touch and Latch—come into play.

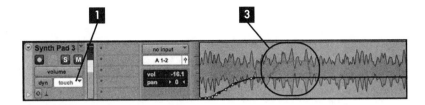

**1** Select the **Touch automation mode** from the Automation Mode Selector menu.

**2** **Play** your **session**. As long as you don't click any parameters, your automation will be read back, and the appropriate controls will move.

**3** When you want to make a change in your automation, just **click** on the appropriate **control** and **adjust it**. Let go of the control when you want to stop writing, and you'll see your parameter move back to the previously written automation line (if you're in Touch mode—if you're in Latch mode, the parameter will continue to write the last value until playback is stopped).

In this example, here's what I got:

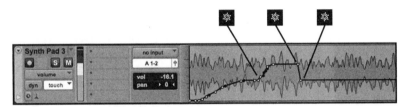

❊ Automation was played back as originally written until this point, when I began moving the volume fader.

❊ At this point, I released the fader. Because I was in Auto Touch mode, the fader began to move back to the previously written automation playlist.

❊ Auto Touch mode will take a little time to go back to the previously written automation (a parameter called AutoMatch time, which you can adjust from the Mixing tab in the Preferences window).

The other update mode, Auto Latch, is written using the same steps that you took in writing with Auto Touch mode, but the mode's behavior is a bit different. Here's how a similar update pass would look with Auto Latch mode:

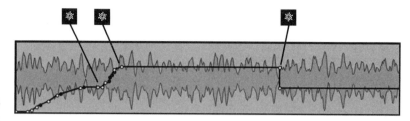

✵ Automation was played back as originally written until this point, when I began moving the volume fader—so far, this is the same behavior as you saw with Auto Touch mode.

✵ At this point, I released the fader. Since I was in Auto Latch mode, the fader stayed put (instead of going back to previously written automation, as you saw in Touch mode).

✵ When playback stopped, the writing of automation stopped as well.

✵ AUTOMATION INDICATORS

You might have noticed that the track's Automation Mode button turned red as soon as you moved the volume fader—what's up with that? The track's Automation Mode button will turn red when any kind of automation data is being written to it. (When using Auto Write mode, the Automation Mode button will always appear red.)

## The Automation Window

The Automation window will allow you to have a different kind of control over mix automation, allowing you to choose what types of data can be automated in your session.

**1** Click on the **Window menu**.

**2** Click on **Automation**. The Automation window will appear.

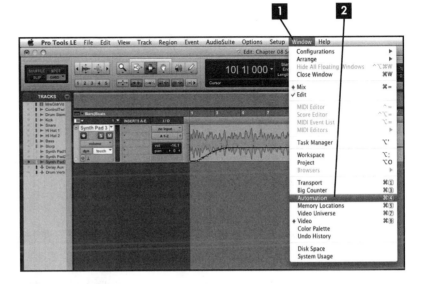

❊ If you click the Suspend button, all automation (writing and playback) will be disabled.

❊ The seven Automation Enable buttons represent automatable mix parameters—volume, pan, mute, plug-in, send volume, send pan, and send mute. An enabled parameter will be indicated by a red button, and if you click on a given button (removing the red highlighting), the parameter will be rendered unwritable (though written automation will still be read).

## New in Pro Tools 8: Automation Lanes

You've already seen track lanes before (playlist lanes for track comping, continuous controller lanes for viewing MIDI data). Let's take another look and see how track lanes can be used to view multiple mix automation parameters.

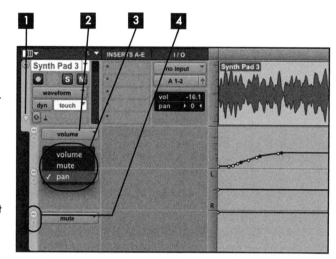

**1** **Click** the **Show/Hide Automation Lanes icon** to reveal (or hide) a track's additional lanes.

**2** Choosing a lane's view is very similar to what you've done already in the main body of the track—just **click** the **Lane View Selector button**, and a list of available views will appear.

**3** **Choose** the desired **automation type** from the list. The currently visible type is indicated by a check mark.

**4** You can add an automation lane by **clicking** the **Add Automation Lane below This One button** (indicated by a plus (+) icon) or remove one by **clicking** the **Remove This Automation Lane button** (shown as a minus (−) icon).

## Plug-In Automation

Virtually every knob or button of a plug-in can be automated, allowing you to change tonal color, ambience, and more!

❋ WORKING WITH THE TUTORIAL SESSION

If you're following along with this chapter's tutorial session, there's a good example of plug-in automation in store for you—automating a frequency sweep on a drum loop. It's a popular effect these days, and it's very easy to create.

Solo the Drum Stem track. You'll find that there's a 1-Band EQ3 already instantiated for you. Once you open the plug-in window, you'll also notice that there is a very strong and very narrow frequency range being emphasized in the plug-in. Your job: Automate that frequency up and down.

## Enabling Plug-In Parameters: Method One

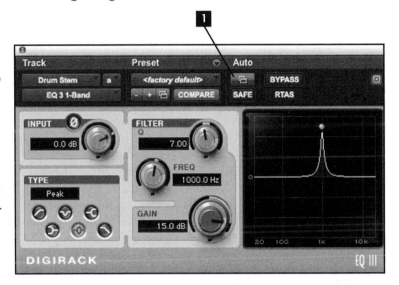

**1** Click on the **Plug-In Automation Enable button**. The Plug-In Automation dialog box will open.

The Plug-In Automation dialog box is structurally similar to the Create Group dialog box that you worked with earlier in this chapter, with a list of available parameters on the left side of the window and a list of enabled parameters on the right.

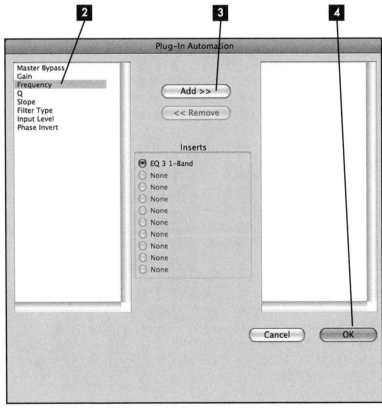

**2** Click the **effects parameter(s)** that you wish to automate. (In this case, you'll want to automate the plug-in's Frequency parameter.) Selected parameters will be highlighted.

**3** Click the **Add button**. The selected parameters will move from the left list to the right list.

**4** When you're finished, **click OK**.

> ※ DISABLING A PARAMETER
>
> You can disable a plug-in parameter using similar steps: Just click the desired parameter(s) in the right-hand list and click the Remove button.

## Enabling Plug-In Parameters: Method Two

**1** Press and hold the **Control+ Option+Command keys (Mac) or the Ctrl+Start+Alt keys (PC)** and click on the **parameter** you want to automate (in this case, FREQ). A menu will appear, giving you two options:

**2a** Click on **Enable Automation for <parameter name>** to immediately enable the parameter for automation.

OR

**2b** Click on **Open Plug-In Automation Dialog** to open the Plug-In Automation dialog box that you saw in the previous section. At this point, you can follow Steps 2 through 4 from the "Method One" section.

> ※ Parameters enabled for automation will be indicated by a color. (Sometimes it's an outline, a box, or in this case a small light beneath the parameter.) Note that this color will only appear when you're in an automation mode in which automation can be written (Auto Write, Auto Touch, or Auto Latch).

### ❈ ENABLING ALL PLUG-IN PARAMETERS

Here's a quick way to enable all the parameters on a specific plug-in: Press and hold the Control+Option+Command keys (Mac) or the Ctrl+Start+Alt keys (PC) and click on the plug-in window's Plug-In Automation Enable button.

You can also automatically enable all parameters for automation as soon as a plug-in is instantiated, through the Preferences window. Just go to the Mixing tab and click the Plug-In Controls Default to Auto-Enabled check box. Once this box is checked, all plug-ins created from that point on will have all their parameters enabled for automation.

## Writing Plug-In Automation

Plug-in automation is largely similar to any other kind of automation, but before we close this chapter, let's take a quick look at how you can view plug-in automation data.

❈ Once a parameter is enabled for automation, the plug-in and parameter will appear as an option when you click the Track View Selector button. Just choose the desired plug-in (which will reveal a submenu) and then choose the specific parameter that you want to view. (This can be shown in track lanes as well.)

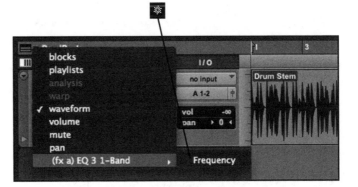

From this point, automation is identical to other kinds of automation—choose your automation mode, begin playback, and change the parameter to start writing automation!

**CHECKING YOUR WORK**

To see many of the steps we've gone over in this chapter, open the session file named Chapter 08 Session-Finished, included on your book's disc.

Next stop...the mixdown!

# 9 } Finishing Touches

Now that you're at the threshold of finishing your first project, it's interesting to look back at all you've accomplished to get here, from setting up your system to recording, editing (and more editing), and on to mixing. Now you're moving to the final stages of creating a deliverable product—good job!

Okay, enough reminiscing—break's over.

Before you can truly consider a project finished, there's usually some tweaking to be done with the mix. Then, when you're satisfied with everything, it's time to do a final mixdown to a file or pair of files that you can listen to on something other than your Pro Tools rig. Last but absolutely not least, there's the business of archiving your session. In this chapter, you'll learn how to:

❋ Tweak your mix automation in the Edit window

❋ Use subgroups and Master Fader tracks

❋ Bounce to disk in a CD-ready format

❄ USING THE TUTORIAL SESSIONS

If you'd like to follow this chapter's examples, please launch the session named Chapter 09 Session, which is included on the disc that came with your book. (Remember to copy it to your hard drive first.) Alternatively, if you worked with the tutorial session for Chapter 8 and you like your mix, you can continue working with that session as well!

# More Fun with Mixing

Though you certainly got a solid start with mixing in the previous chapter, here are a few more techniques that you might find useful.

## Plug-In Power

Learning more about managing your plug-in effects will save time and boost creativity!

### Creating Presets

Suppose you created the *perfect* slap delay for the Delay Aux track, and you'd like to use the same settings in future projects. No problem—saving a preset is an easy process!

Before we go further, though, there's a setting that you should check—one that will affect where your preset will be stored.

**1** Click the **Settings Menu button** (the small circular button immediately to the right of the word Preset). The Settings menu will appear.

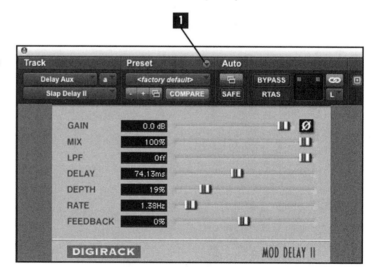

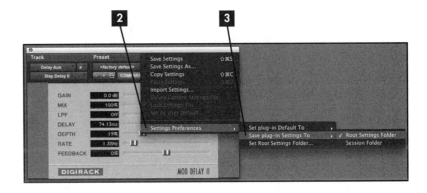

**2** **Choose Settings Preferences.** A submenu will appear.

**3** **Choose Save Plug-In Settings To.** Another submenu will appear, giving you two options:

❋ Choose Root Settings Folder to save your preset to your host computer's Plug-In Settings folder (typically on your computer's primary hard drive). With this option selected, you'll be able to recall your saved presets quickly in any sessions you create or open on this computer.

❋ Choose Session Folder to save your preset to the Plug-In Settings subfolder of the session in which you're currently working. Using this option, the plug-in presets will travel with your session folder, and this preset will be recallable on any computer that you use to open the session.

❋ **IF YOU'RE USING THE TUTORIAL SESSION...**

For the purposes of this example, choose Root Settings Folder.

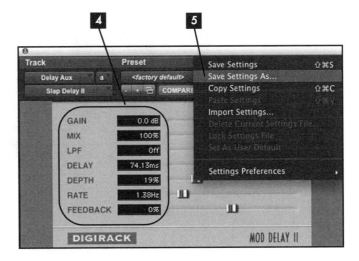

**4** **Adjust** the **settings** for your effect until they're just right.

**5** **Click** the **Settings menu button** once more and then **choose Save Settings As**. The Save dialog box will appear.

**6** **Type** a descriptive **name** for your preset (such as Control Tower Delay, as I've done here).

**7** Click the **Save button.**

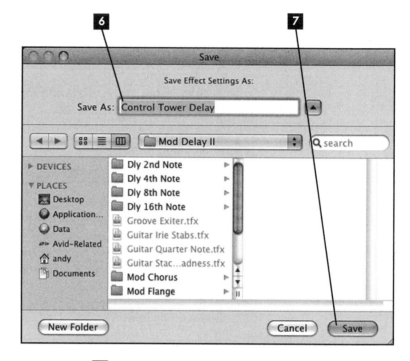

※ Your saved preset will be added to the list of available presets for that plug-in. The more presets you save, the longer that list will become!

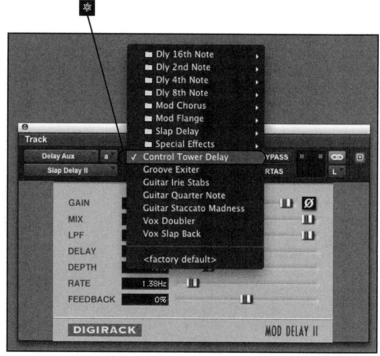

## Setting Up Default Plug-Ins

As you gain experience, you might find that you have some favorite EQ and Dynamic effects that you use time and time again. Setting them up as *default* plug-ins will help you recall them quickly.

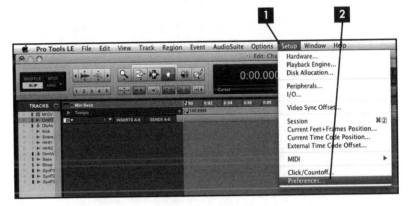

**1** Click the **Setup menu**.

**2** **Select Preferences**. The Pro Tools LE Preferences window will appear.

**3** Click the **Mixing tab** of the Preferences window.

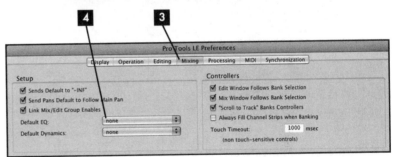

**4** In the Setup section, you'll see two menu buttons, allowing you to select a Default EQ and Default Dynamics plug-in. Let's begin by choosing a favorite EQ—**click** the **Default EQ button**. A menu will be displayed.

**5** Click the **Plug-In menu item**. A submenu will be shown, listing all the EQ plug-ins installed in your system.

**6** Click your favorite **EQ plug-in** (in this case, I've chosen the EQ 3 7-Band). As soon as you choose your favorite plug-in, the menu will close, and your choice will be set as the default EQ for Pro Tools.

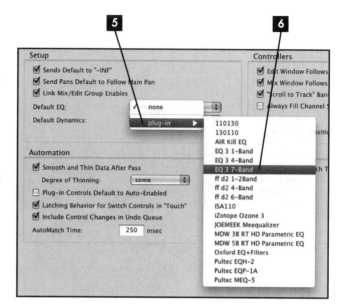

**7** Now let's choose a default *dynamic* plug-in. **Click** the **Default Dynamics button**. A menu will be displayed, as shown here.

**8** The process for selecting a default dynamics plug-in is identical to the steps you took in choosing a favorite EQ—just click the **Plug-In menu item** and **choose** the desired **plug-in** from a list of options. (In this case, I've chosen the Compressor/Limiter Dyn 3.)

**9** When you're finished, just click OK.

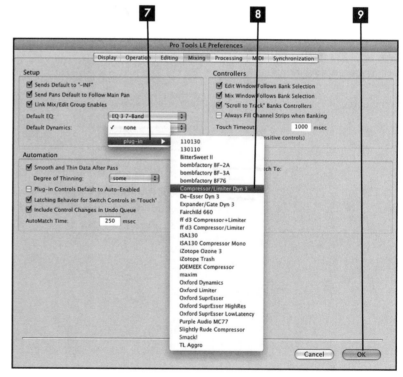

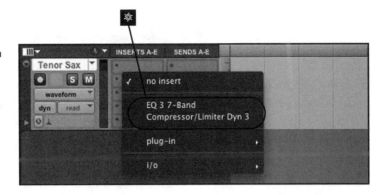

❋ Here's the payoff: Now, when you click on any Insert Selector button, your default plug-ins will appear at the top of the list, easily accessible.

## Using the Workspace Browser with Plug-Ins

You've used the Workspace Browser window before and seen how easy it is to import audio files and sessions. Did you know that you can use the Workspace to import plug-in settings as well?

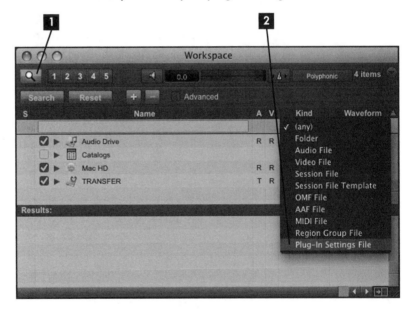

1️⃣ The first step is to locate your desired plug-in preset in the Workspace Browser. You'll find that using the Search function (which you learned about back in Chapter 3) will make the job easier.

2️⃣ Not only can you search by typing in a descriptive name, but you can further refine that search by clicking the menu in the Kind column and choosing Plug-In Settings File. This will exclude other kinds of files from your search.

❋ SEARCHING FOR SETTINGS

If you *don't* type in a name, and you only search by plug-in settings file type, Pro Tools will show *all* your plug-in settings files.

> ❄ **PLUG-IN SETTINGS FILES**
>
> The default location for your plug-in settings files is <boot drive>Library>
> Application Support >Digidesign>Plug-In Settings (Mac), or C:\Program
> Files\Common Files\Digidesign\DAE\Plug-In Settings (PC).

The only thing that you need to do is drag your desired plug-in settings
file into an Insert position on a track. There are two ways to do it:

❄ If you drag the plug-in preset onto an insert that contains a plug-in
(making sure that the plug-in setting matches the plug-in that you're
dragging to), the preset will be loaded in the plug-in.

❄ If you drag the plug-in preset onto an unused insert, Pro Tools will
instantiate the plug-in and load the preset automatically. Job done!

## Making the Most of Automation

Creating mix automation by manipulating knobs, sliders, and
faders is a fantastic advantage of using a DAW, but it'll only take
you so far. When you need to get really specific with your automation, sometimes the only place to do that is back in the Edit window.

**1** If you're not already there, **go**
to the **Edit window**.

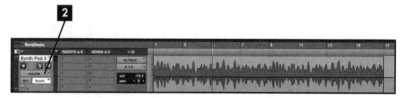

**2** **Click** on the **track display format button** of the track you want to work
with and **choose** the **data** you want to edit. (In this example, I've chosen to view volume automation on the Synth Pad 3 track.)

As you learned in the previous chapter, you'll see a line that represents any parameter movements that have been written to the
track—if you haven't done any automation passes, the automation
playlist will appear as a straight line. Note that you can still see
your regions and waveforms in the background.

## Automation and the Pencil Tool

Now, let's create some new automation data using the Pencil tool.

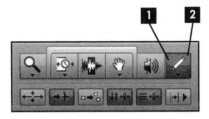

**1** Click on the **Pencil tool**. With the Pencil, you'll be able to write new automation or overwrite previously written automation.

**2** To view the different drawing options available to you, just **click and hold** the **Pencil Tool button**. A menu will appear.

Just like the Trim and Grabber tools, the Pencil has some useful variations. For example, suppose you want to change the Pencil tool from its default freehand mode into a straight line (which in the case of volume automation would create linear changes in amplitude).

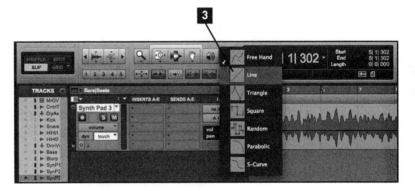

**3** Click on the **option** you want to use (in this case, the Line variation).

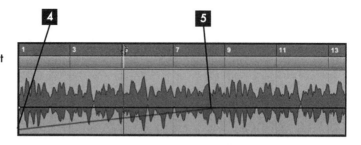

**4** Click and hold the **Pencil tool** at the point at which you want to begin writing new automation.

**5** Drag the **mouse** to the place where you want to stop writing new automation. The Pencil tool will progressively write over preexisting automation. In this example, a straight line will be drawn because the Line option for the Pencil tool was chosen.

**6** Release the **mouse button**. Your new automation will be written.

Of course, you can write more than just volume automation with the Pencil tool. Let's try some pan automation on the "Blorp" track that ping-pongs from left to right.

**1** Click on the **track display format button** and **choose Pan**. The automation data will appear as a line along your track, looking a lot like the volume automation you just worked with. With pan, however, you're not getting louder and softer as the line moves higher and lower—you're panning from left to right.

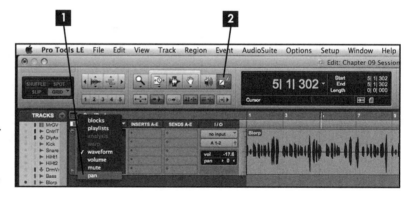

**2** Although you *could* draw a straight line from left to right over and over again to get a ping-pong effect, there's an easier way to do it. **Click and hold** the **Pencil Tool button**. Again, the Pencil tool options will appear.

482
❀ ❀ ❀

**3** This time, **click** on the **Triangle menu item**.

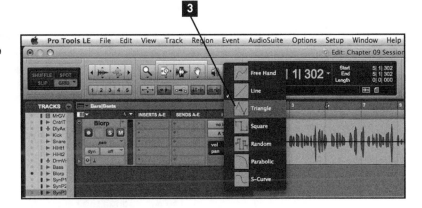

**4** When you're dealing with the Triangle, Square, or Random Pencil tool options, the Grid setting will determine the frequency of the automation changes (even if you're not in Grid mode). In this case, I want to pan from side to side every measure, so I've **chosen 1 bar** as my grid value.

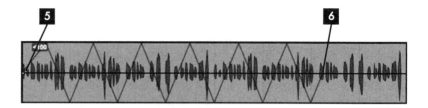

**5** **Click and hold** the **Pencil tool** at the point at which you want to begin writing automation. This time, as you drag horizontally, a triangle wave will be drawn across the track. The frequency of your panning will be the same as your Grid value. (In my case, it's one measure.) You can change the height of the wave by moving your mouse vertically as you drag. In the case of pan automation, a higher and lower triangle wave will translate into a more extreme pan from left to right.

**6** When you're finished, **release** the **mouse button**. The pan automation will be written to your track.

❋ **AUTOMATION AND GRIDS**

Although a triangle wave can be drawn in any of the edit modes, if you want the apex of the triangle wave to fall on a grid line, you must be in Grid mode.

## Copying and Pasting Automation

If you've got a segment of automation that you like, you can cut and paste that automation from one location to another. It's easy!

**1** Click the **Selector tool**.

**2** **Select** the **area of automation** that you want to copy, just as if you were selecting a segment of audio.

**3** Click on the **Edit menu** and **choose** any of the basic **editing functions** you've used before (such as Cut, Copy, Paste, or Duplicate). One thing to keep in mind, though: This will not affect any audio regions or any automation parameters other than the one(s) you have selected.

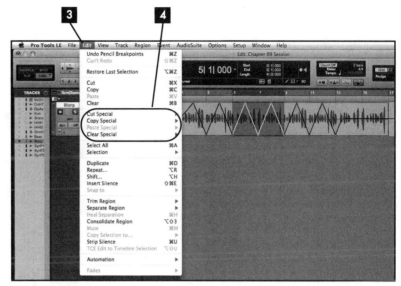

**4** **Clicking** the "special" **editing items**, however (including Cut Special, Copy Special, Paste Special, and Clear Special), will reveal a submenu that will allow you to edit *all* automation, **only pan** automation, or *all plug-in* automation.

❄ SHORTCUT REMINDER

Remember, you can use the regular Cut, Copy, and Paste editing shortcut keys instead of going to the Edit menu.

## Automation Follows Edit

If you move a region, do you want the automation during that time to follow the region, or do you want it to stay put? Either way, Pro Tools has you covered.

**1** Click the **Options menu**.

**2** The feature we're looking for in this case is called Automation Follows Edit. When active, the menu item will appear with a check mark, and you can enable or disable this behavior by **clicking it** in the menu.

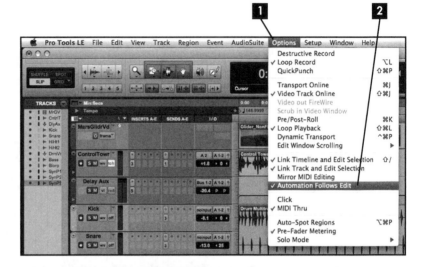

The best way to understand how this feature works is to see it in action. This image shows an example of an unmoved region, showing pan automation in an automation lane below the main playlist. Now, let's say that we move the region. What will happen to the automation?

If Automation Follows Edit is enabled, the automation will be moved along with the region.

If Automation Follows Edit is disabled, the automation will not be moved along with the region and will remain in its original position.

### ❄ SEPARATING REGIONS WHILE VIEWING AUTOMATION

If you want to separate a region, but you are currently in an automation view on the main playlist, it's no problem. Just use the Selector tool to place your cursor where you want to split the region and separate the region as usual (using the processes you learned in Chapter 5). Your region will be separated, just as if you were in Waveform view.

### ❄ SELECTING REGIONS WHILE VIEWING AUTOMATION

If you want to quickly select the area of a region, but you are currently in an automation view on the main playlist, just double-click the region with the Selector tool (just as if you were in Waveform view). The time corresponding to your region will be selected.

### ❄ THE TRIM TOOL AND AUTOMATION

Once you've selected an area of automation, the Trim tool will allow you to scale it proportionally. When the Trim tool is moved into a selected area of automation, it will be shown as downward-facing, allowing you to drag your mouse up and down to increase or decrease the level of the automation in that selected area (while maintaining the shape of the automation line).

Note that when you use the Trim tool to change automation, there will be a small box to the left that will not only show you the level of your new automation, but also a delta value (indicated by a triangle), which lets you know the *amount* of change you're applying.

## Momentary Switches and How to Use Them

Volume, pan, and plug-ins aren't the only aspects of your mix that can be automated—switch-style controls (those that have only an on or off state) can be automated as well. In particular, mute and bypass (for plug-in effects) are often automated in order to get even more control over your mix.

Typically, these controls "latch"—if you click the button once, it will change the state of the parameter until the button is clicked again, like a light switch. However, you might find that changing the behavior of these switches, so that they don't latch (in other words, the state of the switch will only change while you're pressing the button), opens new creative possibilities. This non-latching kind of switch is called a *momentary* switch and is quite useful for adding delay or reverb to individual words or notes but leaving the rest of the track dry.

Here's a scenario for you: If you take a look at your session, you'll see that you have a snare track. What we want to do is to add a large amount of reverb to every fourth snare hit. Here's how to do it using momentary (non-latching) switches.

First, let's set things up (using the traditional time-based techniques we covered in Chapter 8).

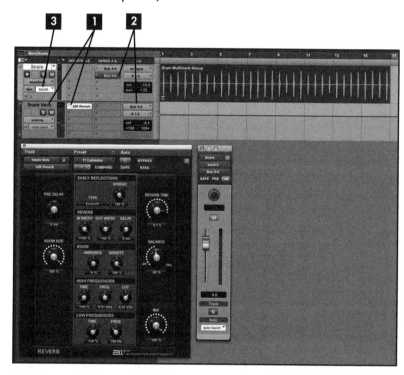

**1** Create a **stereo Aux track** and **instantiate** a **reverb plug-in** on any available insert.

**2** Create a **send** on the Audio track that you want to work with (in this case, the Snare track) and **assign** the **output** to an available pair of busses. (I've chosen Busses 5–6 in this case.) Set the **input** of the **Aux track** to the same busses.

**3** Last but not least, **put** your **Audio track** into Touch automation mode and **mute** the **send**, since this is the state that you'll be starting off with.

**4** In the Preferences window, **go to** the **Mixing tab**.

**5** By default, the Latching Behavior for Switch Controls in "Touch" box is checked. To make the switch momentary, **click** the **box** to remove the check mark.

**6** **Click OK** at the bottom of the Preferences window.

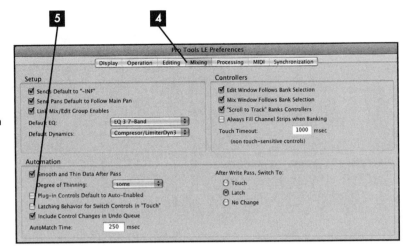

Now you're ready to rock. After you start playback, click and hold on the Send Mute button (which you'll see in the Send Output window) during every fourth snare hit. As soon as the snare hit is finished, release the button (which will put the send back into a muted state).

Though it might take a couple attempts to get it right, here's what you should wind up with. If you look at your send's mute automation playlist, you will see your send alternately mute and unmute. When the send is unmuted, a signal will be sent to the Aux track, and you'll hear the reverb.

This technique is known in many circles as a *dub hit*, and it can be used on any kind of track, from beats to vocals. Now that you understand how the effect is achieved, you'll hear it in all sorts of modern music—the most obvious example is a vocal in which some individual words have reverbs (or echo or delay) but others are relatively dry.

> ❄ **BLUE BREAKPOINTS**
>
> Before we move on from the world of automation, there's one final detail you should be aware of. From time to time you might see an automation breakpoint (the small dots that make up an automation playlist) colored blue. This blue color indicates that the automation data has overflowed (think of it as automation "clipping"), and an automation value was attempted to be written that exceeds the limit of that parameter.

# More Mixing Power with Subgroups

What's a subgroup? Simply put, a *subgroup* is an arrangement whereby the output of a number of tracks is routed to the input of a single track (usually a stereo Aux track). This has the effect of "funneling" the audio through this single track (often referred to as a *subgroup master*), making levels and effects easier to manage. Take a look:

**1** **Create** a **track** to be your subgroup master (in this case, I've chosen to create a stereo Aux track) and **name it** appropriately.

**2** Because you'll be using internal routing in this sort of situation, **choose** available **busses** for the input of the subgroup master. (In this case, I've chosen Busses 7 and 8.)

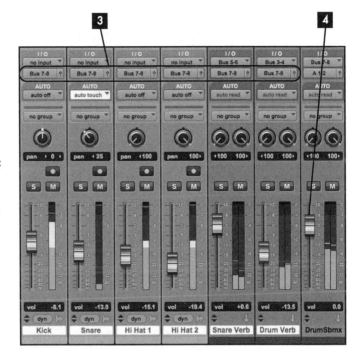

**3** **Assign** the **outputs** of the tracks to be grouped (in this case, I've chosen all of the drum tracks in this session, including the reverb Aux tracks) to the same busses as you've chosen for the input of your subgroup master.

**4** Your subgroup Master track's fader is now in control of the overall volume of your sub-grouped tracks. Note that as you adjust the fader, the relative blend of the drums remains consistent, and the subgroup master controls the overall output.

In addition to making levels more manageable, subgroups can also help you work more efficiently with plug-ins. For example, if you want to apply a compressor to your drums (a very common thing to do), you *could* instantiate a compressor on each of the tracks, but that would be unwieldy to work with and wasteful of your limited processing resources. Instead, just launch one compressor effect on an insert of the subgroup master. There's only one plug-in to adjust, and it's thrifty use of your CPU!

# Using Master Faders

There's one more track type left for us to explore—the Master Fader. Although it looks similar to an Audio or Aux track, its function is substantially different than anything you've seen up to this point.

A Master Fader is a way to control output, and it is commonly used to control the output of an interface channel (though it can be also used to control the output of busses as well, in more complex mix situations). With this simple but powerful track, you can control the entire level of your session.

## Creating a Master Fader

First things first...you need to *create* a Master Fader before you can use it!

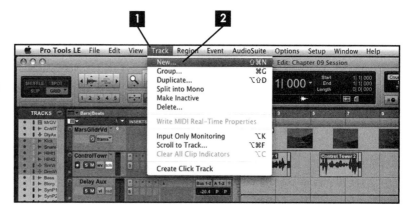

**1** Click the **Track menu**.

**2** Click on **New**. The New Tracks dialog box will open.

**3** Using the techniques you learned back in Chapter 3, **create** a **stereo Master Fader track** (you'll find "Master Fader" listed in the track type menu, as shown here). The new Master Fader track will be created below the last selected track in your session.

The Master Fader looks similar to any other track, but don't be fooled—it's significantly different!

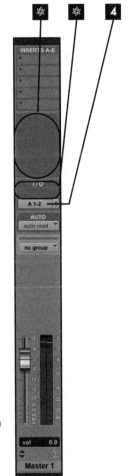

❋ You'll notice that the area on the channel strip that would normally display an Input button is conspicuously blank. That's because there is no input on a Master Fader; it is only a way to control an output.

❋ Notice also that there are no sends on a Master Fader.

❋ If you take a look at a Master Fader track in the Edit window, you'll see that you can't place regions on this track. (In this regard, it's similar to an Aux track.)

❋ **Click** on the **Output Path Selector button** and **select** the **interface output** that you're using to listen to your mix (if it's not already being shown in the button). With this output selected, the Master Fader is in its common role of controlling the output of your entire mix.

## Controlling Your Mix with a Master Fader

Now let's use your Master Fader to control your entire mix. Let's start by creating a linear fade-out for your entire mix in one easy process.

 SETTING THINGS UP

For this section, switch to the Edit window if you're not viewing it already.

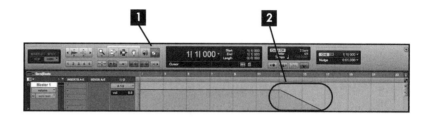

**1** Select the **Pencil tool** and **choose** the **Line option** to create a straight fade-out.

**2** Write a **linear decrease** in volume automation on the Master Fader track, just as you would on any other kind of track. Because this Master Fader is controlling the output of your entire mix, you'll hear a linear change in the volume of all of your tracks, starting at the point at which the Master Fader's automation begins.

### ❋ AUTOMATION AND MASTER FADERS

If you want to write automation onto your Master Fader in the Mix window, it's no problem. Simply write automation just as you would on any other type of track, using any of the automation modes.

## Basic Mastering Techniques Using a Master Fader

*Mastering* is a post-mix process that further refines a session to a professional quality. It's such an exclusive and important process that there is an entire segment of the professional audio community dedicated to the specific task of mastering others' mixes. With that in mind, the task of professionally mastering a mix is certainly not recommended for the non-specialist.

You might, however, want to try your hand at a little basic mastering to punch up your mix for your own enjoyment or to make an evaluation mix a little more palatable for your client. That's where Master Faders can really come in handy, due to another interesting difference between a Master Fader and any other track (one that may not be initially apparent). This difference is in the area of signal flow—the inserts are *after* the fader in the signal chain. Read on...

Advice on Mastering

The discussion in this section relates to the process of mastering a mix *on your own* (as opposed to having your mix professionally mastered by a dedicated mastering engineer). If and when you decide to have your mix professionally mastered, the mastering engineer will want to do the entire job himself (usually with highly specialized and costly gear specific to the process of mastering), so you won't need to go through the steps outlined here. That being said, it's always a good idea to consult with your mastering engineer *before* submitting your mix so you can find out exactly what he or she needs from you.

## Adjusting Dither

Dither is a common mastering tool used to offset some of the negative sonic qualities of digital audio. In simplistic terms, it is a very low-level noise that is added to digital audio to combat distortion that is sometimes associated with very quiet signals. In the mastering process, dither is added when the bit depth of audio is reduced. For example, if you're working in a 24-bit session but will be creating a 16-bit file for an audio CD, you can improve the quality of your audio by instantiating a dither plug-in on a Master Fader.

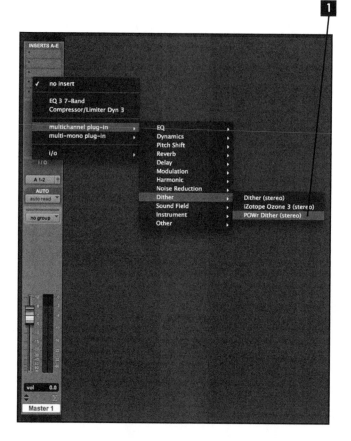

**1** On an available insert on the Master Fader track, **select** a desired **dither plug-in** (in this case, I've chosen POWr Dither) from the Multichannel Plug-In menu. The plug-in's window will appear.

**2** **Click** on the **Bit Resolution button** and **choose** the **final resolution** for your mix from a list. For example, if you want to make a Red Book Audio CD of your mix, you would choose the 16-bit option (as shown here).

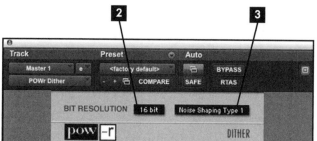

**3** Noise shaping can help make dither "noise" even less audible than it normally is. **Click** the **Noise Shaping button** and **select** a **Noise Shaping Type** from the list. For now, you can safely stick with the default shaping, but be sure to listen to different mixes with different noise shaping later, to determine the one that's best for you.

## Punching Up Your Mix with Compression—Two Ways

Another common step in the mastering process is the application of compression to the entire mix. This is a tried-and-true method employed to narrow the dynamic range of your audio, thereby maximizing its overall "punch." Here's an easy way to get it done:

**1** On your Master Fader, **instantiate** a **compressor plug-in** on an insert before (above) the one you used for dither. The Compressor plug-in window will appear.

**2** **Adjust** your compressor's **parameters** to punch up your mix to suit your taste. It'll take some experimentation to find your ideal settings, of course, but you can start with a preset configuration, like the one shown in this example.

❋ **COMPRESSORS AND DITHER**

If you're using both dither and a compressor on a Master Fader, you'll need to arrange your inserts so that the dither is the last plug-in in the insert signal flow (for example, on the lowest insert). Don't worry if your dither is currently on the top insert; you can just drag it down to a lower insert position (and thus later in the insert's signal path) with your mouse and then launch your compressor in an insert above it.

Those of you with mixing experience might notice a problem with this sort of routing. As you know, a compressor operates by attenuating (or reducing) any level above a certain threshold, which you set up in your plug-in window. Any incoming signal that is below that threshold will not be affected by the compressor. As long as you don't use your Master Fader for fade-ins or fade-outs, there's no problem with using a compressor on the Master Fader, but if you *do* use the Master Fader for any kind of volume automation, you might hear your compressor kick in or out, depending on whether you're fading in or out. (Remember, the inserts on a Master Fader track are post-fader.) How do you get around this problem? I'm glad you asked!

**1** **Reassign** the **output** of all tracks previously assigned to Main Output (in this case, A 1-2) to an available pair of busses. (In this case, I've chosen Busses 9-10.) If you're following the tutorial session, this will include all the tracks *except* your drum tracks. (They're already assigned to a bus, which is routed to a subgroup Aux track. You *will* want to change the outputs on the Drum Subgroup Aux track, though.) Your session should now be completely inaudible, but wait!

**2** **Create** a **stereo Aux track** and **assign** the **input** of that track to the same pair of busses that you used as an output for your other tracks. Essentially, you're creating a huge subgroup. Finally, **drag** the **compressor plug-in** from the Master Fader (with its post-fader inserts) to the new Aux track (which has pre-fader inserts).

**3** The output of this Aux track (in this case, A 1-2) is still ultimately controlled by the Master Fader, making it an ideal place to apply dither. Since the inserts of the Aux track are pre-fader, the signal going to the compressor will be affected by neither the Master Fader nor the Aux track's output level, meaning that you can apply your global fade automation on either track without losing that punchy sound. That's it!

✳ There's one more very important function of a Master Fader track—one for which it is uniquely suited due to its post-fader inserts. Master Faders are great for monitoring the overall levels of your mix, and in addition to the track's own level meters, there are a variety of metering plug-ins available to you. A good example of this is the Bomb Factory Essential Meter Bridge shown here. (You'll find it in the Other category of the Multichannel Plug-Ins insert menu.)

# Bouncing to Disk

When you're working with a Pro Tools session, you're in a multitrack environment. Even though you may be listening through stereo monitor speakers, you're actually hearing many component tracks, artfully combined by Pro Tools' software mix engine. From a production standpoint, it's a very cool way to work, but if you ever want to hear your song *outside* of the Pro Tools environment, you'll have to somehow render the mix down to a format that is compatible with the outside world.

The Bounce to Disk function will allow you to "mix down" your session to a final format (for example, a stereo file that can be heard through your computer speakers). It's a simple process, but one that demands attention to detail, so we'll go over each step carefully. For the purpose of demonstration, here's how to go about bouncing to disk so you can create a file that you could burn onto an audio CD (Red Book format).

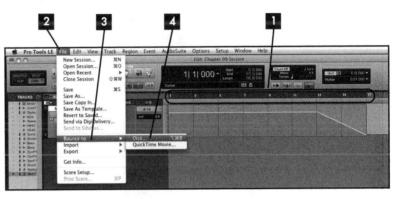

**1** Using the Selector tool, **select** the **area** of your session you want to bounce to disk in the Ruler area. (In this case, I'll select from the beginning of my session to the end of my Master Fader's fade-out.)

**2** Click on the **File menu**.

**3** Click on **Bounce To**. A submenu will be displayed.

**4** Click on **Disk**. The Bounce dialog box will appear.

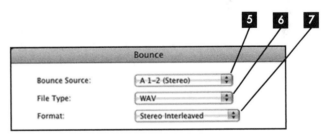

**5** At the top of the Bounce dialog box, you'll see the Bounce Source menu. (The button will display the currently selected bounce source.) To change the source, just **click** the **Bounce Source menu button** and **select** the **output path** that you're using to listen to your mix from a list of options. (In this case, I want to choose A 1-2 as my bounce source, since that's the path that is connected to my monitor speakers.)

> ❊ **BOUNCE TROUBLESHOOTING**
>
> If you do a bounce to disk and then later find that your bounce is a silent audio file, you've probably chosen the wrong bounce source.

**6** The File Type menu button will display the type of file that you will be creating. (In this example, we'll be creating a .wav file.) If you want to change the file type, just **click** the **File Type menu button** and **choose** the desired **type** from the list of available file types.

**7** The Format menu button will display the kind of file(s) that you will be creating with your bounce. (In this case, it's Stereo Interleaved.) Let's take a closer look at this—**click** on the **Format menu button** to reveal a list of bounce options.

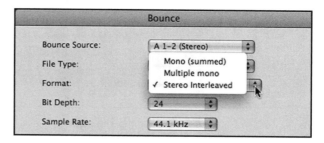

* **Mono (Summed).** With this option selected, your session will be mixed down to a single mono file (even if it's a stereo session).

* **Multiple Mono.** When this is chosen, your stereo mix will be output to a pair of mono files—one for the left channel (with a ".l" after the file name) and one for the right (with a ".r" after the file name). This is particularly useful for bounces that you intend to import into another Pro Tools session.

* **Stereo Interleaved.** Your mix will be rendered to a single stereo file.

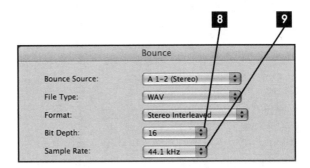

**8** The Bit Depth menu button will display the bit depth of the file that you will be creating. (In this example, we'll be creating a 16-bit file.) If you want to change the bit depth, just **click** the **Bit Depth menu button** and **choose** the desired **setting** from a list of available resolutions.

**9** The Sample Rate menu button will display the sample rate of the file that you will be creating. (In this example, we'll be creating a 44.1-kHz file.) If you want to change the setting, just **click** the **Sample Rate menu button** and **choose** the desired **sample rate**.

❄ RED BOOK CD SETTINGS

If your bounced file is going to be put onto a Red Book Audio CD, here are the settings you'll want to use: The Bit Depth should be set to 16, the Sample Rate should be 44.1 kHz, and the Format should be set to Stereo Interleaved.

✴ If the sample rate or bit depth you've chosen for your bounced file is different from those of your session (or if you've chosen any format other than Multiple Mono), Pro Tools will need to perform a conversion process—this will be done in one of two ways:

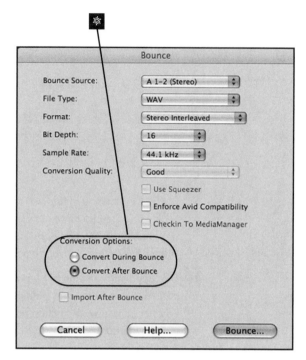

✧ **Convert During Bounce.** Clicking this radio button will direct Pro Tools to convert during the bounce process (as your session plays).

✧ **Convert After Bounce.** This option will allow Pro Tools to apply its conversion after the bounce pass is complete, and it is the recommended setting in most cases.

### ✴ SOME ADVICE ON BOUNCING

In rare cases, choosing Convert During Bounce can cause Pro Tools *not* to play back some types of automation during the bounce pass (as a result of the extra burden of conversion while bouncing). For consistently accurate results, choose the Convert After Bounce option.

❋ **Import After Bounce.** If the file type, sample rate, and bit depth of your bounced file match your session's setup (and if you've chosen Multiple Mono as a format), clicking the Import After Bounce check box will import your bounced file back into your session on an Audio track.

**10** Once you have everything set up properly, **click** the **Bounce button**. The Save dialog box will open.

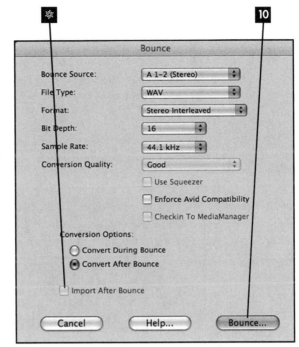

**11** By now, you've seen the Save dialog box in a number of different contexts—in this case, you'll be **choosing** a **name** and **location** for your bounced audio file(s). You can save your file under any name you want, in any drive, and in any folder.

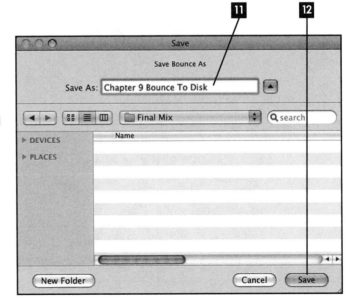

> ❄ THE IMPORTANCE OF GOOD FILE MANAGEMENT
>
> At this point, I want to emphasize again how important it is to know exactly where and under what name your files are saved. (This goes for session files and other audio files as well.) You can save your bounced file anywhere you choose in your system, but with this great flexibility comes the added responsibility of using this power wisely—make sure you can find your files when you need them!

**12** Once you've chosen a name and location for your new file, **click** on the **Save button**, and your bounce will begin.

Your session will begin playing, and a small countdown window will indicate that bouncing is occurring in real time.

If conversion is necessary (and assuming you wisely chose to Convert After Bounce), you'll see a quick conversion progress window after your session is done playing. You're finished!

## Bouncing to a QuickTime Movie

Because this session happens to have a Video track included in it, you also have the option of bouncing your work to a QuickTime movie file. The process is nearly identical to bouncing to disk.

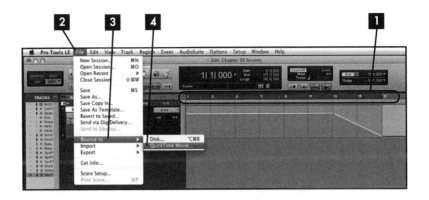

1. Using the Selector tool, **select** the **area** of your session you want to bounce to disk in the Ruler area. (When you're bouncing to a QuickTime movie, a good rule of thumb is to select an area equal to the length of the region on your Video track.)

2. Click on the **File menu**.

3. Click on **Bounce To**.

4. Click on **QuickTime Movie**. The Bounce dialog box will appear.

5. The Bounce dialog box that appears here is nearly identical to the one you encountered when you bounced only your audio. You may notice, though, that you have different options with regard to format and sample rate—this is normal. When you've made your choices, **click** the **Bounce button**. The bounce process will continue just as it did when you were using the Bounce to Disk feature, except that in this case, you'll be creating a QuickTime movie file.

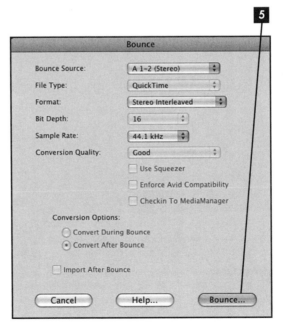

Enjoy your final mix—you've earned it!

# Moving to the Next Level: Tips and Tricks

Pro Tools LE is a complex, professional application, and mastering it requires dedication, inspiration, and time. This book is meant to provide you with a solid basic understanding of how to use this powerful product—a foundation upon which to build greater knowledge as you gain experience. Through mastering this book so far, you've attained that basic understanding.

This chapter is a varied list of next-level functions, designed to allow you to be even more productive. In this chapter, you'll learn how to:

* Get the most out of your system
* Make the most of your recording sessions
* Edit with more efficiency and flexibility
* Understand and use Elastic Audio
* Import and use movie files

> ❋ WORKING WITH THE TUTORIAL SESSION
>
> To follow along with the examples shown in this chapter, launch the session named Chapter 10 Session. You'll note that in this session, features are demonstrated through a series of memory locations. You'll note also that even though the session is extensive in its tracks and complexity, it's only using a few different audio files, keeping the overall session folder size small!

# Boosting Performance with Disk Allocation

When they're starting out with Pro Tools, many people don't set up a dedicated hard drive for recording their audio files. (In fact, they often record to their sole system drives.) Although this will work for relatively simple sessions, you may eventually find that a single hard drive—especially if it's your system drive—just doesn't cut it. Here are a few things that can place added stress on a hard drive:

- ❋ **High Audio track count.** More Audio tracks require more streams of communication to and from your hard drive.

- ❋ **High-resolution audio and/or bit depth.** Higher-quality audio requires a greater bit rate and more of a hard drive's limited bandwidth.

- ❋ **Edit density.** The term *edit density* refers to the frequency with which your session needs to retrieve new audio from your hard drive during playback. Each time you create a region boundary in a track, you require Pro Tools to access a specific location on your hard drive—the more regions you have in a given time, the higher your edit density becomes, and the harder your drive has to work to provide uninter-rupted audio playback. There are a few features that tend to increase edit density in a session, including using Beat Detective and Strip Silence—two tools that we'll talk about later in this chapter.

One solution to hard-drive bandwidth problems is to distribute audio playback among *multiple* hard drives, and that's just what the Disk Allocation window lets you do. But first, let's take a quick trip to the Workspace Browser to set up different drives for different jobs:

❈ Immediately to the right of each drive name, you'll see a column headed with an A (for *audio*), which will allow you to set up how each drive deals with audio files with regard to Pro Tools.

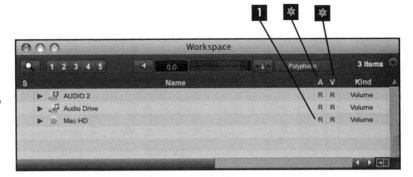

❈ Right next to the A column, you'll see a V (for *video*) column. This does the same thing as the A column, except that it's concerned with the way that Pro Tools works with video files.

**1** Let's start by setting up each drive's audio behavior. Just **click** the **letter** in the A column that corresponds to the drive you want to set up. (In this case, I want to change the behavior of my system drive.) A menu will appear.

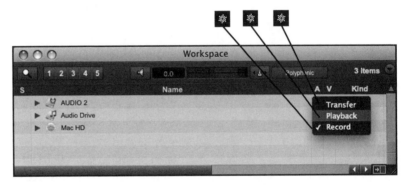

❈ If you set up your drive to be a Transfer volume, your Pro Tools session will not be able to record or play back audio files with that drive. Essentially, the drive is off limits to Pro Tools as far as audio files are concerned (though it is worth noting that you can audition audio files that are stored on Transfer drives). System drives are commonly set up as transfer volumes (assuming that there are dedicated hard drives for audio recording and playback).

❈ A Playback volume will allow Pro Tools to play back audio files, but you may not record new audio to this type of volume. This is a common setting for archive drives, allowing you to listen to your backed-up sessions but not to inadvertently record to that hard drive.

✻ Finally, a Record volume is fully functional with regard to audio and Pro Tools, which means that you can record to it and play back from it. A typical audio drive is set up as a record volume.

The volume designations in the V (video) column work just the same way, only for video files instead of audio files. You can (and should) set up each of your hard drive's accessibility for audio and video files. Here's a common setup for a Pro Tools system with two dedicated audio hard drives:

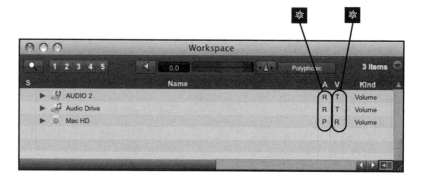

✻ As far as audio recording and playback are concerned, both the Audio Drive and AUDIO 2 drive can record and play back audio files. The system drive (Mac HD) is set up as a playback drive for audio, so that I can play back sessions that are copied to the drive but keep it protected from recording new files.

✻ With regard to video files, I've set up my audio files to be transfer volumes, meaning that I can neither play back nor record video files with those drives. On the rare occasion that I have to record video, I can record video files to my system drive and play them back as well.

When the behavior of the drives has been squared away, it's time to do some disk allocation. In this session, I've created 10 pretty generic tracks, and I'm almost ready to do some recording. This is just the time to set up disc allocation—*before* you record any new audio.

**1** Click the **Setup menu**.

**2** Click **Disk Allocation**. The Disk Allocation window will appear.

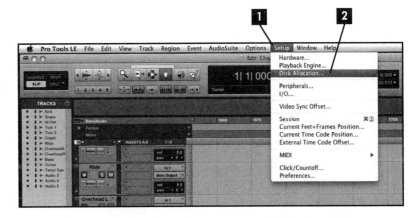

**3** In the Disk Allocation window, you'll see a listing of all the Audio tracks in your session—the track names will be in the leftmost column, and the location to which audio files will be recorded will be shown in the column to the right. From this window, you'll be able to assign individual tracks to available hard drives on a track-by-track basis. Just **click and hold** on the **Root Media Folder column** for a track you want to set up. (In this case, I've chosen the Snare track.) A menu will appear.

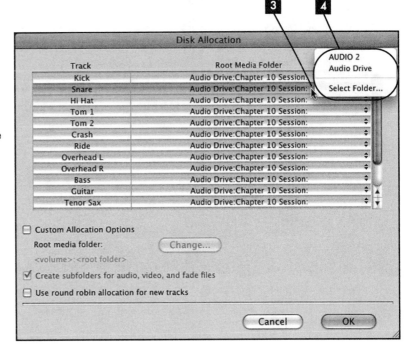

**4** From this menu, you'll be able to choose which drive will store the audio recorded on that track. You can either **choose** one of the **drives** and let Pro Tools create the appropriate folder for you or **click** the **Select Folder option** to choose a specific location. For the purposes of this example, I'll choose AUDIO 2, which will automatically create a session folder on that drive.

The basic goal when assigning disk allocation is to balance the session's audio workload as evenly as possible between the audio drives that you have in your system, to ensure maximum performance. Here's what I've ended up with:

※ In this particular case, I've alternated each track between the two audio hard drives. Basically, each drive is doing about half the work needed to play and record audio for this session.

※ Here's a useful feature: If you check the Use Round Robin Allocation for New Tracks box, Pro Tools will automatically cycle through all the record-enabled volumes for your tracks as they are created. The result would be the same as what you're seeing in this image but would have been done automatically by Pro Tools as you added new tracks.

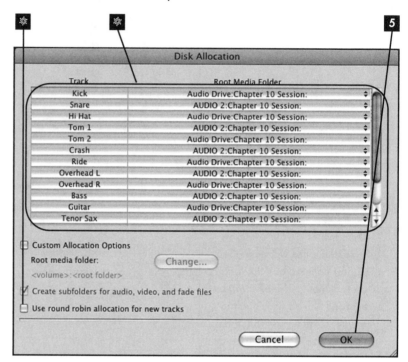

**5** Once you've set things up the way you want them, **click OK**.

### ※ DRIVE VOLUMES AND ROUND-ROBIN ALLOCATION

Note that only the drives that you've designated as Record volumes show up in the drive assignment drop-down menu, and they will be the only drives that will be used when the round-robin allocation box is checked. By setting up your volume designations beforehand, you can make working in the Disk Allocation window quicker, easier, and better.

Now you're ready to record as usual. When you're finished, you'll see regions created in your Regions list. But where have they been recorded to? Let's find out:

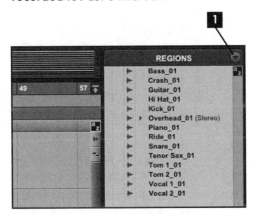

**1** Click the **Regions List Pop-up button**. A menu will appear.

**2** Click on **Show**. A submenu will appear.

**3** This menu will allow you to see different aspects of your regions in the Regions list. (You may find showing the full path very useful in tracking down individual files!) In this case, we want to see what disk they've been recorded to, so click **Disk Name**.

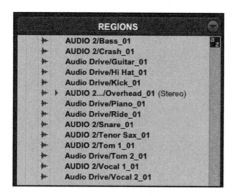

Assuming that you've set up your disk allocation correctly, you should see both drives represented in the Regions list. This means that you've balanced your hard drives' workload and can get extra performance and higher track counts when you need it.

 WHEN TO SET UP DISK ALLOCATION

Remember to set up your disk allocation *before* you start recording. Changing your disk allocation after your audio has been recorded (and files have been created) will have no effect on the performance of your session.

# Recording with Cue Mixes

During the recording process, your artist might want to have a customized mix—something that's different from what the engineer (that's you) in the control room is hearing. In cases where there are multiple musicians, for example, each player will often want their *own* personal mix. Not to worry—creating customized cue mixes is easy to do, using your tracks' sends. Here's a common cue mix process:

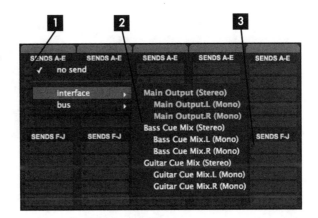

**1** While **holding** the **Option key (on a Mac) or the Alt key (PC), click** an available **send selector button.** (In this case, I've chosen Send A.)

**2** Since our cue mix will be sent out of a physical output, **assign** the send's **output** to an available interface output path. (In this case, I've created a path named Bass Cue Mix.)

**3** If you have additional musicians requiring individual cue mixes, you'll need to **repeat Steps 1 and 2** for each cue mix. In this example, I've got a guitarist that wants his own mix, so I'll create my second send at the Send F position (you'll see why in a moment) and assign it to interface output path Guitar Cue Mix.

If you're following the steps outlined here, when you're finished you should see one cue mix send on Send A (for the bass player) and one on Send F (for the guitar). Holding down the Option or Alt key while I was creating the sends made the job easier by creating sends on all the tracks in the session, as opposed to creating sends one at a time.

In this example I've created two cue mix sends, and while I *could've* put them on adjacent sends (Sends A and B, for example), there's an advantage to having them on different banks.

**4** While **holding** the **Command key (on a Mac) or the Ctrl key (PC), click** on the **send selector button** for Send A (the one I'm using for my bassist's cue mix).

You can now see volume, pan, mute, and pre/post controls for each track's send, allowing you to view and control the cue mix with ease. To get out of this view, just hold the Command key (on a Mac) or the Ctrl key (PC) and click the send selector button again. (You'll see a list from which you can choose to view all the send assignments in that bank or to view another send.)

**5** Here's where setting up the second cue on a different bank will pay off. **Repeat Step 4**, but with the second cue mix send. (In this example, it's on Send F.)

Assuming that the sends' outputs are attached to headphone amplifiers (which are in turn attached to headphones!), you now have the ability to quickly customize a mix for your musicians, as shown here. With Pro Tools' two banks of sends, you can view two cue mixes at once.

# Making the Most of Editing

Let's take a look at some techniques that will make editing even more efficient and fun!

## Identify Beat

One of Pro Tools' greatest strengths is its ability to use MIDI and audio in the same environment. To get them to work well together, though, their tempos should agree. That's where the Identify Beat feature comes in—it will let you quickly determine the tempo of a selected area of audio, and once that's set, your tick-based MIDI tracks will naturally follow the tempo of your Audio tracks.

This memory location (#1—Identify Beat) shows a great example of a very common dilemma. Listen to the region—sounds like eight full measures of drums, right? Now look at the selection length according to the Pro Tools tempo ruler—it says that the region is 6 measures, 1 beat, and 741 ticks! Obviously, your judgment is correct, and here's how to get Pro Tools to agree with you!

**1** Make a **selection** of a specific musical length. (In this example, eight measures have already been selected for you). Use your ears to make a good, loopable selection—*don't* rely on your bars|beats ruler.

**2** Make sure that the **Conductor track** is enabled if it isn't already. When enabled, the Conductor Track button will be colored blue.

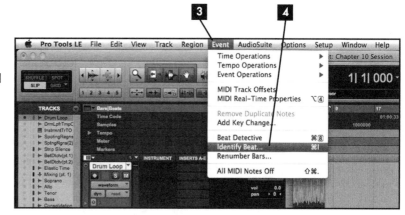

**3** Click on the **Event menu**.

**4** Click on **Identify Beat**. The Add Bar | Beat Markers dialog box will appear.

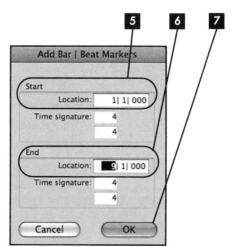

**5** Type the musical **location** of the beginning of the selection in the Location text box in the Start area. Again, let your ears be your guide—in this example, since the selection begins at the beginning of the timeline, the beginning should be 1|1|000.

**6** Type the musical **location** of the end of the selection in the Location text box in the End area. In this example, you are hearing an eight-bar selection, ending at the beginning of Bar 9 (9|1|000).

**7** Click OK. The Add Bar | Beat Markers dialog box will close, and your tempo will change accordingly.

When you're finished, you'll see that your session's bars|beats ruler and your ears are now in agreement as to the tempo of the section of audio, as shown here. Now the grid lines will be aligned with the appropriate musical events (assuming that your grid scale is set to Bars|Beats), and the selection that you made will be correctly displayed in the Edit Selection display (assuming that your main time scale is Bars|Beats).

❊ IDENTIFY BEAT WORKS ANYWHERE!

You can use the Identify Beat function at any point in a session. For example, if you have a live drummer who goes a little faster during the chorus, just select the chorus and enter the correct musical values in the Add Bar|Beat Markers dialog box.

## Timeline versus Edit Selection

Throughout this book, whenever you have made a selection on a track, that selection has been reflected in the Ruler area (also called the timeline) and vice versa. Normally, this is the way to work, but these two selections don't *need* to be linked.

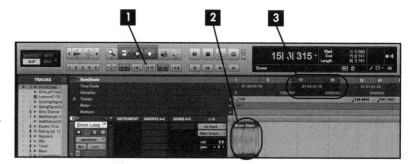

**1** Click on the **Link Timeline and Edit Selection button** (which is normally blue) to deselect it.

**2** Make a **selection** on any track.

**3** Now make a **different selection** in the Ruler area. Note that the two selected areas do not reflect each other.

It's important to take a moment to see just how Pro Tools acts in this situation. If you try to play your session, note that what plays back is your timeline selection. In truth, this always has been the case, though many users don't make any distinctions between the edit selection and the timeline selection and leave the linking enabled all the time.

Unlinking your timeline and edit selections can be handy when you want to hear a different part of your song than the part that you're editing. For example, if you want to hear a little *before* the region that you're working with, *unlink* your timeline and edit selection and make a timeline selection that reflects what you want to hear. Just be careful to *relink* when you're finished with this unusual mode of operation!

### ❄ ANOTHER WAY TO LINK OR UNLINK

In addition to being able to link or unlink the timeline and edit selection with the Edit window button as shown previously, you also have a menu-based option: Just click the Options drop-down menu and choose the Link Timeline and Edit Selection menu item. (When enabled, a check mark will appear to the left of the menu item.)

## Dynamic Transport

You have yet another way to treat your selections and playback independently, through a feature called *Dynamic Transport*. Dynamic Transport gives you the ability to start playback at any point in your session, regardless of either the timeline or edit selection. Take a look:

1 Click the **Options menu**.

2 Choose **Dynamic Transport**.

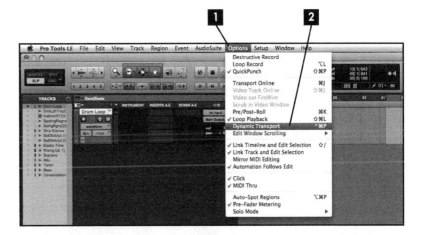

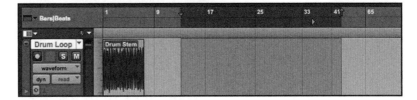

You'll notice that your main timescale ruler has gotten twice as tall as any other ruler. In the bottom half of the main timescale ruler, you'll now see a right-facing blue triangle, which indicates where your playback will begin. Just click and drag the triangle to any location on the timeline, and your session will play back from that point. This point can be *before* a selected area, anywhere *within* a selection (as shown here), or even *after* a selected area.

By default, your timeline and edit selections are automatically unlinked when you turn on Dynamic Transport. (You can re-link them at any time.) When you turn off Dynamic Transport, your timeline and edit selection will be re-linked.

## Samples versus Ticks

You learned back in Chapter 6 about the power of *tick-based* Audio tracks. In this section, we'll talk a little bit more about samples and ticks in a Pro Tools session, and how they interact.

> ❄ SETTING THINGS UP
>
> If you're using the tutorial session, go to Memory Location #2—Tempo Operations.

### MIDI Track Timings

Audio tracks, as you know, are typically created as *sample-based* tracks, meaning that each region is anchored to a specific sample (or real-time) location. The upshot of this is that tempo, bar|beat, and meter changes will have no effect upon the regions of the track.

Instrument tracks and MIDI tracks, on the other hand, are created by default as *tick-based* tracks, which means that regions and notes on these tracks *will* respond to tempo and meter changes. For example, if you increase the tempo of your session, your tick-based tracks will speed up accordingly.

Even though these are the *default* states for each kind of track, there are advantages to working unconventionally!

> ❄ As you saw in Chapter 6, you can change an Audio track to tick-based timing (indicated by a Metronome icon in the Timebase Selector button), allowing you to put your region timing under the control of your MIDI tempo map. In this example, if you were to change the tempo of your session, your regions would move and change your drum audio's "tempo" as a result.

> ❋ Less common, but no less possible, is the practice of changing a MIDI (or Instrument) track to sample-based timing. To do it, just click the track's Timebase Selector button and choose Samples from the list of options (as shown here). In this mode, your MIDI track takes on a very interesting behavior, as your MIDI data will not change when you change tempo!

Though sample-based MIDI is somewhat unusual, it opens up interesting opportunities. For example, if you want to use a sampler or other virtual instrument to "play" a sound effect that needs to be synched to video, a sample-based track does the trick nicely. Since MIDI notes on sample-based tracks will ignore tempo changes, you have the freedom to change musical tempo without affecting the timing of these notes, ensuring that they remain in sync with the video.

## Default Track Timebase

For some users, particularly those primarily doing music production, you might want your tracks to be tick-based as a general rule.

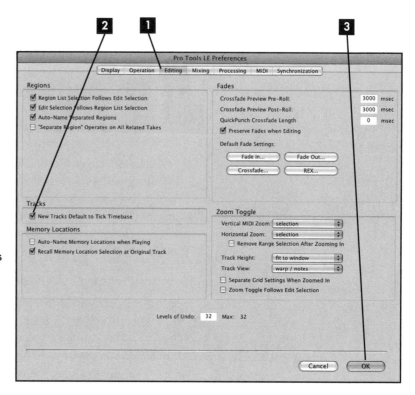

**1** After opening the Preferences window (from the Setup menu), **click** the **Editing tab**.

**2** In the lower-left area of the Editing page, you'll see the New Tracks Default to Tick Timebase option. Just **click** the **check box** to make all your new tracks default to a tick timebase.

**3** **Click OK** to exit the Preferences window.

## Session Linearity

This next bit can get a little tricky: By default, the rulers of your sessions are evenly spaced (or *linear*) based upon real time, which can be broken down into hours, minutes, seconds, frames (in the case of SMPTE time code), and samples. Another way of saying this is that, by default, Pro Tools uses a Linear Sample Display. This works well in many cases, but from time to time, you might want to look at your timeline in a different way....

❄ SETTING THINGS UP

If you're using the tutorial session, go to Memory Location #3—Session Linearity.

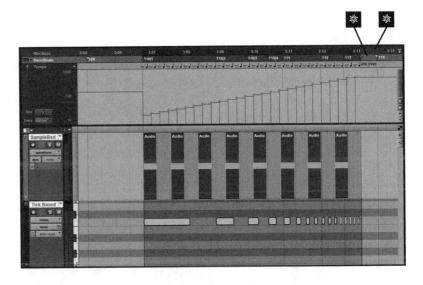

This image shows a Pro Tools session with a Linear Sample Display. Taking a look at your sample-based and tick-based rulers illustrates this mode well.

- ❄ Your real-time rulers will be evenly spaced.
- ❄ Your bars|beats ruler will change its spacing based upon tempo changes in your session. (In this case, the bars and beats get gradually compressed as the tempo increases.)

The regions on the Audio track are clearly evenly spaced in real time. The notes on the Instrument track are all eighth notes, but the duration and spacing of these notes change due to an increasing tempo. Occasionally, it's desirable to be able to see your notes displayed more consistently, regardless of tempo changes. It's very easy to do, and it makes quite a difference in your Edit window's view.

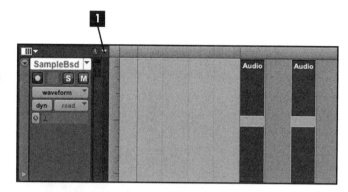

1 **Click** the **Linearity Display Mode down arrow** (located in the upper-left area of the Edit window). A menu will appear.

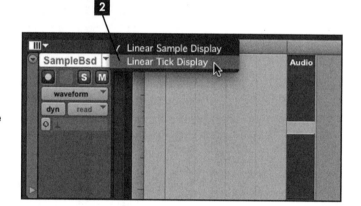

2 **Choose Linear Tick Display.** The Linearity Display Mode icon will change from a blue clock (indicating sample linearity) to a green metronome (indicating tick linearity).

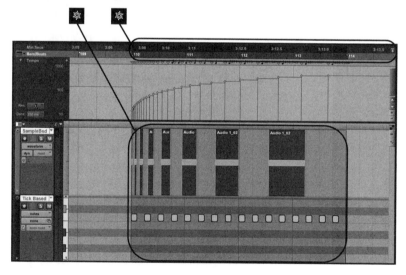

❈ Your bars|beats ruler (top) is now evenly spaced (despite the tempo change), and the min:secs ruler is now unevenly spaced.

❈ The spacing of both your Audio and MIDI tracks has changed. Note that regions on the sample-based Audio track are now not as evenly spaced as they once were, whereas each eighth note in the Instrument track (despite the tempo change) appears at regular intervals.

## 528
❈ ❈ ❈

As you listen to and watch the playback of your session, you'll see that the only change made to your session has been visual. This change in linearity is simply for ease of use (and can be especially useful when working with MIDI data in sessions with radical tempo changes).

# Cool Editing Tricks

We've already covered a bunch of editing processes—here are a few more for your bag of tricks!

## New Ways to Spot Regions

Back in Chapter 5, we talked a little about the Spot edit mode, and how it can make placing regions at specific points in time quick and easy. Spot *mode*, however, is really only useful if you already know the specific numeric position to which you want your region to go. Many times, you'll want your region to go to a specific *selected* place in your session, and Pro Tools makes this easy as well—especially if you have a mouse with a right-click button!

❄ SETTING THINGS UP

For this section, go to Memory Location #4—Spotting Regions.

 Using the Selector tool, **make a selection** or **place** your **timeline insertion cursor** at the place at which you want your region to move.

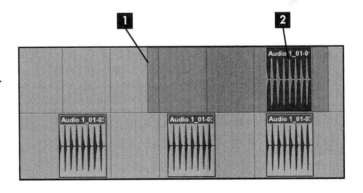

2 **Command-right-click (Mac) or Ctrl-right-click (PC)** on the **region** that you want to move. A menu will appear.

※ The third segment of the list will include three region-moving options:

    ☆ Move Region Start to Selection Start will move the region so that the *beginning* of the region aligns with the beginning of the selection or with the timeline insertion cursor.

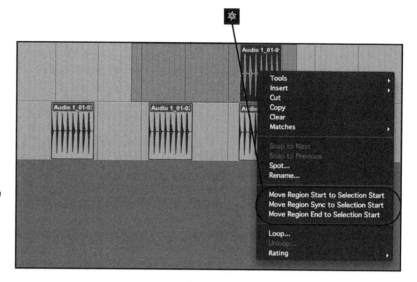

    ☆ Move Region Sync to Selection Start will move the region so that the region's Sync Point (if it has one) aligns with the beginning of the selection or with the timeline insertion cursor. (We'll discuss Sync Points in the next section.)

    ☆ Move Region End to Selection Start will move the region so that the *end* of the region aligns with the beginning of your selection or with the timeline insertion cursor.

If you don't have a mouse with a right-click button, all is not lost. Here are some shortcuts to help you get the job done:

※ To Move Region Start to Selection Start, hold the Control key (Mac) or Start key (PC) and click the region with the Grabber tool (*not* the Smart tool).

※ To Move Region Sync to Selection Start, hold Shift+Control (Mac) or Shift+Start (PC) and click the region with the Grabber tool.

※ To Move Region End to Selection Start, hold Command+Control (Mac) or Ctrl+Start (PC) and click the region with the Grabber tool.

## Sync Points

So far, we've primarily focused on region boundaries (beginning and end) when talking about moving regions. Many times, however, the really interesting part of a region is somewhere *inside* the region. For example, within a drum beat, you might have a specific hit that you want to align with another region, or you might have a specific word in a dialog region that is particularly easy to spot. *Sync Points* will help you mark these places of interest, so that you can align those places to your timeline insertion using the techniques we discussed in the previous section.

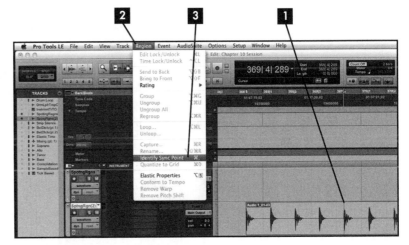

**1** Using the Selector tool (or the Smart tool), **place** your **timeline insertion cursor** at the point within your region where you want to create a Sync Point.

**2** **Click** the **Region menu**.

**3** **Click Identify Sync Point.** A small green triangle will appear at the bottom of the region to indicate the position of the Sync Point.

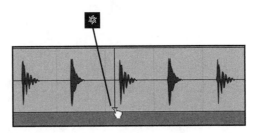

❋ If you need to reposition your Sync Point once you've created it, the Grabber tool will let you move it. Just move your mouse close to the triangular Sync Point icon. When the Grabber tool turns into the "pointing hand" shown here, you're ready to move the Sync Point—just click, drag, and drop the Sync Point to its new location.

Now that you've created your Sync Point, you can utilize the right-click and shortcut commands described in the previous section!

✳ SYNC POINT PRACTICE

Using Sync Points is a skill that can be refined through repetition, so I've included a session to help you do just that. If you open the session named Chapter 10 – Sync Point Practice, you'll see a number of tracks that aren't lined up properly. (These tracks should look familiar—you worked with them back in Chapter 4.) By creating a Sync Point at the first beep of each track's region and then aligning each Sync Point to the beginning of the region on the top track, you can fix this problem. I've included a finished version of the session (named Session 10 – Sync Point Practice – Finished) so that you can see how using your session should look when you're finished.

## Snapping Regions

Sometimes you'll want a region to move adjacent to the region before or after it. Again, the right-click mouse comes to the rescue!

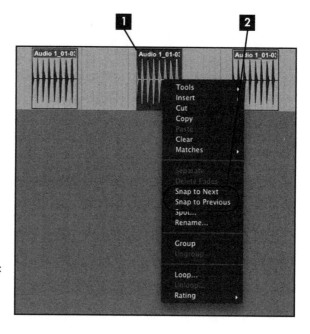

**1** Right-click the **region** that you want to move.

**2** A menu will appear, including two region-snapping options:

✳ Choosing Snap to Next will move the region so that the *end* of the region aligns with the beginning of the region to the *right*.

✳ Clicking the Snap to Previous menu item will move the region so that the *beginning* of the region aligns with the end of the region to the *left*.

✳ SPOT

The menu item just below the Snap to Previous menu item, named Spot, will open the Spot Dialog box (the same box you would normally encounter in the Spot edit mode).

Before we leave this section of the chapter, a word on region moving and nudging: Beginning with Pro Tools LE 7.3, you now have the ability to select fade regions (including crossfades), move them with the Grabber tool, or nudge them just as you would any normal region (using the +/2 keys).

## Using Strip Silence

Strip Silence is a nifty little editing tool that acts upon regions similar to how a noise gate acts upon audio. When you use Strip Silence, any audio below a specified volume threshold can be removed from your selection, leaving discrete regions that you can move and edit separately.

❄ SETTING THINGS UP

Please go to Memory Location #5—Strip Silence.

**1** Select an **area** in your session that you would like to strip.

**2** Click on the **Edit menu**.

**3** Click on **Strip Silence**. The Strip Silence dialog box will open.

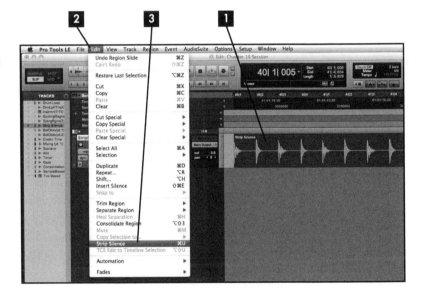

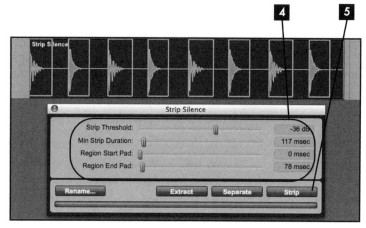

**4** At this point, your goal is to adjust the parameters in the Strip Silence dialog box and separate the useful audio from the audio that you don't want to keep. (As you **adjust** these **parameters**, you will see boxes indicating where new region boundaries will be created, as shown here.) This can take a little time to get just right, as these values are interrelated, so be patient. The four parameters available to you are:

* **Strip Threshold.** This indicates the minimum volume of the audio that you want to keep (with a range from 296 dB to 20 dB). Portions of audio with volume levels *under* the Strip Threshold can be stripped from your region. As you move the fader from left to right, you'll see that you'll be stripping more and more of the audio.

* **Min Strip Duration.** This value determines the shortest region able to be created by Strip Silence. As you move the fader from left to right, you'll see smaller boxes combine to make larger ones.

* **Region Start Pad.** This slider will move the left boundary of each box earlier in time. If you find that by using Strip Silence, you're cutting off the beginning of words or notes, a small amount of Region Start Padding will fix the problem.

* **Region End Pad.** This slider will move the right boundary of each box later in time. If you find that by using Strip Silence, you're cutting off the end of words or notes, a small amount of Region End Padding will fix the problem

**5** Once you've adjusted these parameters to your liking, **click** on the **Strip button**. Your selection will be chopped into discrete regions, and the unwanted portions of audio will be removed from the track altogether. These newly created regions will be shown in the Regions list.

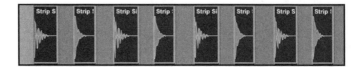

Don't worry; you haven't actually deleted any audio. If you find that you've stripped too much or too little from your track, you can use the Trim tool to adjust individual region boundaries.

❋ In addition to being able to strip away unwanted audio (by clicking the Strip button), you have a few other options when using Strip Silence:

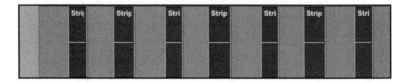

 ✧ **Extract.** This does the *opposite* of the Strip button and will create only regions of audio that are *below* the strip threshold.

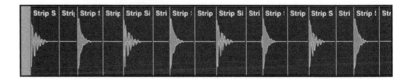

 ✧ **Separate.** This mode will not strip any audio, but will only separate your selected area, resulting in alternating regions of sound and silence.

 ✧ **Rename.** The Rename option will allow you to automatically rename selected regions. When you click the Rename button, the Rename Selected Regions dialog box will open.

❄ The Name field will allow you to type a descriptive name for your selected regions.

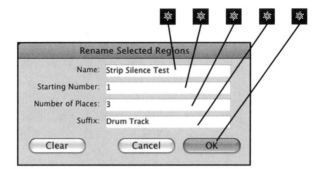

❄ You can choose a starting number for your regions as well. For example, in some situations you might want to have the first region be numbered 0, and in other cases you'll want to start your numbering with the number 1 (as shown here).

❄ The Number of Places field will allow you to set the number of digits that will be used in your region renumbering. In this case I've chosen three places, so my files will be numbered 001, 002, 003, and so on.

❄ Finally, you may want to add a suffix to your file names.

❄ When you've set up your renaming scheme, click the OK button. Based on the settings shown here, the selected regions will be renamed Strip Silence Test001Drum Track, Strip Silence Test002Drum Track, and so on.

## Beat Detective

One of the most interesting music production tools in Pro Tools' bag of tricks is Beat Detective. Based upon the same technology that makes the Tab to Transient feature work so well, Beat Detective can be used in a variety of ways. Essentially, it's used for aligning MIDI and audio, and though it's most commonly used in conjunction with drum tracks, it can be applied to any audio with clearly defined transients (or MIDI). Let's take a look at some basic Beat Detective workflows.

❄ SETTING THINGS UP

If you're following along with the tutorial session, go to Memory Location #6—Beat Detective (pt.1).

The first Beat Detective workflow is based on the idea that, in many cases, a musical groove is not mathematically uniform. This "human" element is in opposition to the mathematical precision of a static MIDI tempo. If you're following along with the tutorial session, you'll see just what I mean—though the Audio track and the Instrument tracks are at the same tempo, they certainly aren't playing well together.

To get our audio and MIDI to groove together, we'll want to create a complex MIDI tempo map (based on the live drum track), and Beat Detective will help us do just that!

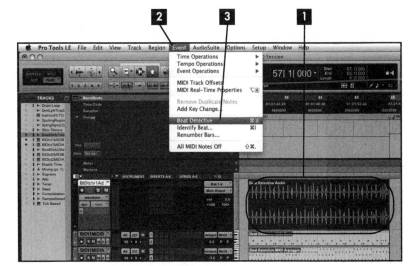

1 **Select** the **segment of drums** that you want to analyze. (If you're following along with the tutorial session, that selection has been made for you.)

2 **Click** on the **Event menu**.

3 **Click** on **Beat Detective**. The Beat Detective window will appear.

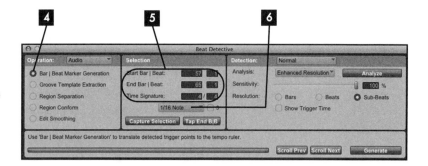

**4** The mode you'll use for this sort of work is Bar|Beat Marker Generation. **Click** the **top radio button** to enter this mode.

**5** This step is *very* important: **Make sure** that the **values** in Beat Detective's Selection area correctly reflect the musical start, end, and meter of your selected area. Just as when you used Identify Beat earlier in this chapter, let your ears be your ultimate guide.

**6** **Choose** the smallest **musical note value** of your audio (in this case, sixteenth notes).

### ✿ USING CAPTURE SELECTION

Assuming that your selection is known to be in general agreement with the MIDI tempo, you can click the Capture Selection button in the Selection area of Beat Detective. This is an easy way to go with audio in which the beat has already been identified.

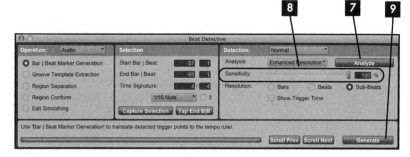

**7** **Click** the **Analyze button**. Beat Detective will search your selected audio for transient events.

**8** Slowly **slide** the **Sensitivity slider** from left to right. Note that as your sensitivity percentage increases, you will begin to see vertical lines intersecting the transients of your audio. (The loudest transients will be marked first.) Once you are satisfied that the important transients have been marked (and no others), stop moving the slider.

**9** **Click** the **Generate button**. The Realign Session dialog box will open.

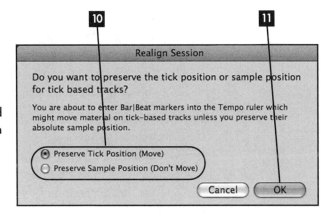

**10** The Realign Session dialog box is fairly self-explanatory. The two radio buttons will determine how your tick-based tracks will react to the creation of the new bar|beat markers.

❊ If you want the timing of your session's tick-based tracks (such as a drum part on a MIDI track) to move to match the timing of the Audio track, choose Preserve Tick Position (Move). This is what we'll choose in this case.

❊ If your tick-based data doesn't need to be matched to your new tempo map, choose Preserve Sample Position (Don't Move). The data on your tick-based tracks will not be changed in any way.

**11** When you've made your choice (in this case, **choose Preserve Tick Position**), **click** the **OK button**.

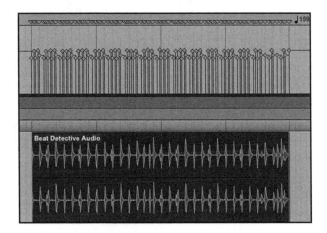

You will see now that a great number of small tempo changes have been added to your tempo ruler (each shown as a blue triangle in the collapsed tempo ruler or as tempo events in the expanded tempo ruler). What you've done is create a tempo map that changes constantly to match the groove of the drum audio, which has effectively created a MIDI *grid* that also reflects these changes. Because things such as Grid mode and MIDI Quantize rely on this grid for their timing, you can now conform any additional MIDI and audio to this original drum beat, and they will all groove together!

But that's not all that Beat Detective can do—not by a long shot. Let's reverse the process: Let's say that instead of creating a new tempo map based on your Audio track (so that the rest of your session can conform to that audio), you instead want to conform your audio to the *current* tempo of the session. Beat Detective can do that, too. In this example, we'll take the same audio region and conform it to the mathematically static tempo of the session, effectively quantizing it to a sixteenth-note grid.

⁂ **SETTING THINGS UP**

Please go to Memory Location #7—Beat Detective (pt. 2).

**1** Select the **segment of drums** that you want to analyze. (If you're following along with the tutorial session, that selection has been made for you.)

**2** The mode you'll use for this sort of work is Region Separation. **Click** the **third radio button** to enter this mode.

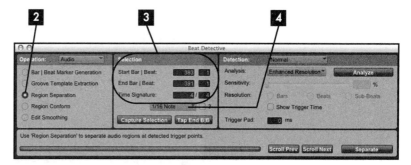

**3** Again, **make sure** that the **values** in Beat Detective's Selection area correctly reflect the musical start, end, and meter of your selected area. Be careful—Beat Detective does not automatically update its selection values (and if you're using the tutorial session, this memory location is at a different section of your session)!

**4** **Choose** the smallest **musical note value** of your audio (in this case, sixteenth notes).

**5** Click the **Analyze** button. Beat Detective will search your selected audio for transient events.

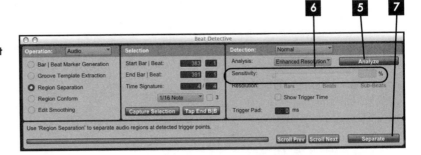

**6** Slowly **slide** the **Sensitivity slider** from left to right. Note that as your sensitivity percentage increases, you will begin to see vertical lines intersecting the transients of your audio. (The loudest transients will be marked first.) Once you are satisfied that the important transients have been marked (and no others), stop moving the slider.

**7** Click the **Separate button**. Your region will be separated into a number of smaller regions. Not only will you see these regions represented on your track, but they will also be shown in the Regions list.

**8** Now that you've chopped up your beat, it's time to get the smaller regions in line. **Click** the **Region Conform radio button**.

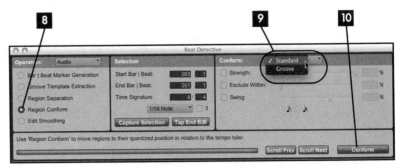

**9** If you click on the Conform menu button, you'll see that you can move your regions in the standard way (the regions will be quantized to the nearest grid line) or with a Groove (using a groove template, similar to MIDI Groove Quantize). For our purposes, **choose** the **Standard mode**.

**10** Click the **Conform button**. The regions will move subtly to match the existing tempo map. If you listen to the selected area, you'll hear a change in the feel.

**11** As a byproduct of the conforming process, some gaps will be produced between regions, and there may also be a few clicks and pops. Beat Detective's final mode will help us clean things up. **Click** the **Edit Smoothing radio button.**

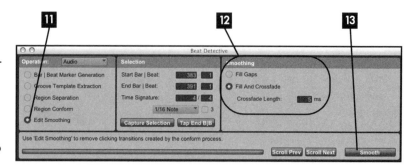

**12** The Smoothing section gives you two options:

* If there are no problems with clicks or pops, click the Fill Gaps radio button. Region boundaries will be adjusted to minimize gaps between regions.

* If there *are* clicks and pops, a quick crossfade between regions will fix the problem in most cases. Set the Crossfade Length (this will vary from situation to situation—in this case, 5 ms sounds good) and then click the Fill and Crossfade radio button.

**13** **Click** the **Smooth button.**

Your audio will now have a significantly different feel and no gaps!

There's one more mode included in Beat Detective, called *Groove Template Extraction.*

**1** Click the **Groove Template Extraction radio button**.

**2** Here again, the values you enter in the Selection area of the Beat Detective window are crucial. Once you've done that, **click** the **Analyze button** and **adjust** the **Sensitivity slider**, just as you've done before.

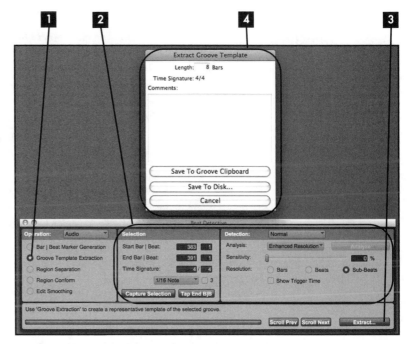

**3** Click the **Extract button**. The Extract Groove Template dialog box will appear.

**4** In the Extract Groove Template dialog box, you can either Save to Groove Clipboard for immediate use or Save to Disk for more long-term storage.

What exactly have you done? Essentially, what you have extracted is the same sort of timing information that you used in bar | beat marker generation, except that in this case you've added this information to your list of available MIDI Groove Quantize options. More simply put, you've given yourself the option to quantize MIDI data (now or in the future) to have the same feel as these drums you've just analyzed!

### ❄ MIDI DETECTIVE

Beat Detective can also analyze MIDI data and perform similar operations. To use Beat Detective with MIDI, just click the Operation Menu button in the upper-left corner (which currently reads Audio) and choose MIDI from the list that's shown. Some subtle changes in the window will appear (and only the first two operation mode radio buttons are relevant to MIDI), but the overall workflow is the same as what we've gone through in this chapter.

### ❄ FOR MORE INFORMATION...

The complex applications of Beat Detective go beyond the scope of an introductory book like this one. If you want to go through every button in Beat Detective, you might want to check out a book called *Working with Beats in Pro Tools: Skill Pack*, written by yours truly and published by Thomson Course Technology PTR (2007).

### ❄ ONE MORE EDITING SHORTCUT

Before we close this discussion on editing, here's one more useful shortcut (one that can be used in a variety of situations). On either a Mac or a PC, hold the Shift key while starting playback to play back your session at half-speed. This comes in particularly handy when you're setting punch-in or punch-out points for a particularly tight spot. (Be careful when recording that way, though, as your recorded audio will be twice as fast and twice as high in pitch!)

# Elastic Audio

Elastic Audio is a relative newcomer to the Pro Tools arsenal of features, and it's already a favorite for Pro Tools users worldwide. On its face, Elastic Audio allows the user to change the timing and pitch of audio in a flexible and nondestructive way and can even give you the same kind of control over your audio that you have over MIDI! When you dig deeper, though, you'll see that Elastic Audio can be a tweaker's paradise!

Like any powerful new feature in Pro Tools, users will be discovering new tricks and workflows for years, but even the standard applications of it are very exciting. Let's take a look at the way Elastic Audio works and some ways to use it, just to get you started!

Please go to Memory Location #8—Elastic Time.

# Basic Operation

**1** You can enable, disable, and customize Elastic Audio on a track-by-track basis. In this image, the track is currently disabled for Elastic Audio (indicated by an empty cell below the track's Automation Mode Selector button). To activate Elastic Audio on an Audio track, just **click** the **Elastic Audio Plug-in Selector button**. A menu will appear.

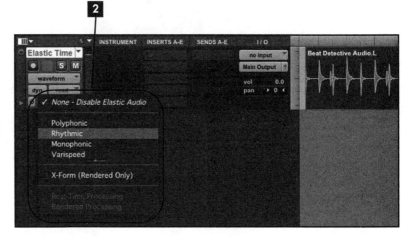

**2** From this list you can **choose** the appropriate **plug-in** for the job. You have five options:

❈ Polyphonic mode is a good general choice and well suited to audio in which multiple pitches are being played simultaneously.

❈ Rhythmic mode is a good choice for drum tracks and other percussive audio.

❈ Monophonic is great for Audio tracks in which only one note is being played at a time (for example, wind instruments or vocals).

❈ Varispeed is fundamentally different from the other plug-ins. Elastic Audio's other modes will maintain the original pitches of your audio regardless of whether they're being sped up or slowed down. Varispeed mode, on the other hand, will raise the pitch of your audio when it is being played faster than normal or lower the pitch when it's being played slower. This is particularly handy for turntable or tape-type effects.

❉ X-Form (Rendered Only) is a high-quality algorithm overall and is often my personal choice, but it is only available as a "rendered" plug-in, as opposed to being real time. (We will discuss the difference between real time and rendered in a moment.)

**IF YOU'RE USING THE TUTORIAL SESSION**

If you're following along with the Chapter 10 tutorial session, you'll note that the track shown is a drum loop, so let's choose the Rhythmic plug-in.

You'll notice that once you choose an Elastic Audio plug-in, a button showing your choice will be displayed. Within that button, and next to the name of the algorithm (in this case, Rhythmic), you'll see a small rectangle, which will be either lit with a green color or dark. This will indicate whether Elastic Audio for that track is being processed in real time or in a rendered mode.

**3** Click the **Elastic Audio Plug-In Selector button** once more, so we can take a second look at the Elastic Audio plug-in list.

**4** The bottom segment of the Elastic Audio plug-in list will allow you to choose the processing mode for Elastic Audio on that track. (The currently selected mode will be indicated by a check mark.) You have two options in most cases:

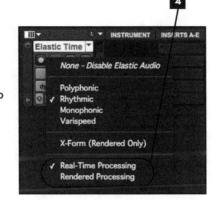

❋ Selecting Real-Time Processing will give you the quickest performance, and any changes that you make to your audio will be applied immediately. That being said, processing in real-time will place an additional load on your computer's CPU, which can be an issue particularly with less powerful computers.

❋ Choosing Rendered Processing means that your changes will not be immediately applied, but rather will take some amount of time (depending upon the speed of your computer) to apply the change. During that time, the track will not be audible. Your changes will be written (or "rendered") to new files that are saved in your session's Rendered Files subfolder.

### ELASTIC AUDIO AND THE TCE TRIM TOOL

One of the first things you'll notice when you enable Elastic Audio on a track is that the TCE Trim tool works a bit differently. When Elastic Audio is set up with real-time processing, instead of creating a new file and region each time you use the TCE Trim tool, your audio will simply be time compressed or expanded immediately. (New files will *not* be created.) Regardless of the processing mode chosen, you might also notice that as you use the TCE Trim tool repeatedly on the same region, the region's audio quality won't progressively degrade (something that can happen with non-Elastic Audio tracks).

This party's just getting started—let's now set up our Audio track to follow tempo changes.

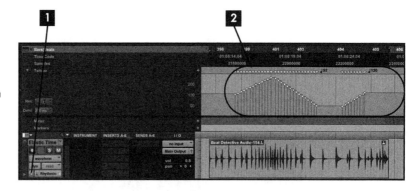

**1** **Change** the **Audio track** from being sample-based to being tick-based. (For a refresher on how to do this, take a look at Chapter 6.)

**2** Using the Pencil tool, **draw** some **tempo change events** onto the expanded tempo ruler, as shown here.

❋ If you play back your session, you'll hear that the region has been compressed or expanded to follow your session's tempo ruler. You'll also notice a small icon in the upper-right corner of the region, indicating that it has been "warped" (something we'll talk about in just a moment).

❋ **IF YOU'RE USING THE TUTORIAL SESSION**
If you're following along with the Chapter 10 tutorial session, please undo any tempo changes you've just made, in preparation for the next section.

With Elastic Audio, not only do you have the ability to have your audio follow tempo changes, but you can also quantize it as if it was MIDI!

**1** **Select** the **area** that you want to quantize.

**2** **Click** the **Event menu**.

**3** **Select Event Operations**. A submenu will appear.

**4** **Click Quantize**. The Event Operations/Quantize window will appear.

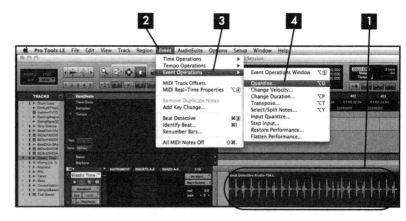

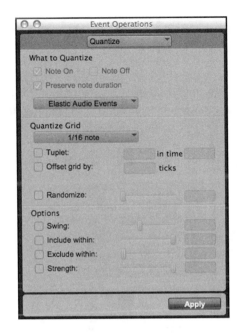

Since you've selected a region on an Elastic Audio-enabled track (which contains Elastic Audio events, which we'll cover next), you have the option of quantizing this drum region, almost as if it was MIDI! You can choose to quantize to either a grid increment (such as sixteenth notes, as shown here) or a Groove Template, just as you did back in Chapter 7 when quantizing MIDI.

### ※ COMBINING TOOLS

Now that you've got both Beat Detective and Elastic Audio under your belt, you'll soon find ways to get them to work together. Here's one scenario: Suppose you've got two drum regions that you want to have the same feel. Here's one way to go—choose the drum region whose feel you prefer and use Beat Detective's Bar|Beat Marker Generation mode to change your session's tempo map. Just quantize the other drum region to the new grid (the track needn't be tick-based to do this), and you're all set!

## Event and Warp Markers (and How to Use Them)

When Elastic Audio is enabled on a track, you'll notice that there are two new track views that are available to you—Analysis and Warp. Both of these track views have their parts too—let's take a look at them one at a time.

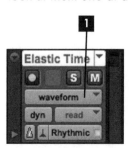

**1** Click the **Track View Selector button** (which in this case currently reads Waveform). The Track View menu will appear.

**2** **Choose Analysis** from the list of view options.

✳ You'll immediately note that there are vertical lines marking transients in your audio (even the very low-level ones). Each of these lines is called an *event marker*.

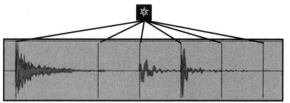

Event markers are loosely analogous to the beat markers that you saw earlier in this chapter when you worked with Beat Detective. These markers determine the locations within an audio region that will move as the audio follows tempo changes or when the audio is quantized, as you did earlier in this section.

If you need to, you can move, delete, and add event markers. The Grabber tool will help you do this.

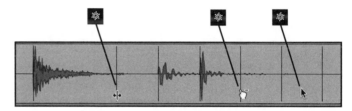

❄ Using the Grabber tool, move your cursor over an existing event marker. Your cursor will change to the double-arrow shown here, and you may click and drag the event marker to a new location.

❄ You can delete an existing event marker by holding down the Option (Mac) or Alt (PC) key and clicking it using the Grabber tool. (The cursor will be shown as a pointing hand with a minus (2) sign next to it.)

❄ If you want to create a new event marker, just double-click where you want to create it!

Now, let's move on to the Warp view:

**1** Click the **Track View Selector button** (again) and **choose Warp** from the list of options.

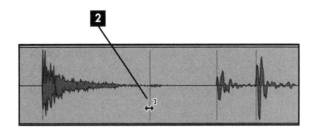

**2** Here again, the Grabber tool will be your greatest ally. Move your mouse over any event marker. (Yes, you can still see your event markers, even though you're in Warp view.) The cursor will turn into the icon shown here, indicating that you're ready to use the Telescoping Warp. Just **click and drag** to the **left** or the **right** to proportionally compress or expand the entire region.

To make the most of the Warp view, you'll need to create a new kind of marker, called a *warp marker*. Conceptually, you can think of a warp marker as being a "handle" with which you can grab and stretch your audio. Warp markers can be identified by their darker color and the small blue triangle at the base of the marker.

Just as you saw with event markers, you will find that the Grabber tool helps you get started easily:

✳ Here's a common starting point: Double-click an existing event marker to change it into a warp marker (shown here).

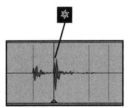

Here are a few other ways to create warp markers:

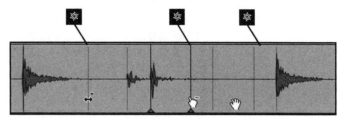

❋ If you have an existing warp marker to the right of an event marker that you want to promote to being a warp marker, you'll see a small plus (+) sign next to the cursor. In these cases, a single-click will create a warp marker.

❋ You can delete an existing warp marker by holding down the Option (Mac) or Alt (PC) key and clicking it using the Grabber tool. (The cursor will be shown as a pointing hand with a minus (−) sign next to it.)

❋ If there are no existing event markers at the location where you want to create a new warp marker, no problem—just double-click where you want to create one!

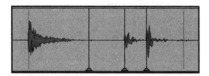

Here's a typical warp marker setup: The center warp marker in this scenario is the point of audio that I want to move. The warp markers to the left and right of the center warp marker, though they can also be moved, will act as "anchors" in this case. Now we're ready to do some serious warping!

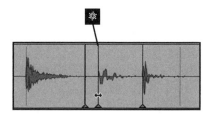

❋ Click and drag the center warp marker left or right. You'll immediately see that the audio is being pulled like taffy, giving you control over minute aspects of your audio region, with the adjacent warp markers acting as anchors. Warp markers can be dragged smoothly if you're in Slip, Shuffle, or Spot mode—if you're in Grid mode, you'll see that your warp marker "snaps" according to your grid resolution.

Here's a quicker way to create the warp markers you need for this kind of work:

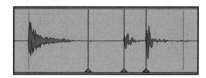

**1** **Hold down** the **Shift key** and **move** your **mouse** over an event marker that you want to promote to being a warp marker and then move. The cursor shown here is called an *individual warp* cursor.

**2** **Click** on the **event marker**.

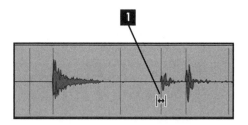

You'll notice that not only has the event marker you clicked changed to be a warp marker, but the markers immediately adjacent to it have also changed to be warp markers. This puts you in position to adjust the center warp marker, just as you did earlier in this section.

From time to time, moving a warp marker can cause audible side effects. While one possible solution is to change the Elastic Audio plug-in to one more suited to the job, you can also tweak the current plug-in a bit to improve its performance.

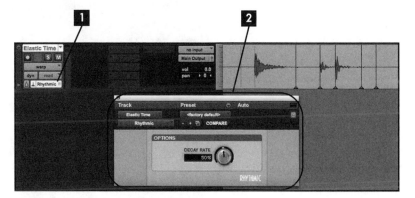

**1** Click the **Elastic Audio Plug-In button** (which in this image reads "Rhythmic," the currently selected Elastic Audio plug-in). The plug-in window will appear.

**2** The appearance of the Elastic Audio plug-in window will vary depending on the Elastic Audio plug-in you're using, allowing you to adjust parameters that are most relevant to each one. In the case of the Rhythmic plug-in shown here, you can just **adjust** the **decay rate**, which can remove unwanted artifacts that sometimes accompany this particular plug-in.

You also have the ability to adjust specific Elastic Audio settings on a region-by-region basis.

**1** **Select** the **region** that you want to work with.

**2** **Right-click** the **region**. A menu will appear.

**3** **Select Elastic Properties**. The Elastic Properties window will appear.

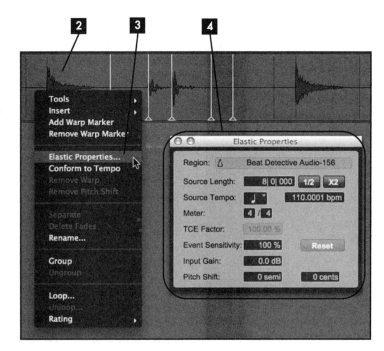

**4** The Elastic Properties window will give you overall information about the region (which will vary depending on whether the track is sample-based or tick-based) in the upper part of the window. In the bottom half, you'll see more specific data, including Event Sensitivity (which is similar in function to the Sensitivity slider you worked with in Beat Detective), Input Gain (which you can adjust downward if you find that your region clips as a result of warping), and Pitch (which we'll discuss later in this section). You can easily enter new settings here by typing new values into the appropriate fields.

## Elastic Audio and the Workspace

Elastic Audio is at work not only in your session, but in the Workspace, Volume, and Project Browsers as well. Within these browsers, audio files that are analyzed by Elastic Audio and are determined to have a musical pattern (such as a drum beat) are listed as being tick-based files (indicated by a green Metronome icon in the Kind column). Files that are analyzed and found not to have this sort of pattern (for example, a single drum hit or a spoken sentence) will be listed as being sample-based (indicated by a blue Clock icon in the Kind column).

**1** At the top of the Workspace window, you'll see the green Audio Files Conform to Session Tempo button. When you **click** this **button**, your tick-based audio files will play at your session's tempo (rather than at their original tempo) when previewed.

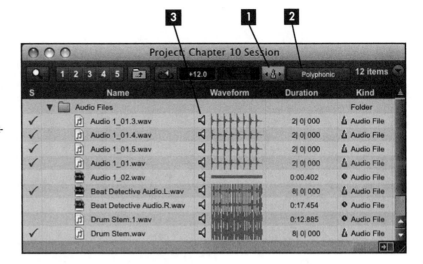

**2** The button to the immediate right of the Audio Files Conform to Session Tempo button will display the currently chosen Elastic Audio plug-in (the one being used for previewing audio files in the browser). **Click** this **button** to reveal a list of all the real-time Elastic Audio plug-in options, from which you can choose the algorithm that sounds best to you.

**3** Just **click** the **speaker icon** next to the region waveform that you want to preview.

The Audio Files Conform to Session Tempo feature also has an effect upon the process of importing files into your session. When the feature is active, a tick-based file will be imported to a tick-based, Elastic Audio–enabled track, with the same plug-in algorithm that you had in your Workspace window being applied to that track.

## Making the Most of Elastic Audio

As we discussed earlier, using Elastic Audio in real-time processing mode will consume some of your computer's limited CPU resources. While switching tracks over to rendered processing whenever possible will give your CPU a break, you can also coax more power out of your computer with the help of the Playback Engine window.

**1** Click the **Setup menu**.

**2** Click **Playback Engine**. The Playback Engine window will open.

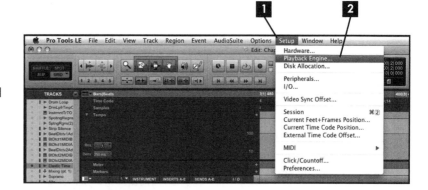

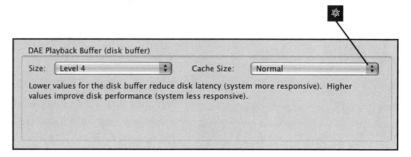

❋ The Cache Size button (which you'll find in the center-right area of the Playback Engine window) will allow you to choose how much memory will be allocated specifically for the playback of Elastic Audio regions. When you click the Cache Size menu button, you'll see that you have three options:

 ☆ Minimum (reduces memory use)

 ☆ Normal

 ☆ Large (improves performance)

You can also tweak the behavior of Elastic Audio through the Preferences window.

**1** Click the **Setup menu**.

**2** Click **Preferences**. The Preferences window will open.

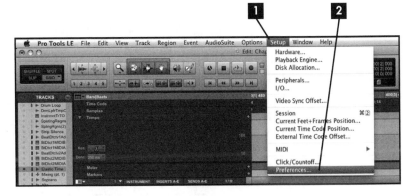

**3** In the Preferences window, click the **Processing tab**.

**4** In the Elastic Audio section of this page, you'll see three useful options:

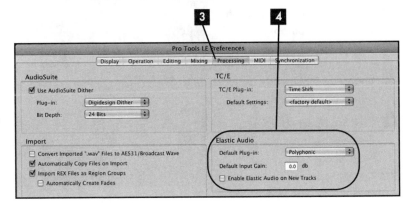

❊ **Default Plug-in.** Here you can choose the initial plug-in used for auditioning files in the browser windows, as well as the plug-in that is initially used if new tracks are created as Elastic Audio tracks.

❊ **Default Input Gain.** This will allow you to automatically reduce the volume of Elastic Audio regions, to prevent the clipping that can sometimes occur when a region is warped.

❊ **Enable Elastic Audio on New Tracks.** When this box is checked, new Audio tracks will be created with Elastic Audio enabled (using the Default Plug-In type).

## New in Pro Tools 8: Elastic Pitch

Beginning with Pro Tools 8, Elastic Audio can adjust not only the timing of your audio, but its pitch as well. Using Elastic Audio, you can easily change pitch on a region-by-region basis.

❄ ELASTIC PITCH LIMITATION

Adjusting pitch with Elastic Audio can currently only be done when using the Polyphonic, Rhythmic, or X-Form Elastic Audio plug-ins.

There are two different methods by which you can adjust the pitch of a selected region, each with its particular advantages. Let's start by looking at a way to *transpose* a region, just as you did with MIDI back in Chapter 7.

1 **Select** the **region** whose pitch you want to transpose.

2 **Click** the **Event menu.**

3 **Choose Event Operations.** A submenu will appear.

4 **Click Transpose.** The Event Operations/Transpose dialog box will appear.

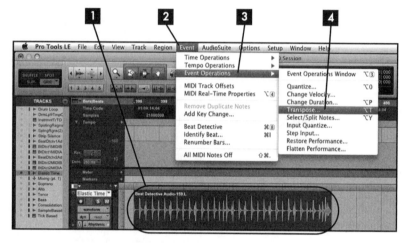

5 **Adjust** the **transposition parameters** just as you did when working with MIDI data.

6 **Click** the **Apply button**, and you're finished!

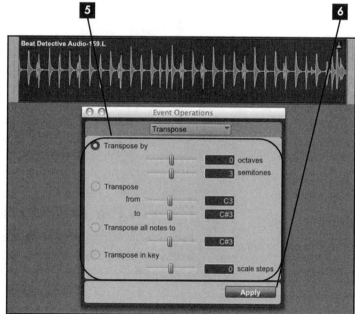

The previous workflow is very handy in situations where you want to make relatively large changes in pitch, but what if you just want to tweak the pitch of a flat note? No problem—you can make those kinds of fine adjustments in the Elastic Properties window.

**1** Right-click the **region** that you want to change. A list of options will appear.

**2** Choose **Elastic Properties**. The Elastic Properties dialog box will open.

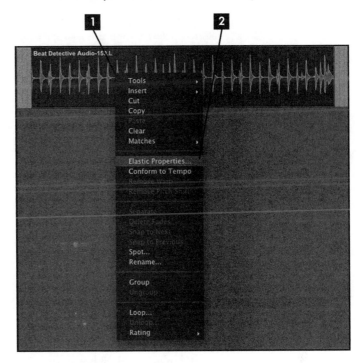

❋ The bottom section of the Elastic Properties dialog box will allow you to adjust pitch not only in semitones (something you could also do in the Transpose dialog box), but also in cents, which are very small units of pitch. (There are 100 cents in a semitone, or half-step.) You will find that by adjusting pitch in terms of cents, you have very fine control over the pitch of the audio.

561

※ ARE YOU WARPED?

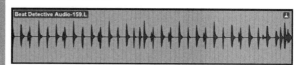

If you're unclear as to whether a given region has been altered through the application of Elastic Audio, the region itself will give you a clue: Regions changed by Elastic Audio (including pitch changes) will be indicated by a small icon in the upper-right corner of the region, as shown here.

※ ELASTIC WARNINGS

One final point: From time to time, you might see sections of your audio turn red when dragging warp markers. Not to worry—Pro Tools is just letting you know that you've applied a good deal of time compression or expansion. Technically speaking, you've gone beyond Pro Tools' recommended limits, but if it sounds good to your ears, go for it!

# Making the Most of Mixing

Here are a few tips to help you make your mixes *rock*!

## Using the Edit Tools

So far, you've primarily used the Pencil tool to edit your automation. Let's take a look at how you can use a couple other tools as well.

※ SETTING THINGS UP

Please go to Memory Location #9—Mixing (pt. 1).

You've seen how useful the Grabber tool can be when working with Beat Detective and Elastic Audio—here's how you can use it to create, modify, and even delete automation breakpoints.

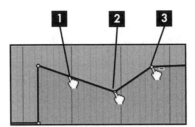

**1** To create an automation breakpoint, just **click where you want it to be**.

**2** To change the time or value of an existing automation breakpoint, **click and drag** the **breakpoint** to the desired location.

**3** You can delete an existing automation breakpoint by **holding down the Option (Mac) or Alt (PC) key** and **clicking it**. (The cursor will be shown as a pointing hand with a minus (−) sign next to it.)

The Trim tool can also come in very useful when you want to proportionally scale your automation (raise or lower the automation line without changing its shape):

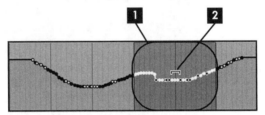

**1** **Make** a **selection** of the area that you want to change (using the Selector tool).

**2** **Move** the **Trim tool** into the selected area. The Trim tool will be shown downward-facing, indicating that it's ready to change your automation.

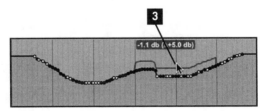

**3** **Click and drag** your **mouse** up or down to adjust your automation proportionally. Above your cursor, you'll see a delta value (the amount of change) shown in parentheses next to a triangle (the Greek letter *delta*).

**4** **Release** the **mouse button**. The automation will be proportionally changed in the selected area.

## Toggling Groups

Here's a way to change the balance of a mix (fader) group without the hassle of first having to deactivate the group!

 **SETTING THINGS UP**

For this section, please go to Memory Location #10—Mixing (pt. 2).

In this example, we've got four vocal parts that are grouped together in an active fader group.

1. **Press and hold** the **Control key (Mac)** or the **Start (Windows) key (PC)**, *and then* **click and drag** the **fader** you want to change. Note that though the group is still being shown as active in the Groups list, you can change individual tracks without affecting the rest of the group.

2. **Release** the **key**. Your group will be re-enabled.

❋ MY FAVORITE MIX WINDOW SHORTCUT

Before we finish our discussion on mixing, here's a useful shortcut (especially for those complex sessions with many groups): To quickly show only the tracks in a given group, hold down the Control key (Mac) or the Start key (PC) and click the name of the group that you want to see in the Groups list. (This works in either the Mix or the Edit window.) All tracks that are not members of that group will be hidden.

# Advanced Resource Management

Yet more ways to view and manage your data!

## The System Usage Window

First, let's take a look at a new window—the System Usage window—which will help us monitor our CPU resources.

**1** Click on the **Window menu**.

**2** Click on **System Usage**. The System Usage window will appear.

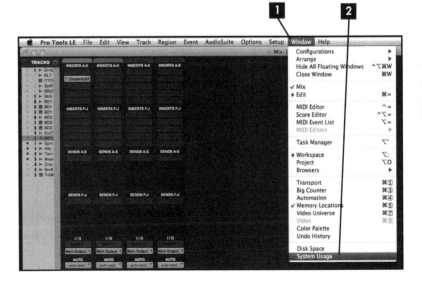

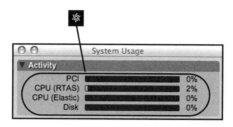

✻ The four graphs in this window will help you to view your memory and PCI bandwidth consumption. When it comes to resource management, though, perhaps the most important graphs to watch are the CPU (RTAS) and CPU (Elastic) meters.

## Inactive Elements

There's a difference between elements in your session that are offline and those that are inactive. An offline region occurs when source media is not found when you open a session. When that happens, a region will appear on a track, but that region will be empty, with the region name in italics. Inactive elements, on the other hand, are processes that are somehow disabled (either as a result of not having the appropriate plug-in installed on a system or deliberately by the Pro Tools user).

There are a few good reasons to make a plug-in or track inactive.

✻ Making a plug-in inactive will free up valuable CPU resources while maintaining automation and preset settings.

✻ Making tracks inactive can allow you to work with tracks beyond the 48 Audio track limitation of a Pro Tools LE system (though an inactive track will not be audible).

There are two easy ways to make a plug-in inactive.

**1** **Right-click** the **Insert button**. A list will appear.

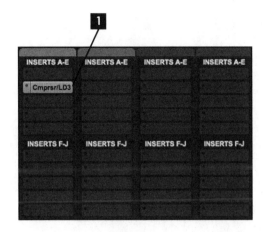

**2** **Choose Make Inactive**.

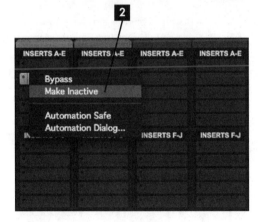

Here's another way to do it:

**1** **Press and hold** the **Command+Control keys (Mac) or the Ctrl+Start keys (PC)** and **click** on the **Insert button** for the plug-in you want to disable.

Regardless of the method you choose, here's what you'll see:

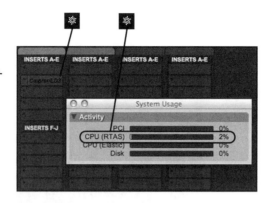

※ The Insert button's text will be shown in *italicized* text, indicating that the plug-in is inactive.

※ For every RTAS plug-in you disable, your CPU usage will decrease, leaving more processing room for new effects.

※ OPENING A SESSION WITH PLUG-INS INACTIVE!

Holding the Shift key while opening a session will cause the session to open with all plug-ins inactive. This can drastically reduce the time it takes to open many sessions (particularly sessions with a high plug-in count).

Similarly, there are multiple ways to deactivate an entire track.

**1** Select the track(s) that you want to deactivate.

**2** Click the Track menu.

**3** Choose Make Inactive.

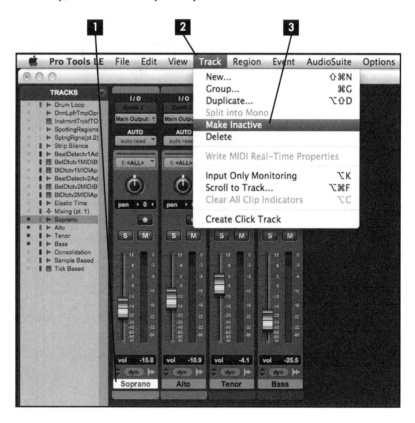

Here's another way to do it:

**1** Right-click the **name** of the track(s) that you want to deactivate. (You can make this selection in the Mix window, the Edit window, or the Tracks list.) A list will appear.

**2** Choose **Make Inactive** (or **Hide and Make Inactive**).

Here's what you'll get:

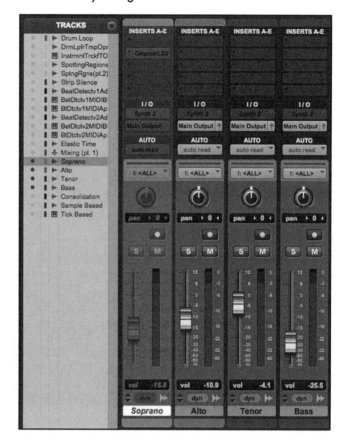

An inactive track's channel strip will be grayed out (and the track name will be italicized).

### WORKING WITH HD SESSIONS

When you open a session used on an HD system, you might find that some of your tracks are inactive (since HD systems support more active tracks than LE systems). You can still use them by deactivating any of the currently active tracks and then activating one of the currently inactive tracks.

## Edit Density and Consolidation

One way to increase the efficiency of your session is to minimize its edit density. Edit density refers to the number of times your system must acquire audio data from your hard drive during playback. If your session has many small audio regions, it might be said that it has higher edit density than a session with just a few large regions.

In extreme cases, high edit density can cause playback problems. The trick in those cases is to decrease the number of regions without changing the sound of your session, and the Consolidate function is the key.

### ※ SETTING THINGS UP

For this demonstration, go to Memory Location #11—Consolidation. You'll see a section of drums to which Beat Detective's Region Separation feature has been applied, creating lots of regions!

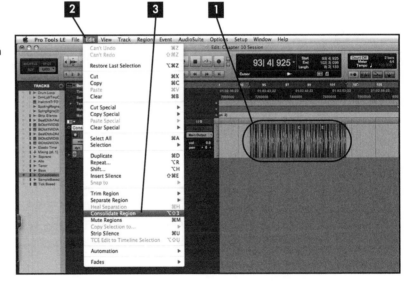

**1** Select a section of your session that is particularly dense with regions. (If you're working with the tutorial session, this has been done for you.)

**2** Click on the Edit menu.

**3** Click on Consolidate Region.

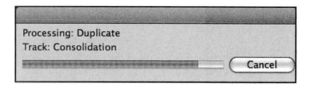

A window will display the progress of the consolidate process.

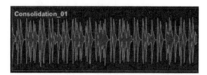

Your selection of multiple regions has been rendered into a *single* region (and a single audio file on your hard drive).

 **CONSOLIDATING SILENCE?**

When you use the Consolidate feature, any selected space that is not occupied by a region will be rendered as silent audio, as will any gaps in between regions in your selected area.

**CONSOLIDATING MIDI?**

Beginning with Pro Tools 8, MIDI regions can be consolidated as well as audio regions. Note that, although convenient, consolidating MIDI data won't affect your edit density.

# Working with Video

Although Pro Tools is certainly an audio-centric program (as are most DAWs), that doesn't mean you can't incorporate video into your sessions. In fact, working with video in your session is a very straightforward process.

❄ DV TOOLKIT 2

In a basic Pro Tools LE system, there are a few limitations with regard to video (ways that a video track can be edited, SMPTE timelines, and so on). For the purpose of this book, we'll limit our discussion on video to basic operations, and these limitations won't present a problem in this chapter.

For those of you who are in need of more advanced video features within Pro Tools LE, there is a software addition to Pro Tools called the DV Toolkit 2, which adds video-related features and plug-ins to your system. You can learn more about the DV Toolkit 2 and what it offers by visiting Avid's website (www.avid.com).

# Importing Video

Let's start off with a look at the process of importing a QuickTime movie, which couldn't be easier.

1 Click on the **File menu**.

2 Click on **Import**, and another menu will appear.

3 In this submenu, **click** on **Video**. The Open/Select Video File to Import dialog box will appear.

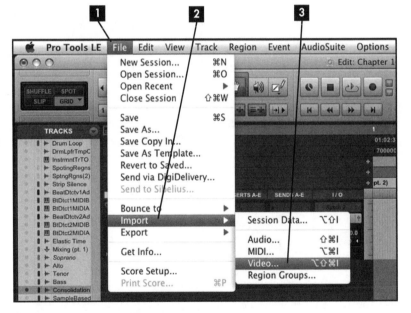

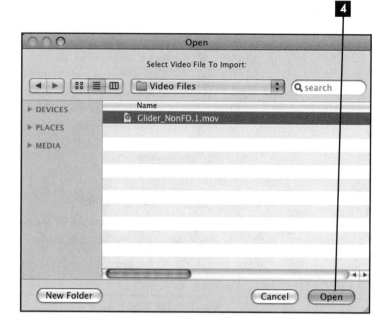

**4** **Navigate** to the **file** you want to import and **click** the **Open** button.

## DON'T HAVE ANY VIDEO FILES? NO PROBLEM!

If you don't have any other video files to import, you can import the video file from the Chapter 09 session. Just go into the Chapter 09 Session folder and then open the Video Files folder.

You can also import video via any of the Pro Tools browser windows (including the Workspace, Volume, and Project browsers). This is perhaps the quickest and easiest way to bring video into your session.

**1** **Locate** the **file** that you want to import.

**2** **Drag and drop** the **file** into your session. You can drag it to your session's Playlist area, to the Tracks list, or to the Regions list.

Regardless of which import method you choose, the Video Import Options dialog box will appear.

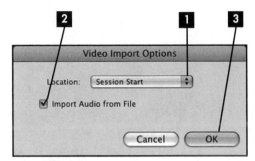

**1** If you **click** the **Location menu button**, you'll be presented with a list of options as to when to position your Video region:

❉ **Session Start.** This will place the Video region at the very beginning of the Video track.

❉ **Song Start.** You can set your song to start at a place other than the beginning of your session (something we covered back in Chapter 6). If you have done this, you have the option to place your Video region at the song start.

❉ **Selection.** Choosing this option will place your Video region at the beginning of the currently selected area.

❉ **Spot.** Choosing this option will open the Spot dialog box, allowing you to type a specific time location for your Video region.

**2** If you **click** the **Import Audio from File check box**, any audio that is included with the video will be imported to a new Audio track.

**3** To import the video into your session, **click** the **OK** button.

Although a Video track isn't an Audio track to be sure, you'll still see it displayed in the Edit window. You can arrange the track in the Edit window just as you would any other track, and you can move the Video region just as you would move any Audio or MIDI region.

## Viewing Video

You can easily show or hide Pro Tools' Video window:

**1** Click the **Window menu**.

**2** Choose **Video** to show the Video window (or to hide it, if it's currently being shown).

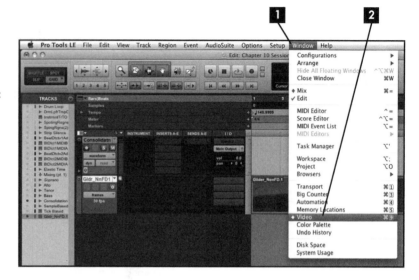

---

❄ **RESIZABLE VIDEO**

Just move your cursor to any of the Video window's boundaries and click and drag the window to the desired size. If you want the Video window to fill your entire screen, just right-click the Video window and choose Fit Screen from the list of sizing options that will appear.

## Bouncing to QuickTime

Bouncing your session to a QuickTime movie is similar to the Bounce to Disk process that we covered in Chapter 9. Before we close our discussion on using video, let's take a quick look.

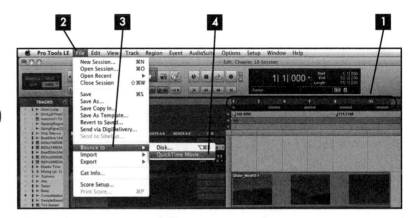

**1** Using the Selector tool, **select** the **area** of your session you want to bounce. (In this case, I'll select from the entire video.)

**2** Click on the **File menu**.

**3** Click on **Bounce To**. A sub-menu will be displayed.

**4** Click on **QuickTime Movie**. The Bounce dialog box will appear.

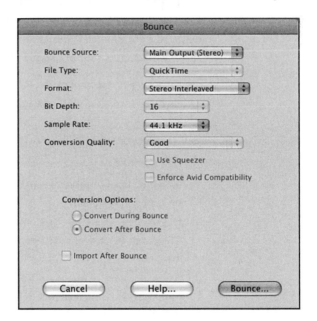

The Bounce dialog box when bouncing to a QuickTime movie is nearly identical to the window you worked with when bouncing audio in Chapter 9. (Refer to the previous chapter for a rundown of the dialog box's options.)

> **CHECKING YOUR WORK**
>
> To see this chapter's steps in their completed form, check out the Chapter 10 Session - Finished session.

# Interoperability: Making Shared Sessions Work

Perhaps the most compelling reason to learn and use Pro Tools is its position as the global standard in the DAW world. From bedroom studios to multimillion-dollar facilities, Pro Tools allows for greater collaboration for amateurs and professionals alike than perhaps any other application. Take your humble author, for example—I wrote a good portion of this book in airports with an Mbox 2 Micro LE system, and I could easily open this book's sessions in any professional studio with a minimum of muss and fuss!

The best way to maximize the interoperability of Pro Tools is to take efforts to ensure that your session can be opened and heard properly on a wide variety of systems and that collaborators can easily understand your work. Here are some recommendations on how to make this happen:

* Name all tracks before recording, and name them in a way that anyone can understand.
* Use the Comments view in both the Edit and Mix windows. The Comments column of every track and the Comment field of memory locations are valuable sources of information to others.
* Use your memory locations. Identify each section of your work and descriptively name it so that anybody can understand the overall layout of your session.
* Internally record (using a bus) all of your virtual Instrument tracks to Audio tracks. This ensures that even if your collaborator doesn't have the same virtual instruments installed in his system, he will still be able to hear your session the way it was meant to be heard.
* Use AudioSuite plug-ins when appropriate. Just as with internal recording, this will create a new file that can be played back in any Pro Tools situation, even if the actual plug-ins aren't present on other systems.

❊ Use a click track. Recording a great beat is all well and good, but if you're not in sync with the MIDI tempo of your session, features such as Quantize, Beat Detective, and Grid mode can do more harm than good!

❊ Before you archive your session or whenever you're moving it from one system to another, do a Save Copy In of your session and click all appropriate options for saving. This will ensure that all your audio, video, and plug-in settings will be saved in one central location. That's the file you should archive or move to another system for further work. Incidentally, you can also use the Save Copy In feature to save your session as an older version of Pro Tools (if you're collaborating with a user that doesn't have the latest software).

# Good Luck!

Congratulations—you made it! You've gone through a solid introductory tour of Pro Tools' basic operations and features. Although this discussion of Pro Tools is certainly not a comprehensive listing of *everything* that Pro Tools can do, you can rest assured that your creative journey has started well. Over time, you'll not only learn more about Pro Tools, but undoubtedly you will find your own working style—a process that will be constantly refined as you gain experience and speed.

❊ STILL WANT MORE SHORTCUTS?

Over the course of this book we've covered a good number of useful shortcuts, but there are still many more for you to discover. Fortunately, there's a resource for your shortcut-browsing pleasure—the Pro Tools Help menu, which is ready for you to use. From the Help drop-down menu, choose the Keyboard Shortcuts menu item to view a comprehensive list of shortcuts. You might also want to take a look at the Pro Tools Reference Guide, which you'll also find in the Help menu. You can find updated versions of these documents on the Avid website.

As your skills grow, you may crave more in-depth knowledge. Fortunately, Avid has an excellent training program, which they offer through their worldwide network of training partner schools. Avid's Training and Education Program is a constantly evolving curriculum that can take you from where you are now all the way up to an elite Expert Certification, complete with worldwide listing! For more information, visit www.avid.com/training.

You've begun a great exploration—and a worthwhile endeavor, in my humble opinion. I personally believe that artistic pursuits nourish the soul not only of the patron, but of the artist as well. It's my fond wish that this book has served to inspire you to push the limits of your creativity and to share your gifts with others.

Good luck!

# } Index

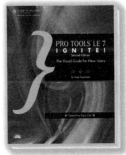

## License Agreement/Notice of Limited Warranty

**By opening the sealed disc container in this book, you agree to the following terms and conditions. If, upon reading the following license agreement and notice of limited warranty, you cannot agree to the terms and conditions set forth, return the unused book with unopened disc to the place where you purchased it for a refund.**

### License:

The enclosed software is copyrighted by the copyright holder(s) indicated on the software disc. You are licensed to copy the software onto a single computer for use by a single user and to a backup disc. You may not reproduce, make copies, or distribute copies or rent or lease the software in whole or in part, except with written permission of the copyright holder(s). You may transfer the enclosed disc only together with this license, and only if you destroy all other copies of the software and the transferee agrees to the terms of the license. You may not decompile, reverse assemble, or reverse engineer the software.

### Notice of Limited Warranty:

The enclosed disc is warranted by Course Technology to be free of physical defects in materials and workmanship for a period of sixty (60) days from end user's purchase of the book/disc combination. During the sixty-day term of the limited warranty, Course Technology will provide a replacement disc upon the return of a defective disc.

### Limited Liability:

THE SOLE REMEDY FOR BREACH OF THIS LIMITED WARRANTY SHALL CONSIST ENTIRELY OF REPLACEMENT OF THE DEFECTIVE DISC. IN NO EVENT SHALL COURSE TECHNOLOGY OR THE AUTHOR BE LIABLE FOR ANY OTHER DAMAGES, INCLUDING LOSS OR CORRUPTION OF DATA, CHANGES IN THE FUNCTIONAL CHARACTERISTICS OF THE HARDWARE OR OPERATING SYSTEM, DELETERIOUS INTERACTION WITH OTHER SOFTWARE, OR ANY OTHER SPECIAL, INCIDENTAL, OR CONSEQUENTIAL DAMAGES THAT MAY ARISE, EVEN IF COURSE TECHNOLOGY AND/OR THE AUTHOR HAS PREVIOUSLY BEEN NOTIFIED THAT THE POSSIBILITY OF SUCH DAMAGES EXISTS.

### Disclaimer of Warranties:

COURSE TECHNOLOGY AND THE AUTHOR SPECIFICALLY DISCLAIM ANY AND ALL OTHER WARRANTIES, EITHER EXPRESS OR IMPLIED, INCLUDING WARRANTIES OF MERCHANTABILITY, SUITABILITY TO A PARTICULAR TASK OR PURPOSE, OR FREEDOM FROM ERRORS. SOME STATES DO NOT ALLOW FOR EXCLUSION OF IMPLIED WARRANTIES OR LIMITATION OF INCIDENTAL OR CONSEQUENTIAL DAMAGES, SO THESE LIMITATIONS MIGHT NOT APPLY TO YOU.

### Other:

This Agreement is governed by the laws of the State of Massachusetts without regard to choice of law principles. The United Convention of Contracts for the International Sale of Goods is specifically disclaimed. This Agreement constitutes the entire agreement between you and Course Technology regarding use of the software.